Drivers of SME Growth and Sustainability in Emerging Markets

Sumesh Dadwal
Northumbrian University, UK

Pawan Kumar
Lovely Professional University, India

Rajesh Verma
Lovely Professional University, India

Gursimranjit Singh
Dr. B.R. Ambedkar National Institute of Technology, Jalandhar, India

A volume in the Advances in Logistics,
Operations, and Management Science (ALOMS)
Book Series

Published in the United States of America by
    IGI Global
    Business Science Reference (an imprint of IGI Global)
    701 E. Chocolate Avenue
    Hershey PA, USA 17033
    Tel: 717-533-8845
    Fax: 717-533-8661
    E-mail: cust@igi-global.com
    Web site: http://www.igi-global.com

Library of Congress Cataloging-in-Publication Data

Names: Dadwal, Sumesh, 1973- editor. | Kumar, Pawan, 1980- editor. | Verma,
    Rajesh, 1974- editor. | Singh, Gursimranjit, 1987- editor.
Title: Drivers of SME growth and sustainability in emerging markets /
    edited by Sumesh Dadwal, Pawan Kumar, Rajesh Verma, Gursimranjit Singh.
Description: Hershey, PA : Business Science Reference, [2024] | Includes
    bibliographical references and index. | Summary: "The book aims to
    identify the drivers of SME growth and sustainability in emerging
    markets and will provide in-depth insights to the marketeers,
    entrepreneurs and practitioners to unravel the opportunities and
    mitigate the challenges of small and medium enterprises"-- Provided by
    publisher.
Identifiers: LCCN 2023046486 (print) | LCCN 2023046487 (ebook) | ISBN
    9798369301111 (hardcover) | ISBN 9798369301128 (paperback) | ISBN
    9798369301135 (ebook)
Subjects: LCSH: Small business--Developing countries--Growth. | Sustainable
    development--Developing countries.
Classification: LCC HD2346.D43 D75 2024 (print) | LCC HD2346.D43 (ebook)
    | DDC 338.6/42091724--dc23/eng/20231005
LC record available at https://lccn.loc.gov/2023046486
LC ebook record available at https://lccn.loc.gov/2023046487

This book is published in the IGI Global book series Advances in Logistics, Operations, and Management Science (ALOMS) (ISSN: 2327-350X; eISSN: 2327-3518)

British Cataloguing in Publication Data
A Cataloguing in Publication record for this book is available from the British Library.

For electronic access to this publication, please contact: eresources@igi-global.com.

Advances in Logistics, Operations, and Management Science (ALOMS) Book Series

John Wang
Montclair State University, USA

ISSN:2327-350X
EISSN:2327-3518

MISSION

Operations research and management science continue to influence business processes, administration, and management information systems, particularly in covering the application methods for decision-making processes. New case studies and applications on management science, operations management, social sciences, and other behavioral sciences have been incorporated into business and organizations real-world objectives.

The **Advances in Logistics, Operations, and Management Science** (ALOMS) Book Series provides a collection of reference publications on the current trends, applications, theories, and practices in the management science field. Providing relevant and current research, this series and its individual publications would be useful for academics, researchers, scholars, and practitioners interested in improving decision making models and business functions.

COVERAGE

- Computing and information technologies
- Risk Management
- Production Management
- Services management
- Decision analysis and decision support
- Organizational Behavior
- Political Science
- Finance
- Marketing engineering
- Operations Management

IGI Global is currently accepting manuscripts for publication within this series. To submit a proposal for a volume in this series, please contact our Acquisition Editors at Acquisitions@igi-global.com or visit: http://www.igi-global.com/publish/.

Titles in this Series

For a list of additional titles in this series, please visit: http://www.igi-global.com/book-series/advances-logistics-operations-management-science/37170

Critical Examination of the Recent Evolution of B2B Sales
Joel G. Cohn (Everglades University, Boca Raton, USA)
Business Science Reference • © 2024 • 276pp • H/C (ISBN: 9798369303481) • US $255.00

Contemporary Management and Global Leadership for Sustainability
Kannapat Kankaew (Burapha University International College, Thailand) Shilpa Chaudhary (Lovely Professional University, India) and Sarun Widtayakornbundit (Kasetsart University, Thailand)
Business Science Reference • © 2024 • 324pp • H/C (ISBN: 9798369312735) • US $275.00

Innovation and Resource Management Strategies for Startups Development
Neeta Baporikar (Namibia University of Science and Technology, Namibia & SP Pune University, India)
Business Science Reference • © 2024 • 298pp • H/C (ISBN: 9798369320778) • US $275.00

Reskilling the Workforce for Technological Advancement
Oytun Meçik (Eskişehir Osmangazi University, Turkey)
Business Science Reference • © 2024 • 308pp • H/C (ISBN: 9798369306123) • US $265.00

Complex AI Dynamics and Interactions in Management
Paula Cristina Nunes Figueiredo (Universidade Lusófona, Portugal)
Business Science Reference • © 2024 • 360pp • H/C (ISBN: 9798369307120) • US $265.00

Cybersecurity Measures for Logistics Industry Framework
Noor Zaman Jhanjhi (School of Computing Science, Taylor's University, Malaysia) and Imdad Ali Shah (School of Computing Science, Taylor's University, Malaysia)
Information Science Reference • © 2024 • 418pp • H/C (ISBN: 9781668476253) • US $250.00

Perspectives on Innovation and Technology Transfer in Managing Public Organizations
Luan Carlos Santos Silva (Federal University of Grande Dourados)
Business Science Reference • © 2024 • 371pp • H/C (ISBN: 9781668498330) • US $275.00

701 East Chocolate Avenue, Hershey, PA 17033, USA
Tel: 717-533-8845 x100 • Fax: 717-533-8661
E-Mail: cust@igi-global.com • www.igi-global.com

Editorial Advisory Board

Table of Contents

Detailed Table of Contents

    Julius Eziashi, Northumbria University, UK
    Eustathios Sainidis, Northumbria University, UK

The chapter aims to review the current body of knowledge on growth models in manufacturing SMEs within an emerging economy. Empirical evidence on Nigerian manufacturing SMEs, their strategy to grow and develop is discussed. The relevant literature is extensively and systematically reviewed to underpin the theoretical perspective of Nigerian manufacturing SMEs. Qualitative data is used within the empirical discussion. The instrument for the data collection was a face to face semi-structured interview of 17 senior managers and owners of Nigerian manufacturing SMEs. Thematic template analysis has been applied aiming to identify the emerging patterns from the interview to ascertain Nigeria manufacturing SMEs challenges, priorities and key issues considered vital in the development of manufacturing practices. The findings present empirical evidence in understanding SMEs development in dealing with challenges and prioritising their manufacturing practices. The findings have implications on government policy and assists professional practitioners in understanding manufacturing SMEs strategy, priorities and challenges in the emerging economy in the context of Nigeria.

    Luther-King Junior Zogli, Durban University of Technology, South Africa

In developing countries like South Africa, the informal sector plays a crucial role in providing employment opportunities for people are not able to secure formal jobs or establish registered businesses. This undocumented sector accounts for over 65% of the total employment in developing economies. The purpose of this research is to investigate the formalisation experience of informal traders in Durban's central business district, South Africa. Using snowball sampling, the structured interview strategy was used to acquire qualitative data. After completing twelve interviews with informal traders, data saturation was reached. The data was analysed using content analysis. After data analysis, the study revealed that informal traders faced significant challenges in the formalisation process. These challenges were organized into three main themes: lack of support from the municipality, limited access to information on formalisation procedures and their perception that the formalisation process to be expensive and beyond their financial capabilities.

Chapter 3

Gifty Edwin-Akakpo, Coventry University, UK
Alfred Akakpo, University of Northampton, UK
Said Ali, Coventry University, UK

The purpose of this chapter is to examine access to finance for small and medium scale enterprises in emerging markets with a focus on South Korea. This book chapter evaluates the critical role access to finance plays in enabling growth and expansion for SMEs in emerging market economy such as a South Korea. Also, there is critical analysis of the challenges faced by SMEs in securing financing in emerging markets. The lack of funding sources was discussed with a review on innovative models and policy solutions that aim to improve small and medium scale enterprises' access to finance.

Chapter 4

Deepak Bisht, Lovely Professional University, India
Pawan Kumar, Lovely Professional University, India
Lokesh Jasrai, Lovely Professional University, India

Small businesses serve as powerful drivers of sustainability and growth in emerging economies. Their contributions to economic development, job creation, inclusive growth, and environmental sustainability are unparalleled. By overcoming challenges through supportive policies and innovative approaches, governments and stakeholders can unleash the full potential of small businesses, creating a more prosperous and sustainable future for emerging economies. Keeping all these in consideration this chapter delves into the crucial aspects of small businesses and their pivotal role as catalysts of growth and sustainability in emerging economies and aims to provide a comprehensive understanding of the multifaceted contributions of SMEs to economic development, highlighting their significance in driving sustainable growth and promoting social and environmental well-being.

Chapter 5

Mohamad Zreik, Sun Yat-sen University, China

This chapter provides an in-depth examination of the advantages and disadvantages that China's SMEs confront in the country's dynamic economic climate. It begins by outlining the challenges small enterprises confront, including little money, complicated regulations, and the need to update outdated technology. It then examines the methods used by Chinese SMEs, such as the adoption of digital technologies, the creation of novel business models, and the development of non-traditional sources of funding, to achieve scalable growth. Several examples are given, primarily from the fields of agriculture and tourism, to illustrate the usefulness of these methods. SME capacity building and policy recommendations for an enabling environment round out the chapter. Those curious about the factors driving the expansion of China's small and medium-sized enterprises (SMEs) will find this book chapter essential.

Chapter 6

This chapter reveals that SMEs in South Africa are highly vulnerable to electricity crises, with many experiencing significant financial losses and business closures. The impact of power outages and load shedding varies across sectors, with manufacturing and retail businesses particularly affected. SMEs also face challenges in accessing alternative energy sources, such as solar power, due to high costs and limited availability. Factors contributing to SMEs' vulnerability include their reliance on the national electricity grid, limited access to finance for alternative energy solutions, and inadequate government support. Many SMEs are also struggling to compete with larger firms that have the resources to invest in backup power solutions and other resilience measures. Further, the chapter identifies several policy interventions that could support SMEs in mitigating the impact of electricity crises, including incentives for renewable energy, increased access to finance for energy-saving solutions, and targeted business support programs.

Chapter 7

Small and medium-sized enterprises are a critical component of the global economy, contributing significantly to job creation, innovation, and economic growth. The emergence of digitalization has significantly changed the business landscape leading to both challenges and opportunities for SMEs. The study provides new insights into how digital platform service providers may assist SMEs in their transformation and competitiveness. This chapter aims to provide a comprehensive review and analysis of the impact of digitalization on SMEs growth. The study explores the various aspects of digitalization, its effects on SMEs, and strategies that SMEs may use to take advantage of digital technologies to enhance growth and competitiveness. A total of fifteen papers are reviewed; their methodology and findings are summarized. It shows that digital transformation ensures easy accessibility of the business significantly affects customer relationships. The results further indicate online selling and digital marketing as the leading digital platforms successfully implemented by most SMEs.

Chapter 8

The chapter aims to find interdependencies between barriers that hinder adoption of digital transformation technologies in small and medium firms. Barriers were identified using an extensive literature review and finalized after consulting an expert panel. Next, a pairwise questionnaire was developed, and responses from essential stakeholders working with small and medium firms were collected. Data were analyzed using the DEMATEL technique. Salient challenges for implementing digital transformation technologies were identified, and the cause-and-effect relationship between the barriers was established. Lack of proper digital vision and strategy was identified as the most critical barrier that hinders adoption of digital transformation technologies in small and medium firms. Digital technologies help to improve the efficiency of the firms and improve resource utilization by facilitating timely and accurate decision making. Hence, overcoming the identified challenges in transformation will improve the operations of the production system and organizational process.

Chapter 9

Nitsa J. Herzog, Northumbria University, UK
David J Herzog, QA Higher Education, UK

The fast development of information technologies fostered the recent flourishing of intelligent systems. While on the personal or household stratum, the usage of smart devices is quite limited in scope if not in function, on the industrial and geographical levels, various networks allow the creation of a new paradigm: Cyber-Physical space, enabled by the internet of things and smart environments. The phenomenon is truly global, encompassing all walks of life. Small and medium enterprises certainly benefit from the explosive spread of IoT and smart technologies. Industry 4.0 develops manufacturing, smart logistics and smart servitization, which are supported by just-in-time supply-chain operations. The current review of the present-day IoT, IIoT, and smart environments describes operational capabilities for innovative SMEs to expand operations and ride the wave of revolutionary change for profit and society benefits as a whole. A comprehensive assessment of potential drawbacks with technology acceptance by SMEs is done, with prospective solutions in every sphere of activities.

Chapter 10

Bindu Aggarwal, Chandigarh University, India
Ranjeet Verma, Chandigarh University, India
Pawan Kumar, Lovely Professional University, India

The dynamic interaction between tourism and small and medium enterprises (SMEs) as generators of long-term economic growth is explored in this chapter. The chapter investigates methods to unlock the potential synergy between tourism and SMEs, resulting in a paradigm of sustainable and inclusive growth, by looking at case studies, best practices, and emerging trends.

Chapter 11

Manpreet Arora, School of Commerce and Management Studies, Central University of
Himachal Pradesh, Dharamshala, India
Swati Singh, Maharaja Agresen University, Baddi, India

The concept of women entrepreneurship has the ability to transform the whole society, it gains more relevance in emerging economies. Through women's entrepreneurship, not only the economic freedom of women can be ensured but it also fosters creativity innovation, and productivity in emerging nations. One of the best ways to make women empower along with education is "women entrepreneurship." In the process of women entrepreneurship, women not only earn self-respect, but they also understand the peculiarities of economic and social dimensions of life. The abilities of women are many-fold, which can be harnessed easily by adopting the path of women entrepreneurship. The tool of women entrepreneurship can act as a facilitator, motivator as well as moderator of fostering women empowerment. If access to finance through microfinance and other interventions, is provided to women they become empowered in many aspects. This chapter highlights the role of women entrepreneurship for women empowerment in emerging economies. This piece of research highlights various policy implications also in order to nurture women entrepreneurship.

    Sargunpreet Kaur, Lovely Professional University, India
    Anurag Pahuja, Lovely Professional University, India
    Pawan Kumar, Lovely Professional University, India

In the present era, sustainability is the most important aspect in innovation and financing. While the integration of sustainability into financing and innovation has been adopted in large enterprises but when it comes to SMEs, they are still lagging behind. Sustainable financing plays a significant role in driving the growth and success of small and micro enterprises (SMEs). SMEs, being essential contributors to the global economy, often face numerous challenges in accessing finance. Limited access to capital hinders their ability to expand, invest in resources, and innovate. The chapter aims to explore the importance of sustainable financing in promoting the growth and development of SMEs along with highlighting innovative financing models and challenges they pose. Additionally, the chapter discusses government initiatives, best practices, and case studies that demonstrate successful sustainable financing for SMEs. Finally, it throws light upon the future trends and opportunities in sustainable financing that can further support SMEs in their journey towards economic prosperity.

    Sumaya Yeasmin, Varendra University, Bangladesh
    Md. Ataul Gani Osmani, Varendra University, Bangladesh
    Orhan Şanli, Faculty of Economics and Administrative Sciences, Aydın, Turkey
    Laeeq Janjua, International Relations, Poland
    Almas Sultan, National College of Business Administration and Economics, Pakistan

The study investigates the recent trend and relationship between gross investment and agricultural productivity in Bangladesh. The study applies descriptive statistic techniques to describe the recent trend and ARDL bound testing approach to find the causation by using annual time series for the period of 1993 to 2022. In the first step, the study finds that Bangladesh is observing continuous growth in food production, where rice is the dominant crop, with a gradual increase in other seed production. Secondly, the results from the ARDL bound test state that there exists a long-run relationship between gross investment and agricultural productivity, but the exciting fact is that gross investment has a negative impact on agricultural productivity in Bangladesh because the country is observing structural change in policy regime towards industrialization such that increase in gross investment discourages agricultural sector. Therefore, it is recommended to set greater budgetary investment specifically for the agriculture sector to improve agricultural productivity in Bangladesh.

Preface

Drivers of SME Growth and Sustainability in Emerging Markets is a comprehensive book that delves into the intricate dynamics of small and medium-sized enterprises (SMEs) operating in developing economies. With a focus on a keen awareness of the challenges faced by SMEs, this book offers valuable insights for marketers, entrepreneurs, practitioners, and policymakers seeking to unlock the potential of these vital economic contributors. Drawing upon a wide range of topics, this book explores the multifaceted interactions that can either impede or enhance the growth and sustainability of SMEs in emerging markets. From examining the strategic risks SMEs face in relation to climate and sustainability to analyzing the innovative practices and business models that can transform these enterprises into unicorns, the book provides in-depth analyses of critical factors affecting SME success.

Furthermore, the book explores various financing avenues such as crowdfunding and microfinancing and investigates the profound impact of digital transformation and disruptive technologies on SMEs. It also investigates the role of government procurement, artificial intelligence, and state-of-the-art digital solutions, highlighting their potential to propel SMEs forward. With a focus on entrepreneurship capacity building and government schemes designed to support SMEs, this book equips readers with the knowledge and tools to create an enabling environment for sustainable SME growth. Various sectors of emerging markets face unique challenges, largely related to the gap between small and medium-sized enterprise (SME) research and practice. The relationship between SMEs and agriculture, tourism, and other key industries requires a close examination to understand the intricacies of their interplay. An emphasis on the need to bridge this gap, and strategies for scaling up and embedding new sustainability and technology trends into SME strategies is necessary for a healthy growth strategy within emerging markets.

From identifying bottlenecks and challenges to presenting innovative business models and sustainable practices, this book serves as a vital resource for business students, management faculty, and professionals seeking to navigate the complexities of SMEs in emerging markets.

Audience

The primary target audience for the proposed publication is scholars and practitioners who require specialized reference information on the issue mentioned above. The secondary target audience includes educators, lawmakers, managers, consultants, experts in organization development, and undergraduate and graduate business students, all of whom use the same reference materials. Although the book will have a scholarly bent, it is also written in a style that readers outside of academia and professional circles will find interesting and easy to understand.

The readers will gain varied research perspectives on he idea that, in order to remain competitive, small and medium-sized businesses (SMEs) should prioritize sustainable practices. Research on the adoption of sustainable behaviors and the factors that either reinforce or contradict them is lacking. This book closes the knowledge gap by applying different dimesions to comprehend the drivers of and obstacles to sustainable practices in SMEs. so this book is an attempt to provide insights for both industry and academia to assist them in teaching and training the next generation leaders through universities and corporate training. Moreover, this book contributes to the body of knowledge on drivers of SME Growth and Sustainability in emerging economies which can assist policymakers and practitioners to take the necessary steps to enhance sustainable practices in SMEs.

Key Features of The Book

This book includes how Small and medium-sized enterprises (SMEs) are crucial for promoting innovation, job creation, and economic development, especially in developing countries. When taken as a whole, these characteristics offer a thorough grasp of the opportunities, difficulties, and tactics associated with supporting the growth of small and medium-sized businesses in emerging economies.

SMEs are economic engines that significantly boost GDP growth, create jobs, and reduce poverty. Their adaptability, creativity, and agility give them a competitive edge since they enable them to quickly adapt to changing market conditions. In particular, SMEs are essential for fostering economic resilience in sectors including manufacturing, services, and agriculture. SMEs contribute to the development of vibrant, strong economies by promoting entrepreneurship, easing the acceptance of new technology, and promoting environmentally friendly business practices.

ORGANISATION OF THIS BOOK

This book also has taken an approach of integrating knowledge and understanding about
SMEs in a range of countries. The book has explored issues, trends and drivers of sustainable growth of SMEs in emerging markets.

This book is organised into 13 chapters. A brief description of the chapter is given in the next sections.

Chapter 1: Manufacturing SMEs Strategy to Grow and Develop in an Emerging Economy - Evidence from Nigeria

The chapter reviews growth models in Manufacturing SMEs within an emerging economy. In particular, empirical evidence on Nigerian Manufacturing SMEs, their strategy to grow and develop is discussed. Qualitative data is used within the empirical discussion. The instrument for the data collection is face to face semi-structured interview of senior managers and owners of manufacturing SMEs. Thematic template analysis is applied aiming to identify the emerging patterns from the interview to ascertain Nigeria manufacturing SMEs challenges, priorities and key issues considered vital in the development of manufacturing practices. The findings have implications on government policy and assists professional practitioners in understanding manufacturing SMEs strategy, priorities and challenges in the emerging economy in the context of Nigeria.

Chapter 2: Exploring perceptions of street traders about transitioning from the informal to the formal sector in Durban's central business district, South Africa

In developing countries like South Africa, the informal sector plays a crucial role in providing employment opportunities for people who are not able to secure formal jobs or establish registered businesses. This chapter argues that this undocumented informal sector accounts for over 65% of the total employment in developing economies. The purpose of this research is to investigate the formalisation experience of informal traders in Durban's central business district, South Africa. Using snowball sampling, the structured interview strategy was used to acquire qualitative data. After completing twelve interviews with informal traders, data saturation was reached. The data was analysed using content analysis. After data analysis, the study revealed that informal traders faced significant challenges in the formalisation process. These challenges were organized into three main themes: lack of support from the municipality, limited access to information on formalisation procedures and their perception that the formalisation process to be expensive and beyond their financial capabilities.

Chapter 3: Improving Access to Finance to Unlock SME Growth Potential in Emerging Markets-South Korea Example

The purpose of this chapter is to examine access to finance for Small and Medium Scale Enterprises in emerging markets with a focus on South Korea. This book chapter evaluates the critical role access to finance plays in enabling growth and expansion for SMEs in emerging market economy such as a South Korea. Also, there is critical analysis of the challenges faced by SMEs in securing financing in emerging markets. The lack of funding sources were discussed with a review on innovative models and policy solutions that aim to improve Small and Medium Scale Enterprises access to finance.

Chapter 4: Causation between Gross Investment and Agricultural Productivity: A Fresh Inside from Bangladesh

The chapter investigates the recent trend and relationship between gross investment and agricultural productivity in Bangladesh. The study applies descriptive statistic techniques to describe the recent trend and ARDL bound testing approach to find the causation by using annual time series for the period of 1993 to 2022. In the first step, the study finds that Bangladesh is observing continuous growth in food production, where rice is the dominant crop, with a gradual increase in other seed production. Secondly, the results from the ARDL bound test state that there exists a long-run relationship between gross investment and agricultural productivity, but the exciting fact is that gross investment has a negative impact on agricultural productivity in Bangladesh because the country is observing structural change in policy regime towards industrialization such that increase in gross investment discourages agricultural sector. Therefore, it is recommended to set greater budgetary investment specifically for the agriculture sector to improve agricultural productivity in Bangladesh.

Chapter 5: Scaling Up SMEs in China: Overcoming Challenges and Embracing Opportunities for Sustainable Growth

This chapter provides an in-depth examination of the advantages and disadvantages that China's SMEs confront in the country's dynamic economic climate. It begins by outlining the challenges small enterprises confront, including little money, complicated regulations, and the need to update outdated technology. It then examines the methods used by Chinese SMEs, such as the adoption of digital technologies, the creation of novel business models, and the development of non-traditional sources of funding, to achieve scalable growth. Several examples are given, primarily from the fields of agriculture and tourism, to illustrate the usefulness of these methods. SME capacity building and policy recommendations for an enabling environment round out the chapter. Those curious about the factors driving the expansion of China's small and medium-sized enterprises (SMEs) will find this book chapter essential.

Chapter 6: From Power Outages to Business Shutdowns: Exploring the Fate of Small and Medium-sized Enterprises SMEs in South Africa's Electricity Crises

This chapter reveals that SMEs in South Africa are highly vulnerable to electricity crises, with many experiencing significant financial losses and business closures. The impact of power outages and load shedding varies across sectors, with manufacturing and retail businesses particularly affected. SMEs also face challenges in accessing alternative energy sources, such as solar power, due to high costs and limited availability. Factors contributing to SMEs' vulnerability include their reliance on the national electricity grid, limited access to finance for alternative energy solutions, and inadequate government support. Many SMEs are also struggling to compete with larger firms that have the resources to invest in backup power solutions and other resilience measures. Further, the chapter identifies several policy interventions that could support SMEs in mitigating the impact of electricity crises, including incentives for renewable energy, increased access to finance for energy-saving solutions, and targeted business support programs.

Chapter 7: A Study on the Impact of Digitalization on SME Growth

The chapter explores the various aspects of digitalization, its effects on SMEs, and strategies that SMEs may use to take advantage of digital technologies to enhance growth and competitiveness. Small and Medium-sized Enterprises are a critical component of the global economy, contributing significantly to job creation, innovation, and economic growth. The emergence of digitalization has significantly changed the business landscape leading to both challenges and opportunities for SMEs. The study provides new insights into how digital platform service providers may assist SMEs in their transformation and competitiveness. This research paper aims to provide a comprehensive review and analysis of the impact of digitalization on SMEs growth. A total of fifteen paper are reviewed, summarised their methodology, and findings. It shows that digital transformation ensure easy accessibility of the business significantly affects customer relationships. The results further indicate online selling and digital marketing as the leading digital platforms successfully implemented by most SMEs.

Chapter 8: Barriers Hindering Digital Transformation in SMEs

The chapter aims to find interdependencies between barriers that hinder the adoption of digital transformation technologies in small and medium firms. Barriers were identified using an extensive literature review and finalized after consulting an expert panel. Next, a pairwise questionnaire was developed, and responses from essential stakeholders working with small and medium firms were collected. Data were analyzed using the DEMATEL technique. Salient challenges for implementing digital transformation technologies were identified, and the cause-and-effect relationship between the barriers was established. Lack of proper digital vision and strategy was identified as the most critical barrier that hinder the adoption of digital transformation technologies in small and medium firms. Digital technologies help to improve the efficiency of firms and improve resource utilization by facilitating timely and accurate decision-making. Hence, overcoming the identified challenges in transformation will improve the operations of the production system and organizational process.

Chapter 9: IoT and Smart Environment Solutions for SMEs

The fast development of information technologies fostered the recent flourishing of intelligent systems. While on the personal or household stratum, the usage of smart devices is quite limited in scope if not in function, on the industrial and geographical levels, various networks allow the creation of a new paradigm: Cyber-Physical Space, enabled by the Internet of Things and smart environments. The phenomenon is truly global, encompassing all walks of life. Small and medium enterprises certainly benefit from the explosive spread of IoT and smart technologies. Industry 4.0 develops manufacturing, smart logistics and smart servitization, which are supported by just-in-time supply-chain operations. The current review of the present-day IoT, IIoT and smart environments describes operational capabilities for innovative SMEs to expand operations and ride the wave of revolutionary change for profit and society benefits as a whole. A comprehensive assessment of potential drawbacks with technology acceptance by SMEs is done, with prospective solutions in every sphere of activities.

Chapter 10: Unlocking the Potential Exploring the Synergy Between Tourism and SMEs for Sustainable Economic Growth

This chapter Unlocking the Potential: Exploring the Synergy between Tourism and SMEs for Sustainable Economic Growth discusses a dynamic interaction between tourism and Small and Medium Enterprises (SMEs) as generators of long-term economic growth is explored in this chapter. The chapter investigates methods to unlock the potential synergy between tourism and SMEs, resulting in a paradigm of sustainable and inclusive growth, by looking at case studies, best practices, and emerging trends.

Chapter 11: Women empowerment Through Entrepreneurship in Emerging Economies: Analysing the Dimensions and Policy Implications

This chapter highlights the role of women entrepreneurship for women empowerment in emerging economies. The concept of women's entrepreneurship has the ability to transform the whole society, it gains more relevance in emerging economies. Through women's entrepreneurship, not only the economic freedom of women can be ensured but it also fosters creativity innovation, and productivity in emerging nations. One of the best ways to make women empower along with education is "women entrepreneurship". In the process of women's entrepreneurship, women not only earn self-respect, but they also understand the peculiarities of economic and social dimensions of life. The abilities of women are many folds which can be harnessed easily by adopting the way of women's entrepreneurship. The tool of women's entrepreneurship can act as a facilitator, learner as well as reaper. If access to finance through microfinance and other interventions, is provided to women they become empowered in many aspects. The findings highlights various policy implications to nurture women's entrepreneurship.

Chapter 12: Sustainable Financing: A Key Driver for Growth of Small and Medium Enterprises

This chapter explains the role of Sustainable financing in driving the growth and success of Small and Micro Enterprises (SMEs). In the present era, sustainability is the most important aspect in innovation and Financing. With the Integration of Sustainability into Financing and Innovation has been studied in large Enterprises but when it comes to SME's, they are still lagging behind. Sustainable financing plays a significant role in driving the growth and success of Small and Micro Enterprises (SMEs). SMEs, being essential contributors to the global economy, often face numerous challenges in accessing finance. Limited access to capital hinders their ability to expand, invest in resources, and innovate. This paper aims to explore the importance of sustainable financing for SMEs and shed light on the various challenges they encounter. It further delves into the role of sustainable financing in promoting the growth and development of SMEs along with highlighting innovative financing models. Additionally, the paper discusses government initiatives, best practices, and case studies that demonstrate successful sustainable financing for SMEs.

Chapter 13: Role of Small Businesses in Emerging Economies as Drivers of Sustainability and Growth

The focus of this chapter is on the contributions to economic development, job creation, inclusive growth, and environmental sustainability etc. By overcoming challenges through supportive policies and innovative approaches, governments and stakeholders can unleash the full potential of small businesses, creating a more prosperous and sustainable future for emerging economies. Keeping all these in consideration this chapter delves into the crucial aspects of small businesses and their pivotal role as catalysts of growth and sustainability in emerging economies and aims to provide a comprehensive understanding of the multifaceted contributions of SMEs to economic development, highlighting their significance in driving sustainable growth and promoting social and environmental well-being.

Chapter 1

Manufacturing SME Strategy to Grow and Develop in an Emerging Economy:
Evidence From Nigeria

Julius Eziashi
Northumbria University, UK

Eustathios Sainidis
Northumbria University, UK

ABSTRACT

The chapter aims to review the current body of knowledge on growth models in manufacturing SMEs within an emerging economy. Empirical evidence on Nigerian manufacturing SMEs, their strategy to grow and develop is discussed. The relevant literature is extensively and systematically reviewed to underpin the theoretical perspective of Nigerian manufacturing SMEs. Qualitative data is used within the empirical discussion. The instrument for the data collection was a face to face semi-structured interview of 17 senior managers and owners of Nigerian manufacturing SMEs. Thematic template analysis has been applied aiming to identify the emerging patterns from the interview to ascertain Nigeria manufacturing SMEs challenges, priorities and key issues considered vital in the development of manufacturing practices. The findings present empirical evidence in understanding SMEs development in dealing with challenges and prioritising their manufacturing practices. The findings have implications on government policy and assists professional practitioners in understanding manufacturing SMEs strategy, priorities and challenges in the emerging economy in the context of Nigeria.

DOI: 10.4018/979-8-3693-0111-1.ch001

INTRODUCTION

The significance of manufacturing SMEs in the creation of jobs is well established in the literature (Daniel et al., 2022). However, we lack understanding of how SMEs growth strategy is being sustained over time in an emerging economy context (Esteve-Pérez et al., 2022). Manufacturing managers quest for growth is recognized a key strategic priority irrespective of organizational formation and size (Daniel et al., 2022). Subsequently, high growth firms have become the focal point of debate for managers and policy makers (Demir et al., 2017). The chapter presents empirical evidence and insight on the Nigeria manufacturing Small Medium Enterprises (MSMEs) sector, its strategy, growth and development potential. The growing global competitiveness of the world economy over the last decade has urged Nigeria MSMEs to implement growth and development-oriented strategic measures aimed at increasing their market share. The fundamental shift in global competition for market share, means manufactured products from Nigeria must compete with manufactured goods from other emerging economies such as the Brazil, Russia, India, China, South Africa (BRICS), Singapore Indonesia and Malaysia (Dodd, et al, 2019; UNIDO, 2013). The need then arises for developing a strategy to mitigate on manufacturing challenges, reduce the cost of production, and improve product quality and output (Ehie and Muogboh, 2016). The challenges of Nigerian MSMEs are comparable to that of most developing economies (Africa Development Bank, 2023). This book chapter presents valuable insight for managers and policy makers pursuing capable ways to create jobs, deal with business challenges and strategically sustain macro- and micro-economic growth. The contribution of our study includes identifying manufacturing SMEs priorities and business challenges that confront managers and provide theoretical and practice-led knowledge that are both relevant to academic scholars and management practitioners. The discussion provides a framework to understand SMEs growth strategy in the emerging economy.

LITERATURE REVIEW

Growth Models of Manufacturing SMEs in Emerging Economies

The growth of SMEs has contributed extensively to the development of emerging economies as measured by GDP and the creation of employment (Dube and Chipumho, 2016; Mamman et al, 2019). SMEs growth is often assumed on the basis of their owners obtaining some financial support (Bouri et al., 2011), without much consideration given to their internal capabilities (Hitt et al., 2015). In emerging economies, manufacturing SMEs growth has been attributed to their internal capabilities such as low cost of production, quality products, product delivery speed, product design and innovation (Theresa et al, 2016). Also, manufacturing SMEs growth has been credited to their process efficiency and their ability to bring their product to the market within a short period of time (Kang et al., 2016; Ghobakhloo, 2018). The majority of SMEs in emerging economies, growth simply means their capability to survive and remain in business, data however points to most SMEs going into administration soon after their start-up phase (Okpara, 2011). Product pricing strategy also plays a major role, based on the SME ability to lower manufacturing costs and offer products at a competitively low price in the marketplace (Hitt et al., 2015). Manufacturing SMEs have also achieved growth strategy through their ability to design and develop new products within a short period of time (Theresa et al, 2016).

In the world of contemporary business practices, innovation has become a requirement for manufacturing SMEs growth operating in an emerging economy to survive global competition. The manufacturing SMEs growth model of innovation involves the use of technology, good managerial practice to address customer needs and accomplish operational improvement (O'Regan and Ghobadian, 2006; Adam and Alarifi, 2021). The role of managers in SMEs in growth strategy is well acknowledged in saving the cost of production, hiring skillful employees and reducing material waste (Mamman et al, 2019).

Nigeria Manufacturing SMEs in Perspective

The SMEs sector has played substantial role in the socio-economic development of many nations in the emerging economies (Africa Development Bank, 2023). The definitions of what makes an SME varies across different countries (Mutula and Brakel, 2007). Empirical studies have shown that there is no generally accepted definition for SMEs as some of the given definitions are country specific based on their degree to economic growth and development (Aruwa and Gugong, 2007). The two most common variables in defining SMEs are the number of employees and financial turnover (Jutla et al., 2002). Additional variables may include business configuration, location, size and their number of sales (Rahman, 2001). In the UK for instances, the Department of Business, Enterprise and Regulatory Reform (BERR, 2009) states that micro firms are less than 10 employees, small firms are not more than 50 employees' medium firms are more than 50 employees, but less than 250 employees and large firms are above 250 employees. The European Union (2003) have defined SMEs in the same way to BERR, nevertheless they included their annual business earnings The size of micro firms as less than 10 employees with annual income not exceeding €2 million, small firms as having not less than 50 employees and annual income of not more than €10 million, medium firms less than 250 employees with annual income not exceeding €43 million (European Commission 2013). The body that represents SMEs in Nigeria, SMEDAN, defined SMEs as small firms employing less than 50 and total asset less than $3200, medium firms between 50-199 employees with asset less than $3.200000 (SMEDAN, 2011; Apulu et al., 2011).

Manufacturing SMEs Strategy

Empirical evidence has shown that SMEs make substantial contribution to the economic growth and development of national economies (European Commission, 2007; Aremu and Adeyemi, 2011; Löfving et al., 2014). As businesses around the world globalise and internationalise, manufacturing SMEs must have to respond quickly to the growing technological changes to be able to survive the ever-competitive market environment (Laforet and Tann, 2006; Hitt et al., 2007; Löfving et al., 2014). To discuss manufacturing SMEs strategy, we must also understand their manufacturing priorities that supports their competitive advantage (Hill, 2000; Cagliano and Spinna, 2002; Groeßler, 2007; Hill and Hill, 2009). In the business and management discipline the study of strategy has been of complex nature (O'Regan and Ghobadian, 2006; Raymond and Croteau, 2006; Ates, 2008; Bellamy, 2009). However, SMEs strategy should be centered on their manufacturing priorities aiming to serve their competitive advantage (Barad and Gien, 2001; Barnes, 2002a, 2002b; Sa¨fsten and Winroth, 2002; Löfving et al., 2014). It is very timely and of geopolitical importance to understand the Nigerian manufacturing SMEs strategy as they have gradually become a major force driving every facet of the Nigeria economic growth and development (Ehie and Muogboh, 2016).

SMEs Manufacturing Priorities

Manufacturing SMEs strategy within the setting of operations and production management literature is divided into manufacturing content and process (Hill, 2000; Amoaka-Gyampah and Acquaah, 2008). Manufacturing content includes a set of capabilities of the manufacturing function which gives SMEs a competitive advantage (Swamidass and Newell, 1987; Hill, 2000; Amoaka-Gyampah and Acquaah, 2008). In the production and operation management literature (Ahmad and Schroeder, 2002; Tarigan, 2005; Rusjan, 2006; Sarmiento et al., 2008; Hallgren et al., 2011; Lin et al., 2012) the term *manufacturing priorities* has been attached to different definitions: competitive priorities (Hayes and Wheelwright, 1984) or manufacturing dimensions (Groeßler and Grübner, 2006; Schroeder et al., 2006) or capabilities and competitive priorities (Gonzalez-Benito and Suarez-Gonzalez, 2010). Manufacturing priorities in an SMEs context defined as are future planned objectives such as manufacturing cost, manufacturing delivery, manufacturing flexibility and manufacturing innovation (Hallgren et al., 2011). Manufacturing cost as a priority is referred to as the incurred expenditure during the provision of the product and service to the customers in the most cost-effective way to a business which outcome is a low price (Lin et al., 2012). Manufacturing quality priority indicates the delivery of product at the highest possible standard that will bring additional value to customers in terms of conformance, durability, reliability and performance (Garvin, 1987; Sarmiento et al., 2007; Lin et al., 2012). The aim of every manufacturer is to get their product as quickly as possible to the consumers. Manufacturing delivery priority offers the reduction in lead time and the capability to quickly carry out the order of customers (Sarmiento et al., 2007; Hallgren et al., 2011; Lin et al., 2012). Finally, the manufacturing priority of flexibility is the capability of manufacturing firms to systematically respond to the unpredictable ever changing manufacturing environment in terms of product volume, range and design (Hallgren et al., 2011; Lin et al., 2012; Oke, 2013).

Challenges of the Nigerian Manufacturing SMEs

There are numerous challenges confronting Nigeria MSMES, which can be compared to that of most Sub-Sahara African countries and emerging economies of the world. The MSMEs challenges includes inadequate financing, skill shortages, inadequate infrastructures, multiple taxation, exchange rate and raw material cost. Despite these challenges Nigerian SMEs are drivers of job creation and growth of the economy the challenges are not given good policy attention.

Inadequate Infrastructure

This has become one of the greatest challenges faced by Nigeria MSMEs due to its effects on every aspect of the manufacturing operations. Public infrastructure such as electricity grid and transportation are not well maintained to support the increase in its demands. The current situation of the electricity grid supply has become a major setback to the Nigeria industrial policy. The electricity demand has increased significantly due to the increase in population and the urbanisation agenda of many states in Nigeria. Empirical evidence has shown that Nigeria needs 12000-15000 megawatts of electricity supply to meet the needs of its manufacturing firms as the present estimated production of electricity is between 2000-3000 megawatts leaving a shortage of 10000-12000 megawatts of electricity (Ayanruoh, 2013). The Nigeria manufacturing firms have no other choice than to produce their own electricity using generators, leading to high increase in the cost of manufacturing operations and production (Olugbenga et al; 2013). The higher cost is absorbed by the manufacturing SMEs will reduce their ability to grow and develop (Malik et al; 2006). Hence, the cost is transferred to their customers and consumers of their products (NIRP, 2014). The resultant effect is that it makes locally manufactured products more expensive than most manufactured product from other parts of the world (Mckinsey, 2013, UNIDO, 2013; NIRP, 2014).

In general terms a transport system that is good and dependable, can help in the sustenance of the economic development of the country (Malik et al., 2002; Adeyemi, 2014). The function that the transportation system plays in the movement of goods and delivery of manufactured products around the world needs to be recognised, as it is of paramount important for global supply chain (Wieland and Wallenburg, 2013). Due to poor road and rail network, it has become very difficult to move goods across the country. The cost to freight goods within Nigeria has become very expensive due poor road infrastructures across the six geopolitical zone and states of Nigeria (Adeyemi, 2014). The delays encountered when moving goods form the plant to consumers has increased the manufacturing cost significantly and impacted on the flow and dispersion of manufactured products to their destination (Malik et al., 2002; Onuorah, 2009).

Insufficient Laboratories

The demand for more product testing laboratories is well established among many Nigeria manufacturing SMEs. These test facilities are needed for testing both imported products and the ones that are locally manufactured, as the imported products are perceived to more superior in quality which is not always the case (Akanya, 2011). The lack of laboratories in commercial scale means that substandard and counterfeit products cannot be easily detected as they make their way into the marketplace (Nwosa and Oseni, 2013). The influx of counterfeit products in circulation is a major concern for most manufacturers and importers of finished goods (Akanya, 2011). The lack of these test laboratories might result in lack of quality controls and some dubious manufacturers are taking advantage of the situation to counterfeit high selling products which present a danger to the consumers of such products (Okorie and Humphrey, 2016).

Sub-Standard Products

The influx of substandard and counterfeit product in the marketplace has had an enormous impact on the survivability of the manufacturing SMEs in Nigeria. Globally the losses from counterfeit and substandard products amount to about USD461 billion and represent 2.5% of the world trade in the year 2013 which is greater than the GDP of Ireland and Czech Republic combined (Stryszowski and Kazimierczak, 2016). The Nigeria manufacturing SMEs are not alone on the issue of substandard products which has become a global concern, many progressive and developed economies in the European Union have greatly experienced economic loss of EUR 85 billion in 2013 which represent 5% of the whole import (Stryszowski and Kazimierczak, 2016). Empirical evidence has shown that most consumers of counterfeit and substandard products were not able to distinguish them from authentic and genuine products, however price was noted to be the main reason purchasing substandard products (Qian, 2008; Mishra and Shukla, 2015). The greatest challenges faced by manufacturing SMEs is that counterfeit and substandard products harm the economic prospect of many nations, as earnings are lost to some criminal associations (Treadwell, 2011; Penz et al., 2009). Quality product manufacturing is good for economic growth and development (Nwosa and Oseni, 2013). Studies have shown that the manufacturing of substandard product starts from a substandard production planning process, this can be changed by having the right manufacturing personnel that are well trained to enforce the quality assurance and control policy of the manufacturing firms Mishra and Shukla, 2015). Substandard product importation has had devastating effect on the competitiveness of Nigeria manufacturing SMEs. It has become dangerous to the survival of most SMEs, which has made the government to take urgent policy steps for outright ban of such products (Nwosa and Oseni, 2013).

Multiple-Taxation

In the taxation management, multiplicity of taxes is not a term that is well-recognised however, it is generally used where tax levy collected is charged on the same person or business in regard of the same tax by several government bodies such as state and local government (Sanni, 2012). The complexity of this tax scheme has become a burden to many SMEs who are forced out of their business (Ocheni and Gemade, 2015). Taxes are of economic importance to the development of many nations, creating funds for public services and employment (Adeniran et al; 2014). However, SMEs income should be put into consideration when administering taxes to ensure their operational and business survival (Adebisi and Gbegi, 2013). Intimidation and harassment from thugs, presenting themselves as different government agencies have led to closure of many SMEs businesses within 5 years of start-up (SMEDAN, 2013). The emergence of different types of tax collection processes have led to SMEs being taxed multiple times leading to their business collapse (Ihua, 2009; Apulu, 2011).

Funding Issues

In Nigeria MSMEs are well acknowledged as the major force driving the economic growth and development (CBN, 2013). The funding and financial resources of Nigerian MSMEs are essential for the growth, development and expansion of the business enterprise through capital investment, as they lack the required financial capability to support their business operations (Fatai, 2009). The registered successes achieved by various Nigerian MSMEs can be attested to as the funding and financing received (Achua, 2008). Most SMEs in the emerging economies do not have the financial capability to expand their businesses (Ihua, 2009). Nigeria MSMEs are in the same precarious situation as the banks are not lending to them for fear that they are not able to repay back, as result most MSMEs unexpectedly shut their businesses (SMEDAN, 2013). The apparent financial discrimination faced by MSMEs from the Nigeria commercial banks are enormous (Luper, 2012), charging interest rate at 30% above the average given to big manufacturing companies (Fatai, 2009). Despite the economic contribution of MSMEs to the Nigeria economy, they are not getting the required loans from the bank (Onugu, 2005, Aremu and Adeyemi, 2011). The MSMEs that can secure a loan, are given a short period of time to repay, which have also discouraged many MSMEs from loaning from the banks (Luper, 2012).

Foreign Exchange

The price rate at which a country's currency is being exchanged for another, has become a very vital economic measure that changes the mechanism of performance of the manufacturing economy when the currency is depreciated and appreciated (Hashim and Zarma, 1996; Odili, 2014). The Nigeria MSMEs is continuously faced with the impact created by the decline in Nigeria Naira exchange rate, against other notable currencies such as the dollar and pounds sterling which then increases the cost of imported raw materials in the manufacturing budget (Odil, 2014). The uncertainty in the exchange rate have shown to slow down growth, economic activities and the reduction in productivity of the manufacturing firms in emerging economies (Ojo, 2009). The currency Naira depreciation has led to increase in the exchange rate which has impacted MSMEs depending on the importation of raw from other countries abroad (Adeniran et al.,2014). The shortage in the import of raw materials needed for manufacturing has led to the decrease in production and export of MSMEs (Aliyu, 2011).

Shortage of Skilled Workforce

The existential gap in skill, the ineffective on-the-job learning and poor supervision among manufacturing SMEs in Nigeria has led to the lack of a quality workforce which is common to SMEs in developing economies (Abor and Quartey, 2010). SMEs require quality workforce to achieve their manufacturing and operational objectives (Aremu and Adeyemi 2011; Agwu and Emeti,2014). Manufacturing SMEs in Nigeria essentially, do not have the required training infrastructures for the acquisition of skill and for the progressive development of its businesses and manufacturing operations (UNIDO, 2012). The lack of the necessary training required for manufacturing practices can lead to incompetence in manufacturing process. Skill is very useful in improving the manufacturing process and enable SMEs to effectively compete (Chatha and Butt, 2015)

SMEs as Drivers of Economic Growth and Development in Nigeria

Empirical evidence has shown that the SMEs segment of the Nigeria manufacturing industry have become an essential component for the sustainable growth and development of Nigerian economy (Ogboru, 2005; Fida, 2008; Eniola, 2014). In terms of distribution of wealth and growth of the GDP, Nigeria MSMEs has been the backbone of the manufacturing segment of the economy (Aremu and Adeyemi, 2011). The reduction in poverty from the job creation, have enabled the Nigeria MSMEs to improve living standards and changed the indigenous technology which were concerns to most emerging economies like Nigeria (Kongolo, 2010). Deciding from an economic standpoint MSMEs create good jobs (Edmiston, 2007).

Economic Contribution of SMEs

The SMEs are renowned for making huge contributions to the Nigeria economic growth and development of the manufacturing segment of the economy (Lukacs 2005; Abor and Quartey, 2010). SMEs in the global perspective provides a lot of economic advantage (Levine 2005; Newberry 2006). For quite some time the Nigeria MSMEs have been considered as the avenue to accomplish manufacturing growth and the development objectives of creating valuable jobs to the economy (Advani, 1997, Abor and Quartey, 2010).

SMEs Job Creation

The SMEs have made considerable contribution to the improvement growth and development of the economy, especially in Nigeria due to their ability to create jobs for employment (Onuorah, 2009; Abor and Quartey 2010; Aremu and Adeyemi, 2011). SMEs have become an essential channel for providing the needed employment. Therefore, SMEs are progressively perceived as creator of new jobs (Swierczek and Ha, 2003; Lukacs, 2005). SMEs have become the powerhouse that create jobs globally; in the European Union (EU) they provide employment to about 65 million people (Lukacs, 2005). Respectively in Nigeria and Ghana SMEs have created about 80 to 85 percent of manufacturing employment. (Abor and Quartey 2010; Aremu and Adeyemi, 2011). The employment by SMEs in Malaysia is about 38.9 percent of the entire employees (Salah and Ndubuisi, 2006). The same applies in Thailand, where it is estimated that the SMEs employment is about 38.9 percent of the whole manpower (Chittithaworn et al., 2011).

SMEs Capability

The flexible business composition of SMEs makes it possible for them to react to their customer needs, make economic contribution and the ability to align to the dynamic business environment and the economic situation than the bigger firms (Beaver and Prince 2004; Newberry 2006). It is well noted that SMEs have an advantage over bigger firms, as bigger firms have less flexible business structure, which frequently create bureaucracy, limiting their capability to act quickly (Beaver and Prince 2004). There is quick decision procedure made by SMEs managers and owner that enables them to change the processes of production within a short period of time, which might not take place in bigger firms (Raynard and Forstater, 2002; Erixon, 2009). It is much debated that new product and innovation happen in SMEs probably more than in bigger firms as SMEs makes little investment infrastructure and less expenses in general economic situation (Erixon, 2009).

SMEs in Poverty Alleviation

SMEs are considered agents of change in the reduction of poverty and has turned the most crucial contributing economic prospect in various nations of the world, especially in the emerging and developing countries (Indarti and Langenberg 2004; Pansiri and Temtime 2008; Chittithaworn et al., 2011). It has been noted that most SMEs investment cost is very little due to its small size and might not require any expert knowledge (Chittithaworn et al., 2011). In essence SMEs have become the potential of employment for millions of poor people all over the globe (Lukacs, 2005). The correlation between SMEs and poverty alleviation is well recognized, for its ability to create jobs in Nigeria (Edom et al., 2015).

EMPIRICAL STUDY: RESEARCH METHODOLOGY

The study presented in this chapter embraced the qualitative research approach due to its usefulness and unique features that are used to address the what, why and how questions (Easterby-Smith et al; 2012) to understand from a different perspective the Nigeria manufacturing SMEs strategy, priorities and challenges. The research approach is utilised in gathering useful information for analysis (Zikmund, 2003). This exploratory study presents empirical evidence, with a qualitative research method, where theoretical development is established (Easterby-Smith *et al.*, 2012). The study empirically presents an understanding of the manufacturing SMEs strategy practice and process in the emerging economy within the context of Nigeria manufacturing SMEs, identifying their business priorities and operational challenges through the experiences of SMEs owners and senior managers underpinned in the interpretive epistemology where interpretation of the study is from the participants (Creswell, 2009; Denzin and Lincoln, 2011; Bryman, 2012).

Data Evaluation

The book chapter is based on an empirical study which aimed to the capture the knowledge and experience of manufacturing SMEs senior manager and owners in identifying their strategy, business priorities, manufacturing and operational challenges in Nigeria. Semi-structured interviews were used as the data collection instrument. 17 senior managers and owners of SMEs were interviewed, representing 17 Nigeria manufacturing SMEs businesses in the six geopolitical zones across Nigeria. The interview approach provided an understanding of the manufacturing SMEs strategy, priorities and challenges in the emerging economies within the context of Nigeria. The data was analysed by building textual data from the interview transcriptions, using template analysis (King, 2009) to code the emerging themes from the transcribed interview data to explain the experiences of SMEs owners and senior managers in understanding the manufacturing strategy process and practice of Nigeria manufacturing SMEs. Nvivo was used as QUAL data analysis software tool which works well with template analysis in order to construct theoretical conclusions grounded in the data. Template analysis offers flexibility in its approach in qualitative data analysis (King, 2009) and offers insightful explanations on the study participant's understandings that are frequently ignored in other data analysis. Template analysis is considered useful where the textual data is obtained from where the research instrument includes interview (Goldschmidt *et al.* 2006; Thompson *et al.*, 2010; Lockett *et al.*, 2012; Brooks 2014 King *et al.*, 2015). In addition, thematic template data analysis offers structure to the study and showcases the fullness of the textual data as they emerge from the themes unit to be coded for an easy analysis of the data (Crabtree and Miller, 1999). The thematic template analysis employed in the study applied the hierarchical coding procedure to adaptably analyse the textual data to the requirement of the study (King *et al.*, 2015). The development of a prior code is necessary in breaking down the chunk of data. Priori codes are common classifications of the extracted data from the objectives and aims of the data explored to form a simple framework on which to commence the investigation of the data (Gibson and Brown, 2009).

Manufacturing SMEs Strategy

Figure 1. Emerging themes of manufacturing strategy with the Nigerian SMEs sector

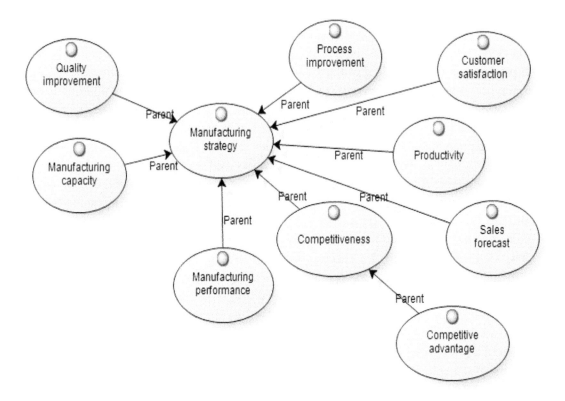

To understand the manufacturing SMEs strategy, senior managers were asked the question: *what is the purpose of manufacturing strategy in your company and how do you formulate this manufacturing strategy?* Their responses were presented in figure 1 transcribed as follows; *"The purpose of our manufacturing strategy is to develop some sort of goals that we want to achieve in setting the direction of the company. Our manufacturing operation involves our daily running of the production process to improve efficiency and reduce manufacturing cost"* (McA). Also the manager of the manufacturing SME McJ spoke that *"our manufacturing strategy and plan is very important to us to manage difficult situation in the manufacturing process to produce products that are of high-quality standard"* (McJ) The manager of manufacturing SME McL in another occasion asserted that *"the purpose of manufacturing strategy is intended to help build a production plan that analyses and examine the productivity and capacity of production process taking into account the human resources, manufacturing equipment and the set out period to accomplish these goals. Our manufacturing strategy includes the process improvement of manufacturing, sale forecast, budgeting, managing operational cost and improving the product quality"* (McL).

During the conducted face to face semi-structured interviews with owners and senior managers of SMEs, it was noted that many of the manufacturing SMEs have a diverse approach to their manufacturing strategy. Some of the managers have reflected their responses based on their current market, financial situation and their customer response. The SME manager state McB stated that, *"our manufacturing strategy is formulated based on the economic situation in the country. The economic situation drives the market and consumer behaviour. This in-turn decides how the company formulate the strategy. From the procurement of machinery, the procurement of raw materials, product development, market expansion, and so on. These are all functions of the economic situations"* (McB).

The Nigeria manufacturing SMEs managers were asked the question during interview: Can you tell me about the overall manufacturing strategy formulation process in your company? The manager McD response was *"my company is not stringent in the process of strategy formulation. As a result, strategy formulation can be because of suggestion received from an external source, internal source, press release, our customer demand, or competitor's move. Regardless of the source, the major process involved in the analysis of this information received and if viable, it can then be adopted and worked on to achieve our manufacturing goals and objectives"* (McD). It is imperative that Nigeria manufacturing SMEs have noted the significance for their strategy to be allied with their business shared values and manufacturing objectives. The SME manager of McH have articulated that *"manufacturing strategy is an essential part of our company's shared values and business strategies, including a well-coordinated manufacturing objectives and action programs designed at accomplishing a lasting sustainable advantage over our company's main competitors"* (McH). In support the manager of McA emphasised that *"over the next few years we want to focus on making our plant, process more efficient, and increase our speed to the market. to enable us to remain competitive and meet our market expectations within the Nigeria and Africa economy, we must support our manufacturing processes, make improvements, and increase our manufacturing abilities"* (McA). One can be persuaded from the interview findings that Nigeria manufacturing SMEs strategy is practiced and deliberate for several motives, comprising of the capability to develop and design new products, satisfy the demands of customers and deliberate on the cost of manufacturing. In that regard the SME manager of McO have expressed *"we have well set out manufacturing plans that enabled us to develop new products, produce quality products, be able to get these products to our customers and the market as quickly as possible"* (McO). Also, in answering the question on manufacturing strategy formulation process in the manufacturing SMEs. The manager of McC communicated that *"in formulating our manufacturing strategy we have taken into consideration, cost of manufacturing, in terms of electricity supply, sourcing raw material, delivering our products and increasing our sales and customer base"* (McC). The empirical findings from the qualitative data analysis have shown that Nigeria manufacturing SMEs require transformational strategy to develop the manufacturing practice. The managers of the manufacturing SMEs in Nigeria were questioned on how they have formulated their manufacturing strategy. In answering the question, the manager of SME McP replied *"we formulate our manufacturing strategy based on so many criteria. We look at our previous set out goals and manufacturing objectives whether they have been accomplished or not. If not accomplished what could have been the reason. Is it as a result of lack of resources or external forces we cannot control such as government policies, we look at our budget and the market in regard to sales forecasts"* (McP). Furthermore, the manager of SME McK asserted *"we have made some strategic changes in our business to reflect our manufacturing strategy and our future manufacturing plans. We must continue with improved production efficiency to reduce the cost, for example, mechanise, automate, improve our manufacturing processes and then upgrade all the manufacturing equipment to meet our future manufacturing and production plans"* (McK). The issues of manufacturing performance in the manufacturing strategy process of the Nigeria manufacturing SMEs were considered. When they were asked about the manufacturing strategy formulation process. The manager of SME McB responded saying *"manufacturing strategy is formulated in consideration to our manufacturing performance. We ask ourselves, are we still competitive, are we still producing at a lower cost, are our machines still good enough to meet our production needs, if not how do we procure another machine to improve our manufacturing process. If we are satisfied with all the questions asked, we then draw up a manufacturing strategy that will sustain all these concerns raised"* (McB).

Manufacturing Priorities

Figure 2. Emerging themes of manufacturing priorities

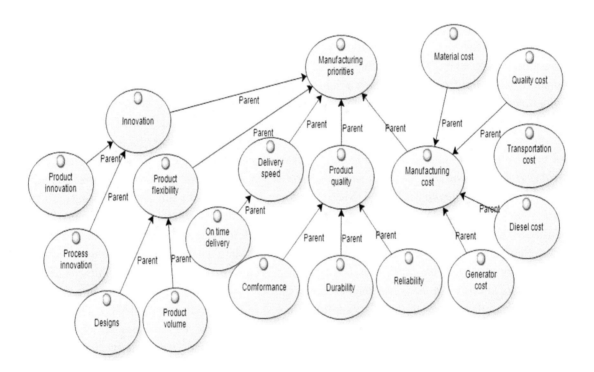

Manufacturing SMEs priorities, the emerging themes in figure 2 were centered on product cost, delivery, flexibility and innovation. The SME manager McA emphasised *"our manufacturing priority is to reduce the cost of manufacturing which is on the high side compared to other manufacturing countries in Africa. The cost of electricity in a year alone is enough to buy new machines and equipment to expand and improve the business"* (McA).

The data from the interviews have shown that the issues of manufacturing cost as a major concern and priority, be it importation cost, electricity cost and product delivery cost. In the interview the SME McK manager emphasised *"we spend lots of money on diesel fuel to generate our own electricity. The electricity supply is less than 8 hours in a day. Can you imagine Nigeria 6th oil producer in the world yet the country import fuel this is not healthy for the economy as the importers pass on the cost to us manufacturers? It cost you more to produce here in Nigeria than many countries of the world.* In support, the manager of SME McD implied that *"the cost of importing raw material is very high as the government keeps increasing import duties. The cost of delivering our products to customers is very high as for result of bad roads and poor transport systems. It takes about 3 to 5 days to deliver goods from Lagos to Kano.''*

Manufacturing Cost

Figure 3. Emerging themes of manufacturing cost

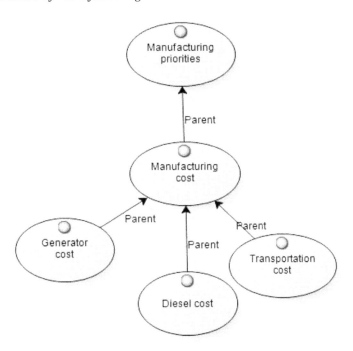

The emerging themes in figure 3 has shown that increasing cost on the manufacturing of products is a concern for manufacturers in the Nigeria SMEs sector. The question what your manufacturing priorities is and do you deal with manufacturing cost were asked. The manager of SME McC noted that *''high manufacturing cost is the major problem facing us manufacturers in Nigeria, even as we continually cut down on our manufacturing costs by recognising the production setback and then applying all the necessary tools and techniques needed to improve the performance of these setbacks''*(McC). In support, the SME manager of McE expressed that *''for the Nigeria manufacturing industry, the challenges around managing the cost of electricity will increase in the nearest future and not do something about it, is not a good choice for any meaningful manufacturing business that wants to succeed''* (McE). The findings have shown that cost of electricity remained an important subject for the Nigeria manufacturers. Several SMEs were forced to close their businesses due to the high cost of manufacturing. The SME manager of McQ state that their *'' manufacturing costs are made up of the raw material costs used in production, labour costs used in converting these raw materials into finished products and other incurred costs which are from diesel cost, generator cost and transportation cost acquired during the production and delivery of these products to customers''*(McQ). Likewise, the SME manager of McA have cautioned that *''if the cost of manufacturing in Nigeria is not properly managed and kept under control, the stability of the entire*

manufacturing sector, as well as the Nigeria economy, will be hurt financially''(McA). Furthermore, the SME manager of McJ emphasized that *''manufacturing generally is not cheap, but in Nigeria, the case is different as it cost almost three times what it cost in neighbouring Africa countries such as Benin, Togo, and Ghana. In other to reduce cost we try as much as possible to minimise and eradicate waste from our manufacturing process''* (McJ). Empirically the evidence presented from the findings have demonstrated that lowering cost is major manufacturing priority for the Nigeria manufacturing SMEs.

Product Flexibility

Figure 4. Emerging themes of product flexibility

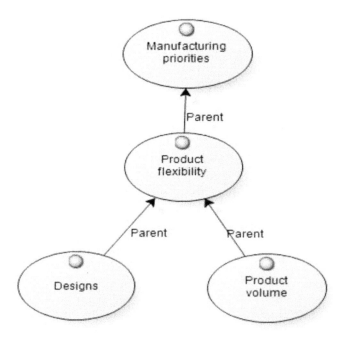

Figure 4 present the emerging themes of flexibility to respond to market demands, in terms of adjusting the production line within short notices, can be very crucial in the competitive manufacturing market environment. Attention has arisen among some Nigerian manufacturing SMEs to respond to radical changes in global technology to improve their products. The SME manager of McK noted "our *product flexibility enables us as manufacturers to be able to respond to the market needs and demands, by bringing in designed new products soon to the market''*(McK).

Product Delivery

Figure 5. Emerging themes of delivery speed

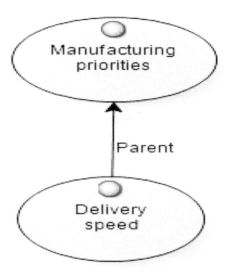

The theme emerging from figure 5 present delivery speed of moving products from one location to another. SME manager of McB expressed that *"as a manufacturing our manufacturing priority is to be able to deliver our products to many of our customers in* time'' (McB). Additionally, the SME manager MCE explained that *''delivering our products quickly to the market is our priority''* (McE). When delivery targets are met, it enabled customers to build a lasting relationship. McO manger reiterate that *''we try everything possible to deliver our products in time, but sometimes the delivery is not under our control, sometimes we have unforeseen delays in the transport, raw material, and power failures''* (McO). Delivery failure can arise from many factors such as poor transportation system, poor road network infrastructures and failures in electricity distribution.

Innovation

Figure 6. Emerging themes of innovation

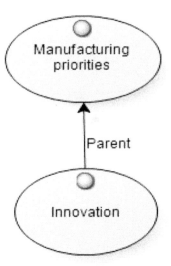

Figure 6 present emerging themes of product innovation as a business priority which is essential for the manufacturing growth and development. The question how often does you develop new products were asked? The SME McA manager responded *"not too often, one of the greatest impediments deterring the manufacturing sector in Nigeria is the lack of manufacturing product innovation as it hampers the industry's ability to apply skills to lessen the effects of other limitations in the country. The Nigerian manufacturing sector of the economy needs new measures, processes, and mechanisation of activities to be globally competitive"*. Likewise, SME manager of McL stated that *"innovation is what that strengthen and sustain the advancement, transformation, and improvements required for our manufacturing performance. The manufacturing industry needs innovation to succeed. The lack of innovation is one of the greatest barriers deterring the smooth running of manufacturing businesses in Nigeria. Innovation is vital to me as a manufacturer as the lack of it obstructs the ability of manufacturers to utilize technology. The Nigerian manufacturing sector needs new ideas for product design, and modification to remain competitive"* (McL).

Nigerian SMEs Challenges

Figure 7. Emerging themes of Nigerian SMEs challenges

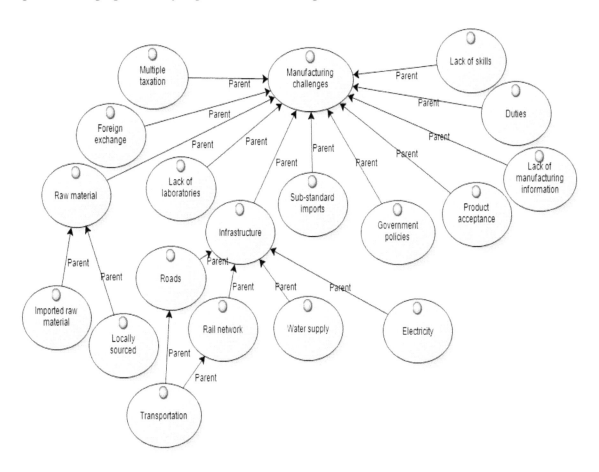

The generated theme from figure 7 shows the challenges of Nigerian SMEs which includes infrastructure, lack of skill, multiple taxations, and funding, sub-standard product, lack of laboratories, lack of raw material, foreign exchange and government policies. The views and comment of manufacturing SMEs McE challenges were note during the interviews- *''the challenges we face as manufacturers in Nigeria are huge. We face challenges of poor electricity supply, infrastructural decay, inadequate security, continuous government policy change, increase in import duty levy, multiple taxations, fuel cost and the declining exchange rate for foreign currency needed for importation of machines and raw materials. It cost more to produce in Nigeria than every other place in Africa. The country currently is generating less than 5000 megawatt of electricity which is far below the demand* (McE).

Infrastructural Challenges

Figure 8. The emerging themes of infrastructure

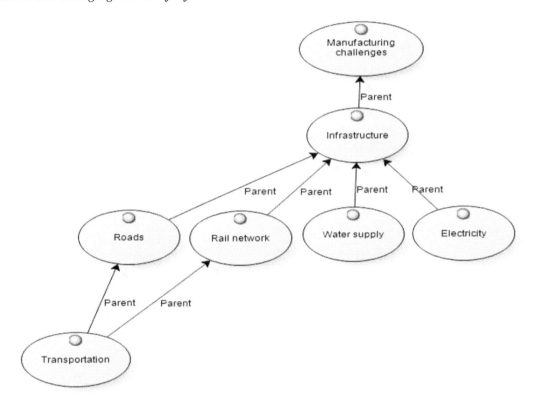

The decline in basic infrastructural amenities is major concerns to many manufacturing businesses in Nigeria (figure 8). SME manager of McD have spoken that, *''in this 21ˢᵗ century the type of the infra-structures in Nigeria is at their worst state. No good roads, no adequate, electricity supply, and even water which are the most needed necessity of most Nigerians''* (McD). Likewise, SME manager of McB emphasises that''the *appalling state of the roads infrastructures is not good for business when it comes to the transportation of manufactured product to other parts of the country. Many lives are being lost on a daily basis as these roads have become death traps to commuters''* (McB). *''The Nigerian government has failed to address the systemic problems affecting the competitiveness of MSMEs such as electricity power supply and high transportation costs''* (McP)

Transportation

Figure 9. Emerging themes of transportation

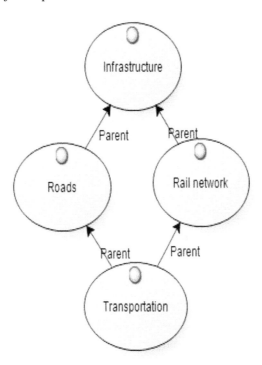

Figure 9 have shown emerging theme of transportation is a hub for economic activities. The lack of good transportation system is major concern to most Nigeria manufacturing businesses The SME Manager of McI emphasised that *''the transport infrastructural development is still not keeping pace with the development of the industrialisation goal of the government. It cost more to transport goods within Nigeria when compared to our neighbouring African countries. The roads are death traps and causes delays to heavy-duty trucks used in transporting our goods and products to a remote area of the country''* (McI). Moreover, SME manager of McD assert *''our transport infrastructure in Nigeria is inadequate, which in essence remains an impediment to the country's development and economic growth. We still lag behind in terms of good road and rail infrastructures. The cost of transportation in Nigeria is sky rocking at moment for the distribution of products to our customers''* (McD).

Multiple Taxation

Figure 10. Emerging themes of multiple taxation

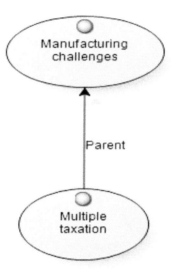

Figure 10 present the emerging themes of Nigeria government complex tax policy. It has become a challenge to many manufacturing SMEs. McQ and McJ managers expressed that *''the tax system is unfair to us manufacturers as it continues to increase our cost as manufacturers. The multiple taxes we pay have increased the cost of doing and establishing businesses in Nigeria. These multiple taxes have put off so many prospective investors''* The multiple tax payment is now a problem to many Nigeria manufacturing SMEs businesses. McG SME manager state that *''the taxes we pay in this country as manufacturers are too much and are not encouraging us to continue to do business in Nigeria. The various government agencies in this country keep levying us with the same levy with different names. On one instance we have to pay for environmental pollution, in another one, we have to pay for environmental waste exposures''* (McG). The findings present empirical evidence that Nigeria manufacturing SMEs paid multiple taxes.

Lack of Skills

Figure 11. Emerging themes of lack of skills

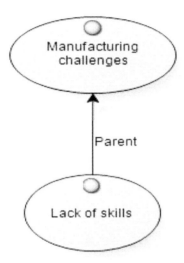

The figure 11 present the emerging theme lack of skills. Quality skill a major asset to most advanced manufacturing nations. The shortage in manufacturing skill presents a great danger to Nigeria manufacturing SMEs. The SME manager of McM emphasised that *''there is a dearth of manufacturing skills in Nigeria'*. This was acknowledged by the manager of SME McK as an *'impediment to the realisation of the full manufacturing potentials and development of the sector of the economy''* (McK). In support SME manager of McN highlighted that *'many people employed do not have the necessary skill set needed to advance manufacturing practice in this country of ours Nigeria, except few of us managers that have been in the manufacturing business for a long period of time...It is important for us manufacturing managers to be aware of the new challenges that might arise as a result of process change or manufacturing plant alterations'* (McN).

Government Policies and Regulations

Figure 12. Emerging theme government policies

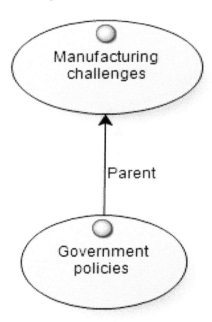

Figure 12 present emerging theme government policies. The government economic policies play an essential role in determining the existence of manufacturing SMEs. The devaluation of the Naira over the years has negative impact of importing manufacturing SMEs. The manager of SME McI asserted that *"Our manufacturing in Nigeria depends mainly on foreign exchange to succeed, given that the large share of the raw materials we use for manufacturing are imported. The present economic situation is not helping our business as the devaluation of the country's currency by CBN means our budget is affected by the Naira fall which leads to spending more money to secure the foreign currency (dollar) needed for importation"* (McI). Likewise, the manager of SME McM said that *"the lack of government support to us manufacturers in this country is on many fronts affecting the manufacturing sector. In the last four years the government have had so many different regulations on manufacturing, ranging from subsidy and the local content act which are supposed to be beneficial to local manufacturers. However, this has not been the case as the local content which is supposed to allow local manufacturers to be competitive, is not being implemented"* (McM).

Funding

Figure 13. Emerging theme of funding

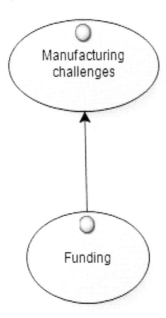

Figure 13 present emerging theme fund, which are not readily made available for SMEs businesses to acquire loans from the banks. Manager of McD recognised the operating cost accompanying manufacturing, by stating that *"in the past one year, we have been generating our own electricity. I can categorically tell you that it is very expensive to run a generating plant for electricity which we all depend on to enable our manufacturing process"* (McD Likewise, SME manager of McJ noted that *''inadequate funding is one of the various challenges we face as manufacturing firms in Nigeria. The banks should make funds available to SMEs for loans, as part of the government stipulated financial provision to support manufacturers. ''...Arguably, the most obvious challenge is lack of financial support. Only short-term funds are available in Nigeria, and those funds are tailored to meet importation (trading) and not manufacturing''* (McJ).

Sub-Standard Imports

Figure 14. Emerging theme of sub-standard imports

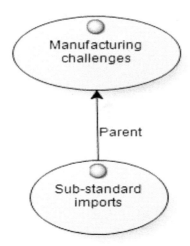

Figure 14 present emerging theme sub-standard import which influx o have increased rapidly, causing a major concern for many manufacturers. *''The country is being flooded with imported fake and sub-standard products that are killing our business. Despite the appalling quality of these products, they are cheaper''* (McH). Another manager stated...*''we must compete with cheap fake sub-standard imports that are coming into this country unchecked''* (McI). The importation and manufacturing of sub-standard products should never be allowed. *''Importations of sub-standard products are dangerous to human consumption and the economic well-being of the country. I think for the good interest of people's well-being, the government needs to ban these products and sanction the importers of such products''* (McH). The findings present evidence about the pact of sub-standard having on manufacturing businesses making them less competitive.

Lack of Laboratories

Figure 15. Emerging theme of lack of laboratories

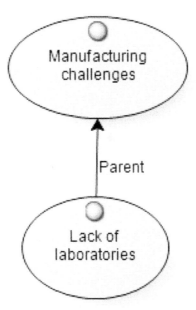

Figure 15 present emerging theme of lack of laboratories where SMEs managers have expressed the challenge and impact on the test of manufactured products. Collectively, SMEs managers of McO and McP have spoken their worries over the absence of commercialised laboratories in Nigeria for good quality control. They stated that *''the charges brought against many Nigerian manufactured products by importers that made in Nigeria product lacks quality cannot be verified as the country lacks laboratories for testing products on industrial scale''*(McO). Also, SME McP manager noted that the... *''lack of commercialised quality control testing laboratories in Nigeria has made it possible for dubious importers to take advantage of the failed system and import fake sub-standard products into the country''*(McP).

Lack of Raw Material

Figure 16. Emerging theme of raw material

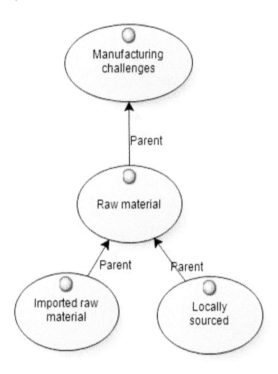

The Figure 16 present emerging theme of of raw material which have resulted in manufacturing SMEs not meeting up with customers demand and production target. Manager of McI stated that "*one of our major challenges is the lack of raw materials, due to high foreign exchange rate slammed on importers. We are cutting down on most of our products due to the scarcity of raw materials. We rely on these importers for the supply of the needed raw material to continue production. The scarcity of raw material is affecting our business as we struggle to meet some of the customers demand*" (McI). Likewise, SME manager of McO communicated that "*the lack of raw materials has made us slow down on our production activities. We are currently searching for alternative suppliers as our present supplier can no longer meet our demands. The lack of information on these raw materials available has made things a bit difficult for us. Some these suppliers do not have websites; we must rely on a conversation with other businesses. Sometimes we go to the addresses provided but we are unable to find any of these suppliers*" (McO).

CONCLUSION

The purpose of the chapter and the empirical study presented here, was to develop an understanding of strategy process and practice of Nigeria manufacturing SMEs. The chapter reviewed and discussed the manufacturing priorities and challenges of SMEs within an emerging economy environment. The empirical findings presented define emerging economy-based manufacturing strategy is deliberate while the local manufacturers build their manufacturing priorities and respond to the challenges in their manufacturing environment. Empirical evidence in the findings have shown that manufacturing SMEs like most other organisations in the emerging economies have many challenges that hinder their abilities to compete. These challenges have major effects on the manufacturing strategic priorities of cost, quality, delivery, innovation and flexibility and the ability to compete with products from the other emerging nations. Emerging economy governments typically aim to introduce regulations and policies which push SMEs to focus on cost reduction strategies and making tradeoffs in quality and flexibility to remain competitive. The findings presented in the chapter have empirically increased the body of knowledge and practice in manufacturing SMEs in understanding strategy, manufacturing priorities and challenges. This has possible implications for managers, policy maker and other business practitioners in the field of manufacturing operation and production management. Emerging economy government policies should be directed towards measures to address the infrastructures, improve their domestic corporate tax system and support capital lending mechanisms for SMEs.

REFERENCES

Abor, J., & Quartey, P. (2010). Issues in SME Development in Ghana and South Africa. *International Research Journal of Finance and Economics*, (39), 218–228.

Accenture. (2014). *Manufacturing Skills and Training Study*. Accenture. http://www.themanufacturinginstitute.org/Research/Skills-and-Training

Achua, J.K. (2008). Corporate social responsibility in the Nigerian banking system. *Society And Business Review 3*(1) 21.

Acur, N., Gertsen, F., Sun, H., & Frick, J. (2003). The formalisation of manufacturing strategy and its influence on the relationships between competitive objectives, improvement goals, and action plans. *International Journal of Operations & Production Management, 23*(10), 1114–1141. doi:10.1108/01443570310496599

Adam, N. A., & Alarifi, G. (2021). Innovation practices for survival of small and medium enterprises (SMEs) in the COVID-19 times: The role of external support. *Journal of Innovation and Entrepreneurship*, *10*(15), 15. doi:10.1186/s13731-021-00156-6 PMID:34075328

Adebisi, J. F., & Gbegi, D. O. (2013). Effect of tax avoidance and tax evasion on personal income tax administration in Nigeria. *American. Journal of the Humanities and Social Sciences*, 1.

Adeniran, J. O., Yusuf, S. A., & Adeyemi, O. A. (2014). The impact of exchange rate fluctuation on the Nigerian economic growth: An empirical investigation. *International Journal of Academic Research in Business & Social Sciences*, *4*(8), 224–233.

Advani, A. (1997). *Industrial clusters: A support system for small and medium-sized enterprises, the private sector development.* (World Bank Occasional Paper No. 32). World Bank, Washington DC.

Agwu, O. M., & Emeti, I. C. (2014). Issues, Challenges and Prospects of Small and Medium Scale Enterprises (SMEs) in Port-Harcourt City. *European Journal of Sustainable Development*, *3*(1), 101–114. doi:10.14207/ejsd.2014.v3n1p101

Ahmad, A., & Schroeder, R. (2002). Dimensions of competitive priorities are they clear, communicated and consistent. *Journal of Applied Business Research*, *18*(1), 77–86.

Aliyu, S. U. R. (2011). *Real exchange rate misalignment: An application of behavioural equilibrium exchange rate (BEER) to Nigeria.* Munich Personal RePEc Archive.

Amoako-Gyampah, K., & Acquaah, M. (2008). Manufacturing strategy, competitive strategy and firm performance: An empirical study in a developing economy environment. *International Journal of Production Economics*, *111*(2), 575–592. doi:10.1016/j.ijpe.2007.02.030

Apulu, I., & Ige, E. O. (2011). Are Nigeria SMEs effectively utilizing ICT. *Internatiom Jourmal Business Management*, *6*(6), 207–214.

Aremu, M. A., & Adeyemi, S. L. (2011). Small and Medium Scale Enterprises as: A Survival Strategy for Employment Generation in Nigeria. *Journal of Sustainable Development*, *4*(1), 200–206.

Aruwa, S., & Gugong, B. (2007) An assessment of Small and Medium Industries Equity Investment Scheme (SMIEIS) Implementation Guidelines. Journal of Humanities, Kaduna State University.

Ates, A. (2008). Strategy process in manufacturing SMEs. [PhD dissertation, University of Strathclyde, Glasgow].

Ayanda, A. M., & Laraba, A. S. (2011). Small and Medium Scale Enterprises as a survival strategy for employment generation in Nigeria. *Journal of Sustainable Development*, *4*(1), 200–206.

Ayanruoh, F. (2013). Why privatising Nigeria 's Refineries. ' *The Guardian* (Nigeria), www.ngrguardiannews.com

Ayuba, B. (2014). Assessment of Factors Influencing Consumer Satisfaction: A Survey of Customers of Nigerian Manufacturing Companies. *World Review of Business Research*, *3*(4), 148–161.

Barad, M., & Gien, D. (2001). Linking improvement models to manufacturing strategies – a methodology for SMEs and other enterprises. *International Journal of Production Research*, *39*(12), 2675–2695. doi:10.1080/0020754001110051824

Barnes, D. (2002a). The complexities of the manufacturing strategy formation process in practice. *International Journal of Operations & Production Management*, *22*(10), 1090–1111. doi:10.1108/01443570210446324

Barnes, D. (2002b). The manufacturing strategy formation process in small and medium-sized enterprises. *Journal of Small Business and Enterprise Development*, *9*(2), 130–149. doi:10.1108/14626000210427384

Beaver, G., & Prince, C. (2004). Management, strategy, and policy in the UK small business sector: A critical review. *Journal of Small Business and Enterprise Development*, *11*(1), 34–49. doi:10.1108/14626000410519083

Bellamy, L. C. (2009). Strategy formulation in SMEs: Indications from a longitudinal study. *International Journal of Entrepreneurship and Small Business*, *8*(4), 534–549. doi:10.1504/IJESB.2009.025697

BERR. (2009). *Manufacturing: New Challenges*. New Opportunities. September.

Bouri, A., Breij, M., Diop, M., Kempner, R., Klinger, B., & Stevenson, R. (2011). *Report on support to SMEs in developing countries through financial intermediaries*. Dalberg Global Development Advisors.

Brooks, J. (2014). Young people with diabetes and their peers - an exploratory study of peer attitudes, beliefs, responses and influences. Project report to Diabetes UK, University of Huddersfield.

Bryman, A. (2012). *Social Research Methods* (4th ed.). Oxford University Press.

Cagliano, R., & Spina, G. (2002). A comparison of practice-performance models between small manufacturers and subcontractors. *International Journal of Operations & Production Management, 22*(12), 1367–1388. doi:10.1108/01443570210452057

Central Bank of Nigeria. (2013). *Statistical Bulletin* (Vol. 23). CBN.

Chatha, K. A., & Butt, I. (2015). Themes of study in manufacturing strategy literature. *International Journal of Operations & Production Management, 35*(4), 604–698. doi:10.1108/IJOPM-07-2013-0328

Chittithaworn, C., Islam, A., & Yusuf, D. H. M. (2011). Factors affecting Business Success of Small and Medium Enterprises in Thailand. *Asian Social Science, 7*(5), 180–190. doi:10.5539/ass.v7n5p180

Crabtree, B. F., & Miller, W. L. (1999) Doing qualitative research, 2nd edn. Thousand Oaks, Calif: London: Sage.

Creswell, J. W. (2009). *Research Design: qualitative, quantitative and mixed approaches* (3rd ed.). Sage.

Daniel, K., Per, C., & Tomas, N. (2022). Challenges for growing SMEs: A managerial perspective, Journal of Small Business Management, Demir, R., Wennberg, K., and McKelvie, A. (2017). The strategic management of high-growth firms: A review and theoretical conceptualization. *Long Range Planning, 50*(4), 431–456.

Denzin, N. K., & Lincoln, Y. S. (2011) The Sage Handbook of Qualitative Research 4th edn. Thousand Oaks, Sage.California

Dodd, N., van der Merwe, J., Bond, P., & Dodd, N. (2019). *BRICS'trade with Africa: Long live the new king, just like the old king. BRICS and Resistance in Africa: Contention, Assimilation and Co-optation.* Zed Books.

Dube, C., & Erinah, C. (2016). Response of the Manufacturing Sector to the Zimbabwe Economic Crisis. In K. George & O. O. Raphael (Eds.), *Economic Management in a Hyperinflationary Environment: The Political Economy of Zimbabwe, 1980–2008.* Academic. doi:10.1093/acprof:oso/9780198747505.003.0003

Easterby-Smith, M., Thorpe, R., & Jackson, P. (2012). *Management Research* (4th ed.). Sage.

Edmiston, K. D. (2007). The role of small and large businesses in economic development. *Economic Review*, 73-97

Ehie, I., & Muogboh, O. (2016). Analysis of manufacturing strategy in developing countries. *Journal of Manufacturing Technology Management, 27*(2), 234–260. doi:10.1108/JMTM-07-2014-0094

Eniola, A. A. (2014). The Role of SME Firm Performance in Nigeria. *Arabian Journal of Business and Management Review, 3*(12), 33–47. doi:10.12816/0016552

Erixon, F. (2009). SMEs in Europe: Taking stock and looking forward. *Centre for European Studies*, *8*(8), 293–300. doi:10.1007/s12290-009-0093-7

Esteve-Pérez, S., Pieri, F., & Rodriguez, D. (2022). One swallow does not make a summer: Episodes and persistence in high growth. *Small Business Economics*, *58*(3), 1517–1544. doi:10.1007/s11187-020-00443-8

European Commision. (2013). *SMEs*. European Commission. https://ec.europa.eu/.../en/opportunities/fp7/calls/fp7-sme-2013.html

European Commission (2003). *Recommendation 2003/361/EC regarding the SME definition*. EC.

Fida, B. A. (2008). The Role of Small and Medium Enterprises (SMEs) in Economic Development. Enterprise Development, Free Online Library.

Garvin, D. A. (1987). Competing on the eight dimensions of quality. *Harvard Business Review*, *65*(6), 101–109.

Ghobakhloo, M. (2018). The future of manufacturing industry: A strategic roadmap toward Industry 4.0. *Journal of Manufacturing Technology Management*, *29*(6), 910–936. doi:10.1108/JMTM-02-2018-0057

Gibson, W., & Brown, A. (2009). Working with Qualitative Data. London.SAGE Publications. *Qualitative Report*, *8*(4), 597–607.

González-Benito, J., & Suárez-González, I. (2010). A study of the role played by manufacturing strategic objectives and capabilities in understanding the relationship between Porter's generic strategies and business performance. *British Journal of Management*, *21*(4), 1027–1043. doi:10.1111/j.1467-8551.2008.00626.x

Groeßler, A. (2007). A dynamic view on strategic resources and capabilities applied to an example from the manufacturing strategy literature. *Journal of Manufacturing Technology Management*, *18*(3), 250–266. doi:10.1108/17410380710730594

Größler, A., & Grübner, A. (2006). An empirical model of the relationships between manufacturing capabilities. *International Journal of Operations & Production Management*, *26*(5), 458–485. doi:10.1108/01443570610659865

Hallgren, M., Olhager, J., & Schroeder, R. G. (2011). A hybrid model of competitive capabilities. *International Journal of Operations & Production Management*, *31*(5), 511–526. doi:10.1108/01443571111126300

Hashim, I. A., & Zarma, A. B. (1996), "The Impact of Parallel Market on the Stability of Exchange Rate: Evidence from Nigeria", NDIC Quarterly, Vol. 7 No. 2.

Hill, A., & Hill, T. (2009). *Manufacturing Operations Strategy* (3rd ed.). Palgrave Macmillan. doi:10.1007/978-1-137-07690-8

Hill, T. (2000). Manufacturing Strategy—Text and Cases 2nd edition. Palgrave.

Hill, T. (2009). *Manufacturing Operations Strategy* (3rd ed.). Palgrave MacMillan. doi:10.1007/978-1-137-07690-8

Hitt, M. A., Ireland, R. D., & Hoskisson, R. E. (2007). *Strategic management: Competitiveness and globalization* (5th edition.). Cincinnati, OH: Southwestern College Publishing Company Houndmills, Hampshire. https://databank.worldbank.org/data/home.aspx

Ho, T. C. F., Ahmad, N. H., & Ramayah, T. (2016). Competitive Capabilities and Business Performance among Manufacturing SMEs: Evidence from an Emerging Economy, Malaysia. *Journal of Asia-Pacific Business*, *17*(1), 37–58. doi:10.1080/10599231.2016.1129263

Ihua, U. B. (2009). SMEs Key Failure-Factors: A Comparison between the United Kingdom and Nigeria. *Journal of Social Sciences*, *18*(3), 199–207. doi:10.1080/09718923.2009.11892682

Indarti, N., & Langenberg, M. (2004). *Factors affecting business success among SMEs: Empirical evidence from Indonesia.* U Twente. http://www.utwente.nl/niks/achief/research/conference/esu/papers/indartilagenbe rg.pdf (Accessed 10 March 2015)

Julta, D., Bodorick, P., & Dhaliwal, J. (2002). Supporting the e-business readiness of small and medium sized enterprises: Approaches and metrics. *Internet Research*, *12*(2), 139–164. doi:10.1108/10662240210422512

Kang, H. S., Lee, J. Y., Choi, S., Kim, H., Park, J. H., Son, J. Y., Kim, B. H., & Do Noh, S. (2016). Smart manufacturing: Past research, present findings, and future directions. *International Journal of Precision Engineering and Manufacturing-Green Technology.*, *3*(1), 111–128. doi:10.1007/s40684-016-0015-5

King, N. (2009). Book review: Phenomenological psychology: Theory research and method. *Qualitative Research in Organizations and Management*, *2*(2).

King, N., Brooks, M., Turley, S., & Emma, L. (2015). The Utility of Template Analysis in Qualitative Psychology Research. *Qualitative Research in Psychology*, *12*(2), 202–222. doi:10.1080/14780887.2014.955224 PMID:27499705

Kongolo, M. (2010). Job creation versus job shedding and the role of SMEs in economic development. *African Journal of Business Management*, *4*(11), 2288–2295.

Laforet, S., & Tann, J. (2006). Innovative characteristics of small manufacturing firms. *Journal of Small Business and Enterprise Development*, *13*(3), 363–380. doi:10.1108/14626000610680253

Levine, R. (2005). "Finance and Growth: Theory and Evidence," Handbook of Economic Growth. In P. Aghion & S. Durlauf (Eds.), *Handbook of Economic Growth*. Elsevier.

Levine, R. (2005). *Does firm size matter for growth and poverty alleviation? Prepared for the Brookings Blum Round table: The Private Sector in the Fight against Global Poverty*. Brown University and the National Bureau of Economic Research. https://www.brookings.edu/global/200508blum_levine.pdf

Lin, Y., Ma, S., & Zhou, L. (2012). Manufacturing strategies for time based competitive advantages. *Industrial Management & Data Systems*, *112*(5), 729–747. doi:10.1108/02635571211232299

Lockett, S. H., Hatton, J., Turner, R., Stubbins, C., Hodgekins, J., & Fowler, D. (2012). Using a semi-structured interview to explore imagery experienced during social anxiety for clients with a diagnosis of psychosis: An exploratory study conducted within an early intervention for psychosis service. *Behavioural and Cognitive Psychotherapy*, *40*(1), 55–68. doi:10.1017/S1352465811000439 PMID:21729340

Löfving, M., Säfsten, K., & Winroth, M. (2014). Manufacturing strategy frameworks suitable for SMEs. *Journal of Manufacturing Technology Management*, *25*(1), 7–26. doi:10.1108/JMTM-08-2012-0081

Lukacs, E. (2005). The economic Role of SMEs in world economy, especially in Europe. *European Integration Studies, Miskolc*, *4*(1), 3–12.

Malik, A., Teal, F., & Baptist, S. (2006). Performance of Nigerian Manufacturing Firms: Report on the Nigerian Manufacturing Enterprise Survey. United Nations Industrial Development Organization (UNIDO), Nigerian Federal Ministry of Industry and Centre for the Study of African Economies, Department of Economics, University of Oxford, United Kingdom.

Mamman, A., Bawole, J., Agbebi, M., & Alhassan, A. R. (2019). SME policy formulation and implementation in Africa: Unpacking assumptions as opportunity for research direction. *Journal of Business Research*, *97*, 304–315. doi:10.1016/j.jbusres.2018.01.044

Mckinsey (2013). *Manufacturing the future: The next era of global growth.* McKinsey. www.mckinsey.com/.../our-insights/the-future-of-manufacturing (Accessed12 November,2015).

Mishra, R., & Shukla, A. (2015). Counterfeit Purchase Intentions Among College Students: An Empirical Investigation. In S. Chatterjee, N. P. Singh, D. P. Goyal, & N. Gupta (Eds.), *Managing in Recovering Markets*. Springer. doi:10.1007/978-81-322-1979-8_16

Mutula, S. M., & Brakel, P. V. (2007). ICT skills readiness for the emerging global digital economy among the SMEs in developing economies: Case study of Botswana. *Library Hi Tech News*, (25), 231–245. doi:10.1108/07378830710754992

Newberry, D. (2006). *The Role of Small and Medium-Sized Enterprises in the Futures of Emerging Economies.* Earth Trends. http://earthtrends.wri.org/features/view

NIRP. (2014). *Nigeria Industrial Revolution Plan.* NIRP. http://www.nepza.gov.ng/downloads/nirp.pdf

Nwosa, P. I., & Oseni, I. O. (2013). The Impact of Banks Loan to SMEs on Manufacturing Output in Nigeria. *Journal of Social and Development Sciences*, *4*(5), 212–217. doi:10.22610/jsds.v4i5.754

O'Regan, N., & Ghobadian, A. (2006). Perceptions of generic strategies of small and medium sized engineering and electronics manufacturers in the UK. *Journal of Manufacturing Technology Management*, *17*(5), 603–620. doi:10.1108/17410380610668540

O'Regan N, Ghobadian A, Sims M. (2006). *Fast tracking innovation in manufacturing.* Research Gate.

Ocheni, S. I., & Gemade, T. I. (2015). *Effects of Multiple Taxation on the Performance of Small and Medium Scale Business Enterprises in Benue State International Journal of Academic Research in Business and Social Sciences*, *5*(3), 345–364.

Odili, O. (2014). Exchange Rate and Balance of Payment: An Autoregressive Distributed Lag (Ardl). *Econometric Investigation on Nigeria Journal of Economics and Finance*, *4*(6), 21–30.

Ogboru, P. L. (2005). *An Evaluation of Funding Arrangements for Small and Medium Scale Enterprises (SMEs) in Nigeria.* [PhD Dissertation, St Clements University].

Ojo, O. (2009) Impact of microfinance on entrepreneurial development: the case of nigeria. *The International Conference on Economics and Administration*. University of Bucharest, Romania. <http://www.itchannel.ro/faa/536_pdfsam_ICEA_FAA_2009.pdf>

Oke, A. (2013). Linking manufacturing flexibility to innovation performance in manufacturing plants. *International Journal of Production Economics, 143*(2), 242–247. doi:10.1016/j.ijpe.2011.09.014

Okpara, J. O. (2011). Factors constraining the growth and survival of SMEs in Nigeria: Implications for poverty alleviation. *Management Research Review, 34*(2), 156–171. doi:10.1108/01409171111102786

Olugbenga, T. K., Jumah, A. A., & Phillips, D. A. (2013). The Current and Future Challenges of Electricity Market in Nigeria in the face of Deregulation Process [March.]. *American Journal of Engineering Research, 1*(2), 33–39.

Onourah, P. (2009). *The role of Small and Medium Sized Enterprises for Economic Growth: A Case Study of Matori LGA in Lagos, Nigeria.* [Master's Thesis, School of Management, Blekinge Institute of Technology].

Onugu, B. A. N. (2005). *Small and medium enterprises (SMEs) in Nigeria: Problems and Challenges.* [PhD Thesis, St. Clements's University]. https://www.stclements.edu/grad/gradonug.pdf

Pansiri, J., & Temtime, Z. T. (2008). Assessing managerial skills in SMEs for capacity building. *Journal of Management Development, 27*(2), 251–260. doi:10.1108/02621710810849362

Penz, E., Schlegemilch, B. B., & Stottinger, B. (2009). Voluntary Purchase of Counterfeit Products: Empirical Evidence from Four Countries. *Journal of International Consumer Marketing, 21*(1), 67–84. doi:10.1080/08961530802125456

Qian, Y. (2008). Impacts of Entry by Counterfeiters. *The Quarterly Journal of Economics*, 123–124.

Rahman, S. (2001). A comparative study of TQM practice and organisational performance of SMEs with and without ISO 900 certification. *International Journal of Quality & Reliability Management, 8*(1), 35–49. doi:10.1108/02656710110364486

Raymond, L., & Croteau, A. M. (2006). Enabling the strategic development of SMEs through advanced manufacturing systems: A configurational perspective. *Industrial Management & Data Systems, 106*(7), 1012–1032. doi:10.1108/02635570610688904

Raynard, P., & Forstater, M. (2002). *Corporate Social Responsibility: Implications for Small and Medium Enterprises in Developing Countries. United Nations Industrial Development Organization.* UNIDO.

Rusjan, B. (2006). The impact of a manufacturing focus on manufacturing and business unit performance: an empirical investigation. *Economic and business review, 8*(1), 5-18.

Saleh, A. S., & Ndubisi, N. O. (2006). An Evaluation of SME Development in Malaysia. *International Review of Business Research Papers, 2*(1), 1–14.

Sanni, A (2012). Multiplicity of Taxes in Nigeria: Issues, Problems and Solutions International *Journal of Business and Social Science 17*(3).

Sarmiento, R., Byrne, M., Contreras, L. R., & Rich, N. (2008). Delivery reliability, manufacturing capabilities and new models of manufacturing efficiency. *Journal of Manufacturing Technology Management*, *18*(4), 367–386. doi:10.1108/17410380710743761

Schroeder, R. G., Flynn, B., & Flynn, E. (2006). *The high-performance manufacturing projects*. (Working Paper) University of Minnesota, Wake Forest University, USA.

SMEDAN. (2009). *Small and Medium Enterprise Development Agency of Nigeria*. Small Business in Nigeria.

SMEDAN. (2013). Small and Medium Enterprise Development Agency of Nigeria, Small Business in Nigeria, Abuja. SMEs. *Technovation*, *26*, 251–261.

Soften, K., & Winroth, M. (2002). Analysis of the congruence between manufacturing strategy and production system in SMME. *Computers in Industry*, *49*(1), 91–106. doi:10.1016/S0166-3615(02)00061-1

Srivastava, R. K., & Jena, D. (2011). *Manufacturing: A Case Based Approach Process Improvement in Precision Component Manufacturing: A Case Based Approach*. IAENG. https://www.iaeng.org/publication/IMECS2011/IMECS2011_pp1269-1274.pdf

Stryszowski, P., & Kazimierczak, M. (2016). *Trade in counterfeit and pirated goods mapping the economic impact*. Office for Harmonization in the Internal Market; Organisation for Economic Co-Operation and Development; European Union. https://euipo.europa.eu/tunnel...the.../Mapping_the_Economic_Impact_en.pdf.

Swamidass, P., & Newell, W. (1987). Manufacturing strategy, environmental uncertainty and performance: A path analytic model. *Management Science*, *33*(4), 509–524. doi:10.1287/mnsc.33.4.509

Swierczek, F. W., & Ha, T. T. (2003). Entrepreneurial orientation, uncertainty avoidance and firm performance: An analysis of Thai and Vietnamese SMEs. *International Journal of Entrepreneurship and Innovation*, *4*(1), 46–58. doi:10.5367/000000003101299393

Tarigan, R. (2005). An evaluation of the relationship between alignment of strategic priorities and manufacturing performance. *International Journal of Management*, *22*(4), 586–597.

Thompson, A. R., Smith, J. A., & Larkin, M. (2011, June). Interpretative phenomenological analysis and clinical psychology training: Results from a survey of the group of trainers in clinical psychology. *Clinical Psychology Forum*, *1*(222), 15–19. doi:10.53841/bpscpf.2011.1.222.15

Treadwell, J. (2011). From the car boot to booting it up? eBay, online counterfeit crime and the transformation of the criminal marketplace. *Criminology & Criminal Justice*, *12*(2), 175–191. doi:10.1177/1748895811428173

UNIDO. (2013). *Emerging trends in global manufacturing industries*. UNDO. https://www.manufacturing-policy.eng.cam.ac.uk/policies-documents-folder/2013-emerging-trends-in-global-manufacturing-industries-unido/at_download/file(Accessed 05/01/15).

Wheelwright, S. (1984). Manufacturing strategy: Defining the missing link. *Strategic Management Journal*, *5*(1), 77–91. doi:10.1002/smj.4250050106

Wieland, A., & Wallenburg, C. M. (2013). The influence of relational competencies on supply chain resilience: A relational view. *International Journal of Physical Distribution & Logistics Management, 43*(4), 300–320. doi:10.1108/IJPDLM-08-2012-0243

World Bank. (2015). *Nigeria economic report. Nigeria economic report; no. 3*. World Bank Group.

World Bank Data (2017). *Sustainable development goals*. World Bank Data.

Zikmund, W. G. (2003). *Business Research Methods* (7th ed.). Thompson South-Western.

Chapter 2
Exploring Perceptions of Street Traders About Transitioning From Informal to Formal Sectors in Durban's Central Business District, South Africa

Luther-King Junior Zogli
Durban University of Technology, South Africa

ABSTRACT

In developing countries like South Africa, the informal sector plays a crucial role in providing employment opportunities for people are not able to secure formal jobs or establish registered businesses. This undocumented sector accounts for over 65% of the total employment in developing economies. The purpose of this research is to investigate the formalisation experience of informal traders in Durban's central business district, South Africa. Using snowball sampling, the structured interview strategy was used to acquire qualitative data. After completing twelve interviews with informal traders, data saturation was reached. The data was analysed using content analysis. After data analysis, the study revealed that informal traders faced significant challenges in the formalisation process. These challenges were organized into three main themes: lack of support from the municipality, limited access to information on formalisation procedures and their perception that the formalisation process to be expensive and beyond their financial capabilities.

DOI: 10.4018/979-8-3693-0111-1.ch002

INTRODUCTION

The term "informal sector" emerged in the 1970s from Keith Hart's research in Ghana. Hart (1973) defined the sector as the unregulated economic enterprises or activities. These are businesses that exist outside government regulation. Like most developing countries, the South African economy is separated into two parts: the formal and informal economies. The latest findings from the International Labour Organization (ILO) (ILO, 2018) show that more than 60% of the world's population is active in the informal economy and in Africa, 85% of the population is employed in the informal sector. These figures will be higher in 2022 due to the impacts of the COVID-19 pandemic.

This high incidence of informal sector activity is a major challenge to the rights of workers, social protection, decent work conditions, inclusive development, and the rule of law. As a remedy, ILO (2015) in its general conference, the 103rd session affirmed that the transition from the informal to the formal economy is vital to achieve inclusive development and to realise decent work for all. Guided by recommendation R204, which was adopted by the general conference, the ILO further suggested that member states take appropriate measures to enable the formalisation of small businesses from the informal to the formal sector.

In their quest to formalise, informal traders face many obstacles which inhibit them and, in some instances, result in them deciding to remain informal. Sandada (2014) found that informal traders face fierce entry barriers in their attempt to join the formal sector, an assertion backed by de Soto (1989) who concludes that a key factor contributing to poverty in emerging countries was obstacles placed by governments in the path of small-scale entrepreneurs. These barriers include unnecessary licensing requirements or outright corruption, making setting up a formal business very costly. These factors discourage many entrepreneurs from starting legal businesses, instead, they set up informal firms. Hillenkamp, Lapeyre, and Lemaître, (2013) emphasised that formalisation is vital for business growth as businesses gain better access to credit and other productive factors, including expanded access to markets through public procurement and linkage programmes. Moreover, firms gain access to imports and exports through formal channels.

The city of Durban is South Africa's third largest city and the city's government estimates that a third of economically active adults are in the informal economy. According to the eThekwini municipality, the informal sector provides employment and contributes over R8 billion annually to the Gross Domestic Product (GDP) (Independent Online, 2021). Notwithstanding the employment and GDP contribution, countries with a large informal sector tend to lack development and are less able to finance public services because of low tax revenue collection (Levy, 2010).

Informality is associated with complex and non-transparent trading systems, which discourages foreign direct investment and undermines trade policy and negatively impacts the international competitiveness of developing countries. Van der Molen (2018) adds that tax evasion because of the informal sector is very severe and adds up to US $ 3.1 trillion annually which is about 5% of the world's GDP and US $ 80 billion in Africa.

In developing countries, the informal sector poses a major challenge to workers' rights, social protection, and inclusive development. Formalisation is a crucial step towards achieving inclusive development and decent work for all. However, informal traders encounter numerous barriers that make setting up a formal business expensive. The study's purpose of examining the transition of street traders from the informal to the formal economy in Durban, South Africa, contributes significantly to empirical understanding. It recognises the importance of supporting informal traders and addressing the challenges they face.

Policymakers and stakeholders interested in promoting the formalisation of the informal sector in South Africa and other developing countries benefit significantly from the study's findings. The insights gained from the research could help identify measures to facilitate the formalisation process for informal traders.

LITERATURE REVIEW

Unemployment and Informal Sector in South Africa

In the second quarter of 2022, South Africa's unemployment rate is about 34% (Stats SA, 2022). South Africa as a BRICS (Brazil, Russia, India, China and South Africa) member benefits from its collective strength by way of consultation and support on economic issues (Lukin and Xuesong, 2019). As far as the BRICS countries are concerned, South Africa's unemployment rate is behind that of its fellow members, with Brazil's at 9.1%, India 8.3%, Russia 3.9% and China at 3.6%. IMF (2020) asserted that, by emerging market standards, the country's unemployment rate is still very high. The emerging market average is in the single digits, whilst South Africa's is at the peak of 30% and more worryingly, figures look even worse when observed through the primacy of youth unemployment. The figure for unemployed youth is above 50%, while the emerging average is close to 15%, which is a great concern for the economy.

To address youth unemployment challenges, the South African government has introduced the draft National Youth Policy for 2020-2030 which will consider expanding and analysing the implementation of Broad-Based Black Economic Empowerment (BBBEE) to tackle the youth unemployment problems in South Africa. However, the South African labour market is characterised by numerous challenges, with racial and gender inequalities still predominant in South Africa's labour market. The enduring legacy of apartheid still affects the ability to find a job, as well as the wages received once employed. Moreover, females find it tougher to secure jobs and they earn 30% less than their male counterparts in the same job (Stats SA, 2020).

Employment opportunities are one of the keyways the informal sector contributes to development in Africa. According to Narula (2020), the informal sector is the main employer in most developing nations, employing over 80% of the labour force. This is especially significant because official employment possibilities are scarce, and the informal sector provides a means for people to earn a living. Moreover, the informal sector helps in the alleviation of poverty and the generation of revenue. In their study of Kenya, Okungu and McIntyre (2019) found that most informal sector employees were married and headed families with approximately five members.

Low-income households, which make up the majority of urban dwellers, are unable to purchase products and services provided by formal sectors as a result of price increases, in particular, for food items. Hence are only able to afford goods provided by informal operators (Desta, 2018). The sector also provides affordable services such as hairdressing, shoe repairs, and tailoring, which are not typically available in formal channels.

To summarise, the informal sector contributes significantly to the development of African countries by offering work possibilities, income creation, and commodities and services that are critical for low-income households' survival. It is, however, confronted with numerous hurdles which limit its potential for growth and development.Top of Form

The high informality and low work security of South Africa's informal sector has been severely exacerbated by the COVID-19 outbreak. Informal operators now suffer even more severe difficulties due to the pandemic. Many people who work in South Africa's informal economy have seen their incomes drop and their access to markets and clients cut because of COVID-19 and the accompanying lockdown measures (Khambule, 2022). According to the ILO (2020), the COVID-19 pandemic led to a 60% reduction in informal sector earnings. This was the case in South Africa as well, where about 70% of informal workers lost their livelihoods (Rogan and Skinner, 2020). Additionally, the pandemic has highlighted the importance of social protection for informal sector workers, with many lacking accesses to formal social protection schemes. In South Africa, while social grants have been enlarged and changed to provide some relief to vulnerable households during the COVID-19 pandemic, Bhorat and Köhler's (2020) study indicates that the targeting of these awards has been insufficient, leaving many informal workers without access to support. The authors went further to state that the grants have limited reach, especially to informal settlements and rural areas, where many informal workers congregate and where the need for assistance is frequently greatest.

In summary, it has been shown that the pandemic has had a severe impact on the informal sector in South Africa, underscoring the need for targeted support and legislative initiatives to protect this vulnerable sector.

Transitioning From the Informal to the Formal Economy

ILO (2017) describes formalisation as a process that firms undertake when transitioning their enterprises from the informal to the formal sector. The crucial goal of enterprise formalisation is to create better jobs, reduce poverty and address the marginalisation of those who are most exposed to poor work conditions in the informal sector. Formalisation has the following dimensions according to the ILO:

- Registration and licensing with national, provincial and local authorities.
- Gaining access to social security for the business owner and employees; and
- Compliance with legal frameworks that include tax, social security and labour laws.

The process of formalizing businesses may not yield immediate growth in the short term, but having more firms operating in the formal economy can provide higher quality and sustainable jobs in the long run, instil investor confidence, and boost investment. Researchers Dzansi and Tasssin-Njike (2014) found that formalised businesses create jobs and make social responsibility contributions. Converting to formal status can also enhance a business's credibility and trustworthiness, allowing it to handle international transactions while providing governments with a broader tax base.

On the other hand, Moyo's (2022) study spanning 22 developing countries revealed the many obstacles that workers in the informal sector face during the formalisation process, including the high costs and complexity of regulatory compliance, limited access to formal financial services, and a lack of trust in government institutions. Moreover, the process of formalisation often requires significant trade-offs for informal workers, such as increased taxes and reduced autonomy and flexibility, which can discourage them from pursuing formalisation. McKenzie and Sakho's (2010) study in Bolivia and Khamis' (2014) study conducted in Brazil, Mexico, and Peru suggests that authorities can persuade informal businesses to formalise by providing more information about the process and streamlining registration procedures. The lack of information on the formalisation process accounts for many firms remaining in the informal economy. Muchichwa's (2017) research shows that methods for formalising the informal economy can take various forms, including registration, taxation, organization, and improving transition to formalisation at a local level. Local authorities must facilitate market access, increase inward investment, and local procurement to achieve this.

Leino's (2009) research on three African countries discovered that one of the key reasons why informal firms remain informal is the taxes imposed on registered businesses. Additionally, according to Aswani's (2007) study, a lack of access to affordable capital or credit presents a significant financial barrier to transitioning from the informal to the formal sector. Furthermore, policy reforms to support the informal sector are often hindered by political opposition and limited resources, thus underscoring the need for increased coordination between government departments and interested parties (Narula, 2020).

In conclusion, formalizing informal enterprises is a complex and difficult process that necessitates a thorough assessment of the challenges and opportunities involved. While formalisation may not result in instant growth, it can have long-term benefits such as higher-quality jobs, social protection, increased investment, and enhanced legitimacy. Informal sector workers, on the other hand, are confronted with various impediments to formalisation, including high regulatory compliance costs and complexity, limited access to formal financial services, and a lack of faith in government institutions. Furthermore, the formalisation process frequently involves major trade-offs, such as higher taxes and less flexibility, which can dissuade informal employees from formalizing their activity.

Conceptual Framework

Many developing nations' economies depend on the informal sector. It employs millions but has poor working conditions, low pay, and minimal social safety. Many informal sector workers are eager to join the formal sector, yet, high regulatory compliance costs, restricted access to funding, and a lack of faith in government institutions make shifting from the informal to the formal sector difficult. The conceptual framework, as shown in **Figure 1** has four components: (1) the informal sector, (2) business growth and sustainability, (3) transitioning to the formal sector, and (4) barriers to transitioning to the formal sector.

The first component, the informal sector, includes unregulated and unregistered industries such as street vending, small-scale manufacturing, and services such as hairdressing and shoe repairs. These firms are operated by individuals who are self-employed or employed by small firms.

Secondly, formalizing informal enterprises improves business sustainability, investor trust, and business growth. Formal businesses gain legitimacy and trust to handle both local and foreign transactions, while governments enhance their revenue base. Formalisation drives long-term corporate growth and sustainability.

The third component, transitioning to the formal sector, acknowledges that most informal sector operators may have a desire to transfer to the official sector. This may entail registering their company, getting licenses and permits, and gaining legitimacy.

The fourth component, barriers to transitioning to the formal sector, indicates that many impediments constrain the formalisation of informal enterprises, including high regulatory compliance costs and complexity, lack of information about the formalisation process, cost of formalisation and a lack of faith in government institutions.

In summary, the conceptual framework offered here emphasises the experience of informal traders when transitioning to the formal sector. While formalisation is required for long-term growth and sustainability, the process is not always simple due to the numerous obstacles encountered. Understanding these limitations and devising measures to overcome them, on the other hand, is critical for encouraging more enterprises to enter the formal sector. The current study is being undertaken against the backdrop of these reasons.

Table 1 in Annexure 1 shows a summary of studies that are mentioned in the introduction and literature review sections.

METHODOLOGY

The current study adopts the qualitative research technique. Qualitative research investigates social issues through subjective experiences, meanings, and interpretations (Arghode, 2012). It analyses words, images, and observations to find themes and patterns. Data was collected using structured interviews. Segal, Coolidge, O'Riley and Heinz, (2006) define structured interviews as a technique for gathering data on a subject that involves asking questions in a predetermined order.

The population under study consisted of street traders located in the Durban CBD. The most recent data states that, the number of informal traders in the Durban city is estimated to be approximately 50,000, while about 4,705 traders are in the inner city (Mkhize, Dube and Skinner, 2017). The snowball sampling method was used to identify participants. This form of sampling works on a referral basis as data-rich sources will recommend other participants to be interviewed (Alvi, 2022). This sampling method works by identifying initial participants who satisfy the requirements and requesting them to recommend other potential participants who may also meet the criteria is the strategy (Heckathorn, 1997).

Data was collected till data saturation was reached. While the foundations for meta-themes may be seen as early as the sixth interview, Guest, Namey, and Chen, (2020) argue that data saturation can be reached by the eighth interview. In this study, data saturation was reached at eight participants. The collected data was analysed using content analysis. Hsieh and Shannon (2005) describe content analysis as a method is organising and gaining meaning from qualitative data collected to draw conclusions from it. This is a research strategy that involves carefully analyzing textual or visual data to uncover patterns, themes, and meanings. This method entails establishing and defining categories depending on the research objectives, and then categorizing the data systematically (Krippendorff, 2018).

Trustworthiness and Credibility

The study's trustworthiness and credibility were prioritised in the development of its research criteria (Bell, Bryman and Harley, 2022). Firstly, this was achieved by ensuring that the respondents in the study were competent, trustworthy, and active in the informal sector of the Durban Central Business District. In addition, inter-coder reliability was also used. Intercoder reliability is an agreement between different coders regarding how the same data should be coded (O'Connor and Joffe, 2020). Intercoder reliability is achieved when both researchers independently code the data similarly. The researcher and a colleague statistician undertook the coding independently and compared the results. Both codings were similar, signifying inter-coder reliability.

RESEARCH FINDINGS

In terms of awareness of the existence of a formalisation process, 7 out of 8 respondents are aware of the formalisation process. Furthermore, all 8 respondents (100%) expressed a strong desire to formalise their businesses, citing job security, financial stability, secured workspace, and improved quality of life as key benefits. They further indicated that formalised businesses are generally more favoured and respected than informal ones. The respondents went on to mention the key issues they face in the formalisation process.

First, there is a perceived lack of government and local municipality support to assist informal businesses in navigating the complex and time-consuming process of formalisation. Respondents noted the need for easy administration and accessible consultants to streamline this process, as well as the loss of potential profit due to time lost during the registration process. Some verbatim quotations from the respondents are as follows:

"I don't think they treat formalisation seriously. The issue of formalisation must treat with importance as formal business owners in town look down on informal traders and don't recognise them as small business owners".

"There is no training provided by the municipality and other government institutions. Also, the Municipality does not consult traders on their development requirements or ask for their views on the kind of training they require."

"I have not heard of any support options available to informal entrepreneurs who wish to formalise but claims she is aware of Companies and Intellectual Property Commission (CIPC)".

From the above comments, it can be seen that the respondents face enormous difficulties they experience in formalizing their enterprises. The lack of government and municipal backing, along with the intricacy and time-consuming nature of the formalisation process, poses considerable barriers to entry for informal traders wishing to formalise their operations.

Another key issue identified is the dearth of information available to respondents via mainstream media channels such as radio, television, and social media regarding the formalisation process. Only one respondent had heard of talks or conferences held by the International Labour Organization, and the Alliance of Street Vendors, known as Streetnet. Even such information was seen to be targeted at people who are highly educated.

One respondent mentioned that:

"This process is designed to suit highly educated individuals and people with money so for someone like me with limited education, formalisation seems impossible as I cannot understand the procedure nor do the paperwork, which is in English."

One more respondent said:

"I know of the Companies and Intellectual Properties Commission (CIPC), the body responsible for registering companies. However, when I approached the body for guidance to register my business, I was pushed from pillar to post, hence I gave up".

Another respondent revealed that:

"I know of SEDA, and the National Youth Development Agency (NYDA) that they help small enterprises, but I do not yet have detailed information on what support mechanism do they really provide to small businesses that are interested in formalizing".

The above comments show a substantial paucity of awareness regarding the formalisation process offered to informal business owners, with only a few respondents aware of programmes or conferences related to formalisation. Even the one who sought formalisation schooling through Streetnet and ILO experienced language and education difficulties, according to the survey, with one respondent commenting that the procedure was geared toward persons with higher levels of education.

Lastly, the study found that 6 out of 8 respondents expressed concern over the high cost of formalizing their businesses, with low profits from their current informal operations making it financially unfeasible. Some verbatim quotations from the respondents are as follows:

"I do not have money to formalise my business, to formalise I would need a lot of money, and no one is willing to finance informal traders. Some years ago, Standard Bank had a Tutuwa fund which was meant to uplift traders, but the funding was discontinued, and I don't know why".

" Formalisation process favours those people who have money as poor informal business owners like me will never formalise their businesses, because we do not have the money and time".

From the responses, it can be seen that the majority of the respondents expressed concern about the high cost of the formalisation process, indicating a considerable financial barrier for informal business owners wishing to formalise their activities. Respondents stated that the poor revenues from their current informal businesses made it difficult to raise the capital required to legalise their operations.

DISCUSSION OF RESULTS

From the results presented in the previous section, three themes emerged. These themes are discussed in the ensuing sections. These themes represent Component Four of the Conceptual Framework (Figure 1) which denotes the barriers of transition from the informal to the formal sector.

No Help From the Municipality

Most of the respondents expressed disappointment with the local municipality for doing nothing to help their cause. This is a similar sentiment shared by informal traders in greater Letaba municipality in Limpopo province in a study conducted by Legodi and Kanjere (2015). According to the respondents in the current study, the municipality is mostly interested in bullying and threatening them although they are made to pay levies. This is an experience similar to what informal traders in Bindura town, Zimbabwe go through daily (Kabonga, Zvokuomba and Nyagadza, 2021). The respondents further reiterated that authorities are not interested in assisting informal traders to facilitate the formalisation process. Hence to attempt formalisation, one must leave their businesses to register to begin the process. The time lost from going to an office to start the formalisation process leads to a reduction in revenue for these street traders who are mostly a one-operator business.

It must be understood that institutionalisation, in this case, formalisation, comes with its difficulties. Institutionalisation involves governments setting rules and checks which mostly makes things "more professional" and "bureaucratic" in different areas (Carey, Braunack-Mayer, and Barraket, 2009). Research by Carey, Buick, and Malbon (2018) shows that ongoing changes in structure increase conflicts. These conflicts happen between the formal rules made by institutions and the informal ways things are usually done. This makes the shift from informal to formal more complicated. When this conflict is exacerbated by institutional neglect as discovered in this research, formalisation becomes near impossible.

Limited Information

In the second emerging theme, the interviews of informal traders reported that there is limited to no information available on how to go about formalising one's business. Only one of the respondents indicated that he had heard about the formalisation process through the Alliance of Street Vendors known as Streetnet, which assisted and educated him about the process. Another respondent indicated that she knows of the Companies and Intellectual Properties Commission (CIPC), the body responsible for registering companies. However, when this informal trader approached the body for support, she mentioned that she was "pushed from pillar to post", hence she gave up. Gatewood and Boko (2009) reiterated in their study that developing countries place an unnecessary burden on informal businesses in their quest to formalise which ends up discouraging them. Most of the bureaucratic measures put in place are not well communicated to traders as Sandada's (2014) study in Harare, Zimbabwe and Olapade's (2015) study in India concluded that informal traders are more willing to transition if they are provided with enough information about process.

Perceive the Formalisation Process to be Expensive

Thirdly, the respondents felt that the money involved in trying to get their businesses formalised is too much. Moyo's (2022) study spanning 22 developing countries revealed that one of the main obstacles that workers in the informal sector face during the formalisation process, is the high costs and complexity of regulatory compliance. This is corroborated by D'Erasmo, Boedo, and Senkal's (2014) study who also discovered that the cost of formalisation is a considerable obstacle to formalisation. Firms may be discouraged from pursuing formal status due to the high expense of complying with formal regulations. As survival-based entrepreneurs, profits made by these informal traders are minimal, so to use most of their meagre earnings to register their businesses is an impossible task according to the informal traders interviewed.

CONCLUSION AND RECOMMENDATIONS

The current study discovered that most informal traders in the Durban CBD are keen to formalise but face an uphill task in their quest to do so.

Respondents indicated there is not much information available, either via radio, television or social media. Furthermore, judging from the responses, most participants are keen to formalise and expressed that transitioning would bring job security, financial stability, and secured workspaces and will improve their quality of life. The respondents also articulated their frustration with the formalisation process and mentioned that excessive financial costs associated with business registration resulted in their decision not to embark on the formalisation process, rather choosing to stay informal.

The current study goes on to recommend some policy strategies that stakeholders can implement to address the research problem at hand. Desta's (2018) study in Ethiopia emphasises that there is a need for a more nuanced and context-specific approach to understanding the informal economy and addressing the challenges.

Attention should be paid to some critical points to make the formalisation process less cumbersome for informal entrepreneurs. Business formalisation education must be a priority for government institutions responsible for regulating and developing this sector, such as the Department of Trade and Industry together with the Department of Small Business Development. This can be done through workshops and, to make sure that the traders are not taken away from their daily operations, the use of mobile education vehicles can be employed. This will ensure that traders go about their daily work while receiving adequate training. Media platforms and all relevant government institutions mandated to develop the informal sector must be more visible and accessible to all informal traders.

Lessons can be learnt from how China went about their formalisation process as indicated by Ishengoma and Kappel (2006). China set up the Street Committee Employment Service Organ (SCESO) which had the task of aiding informal traders in managing various administrative procedures regarding the formalisation process. SCESO's duty was to go to informal traders and register businesses, assist in setting up bank accounts, offer training and support and advise traders on regulations regarding business operations. As smartphone usage is so widespread in 2022, authorities can take advantage of this to register and help informal traders. The Durban Municipality in collaboration with the Department of Small Business Development should develop a mobile application which will be a one-stop-shop for informal traders to go through the formalisation process easily and swiftly without having to leave their business premises. This way will facilitate the formalisation process.

ILO (2015) stated that the burden of red tape is immensely felt by small businesses to the point that they remain informal to avoid compliance costs as well as administration burdens and complicated regulatory requirements. Therefore, in addition to the mobile application, authorities should remove all formalisation costs as it is done remotely. This will encourage more informal traders to formalise.

ACKNOWLEDGEMENTS

The author would like to acknowledge all informal traders who participated in this study and N. Dladla for her assistance.

REFERENCES

Alvi, M. H. (2016). *A Manual for Selecting Sampling Techniques in Research [Internet]*. MPRA. https://mpra.ub.uni-muenchen.de/70218/

Arghode, V. (2012). Qualitative and Quantitative Research: Paradigmatic Differences. *Global Education Journal, 4*, 1–12.

Aswani, F. (2007). *Barriers and facilitators to transitioning of small businesses (SMMEs) from the second to the first economy in South Africa* [Unpublished Masters thesis, Pretoria: University of Pretoria].

Bell, E., Bryman, A., & Harley, B. (2022). *Business research methods*. Oxford University Press. doi:10.1093/hebz/9780198869443.001.0001

Carey, G., Braunack-Mayer, A., & Barraket, J. (2009). Spaces of care in the third sector: Understanding the effects of professionalization. *Health, 13*(6), 629–646. doi:10.1177/1363459308341866 PMID:19841023

Carey, G., Buick, F., & Malbon, E. (2018). The unintended consequences of structural change: When formal and informal institutions collide in efforts to address wicked problems. *International Journal of Public Administration, 41*(14), 1169–1180. doi:10.1080/01900692.2017.1350708

D'Erasmo, P. N., Hernan, J. N., Boedo, M. H., & Şenkal, A. (2014). Misallocation, Informality, and Human Capital: Understanding the Role of Institutions. *Journal of Economic Dynamics & Control, 42*(3), 122–142. doi:10.1016/j.jedc.2014.03.009

de Soto, H. (1989). *The Other Path: The Invisible Revolution in the Third World*. I.B. Tauris.

Desta, C. G. (2018). The urban informal economy in Ethiopia: Theory and empirical evidence. *Eastern Africa Social Science Research Review, 34*(1), 37–64. doi:10.1353/eas.2018.0001

Dzansi, D. Y., & Tasssin-Njike, R. (2014). Understanding the transition from informal to formal business: A conceptual framework. *Mediterranean Journal of Social Sciences, 5*(20), 664–664. doi:10.5901/mjss.2014.v5n20p664

Gatewood, E. J., & Boko, S. (2009). Globalization: Entrepreneurial challenges and opportunities in the developing world. In Z. J. Acs, H. E. Aldrich, & D. B. Audretsch, (Eds.), *The Role of SMEs and Entrepreneurship in a Globalized Economy. Expert Report No. 34 to Sweden's Globalisation Council*. Globalisation Council.

Guest, G., Namey, E., & Chen, M. (2020). A simple method to assess and report thematic saturation in qualitative research. *PLoS One, 15*(5), e0232076. doi:10.1371/journal.pone.0232076 PMID:32369511

Hart, K. (1973). Informal income opportunities and urban employment in Ghana. *The Journal of Modern African Studies, 2*(1), 61–89. doi:10.1017/S0022278X00008089

Heckathorn, D. D. (1997). Respondent-driven sampling: A new approach to the study of hidden populations. *Social Problems, 44*(2), 174–199. doi:10.2307/3096941

Hillenkamp, I., Lapeyre, F., & Lemaître, A. (Eds.). (2013). *Securing livelihoods: Informal economy practices and institutions*. OUP Oxford. doi:10.1093/acprof:oso/9780199687015.001.0001

Horn, A. (2011). Who's out there? A profile of informal traders in four South African city central business districts. *Town and Regional Planning, 59*, 1–6.

Hsieh, H.-F., & Shannon, S. E. (2005). Three Approaches to Qualitative Content Analysis. *Qualitative Health Research, 15*(9), 1277–1288. doi:10.1177/1049732305276687 PMID:16204405

Independent Online. (2021). eThekwini Municipality to host informal traders indaba aimed at boosting local economy in wake of unrest. *Independent Online*. https://www.iol.co.za/mercury/news/ethekwini-municipality-to-host-informal-traders-indaba-aimed-at-boosting-local-economy-in-wake-of-unrest-0b7c6362-7a8a-4c69-b382-fb5354f5e2d0

International Labour Organisation. (2015). *Transitioning from the Informal to Formal Economy [Internet]*. Geneva: International Labour Office. https://www.ilo.org/wcmsp5/groups/public/@ed_dialogue/@actrav/documents/publication/wcms_545928.pdf

International Labour Organisation. (2017). *Enterprise Formalisation*. Geneva: International Labour Office. https://www.ilo.org/wcmsp5/groups/public/---ed_emp/---emp_ent/---ifp_seed/documents/publication/wcms_544828.pdf

International Labour Organisation. (2018). *World employment social outlook*. Geneva: International Labour Office. https://www.ilo.org/wcmsp5/groups/public/---dgreports/---dcomm/---publ/documents/publication/wcms_615594.pdf

International Labour Organisation. (2020). *Brief: Impact of Lockdown Measures on the Informal Economy [Internet]*. Geneva (Switzerland): International Labour Organization. http://www.ilo.org/global/topics/employment-promotion/informal-economy/publications/WCMS_743523/lang--en/index.htm

International Monetary Fund. (2020). *South Africa*. IMF. https://www.tralac.org/documents/news/3097-south-africa-selected-issues-paper-january-2019-imf/file.html (Accessed 21 June 2023).

Ishengoma, E., & Kappel, R. (2006) Economic Growth and Poverty: Does Formalisation of Informal Enterprises Matter. *GIGA Working Papers 20*.

Kabonga, I., Zvokuomba, K., & Nyagadza, B. (2021). The challenges faced by young entrepreneurs in informal trading in Bindura, Zimbabwe. *Journal of Asian and African Studies*, *56*(8), 1780–1794. doi:10.1177/0021909621990850

Khambule, I. (2022). COVID-19 and the informal economy in a small town in South Africa: Governance implications in the post-COVID era. *Cogent Social Sciences*, *8*(1), 2078528. doi:10.1080/23311886.2022.2078528

Khamis, M. (2014) Formalisation of jobs and firms in emerging market economies through registration reform. *IZA World of Labour*. Bhorat, H and Köhler, T., 2020 COVID-19, social protection, and the labour market in South Africa: Are social grants being targeted at the most vulnerable? *Working Papers 202008, University of Cape Town, Development Policy Research Unit.*

Krippendorff, K. (2018). *Content analysis: An introduction to its methodology*. Sage Publications.

Legodi, K., & Kanjere, M. (2015). The challenges faced by informal traders in greater Letaba municipality in Limpopo province, *South Africa. Africa's Public Service Delivery and Performance Review*, *3*(4), 57–75. doi:10.4102/apsdpr.v3i4.98

Leino, J. (2009). *Formal and informal Microenterprises, Enterprise Surveys. Enterprise Note No. 5, Informality*. World Bank.

Levy, S. (2010). *Good intentions, bad outcomes: Social policy, informality, and economic growth in Mexico.* Brookings Institution Press.

Lukin, A., & Xuesong, F. (2019). What is BRICS for China? *Strategic Analysis, 43*(6), 620–631. doi: 10.1080/09700161.2019.1669896

McKenzie, D., & Sakho, Y. S. (2010). Does it pay firms to register for taxes? The impact of formality on firm profitability. *Journal of Development Economics, 91*(1), 15–24. doi:10.1016/j.jdeveco.2009.02.003

Mkhize, S., Dube, S., & Skinner, C. (2013). Stre*et Vendors in Durban, South Africa.* South Africa: Women in informal Employment: Globalizing and Organizing (WIEGO).

Moyo, B. (2022). Factors affecting the probability of formalizing informal sector activities in Sub-Saharan Africa: Evidence from World Bank enterprise surveys. *African Journal of Economic and Management Studies, 13*(3), 480–507. doi:10.1108/AJEMS-06-2021-0304

Muchichwa, N. (2017). *Decent work in the informal economy: towards formalisation of the informal economy.* Labour and Economic Development Research Institute of Zimbabwe (LEDRIZ) / Friedrich-Ebert-Stiftung (FES). https://library.fes.de/pdf-files/bueros/simbabwe/13742.pdf

Narula, R. (2020). Policy opportunities and challenges from the COVID-19 pandemic for economies with large informal sectors. *Journal of International Business Policy, 3*(3), 302–310. doi:10.1057/s42214-020-00059-5

O'Connor, C., & Joffe, H. (2020). Intercoder reliability in qualitative research: Debates and practical guidelines. *International Journal of Qualitative Methods, 19*, 1–13. doi:10.1177/1609406919899220

Okungu, V. R., & McIntyre, D. (2019). Does the informal sector in Kenya have financial potential to sustainably prepay for health care? Implications for financing universal health coverage in low-income settings. *Health Systems and Reform, 5*(2), 145–157. doi:10.1080/23288604.2019.1583492 PMID:30924731

Olapade, M. (2015). *Microfinance and Formalization of Enterprises in the Informal Sector.* (Working Paper No, 62). ILO.

Rogan, M. & Skinner, C. (2020). The COVID-19 crisis and the South African informal economy. *Locked out of livelihoods and employment. National Income Dynamics Study-Coronavirus Rapid Mobile Survey (NIDS-CRAM).*

Sandada, M. (2014). Transition from informality to formality perceptions of informal traders in the Harare Metropolitan Area. *International Journal of Economics. Commerce & Management, 2*(12), 1–11.

Segal, D. L., Coolidge, F. L., O'Riley, A., & Heinz, B. A. (2006). Structured and semistructured interviews. In M. Hersen (Ed.), *Clinician's handbook of adult behavioral assessment* (pp. 121–144). Elsevier Academic Press. doi:10.1016/B978-012343013-7/50007-0

Stats S. A. (2020). *How unequal is South Africa?* StatsSA. https://www.statssa.gov.za/?p=12930 (Accessed 23 September 2022).

Stats, S. A. (2022). *Quarterly Labour Force Survey (QLFS) – Q2:2022*. StatsSA. https://www.statssa.gov.za/?p=15685#:~:text=The%20official%20unemployment%20rate%20was,QLFS)%20for%20Q2%3A%20 2022. (Accessed 23 January 2023).

Van der Molen, P. (2018). Informal economies, state finances and surveyors. *Survey Review, 50*(358), 16–25. doi:10.1080/00396265.2016.1216922

APPENDIX 1

Table 1. Summary of studies*

Author and Year	Setting	Design	Population and Sample	Summary of Findings
Aswani (2007)	Johannesburg	Qualitative interviews	Formal and informal SMME owners	-Major non-financial barrier: Lack of access to information on formalisation -Major financial barrier: Limited access to cash or credit -Major non-financial facilitator: Improved access to information on formalisation -Major financial facilitators: Access to a bigger market and increased access to cash or credit
Bhorat and Köhler's (2020)	South Africa	Secondary study	Stats SA data 2019 to 2022	-Pre-pandemic wage inequality was extremely high. -Real wages rose at the pandemic's onset due to a regressive distribution of job loss. -70% of the rise is explained by this composition effect, with changes in returns to characteristics playing a muted role. -Pandemic temporarily increased wage inequality by 8% or 5 Gini points at its onset. -Wage reductions toward pre-pandemic levels resulted more from lasting changes in returns to characteristics.
Desta, (2018)	Ethiopia	Descriptive Quantitative study	National household survey data	-Informal sector employment significantly rose. -Manufacturing, services, trade, hotels, and restaurant activities decreased, while construction increased. -Capital shortage was the main barrier to work participation, with financing mainly from informal sources. -Income per person varied significantly across sectors.
Dzansi and Tasssin-Njike (2014)	South Africa	Desk research	Studies published on the informal sector	-Success in navigating informal challenges is linked to factors like entrepreneurial orientation, education, and networking abilities. -Failure to graduate keeps businesses informal, providing survival income to owners but depriving the state of taxes and other contributions. -The goal is for graduated businesses to reap benefits of formalisation, contributing to job creation, taxes, and social responsibility.

Continued on following page

50

Table 1. Continued

Author and Year	Setting	Design	Population and Sample	Summary of Findings
Hart (1973)	Ghana	Primary study	Northern migrants in Southern Ghana	- High inflation, insufficient wages, and surplus labour contribute to widespread informality in income-generating activities among the sub-proletariat. - The complexity of income and expenditure patterns challenges conventional economic analyses of poor countries. - Government planning and the application of economic theory in this context face obstacles due to the uncritical adoption of Western categories in African economic and social structures.
Khambule, (2022)	South Africa	Quantitative Survey study	Informal workers in KwaDukuza Municipality	- COVID-19 lockdown intensified the vulnerability of informal workers, leading to a decline in socio-economic status. - Participants reported increased unemployment, poverty, and vulnerability during the lockdown. - Lack of targeted and timely interventions worsened the challenges faced by those in the informal economy amid COVID-induced shocks.
Khamis (2014)	Emerging market economies	Desktop research	Informal sector businesses; World Bank Doing Business Database	- Encouraging registration through information and reducing registration costs and time. - Formalisation benefits include access to formal credit, legal compliance, and avoiding fines. - Formalisation can increase tax revenues. - Formalisation allows formal firms to scale up operations, potentially leading to higher revenues and profits. - Registration reforms may not effectively drive formalisation. - Small-scale firms and low-skilled workers may still find formalisation costs prohibitive. - The perception of taxes as a drawback might hinder formalisation and tax revenue growth.
Lukin and Xuesong, (2019)	China	Desktop research	Information on BRICS, China	- China views BRICS as a key asset in its quest for global power and international system reform. - It aims for a fairer system aligning with the interests of major non-Western states, portraying its stance as collaborative. - China sees the need for developing countries' assistance to address global unfairness. - The strategy involves a gradual evolution through negotiations, not a revolutionary approach.

Continued on following page

Table 1. Continued

Author and Year	Setting	Design	Population and Sample	Summary of Findings
McKenzie and Sakho (2010)	Bolivia	Secondary Quantitative research	Survey of micro and small firms	- Proximity to tax office used as instrument for tax registration's impact on profitability. - Tax registration leads to higher profits, especially for mid-sized firms, contrary to the standard view. - Evidence shows varied effects on profits, increasing for mid-sized but lowering for smaller and larger firms. - Results challenge the conventional belief that formality universally boosts profits.
Moyo (2022)	22 Developing counties	Discrete choice probit model	World Bank informal sector enterprise surveys	- Firms more likely to formalise are young, owned by highly educated individuals, and have registered before. - Governments should target young firms, providing them information about registration benefits. - If owned by experienced and educated individuals, likelihood of registration is high.
Narula (2020)	Developing counties globally	Desktop research	Informal sector of developing counties.	-Notes that large firms subcontract significant activity to informal enterprises, suggesting a precarious relationship. -Proposes active engagement with informal actors in industrial policy during crises, emphasising integration, registration, and state support without taxation. -Advocates for the state's role in matchmaking, incentivizing Global Value Chains to systematically engage with informal actors, and reducing transaction costs for such engagement.
Okungu and McIntyre (2019)	Kenya	Quantitative Survey Research	Informal sector businesses in Mombasa (urban) and Nyeri (rural).	- Income in the informal sector generally low; varied by sectors with health/medical, stationery, entertainment, manufacturing, craft, and transportation having higher incomes. - Mean monthly incomes ranged from 16.7 USD (lowest) to 786.5 USD (highest). - Sustainable entities: stationery, repair/maintenance, food vending, shopkeeping, clothing/beauty products in urban; farming, manufacturing/craft, health/medical in rural. - Key predictors of sustainability: monthly expenditures, gender, marital status, household structure, number of employees, land ownership. - Majority of informal sector entities unsustainable; likely to require subsidies.

Continued on following page

Table 1. Continued

Author and Year	Setting	Design	Population and Sample	Summary of Findings
Rogan and Skinner, 2020)	South Africa	Secondary Quantitative research	National Income Dynamics Study – Coronavirus Rapid Mobile Survey (NIDS-CRAM) Survey	- Around 31% of informal workers experienced employment disruption in April, compared to 26% in formal employment. - Women in the informal economy saw a 49% decrease in typical hours worked, while men experienced a 25% decrease. - Self-employed individuals in the informal sector faced a significant reduction in average and typical hours, with a decrease of over 50% in typical hours. - Average earnings for informal self-employed workers dropped by 27%, and typical earnings by 60%. - Women in informal self-employment witnessed a nearly 70% decrease in typical earnings between February and April.
Sandada (2014)	Zimbabwe	Qualitative Research	Informal traders in Harare	- Four major themes emerged from the interview transcripts: barriers to formality, informality benefits, informality disadvantages, and formality enablers. - Informal traders are conscious of the drawbacks of operating informally and recognize the advantages of formalizing their business activities. - Entry barriers such as high taxes, cumbersome and expensive registration processes, corruption among government and municipality officials, high business premises rentals, insufficient skills, and lack of access to finance hinder the inclination towards formality.
Van der Molen (2018)	General	Desktop research	Information on the informal economy	-People in the informal economy lack decent work. -Governments miss substantial tax revenue. -Government miss information to develop evidence-based policymaking. - Countries with a substantial informal economy, the lack of fundamental datasets hampers any development in these fields.

Source: Author's own compilation
*Reports from bodies (eg., IMF, ILO and Stats SA) and books have been excluded.

Chapter 3
Improving Access to Finance to Unlock SME Growth Potential in Emerging Markets:
South Korea Example

Gifty Edwin-Akakpo
Coventry University, UK

Alfred Akakpo
University of Northampton, UK

Said Ali
Coventry University, UK

ABSTRACT

The purpose of this chapter is to examine access to finance for small and medium scale enterprises in emerging markets with a focus on South Korea. This book chapter evaluates the critical role access to finance plays in enabling growth and expansion for SMEs in emerging market economy such as a South Korea. Also, there is critical analysis of the challenges faced by SMEs in securing financing in emerging markets. The lack of funding sources was discussed with a review on innovative models and policy solutions that aim to improve small and medium scale enterprises' access to finance.

INTRODUCTION

Small and Medium Enterprises (SMEs) are vital drivers of economies in numerous countries, especially in emerging markets like South Korea. SMEs form the majority of businesses worldwide and significantly contribute to contemporary economic growth, job creation and global economic development (Siu, 2005; Nieto and Santamaria, 2010; Mugisha, et al., 2020). Despite their immense importance, SMEs often face obstacles in accessing financial support from sources such as equity financing, traditional banks, ven-

DOI: 10.4018/979-8-3693-0111-1.ch003

ture capitalists and business angels which sets them at a disadvantage compared to larger organizations. Consequently, they often resort to alternative means of financing such as personal savings, contributions from family and friends, and internal funds to initiate and sustain their entrepreneurial ventures.

SMEs face several obstacles in securing financing from investors. A primary factor contributing to this challenge is the relatively low returns offered by SMEs, which makes investment in them less appealing, especially in today's highly competitive global market. Moreover, many SMEs are seen as having limited financial transparency and weak internal controls, elevating the risk and uncertainty associated with investing in them. The absence of an extensive credit history and collateral assets further diminishes their attractiveness to potential investors and lenders (Mugisha, et al., 2020). Adding to the difficulty is the marginalization of SMEs by various stock markets, which impose complex documentation and regulatory requirements, acting as barriers to equity finance. These hurdles make it arduous for SMEs to access the necessary capital from the investor community.

There are numerous studies that have examine access of financial support to SMEs growth and innovation in emerging economies. For example, Pham, et al., (2023) investigated the innovation outcomes on access to finance for SMEs in Vietnam; while Kato (2021) stated that despite proliferation of SMEs in emerging markets, access to sustainable financing for the survival and growth of SMEs is still low and scanty. Further, the International Finance Corporation (IFC) estimates that 65 million organisation, accounting for 40% of formal micro, small and medium enterprises in emerging markets, have an unmet financing need of $5.2 trillion annually, which is equivalent to 1.4 times the current level of the global micro, small and medium enterprises lending (World Bank, 2023). While bank loans are the most available source of external source of finance for many SMEs, however, SMEs finds it difficult to obtain finance from traditional banks.

South Korea, one of the Asian tiger's economic successes has created a large industry of SMEs who act as the backbone of the country's economic performance (Tierno, 2019). Korea has some of the most supportive and vibrant policies for SMEs, including an abundant supply of government-backed loans, due to their role as an engine of growth for employment. Support for SMEs is poised to remain strong as the country undergoes a strategic shift toward inclusive and innovation-led growth (Tierno, 2019). However, critics suggest that government's data and programmes point to poor performance among SMEs.

This book chapter seeks to examine the critical role access to finance plays in enabling growth and expansion for SMEs in emerging market economies with a focus on South Korea. This chapter evaluates the unique financing barriers SMEs face in emerging markets compared to developed economies. Also, the chapter critically discusses how lack of funding sources for SMEs hinders their growth prospects. The rest of the chapter provides a critical overview of SMEs operation in South Korea, overview of emerging Markets and SMEs, SMEs financing gaps in emerging markets with a focus on South Korea. This is followed by a discussion on the risk assessment capabilities, collateral requirements for SMEs lending and the role of government in providing finance to SMEs via grants and other regulations/policies. Further discussion was carried out on the comparison for financing for SMEs in south Korea and Italy.

Emerging Markets and SMEs

Emerging markets represent developing nations that are increasingly participating in the global business arena. They exhibit certain characteristics akin to developed markets, yet they have not fulfilled all the criteria for full development (OECD, 2021b). The identification of emerging markets, as outlined by the International Monetary Fund (2021), relies on attributes such as sustained market access, global economic relevance, and the ability to attain middle-income levels. Given that Small and Medium-sized Enterprises (SMEs) serve as engines of growth and form the backbone of every economy, their significance and influence within emerging economies cannot be overstated (Abbasi, et al., 2017). SMEs play a pivotal role in the development of economies, particularly in developing and underdeveloped regions, and their contributions to emerging markets are of paramount importance. These contributions encompass job creation, economic development, and income generation, as emphasized by the International Labour Organization (2019), which refers to SMEs as "engines for economic growth and social development."

The global significance of SMEs, with a specific focus on emerging markets, is closely tied to their contributions and the imperative for these enterprises to expand. These drivers span both economic and social realms. Emerging markets are poised for advancement and require additional impetus to progress to the next phase of development (Duttagupta & Pazarbasioglu, 2017). To facilitate and sustain this progress, supportive structures and institutions are essential, with SMEs playing a central role.

The multifaceted roles of SMEs extend from employment creation to fostering innovation, reflecting the inherently entrepreneurial nature of these businesses. In emerging economies, a significant portion of the workforce is employed by small and medium-sized enterprises, with the World Bank estimating that 70% of formal jobs are generated by SMEs (World Bank, 2023).

Another pivotal function of SMEs is their support for local communities. Many SMEs are rooted in these local communities, and their contributions to these areas are of paramount importance. Unlike larger corporations, SMEs can thrive in smaller communities due to their size and operational characteristics. SMEs in local and small communities often collaborate and support each other's growth, relying on fellow smaller businesses for raw materials and other supplies. This interconnectedness fosters community development and economic resilience.

Overview of SMEs Operation in South Korea

This section offers a concise overview of Small and Medium-sized Enterprises (SMEs) and their operational characteristics. According to the World Bank (2023), majority of global businesses fall within the SME category, accounting for approximately 90% of all businesses and generating nearly 50% of job opportunities in most countries (Yoon, 2023).

In the year 2020, South Korea boasted around 7.3 million SMEs, while the count of larger corporations stood at approximately 9,300 (Yoon, 2023). SMEs are primarily characterized by their financial metrics, including revenue, assets, and the number of employees, which typically fall below specified thresholds (Liberto, et al., 2023). It's worth noting that these thresholds can vary among different jurisdictions, with individual countries often establishing unique guidelines for SME classification based on sector-specific or industry-specific criteria.

For instance, the United States classifies SMEs by considering ownership structure, employee count, earnings, and industry. In the U.S., a manufacturing firm with fewer than 500 employees fall within the SME category (U.S. Small Business Administration, 2023). In contrast, South Korea employs a different criterion, defining SMEs in terms of the revenue they generate. Specifically, not-for-profit enterprises with total assets not exceeding 500 billion South Korean won are classified as SMEs (Yoon, 2023).

South Korea, like many emerging economies, exhibits a sizable population of less productive businesses coexisting with large, highly productive conglomerates. It is estimated that the SME sector in South Korea contributes significantly to employment, representing approximately 86% of the workforce, while 99% of enterprises fall into the SME category (OECD, 2021a). Ownership structures in these businesses commonly involve partnerships or family ownership, where management and ownership interests are often closely intertwined. As noted by Liberto, et al. (2023), the conventional concept of separating ownership from management may not be readily applicable to these enterprises, as owners frequently maintain active involvement in the day-to-day operations of their businesses.

SMEs Financing Gaps in Emerging Markets With a Focus on South Korea

One of the primary roles of the financial sector is to facilitate the provision of funding to individuals, as well as private and public organizations. Periodically, disparities may arise between the amount of funding required and the availability of financial resources. When the financial sector is unable to adequately supply funding to small and medium-sized businesses, it is referred to as a "financing gap" (OECD, 2021a). While financing gaps exist in all economies and sectors, they tend to be more pronounced in emerging markets.

In the context of SMEs operating within emerging markets, a financing gap denotes the difference between the financial resources SMEs need for their operations and growth, and the amount of funding that is accessible to them (Parrott, 2023). SMEs encounter greater challenges in securing bank loans and other forms of credit when compared to larger corporations. The magnitude of this financing gap varies from one region to another. According to the International Finance Corporation (IFC), SMEs in developing countries grapple with an annual financing gap of approximately $5.2 trillion (World Bank, 2023). This gap is attributed to factors unique to SMEs and the broader economic contexts in which they operate. In the case of South Korea, a multitude of factors hinders most SMEs from accessing financial resources from banks, capital markets, and other financing providers and these factors include (IMF, 2020):

Undeveloped financial structure: the financial structures in Korea like many emerging markets is not well developed and this hinders SMEs in accessing finance. Banks and other financial institutions are mostly based in the towns and cities and SMEs may not have access as they are prevalent in the rural areas with no or limited banking facilities.

Regulatory barriers: Strict regulations and complex documentations can restrict SMEs from access finance from formal financial institutions as small business do not have robust system to enable them to meet these regulatory requirements.

Volatility and Uncertainty: Emerging markets such as Korea have unstable economies with volatility in market. Providers of finance are unwilling to offer credit to SMEs in these economies due to the high risk of default.

Lack of Financial Literacy: Financial management is core to the sourcing of funding for every business. However, SMEs owners in Korea do not have the financial literacy to understand financial management and therefore unable to navigate the complexities of financial sector financing.

Lack of collateral: Most financial institutions may require collateral as a form of security to secure a loan. SMEs have limited asset base and may not be able to provide sufficient and appropriate collateral required for a traditional loan.

As SMEs operate on a small to medium scale, there are prevailing issues with resource acquisition. These constraints include limited access to finance, capital, and human resources. One of the key constraints facing SMEs is access to finance. The next section discusses the barriers to accessing finance by SMEs.

Barriers to Accessing Debt Financing From Banks and Creditors by SMEs in South Korea

Small- and medium-sized enterprises (SMEs) often encounter challenges when seeking to obtain debt financing from financial institutions and creditors. These impediments can encompass stringent eligibility criteria, such as elevated credit score thresholds and collateral prerequisites, which may pose formidable obstacles for smaller enterprises to satisfy. Additionally, the absence of a robust financial track record or limited business history can serve as formidable barriers to securing debt financing (OECD, 2019).

The economic progress of South Korea is predominantly steered by large enterprises; nevertheless, SMEs continue to hold a pivotal position within the economy. They constitute a staggering 99.9% of all enterprises and contribute to 87.5% of the nation's workforce (Liang, 2017; Kim & Lee, 2018). The total count of domestic SMEs in South Korea stands at 7.3 million, collectively employing 17.3 million individuals, constituting 87.9% of the total employment as at 2023 (Yoon, 2023). These statistics underscore the significant role played by local SMEs in the Korean economy. The substantial workforce engaged by SMEs underscores their vital role in generating employment opportunities and propelling economic growth. However, hindered by financial barriers, these indispensable contributors to the economy may encounter difficulties in their expansion endeavors. Limited access to funding can impede their capacity to invest in cutting-edge technologies, recruit additional personnel, and expand their operations, potentially leading to a deceleration in economic development and a dearth of employment opportunities in South Korea.

In South Korea, where the establishment of venture capital remains underdeveloped, banks serve as the primary source of financing for SMEs (Yoshino et al., 2019). SMEs encounter heightened financing constraints in comparison to larger corporations, attributed to factors such as information opacity and the absence of audited financial statements (Hasan et al., 2017; Lu et al., 2022). This lack of transparency poses formidable hurdles for SMEs in attracting potential investors and securing loans from financial institutions. As noted by Pan et al. (2017), small businesses grapple with difficulties in accessing both financial and non-financial credit information, leading to suboptimal credit assessments within credit guarantee systems due to limited collateral and information acquisition challenges.

The dearth of audited financial records further diminishes SMEs ability to establish creditworthiness and financial stability, exacerbating their financial constraints. Moreover, SMEs in Korea confront additional hurdles stemming from the dominance of large conglomerates in the market. These conglomerates often enjoy preferential treatment from financial institutions, thereby intensifying the challenges faced by SMEs in securing funding. Consequently, numerous SMEs grapple with impediments to their expansion and growth, which, in turn, hinder the overall economic development of the nation.

Another major barrier to accessing debt financing from banks and creditors by SMEs is the lack of collateral or assets that can be used to secure loans. This is particularly challenging for women entrepreneurs, who may face cultural norms that limit their access to assets, as highlighted by Ahmetaj et al. (2023). Furthermore, the larger financial market framework can pose impediments to the accessibility of equity financing for SMEs. These obstacles encompass information imbalances between SME management and financial institutions, elevated transaction expenses, and substantial interest costs, all of which can act as limitations for SMEs.

The challenges confronting SMEs extend beyond banking obstacles, encompassing a broad spectrum of barriers that are contingent on factors such as size, geographic location, and their position within the supply chain (Hong et al., 2019; Migilinskas et al., 2013; Vidalakis et al., 2020; Saka & Chan, 2020). As noted by Blach (2020), among the most formidable impediments encountered by SMEs are the ambiguities within tax regulations and accounting standards. These hurdles introduce an element of unpredictability and intricacy into SMEs' financial operations. Furthermore, the lack of clarity in tax legislation and accounting standards amplifies the administrative burden on SMEs, diverting their attention and resources away from innovation and constraining their ability to effectively compete in the market. To effectively address these challenges, it is imperative for South Korean policymakers to establish clear and consistent tax regulations and accounting standards tailored to the specific needs of SMEs.

3.4 Risk Assessment Capabilities and Collateral Requirements for SMEs

Risk assessment capabilities and collateral requirements for SMEs are critical for lenders to make informed lending choices to small and medium enterprises. Lenders may be hesitant to grant credit to SMEs unless they have a thorough understanding of the risks involved and adequate collateral to minimize those risks. Research indicates that SMEs are riskier than larger enterprises, making it even more vital for lenders to thoroughly examine the amount of risk before issuing a loan to an SME (Long et al., 2022).

Risk can be assessed by examining criteria such as the SME's financial records, credit history, and industry performance. Lenders may also analyze SME's company plans, management teams, and market competitiveness to assess their prospects for success and payback. Lenders can make better-informed judgements and reduce the risk of default or financial loss by properly analyzing these factors. Researchers typically assess credit risk by analyzing firm data and identifying three main groups: demographic, financial, and credit history (Long et al., 2022). These three categories offer vital insights into the possibility of a default and assist lenders in making informed decisions. Age, income level, and work stability are examples of demographic data that may reflect a person's ability to repay debt. On the other hand, financial data are concerned with a company's financial health, such as profitability, liquidity, and leverage ratios. Credit history analyses previous borrowing and repayment trends to assess an individual's dependability to satisfy financial obligations. Researchers collectively examine these three groups.

Several methodologies are employed when assessing risks in SME financing. Some methods include qualitative risk assessment, which focuses on subjective evaluations and descriptions of the risk likelihood and effect. Another method is quantitative risk assessment, which includes assigning numerical values to risks based on the likelihood and probable consequences. Researchers employ a network approach to evaluate credit risk in SMEs, incorporating relational risk features that aid in modelling complex systems, understanding the system structure, trust propagation, and contagion risk (Buldyrev et al. 2010; Zha et al. 2021 and Long et al., 2022).

Collateral is security for lenders, providing insurance in case of borrowers' inability to repay loans. SME's collateral positively impacts their creditworthiness according to Wasiuzzaman et al. (2020). This means that the more collateral a SME possesses, the more likely it is for banks to view it as creditworthy. In the case of a default, the lender may take and sell assets such as property, equipment, or inventory.

Role of Government in Providing Finance to SMEs via Grants and Other Regulations/Policies

SMEs are crucial in any economic growth of countries. As with most governments, the South Korean government has continually emphasized support for these businesses. Thus, various programs, policies and financial incentives have been implemented by the government to support the growth of SMEs and make them more competitive (IMF, 2020). Some of the financial support provided by the Korean government include the following:

Start-up Centres

There are start-up centres established by South Korean government which serves as innovation centres which offer support services to SMEs. The support include access to networking, finance and mentoring (Yoon, 2023).

For example, in 2017, Korea established the Ministry of SMEs and Start-ups, this was to replace the previous Small Medium Business Administration. The Ministry operates in 13 regional offices and their mandate is to coordinate the policies of the national SMEs and micro enterprise policies (OECD, 2023).

Low Interest Loans

The government in collaboration with financial institutions (both government and private owned banks) with low interest loans and specialised lending facilities. Credit guarantee programs are available to SMES, they aim at enhancing access to loan in the form of acting as partial guarantors of loans. Thus, government guarantees loan for SMEs who meet all the requisite requirements. For example, between 2017 and 2018, the Korean government guaranteed loans increased by 2.8%. The overall amount of lending to SMEs is estimated to be KRW 4.4 trillon in 2018 (OECD, 2023).

Tax Incentives

The provision of tax incentives is also a means of supporting SMEs. According to Yoon (2023) the Korean government provides reduced tax rates, tax incentives, reductions in local taxes and tax rebate for research and development projects.

Research and Development Subsidies

One important aspect of businesses is the ability to develop through research. Most research project can be very expensive and become a constraint for most SMEs. IMF (2020) stated that there are subsidies available in Korea which supports and encourage small business to pursue various research programs. The support is in the form of grants, subsidies to cover research and development costs incurred.

Potential Solutions to Address Challenges Facing SMEs in South Korea

Faced with numerous barriers and challenges that hinder the progress and performance of SMEs in accessing finance for their operations, the following potential solutions can be implemented to address these issues. Some of the potential solutions to mitigate SMEs financial challenges could include establishment of more specialised banks for SMEs financing with support from government; establishment of credit union for SMEs; provision of adequate training of SMEs staff to enhance their skills in finance sourcing and government credit guarantee schemes to SMEs.

Establishment of More Specialised Banks for SMEs Financing With Support From Government

There is the need to diversify the financing channels of SMEs in Korea by establishing specialised bank that deals mainly with SMEs financing, At the moment there are very limited financial institutions in this area, one good example is the Industrial bank of Korea (IBK) which acts as an SME bank. The bank was established in 1961 as a public bank under the industrial Bank of Korea Act to provide 70% of its loan portfolio directly to SMEs whose access to finance is limited and constrained (Niazi, et al., 2021). Since its establishment, the bank has issued policy loan, credits and financial bonds to SMEs until its privatization in 1994.

This is what one specialised bank can achieve. It is therefore justified to conclude that having a sizeable number of specialised banks focusing on SMEs finances can be a good remedy for tackling SMEs difficulty in accessing finance.

Establishment of Credit Union for SMEs

Another potential solution to SMEs financing problems is for SMEs to address the problem themselves and this can be solved by the establishment of Credit Unions to provide credit and guarantee collaterals for SMEs who want to source finance from other financial institutions. According to McKillop and Wilson (2015) credit unions are cooperative financial institutions with no profit motives providing financial services to their members. Credit unions distinguish themselves from traditional financial institutions by focusing on building social capital and empowering their members. Their primary function involves mobilizing savings and allocating resources to benefit their members. When SMEs unite to establish credit unions, members can secure sufficient funds for their operations, circumventing some of the challenges associated with obtaining financing from traditional banks. Members of SME credit unions stand to gain advantages such as enjoying low interest rates.

As of 2020, there are about 888 credit unions in South Korea with 6.15 million members and assets of US8.1billion (Ahn 2020). The members of these credit unions are primarily individuals and SME membership is nonexistent.

In alignment with the ethos of the Credit Union movement, Credit Unions actively participate in corporate social responsibility (CSR) initiatives, extending social financing, and bolstering the social economy to foster the creation of social value. Ahn (2020) emphasizes that the fundamental philosophy of credit unions centers around providing financial support to members and facilitating the generation of social value. This philosophy is consonant with the objectives of SMEs, which typically operate with the aim of benefiting society and are regarded as the backbone of economies. Collaborating with credit unions is posited as a strategic approach to addressing financing challenges and promoting the shared goals of social contribution.

Adequate Training of SMEs Staff to Enhance Their Skills in Finance Sourcing

There is always a financing gap when discussing accessibility of finance; and SMEs are usually squeezed out as investment in SMEs are perceived as high risk (Parrott 2023). One of the reasons is limited or non-existent internal controls, financial reporting and sourcing skills of employees of SMEs. It is therefore important that employees of SMEs are given the necessary training to improve on their financial reporting skills thereby enhancing their chances of accessing finance from the traditional financial sector. Extensive research has shown that there are clear benefits for SMEs who engages in skill training and development for their employees. For example, Vos and Willemse (2011) acknowledges innovation through knowledge and education is the way forward for the worldwide economy and for SMEs, a proper way out of the crisis. SMEs in South Korea must therefore focus on leveraging training skills of their workers. Only 43% of the SME's have a training and development plan for their employees, and 39% reported that some desired training skills have not been carried out (Vos and Willemse 2011; Lee 2016). Thus, limited financial and credit situation does not allow SMEs to invest in training programmes for their workers compared with bigger organizations to merit government assistance. Therefore, there should be a targeted approach by the Korean government to promote training of SMEs to enhance their accessibility of finance.

Government Credit Guarantee Schemes to SMEs

Another solution to mitigate the impediments face by SMEs in accessing credit facility within South Korea involves augmenting the allocation of credit guarantee schemes by the government specifically tailored for SMEs. For example, in 1976, the South Korean government established the Korea Credit Guarantee Fund (KODIT) with a focus to provide credit guarantee to SMEs in South Korea. As of 2022, its total capital fund stands at S8.3 billion (Korea Credit Guarantee Fund, 2022). Government-backed guarantee loans constitute a form of credit subsidized by the government, shielding lenders from the risks associated with loan defaults. While the overall provision of government guarantee loans across various sectors in South Korea has shown an upward trend since 2011, the proportion of these loans directed towards SMEs has exhibited a decline since 2012 (OECD, 2020). Addressing the hurdles faced by SMEs necessitates the South Korean Government to augment the allotment of government guarantee loans specifically allocated to SMEs. This strategic initiative aims to empower lenders to offer loans to SMEs at reduced interest rates, fostering a more conducive environment for their growth and sustainability.

Comparing South Korea's SME FINANCING LANDSCAPE WITH ITALY

South Korea has traditionally been perceived as a significant business economy, with a reliance on conglomerates referred to as chaebols, whereas Italy boasts a considerable presence of small and medium-sized enterprises within its economy (Albert, 2018). The differences in the nature of respective economies have resulted in variations in the financial landscape for SMEs in both countries (Lee 2015). In South Korea, the government has been expanding policies for SMEs and startups by streamlining the startup process and providing better opportunities to attract investment (Lee 2015). These regulations have resulted in an increase in the number of start-ups and enhanced access to capital among South Korean SMEs. In 2020, the number of SMEs in South Korea increased to 7.3 million from 6.9 million from the previous year (Statista, 2023). This growth in the number of SMEs indicates a positive impact of the government's initiatives on South Korea's entrepreneurial ecosystem. Increased access to financing has enabled SMEs to develop and contribute to the nation's economic growth.

Small and medium-sized businesses account for 99.9% of Italian corporations, with micro-businesses accounting for about 95% (OECD, 2022). In Italy, trade credit is a vital source of funding for Italian businesses (Agostino and Trivieri, 2014). Trade credit allows businesses in Italy to obtain goods and services from suppliers without immediate payment, providing them with flexibility and liquidity. This form of financing is particularly important for small and medium-sized enterprises (SMEs) in Italy as it helps them manage their cash flow and maintain their operations smoothly. Similar to South Korea, the Italian financial system is bank-based, with stock markets playing an insignificant role (Deloof and La Rocca, 2015). Due to strict lending standards and a lack of collateral, SMEs in Italy may experience difficulties obtaining traditional bank loans. According to OECD (2022), a Bank of Italy survey on Industrial and Service Firms found that the SME rejection rate rose to 6.1%, half the peak reached in 2012 but 2 percentage points higher than the previous year. Thus, Italian SMEs could also benefit from bank financing by using it to create relationships with suppliers and negotiate better terms and prices.

Case Study of SMEs in South Korea that Faced Financial Challenges

After the Asian financial and economic crisis of 1997/1998, there were series of bankruptcies among major corporations which significantly impacted on Korean SMEs (Gregory et al., 2002). This downturn forced many SMEs into bankruptcy due to a credit shortage stemming from policies aimed at stabilizing the exchange rate, tight monetary measures, and a steep decline in both domestic and regional demand and sales, particularly in 1998. To illustrate the gravity of the situation, SME bankruptcies surged from 11,600 in 1996 to 17,200 in 1997, peaking at 22,800 in 1998 during the height of the recession (Gregory et al., 2002). Despite these challenges, the economy exhibited an impressive recovery from 1999 to mid-2000. However, economic growth has since decelerated, compounded by the aftermath of the events in New York in September 2001.

CONCLUSION

SMEs face significant financial gaps that impacts on their economic growth, expansion, and innovation. There are many areas of economic policy by the South Korea government effort which has helped to improve financial access to SMEs including tax incentives, low interest loans and start-up centres which act as incubation centres for SMEs to access financial support and training. Financial policies for SMEs in South Korea were the effort of political and economic choices of modernization strategy of the Korean government's control of the economy and social matters. However, challenges still exist for SMEs growth and innovation in emerging economies. However, these efforts are with some challenges such as government guarantee credits and collaterals to secure bank loans.

REFERENCES

Abbasi, W. A., Wang, Z., & Abbasi, D. A. (2017). Potential Sources of Financing for Small and Medium Enterprises (SME s) and Role of Government in Supporting SMEs. *Journal of Small Business and Entrepreneurship Development*, *5*(2), 39–47. doi:10.15640/jsbed.v5n2a4

Agostino, M., & Trivieri, F. (2014). Does trade credit play a signaling role? Some evidence from SMEs microdata. *Small Business Economics*, *42*(1), 131–151. doi:10.1007/s11187-013-9478-8

Ahmetaj, B., Kruja, A., & Hysa, E. (2023). Women entrepreneurship: Challenges and perspectives of an emerging economy. *Administrative Sciences*, *13*(4), 1–20. doi:10.3390/admsci13040111

Ahn, S. Y. (2020, December 12) *"Korean Credit Unions CSR and Social Finance"*. *South Korea*. IRU. https://www.iru.de/wp-content/uploads/2020/06/RaiffeisenToday_Chapter14_South-Korea.pdf

Albert, E. (2018, December 12). *South Korea's Chaebol Challenge*. IRU. https://www.cfr.org/backgrounder/south-koreas-chaebol-challenge

Błach, J. (2020). Barriers to financial innovation: Corporate finance perspective. *Journal of Risk and Financial Management, 13*(11), 1–23. doi:10.3390/jrfm13110273

Buldyrev, S., Parshani, R., Paul, G., Stanley, H., & Havlin, S. (2010). Catastrophic cascade of failures in interdependent networks. *Nature, 464*(7291), 1025–1028. doi:10.1038/nature08932 PMID:20393559

Deloof, M., & La Rocca, M. (2015). Local financial development and the trade credit policy of Italian SMEs. *Small Business Economics, 44*(4), 905–924. doi:10.1007/s11187-014-9617-x

Duttagupta, R. & Pazarbasioglu, C. (2017). *Miles to Go: The Future of Emerging Markets – IMF F&D*. Finance and Development World Bank blog.

Gregory, G., Harvie, C., & Lee, H. H. (2002). *Korean SMEs in the Wake of the Financial Crisis: Strategies, Constraints, and Performance in a Global Economy*. Department of Economics, University of Wollongong, 2002. https://ro.uow.edu.au/cgi/viewcontent.cgi?referer=&httpsredir=1&article=1057&context=commwkpapers

Hasan, I., Jackowicz, K., Kowalewski, O., & Kozłowski, Ł. (2017). Do local banking market structures matter for SME financing and performance? New evidence from an emerging economy. *Journal of Banking & Finance, 79*, 142–158. doi:10.1016/j.jbankfin.2017.03.009

Hong, Y., Hammad, A., Sepasgozar, S., & Akbarnezhad, A. (2019). BIM adoption model for small and medium construction organisations in Australia. *Engineering, Construction, and Architectural Management, 26*(2), 154–183. doi:10.1108/ECAM-04-2017-0064

IMF. (2020). Republic of Korea: Financial System Stability Assessment and Press Release for the Republic of Korea. *IMF Country Report, 20*(120).

International Labour Oorganisation. (2019, September 10) *The power of small: Unlocking the potential of SME*. ILO. https://www.ilo.org/infostories/en-GB/Stories/Employment/SMEs#footer

International Monetary Fund. (2021, September 20). *Emerging markets must balance overcoming the pandemic, returning to more normal policies, and rebuilding their economies*. IMF. https://www.imf.org/external/pubs/ft/fandd/2021/06/pdf/the-future-of-emerging-markets-duttagupta-and-pazarbasioglu.pdf

Kato, A. I. (2021). A Literature Review of Venture Capital Financing and Growth of SMEs in Emerging Economies and a Agenda for Future Research. *Academy of Entrepreneurship Journal, 27*(1), 1–17.

Kim, C., & Lee, J. (2018). The Effect of Network Structure on Performance in South Korea SMEs: The Moderating Effects of Absorptive Capacity. *Sustainability (Basel), 10*(9), 3174. doi:10.3390/su10093174

Korea Credit Guarantee Fund. (2022, December 11). *Annual Report*. Kodit. https://www.kodit.co.kr/ synap/skin/doc.html?fn=2022%EB%85%84%EB%8F%84%20%EC%98%81%EB%AC%B8%20 %EC%97%B0%EC%B0%A8%EB%B3%B4%EA%B3%A0%EC%84%9C.pdf&rs=/serverFiles/syn- ap/20230807181004788_4392/output

Lee, D.-H. (2015). *Commercializing Excellent Ideas for Creative Economy: Focusing on the Six Months Challenge Platform Project. Research Report 2015–047.* Korea Institute of SandT Evaluation and Planning.

Lee, K. W. (2016, December 12). *Skills Training by Small and Medium-Sized Enterprises: Innovative Cases and the Consortium Approach in the Republic of Korea.* (ADBI Working Paper Series). ADBI. https://www.adb.org/sites/default/files/publication/188802/adbi-wp579.pdf

Liang, L., Gao, Y., Huang, B., & Liao, C. (2017). The impact of SMEs' lending and credit guarantee on bank efficiency in South Korea. *Review of Development Finance*, 7(2), 134–141. doi:10.1016/j. rdf.2017.04.003

Liberto, D., James, M., & Kvilhaug, S. (2023, September 10) *Small and Midsize Enterprise (SME) Defined: Types Around the World the World.* Investiopedia. https://www.investopedia.com/terms/s/ smallandmidsizeenterprises.asp#citation-8

Long, J., Jiang, C., Dimitrov, S., & Wang, Z. (2022). Clues from networks: Quantifying relational risk for credit risk evaluation of SMEs. *Financial Innovation*, 8(1), 1–41. doi:10.1186/s40854-022-00390-1

Lu, Z., Wu, J., Li, H., & Nguyen, D. (2022). Local Bank, Digital Financial Inclusion and SME Financing Constraints: Empirical Evidence from China. *Emerging Markets Finance & Trade*, 58(6), 1712–1725. doi:10.1080/1540496X.2021.1923477

McKillop, D. G., & Wilson, J. O. S. (2015). Credit Unions as Cooperative Institutions: Distinctiveness, Performance and Prospects. *Social and Environmental Accountability Journal*, 35(2), 96–112. doi:10. 1080/0969160X.2015.1022195

Migilinskas, D., Popov, V., Juocevicius, V., & Ustinovichius, L. (2013). The Benefits, Obstacles and Problems of Practical Bim Implementation. *Procedia Engineering*, 57, 767–774. doi:10.1016/j.pro- eng.2013.04.097

Mugisha, H., Omagwa, J., & Kilika, J. (2020). Short-Term Debt and Financial Performance of Small and Medium Scale Enterprises in Buganda Region, Uganda. *International Journal of Finance & Banking Studies*, 9(4), 58–69. doi:10.20525/ijfbs.v9i4.910

Niazi, T., Cole, R., Lee, L., Kim, S. S., & Han, J. (2021, December 11). *Public Lending Schemes for SMEs in Asia and the Pacific: Lessons from the Republic of Korea and the United States.* ADB. https:// www.adb.org/sites/default/files/publication/753586/adb-brief-201-lending-smes-asia-pacific-lessons- rok-usa.pdf

Nieto, M. J., & Santamaria, L. (2010). Technological collaboration: Bridging the innovation gap be- tween small and large firms. *Journal of Small Business Management*, 48(1), 44–69. doi:10.1111/j.1540- 627X.2009.00286.x

OECD. (2019, September 16) *"Access to Finance". SME and Entrepreneurship Outlook*. OECD. https://www.oecd-ilibrary.org/sites/8082995b-en/index.html?itemId=/content/component/8082995b

OECD. (2020, December 11). *Key Facts on SMEs Financing-Korea*. OECD. https://www.oecd-ilibrary.org/sites/9fd590e7-en/index.html?itemId=/content/component/9fd590e7-en

OECD. (2021a, September 20). *The SME Financing Gap: Theory and Evidence*. OECD. https://www.oecd-ilibrary.org/finance-and-investment/the-sme-financing-gap-vol-i_9789264029415-en#:~:text=The%20lack%20of%20funding%20available,countries%20and%20non%2DOECD%20economies

OECD. (2021b, September 19). *Business Insights on Emerging Markets 2021. OECD Emerging Markets Network*, OECD Development Centre, Paris. https://www.oecd.org/dev/oecdemnet.htm

OECD. (2022, December 7). *Financing SMEs and Entrepreneurs 2022: An OECD Scoreboard*. OECD.

OECD. (2023, September 20). *Financing SMEs and Entrepreneurs 2020: An OECD Scoreboard*. OECD. https://www.oecd-ilibrary.org/sites/9fd590e7-en/index.html?itemId=/content/component/9fd590e7-en#wrapper

Pan, H., Kang, M., & Ha, H. (2017). Do trade area grades really affect credit ratings of small businesses? An application of big data. *Management Decision*, 55(9), 2038–2052. doi:10.1108/MD-11-2016-0834

Parrott, W. (2023, September 20) *What is an SME?* Acca Global. https://www.accaglobal.com/gb/en/student/exam-support-resources/fundamentals-exams-study-resources/f9/technical-articles/sme-finance.html Accessed 18/09/2023

Pham, T. T. T., Nguyen, T. V. H., Nguyen, S. K., & Nguyen, H. T. H. (2023). Does planned innovation promote financial access? Evidence from Vietnamese SMEs. *Eurasian Business Review*, 13(2), 281–307. doi:10.1007/s40821-023-00238-3

Saka, A., & Chan, D. (2020). Profound barriers to building information modelling (BIM) adoption in construction small and medium-sized enterprises (SMEs). *Construction Innovation*, 20(2), 261–284. doi:10.1108/CI-09-2019-0087

Siu, W. S. (2005). An institutional analysis of marketing practices of small and medium-sized enterprises (SMEs) in China, Hong Kong and Taiwan. *Entrepreneurship and Regional Development*, 17(1), 65–88. doi:10.1080/08985620520000330306

Statista. (2023). *Number of small and medium-sized enterprises (SMEs) in South Korea from 2017 to 2020 (in 1,000s)*. Statista. https://www.statista.com/statistics/1223066/south-korea-small-and-medium-enterprises-number/#:~:text=In%202020%2C%20there%20were%20around,million%20in%20the%20previous%20year

Tierno, P. (2019, July 29). *Can Korea Move Beyond Government-Backed Small Business Lending?* FRBSF. https://www.frbsf.org/banking/asia-program/pacific-exchange-blog/beyond-small-business-lending-korea/

U.S Small Business Administration. (2023, September 10). *"Size Standards"*. SBA. https://www.sba.gov/federal-contracting/contracting-guide/size-standards

Vidalakis, C., Abanda, F., & Oti, A. (2020). BIM adoption and implementation: Focusing on SMEs. *Construction Innovation, 20*(1), 128–147. doi:10.1108/CI-09-2018-0076

Vos, A., & Willemse, I. (2011, December 12). *Leveraging Training Skills Development in SMEs:An Analysis Of East Flaunders*. OECD. https://www.oecd.org/cfe/leed/49180408.pdf

Wasiuzzaman, S., Nurdin, N., Abdullah, A., & Vinayan, G. (2020). Creditworthiness and access to finance: A study of SMEs in the Malaysian manufacturing industry. *Management Research News, 43*(3), 293–310.

World Bank. (2023, July 29). *Small and Medium Enterprises (SMEs) Finance: Improving SMEs' access to Finance and Finding Innovative Solutions to unlock Sources of Capital*. World Bank. https://www.worldbank.org/en/topic/smefinance

Yoon, L. (2023, September 20). *SMEs in South Korea -Statistics and Fact*. Statista. https://www.statista.com/topics/10036/smes-in-south-korea/#topicOverview

Yoshino, N., & Taghizadeh-Hesary, F. (2019). *Unlocking SME finance in Asia: Roles of credit rating and credit guarantee schemes (First ed.)*. SAGE Publications

Zha, Q., Kou, G., Zhang, H., Liang, H., Chen, X., Li, C., and Dong, Y. (2021). Opinion dynamics in finance and business: A literature review and research opportunities. *Financial Innovation (Heidelberg), 6*(1), 1-22.

Chapter 4
Role of Small Businesses in Emerging Economies as Drivers of Sustainability and Growth

Deepak Bisht
Lovely Professional University, India

Pawan Kumar
 https://orcid.org/0000-0001-7501-3066
Lovely Professional University, India

Lokesh Jasrai
Lovely Professional University, India

ABSTRACT

Small businesses serve as powerful drivers of sustainability and growth in emerging economies. Their contributions to economic development, job creation, inclusive growth, and environmental sustainability are unparalleled. By overcoming challenges through supportive policies and innovative approaches, governments and stakeholders can unleash the full potential of small businesses, creating a more prosperous and sustainable future for emerging economies. Keeping all these in consideration this chapter delves into the crucial aspects of small businesses and their pivotal role as catalysts of growth and sustainability in emerging economies and aims to provide a comprehensive understanding of the multifaceted contributions of SMEs to economic development, highlighting their significance in driving sustainable growth and promoting social and environmental well-being.

INTRODUCTION

Small businesses around the globe work as the backbone of any self-reliant nation's economy. Its significance is not just limited to the number of jobs it creates but, in driving the growth through innovation and fostering community development (Acs & Szerb, 2007). As per the World Bank SME's account for 90 per cent of businesses and 50 per cent of total employment generated around the globe. Further

DOI: 10.4018/979-8-3693-0111-1.ch004

SMEs contribute nearly 40 percent GDP of emerging economies. These statistics evidently reveal the very essence of small businesses and also put forward the kind of impetus it requires from governments to empower diverse groups such as the working poor, women, youth, and vulnerable populations. Thus entrepreneurial ecosystem in the form of SMEs plays a vital role in creating an economic ecosystem which positively impacts the overall economic performance parameters related to per capita income (Audretsch & Keilbach, 2004).

As catalysts of economic growth small businesses create new job opportunities, boost productivity, and foster healthy market competition. Small businesses foster innovation and entrepreneurship resulting in the creation of novel products, services and business strategies (Wennekers et al., 2005). By identifying and addressing unmet needs in the market, these enterprises drive disruptive innovations that positively impact entire industries. In emerging economies, small businesses are critical agents of inclusive growth and poverty alleviation as they provide opportunities for marginalized communities, and vulnerable populations, to be a part of economic activities and participate actively in the workforce (Storey, 2016). By offering employment and income generation opportunities, small businesses empower individuals to escape poverty and improve their overall well-being (Sharafat, Rashid & Khan, 2014). Further, small businesses tend to operate in local communities, strengthening the local supply chain and fostering economic development in previously neglected regions (Muske & Woods, 2004). Their contribution to rural economies is particularly vital, as they help bridge the urban-rural divide by promoting decentralized economic growth (Robinson, Dassie & Christy, 2004).

Small businesses have the potential to expand market reach beyond their domestic borders, contributing to export-oriented growth in emerging economies (Wagner, 2007). As per Government of India statistics the share of MSME exports in India is in excess of 34 percent which has led small businesses to explore international markets, drive economic growth and foreign exchange earnings. Moreover, the diversification of markets reduces the dependency on a single market and mitigates risks associated with economic fluctuations. Small businesses can expand their reach by tapping into markets, which not only opens up new opportunities but also helps them strengthen their resilience in the face of economic challenges (Masarira & Msweli, 2013).

Sustainability is a major issue for the small businesses as they have to deal with the changing needs in the marketplace where obligation for environmental and social responsibility is increasingly becoming more unrelenting. Looking at their relevant size it is a tedious but needed to be done task for the small businesses from which they cannot get away (Loucks, Martens & Cho 2010). However, in spite of having fewer resources in comparison to big corporation's small businesses can play their role in sustainability. SME's nimbleness, flexibility and linking to local communities can play an important role in aligning to sustainability goals. Many small businesses incorporate sustainable practices into their operations, such as energy conservation, waste reduction, and responsible sourcing. By adopting green practices, these enterprises contribute to a more sustainable future while attracting environmentally conscious consumers (Shields & Shelleman, 2015).

Emerging Economies

As per IMF there is no set definition of emerging economies or markets. World outlook Report (October 2023) by IMF identifies 41 countries as advance economies and 155 economies as emerging and developing economies amongst 196 countries round the globe on the basis of their share in aggregate GDP, exports of goods and services and population. Out of these 155 economies representing 58.3 percent of total GDP of world, 95 belong to emerging market and middle income economies, 59 belong to low income developing economies and remaining 39 belong to heavily indebted poor economies. 95 countries in this block of emerging market and middle income economies together represent 53.4 percent of the world GDP. Countries like China, India, Russia, Brazil, Mexico, Saudi Arabia, South Africa, Argentina, Turkiye, Thailand and others are some of the fast-paced developing economies. China and India housing more than 36 percent of world population are the major contributors amongst this group.

In decades the role of emerging economies, in the economy has gone through a significant transformation. These nations have become increasingly important in shaping the world economy due to factors like their industrialization, technological advancements and large populations (Pandya, 2012). What's truly impressive is how much these emerging economies contribute to growth. Countries like China, India, Brazil and many others have experienced expansion that has had a profound impact on the overall global GDP. They have essentially become engines of growth that generate opportunities, for trade, investment and economic collaboration on a scale (Saah, 2021).

Emerging economies are also crucial players in international trade. Their growing middle classes and rising consumer demand make them attractive markets for businesses worldwide. They are both significant importers and exporters, fostering economic interdependence across borders. Moreover, these countries have assumed positions, in supply networks providing efficient production capacities and contributing to the manufacturing of various goods and services Keskġn et al., 2010).

SIGNIFICANCE OF SMALL BUSINESSES IN EMERGING ECONOMIES

Small businesses contribute heavily to overall development of a nation's economy. Small businesses are helping developing economies greatly by creating employments, decreasing income disparities, reducing poverty and elevating overall economic growth (Ayyagari, Demirgüç-Kunt & Maksimovic 2011; Agyapong, D 2010). All the major emerging economies depends heavily on SMEs because of their indispensable presence which is required to foster the nation economy. Significance of SME's has been put forth by various academic researchers in the past too. Some of them are enlisted as:

Economic Growth and Development

Small businesses are pivotal in driving economic growth, especially in emerging economies. They are instrumental in creating jobs, fostering entrepreneurial spirit, and contributing significantly to the Gross Domestic Product (GDP) (Beck, Demirguc-Kunt & Levine, 2005). By offering diverse products and services, they stimulate local demand, enhance productivity, and promote economic diversification. In developing economies like India, small businesses contribute nearly 30% of the overall GDP and almost 42% of employment. Similarly, in Africa, they contribute nearly 80% of jobs, while in Latin America and the Caribbean, they represent 99.5% of businesses, accounting for 60% of employment and 20% of GDP, highlighting the substantial impact of small businesses on the economic landscape of emerging economies (Sharma, Ilavarasan, & Karanasios 2023). The literature consistently highlights the critical role of small businesses in generating employment, particularly in developing countries where they provide livelihoods for millions. In nations like India, Kenya, and Brazil, small businesses significantly contribute to both urban and rural employment, demonstrating their capacity to respond rapidly to market demands and leading to local economic growth (Pendleton, 2013). This is further supported by findings that small enterprises often play a pivotal role in community development and social integration, despite facing significant barriers such as access to finance, regulatory environments, and infrastructure challenges. Researches also delves into the growth dynamics of small businesses, indicating that growth is a complex phenomenon influenced by various factors including the firm's size, age, internationalization efforts, network, innovation, public institutions, and capital structure. These factors are interrelated and significantly impact small firms' growth and performance, suggesting that smaller firms tend to expand and grow more than larger ones, as they strive to reach a minimum size for survival (Arofatkhan, 2023). However, some studies present contradictory evidence about the role of small businesses, suggesting that while they exhibit higher growth rates in percentage terms, most new firms do not grow at all, and large startups account for a larger share of new firm growth (Rowinski, 2022).

Employment Generation

Small businesses are vital to the economic fabric of emerging economies, primarily due to their significant contribution to employment generation. Small businesses act as engines of economic growth, particularly in developing countries, where they serve as crucial catalysts for development. They are recognized for their ability to drive economic expansion, employment creation, poverty reduction, and social integration. Small businesses significantly contribute to both urban and rural employment, demonstrating their capacity to respond rapidly to market demands, which leads to local economic growth. This is further supported by the fact that Micro, Small, and Medium Enterprises (MSMEs) constitute 95-98% of all businesses, generate 50% of GDP, and create between 60-70% of all jobs in emerging markets (Billen, 2023). Small Businesses not only contribute to reducing unemployment rates but also offer livelihoods to millions, thereby supporting economic development and social integration. Despite facing challenges such as access to finance and regulatory burdens, their impact on employment generation is undeniable. Policymakers should therefore focus on creating an enabling environment that supports the growth and sustainability of small businesses, thereby leveraging their potential to contribute more significantly to employment and overall economic growth (Karadaq, 2015).

Innovation and Technological Advancement

Small businesses are often lauded for their role in fostering innovation, particularly in emerging economies. Their agility and flexibility allow them to experiment with new ideas and technologies, which can be crucial for technological advancement and economic progress. The World Bank emphasizes the importance of Small and Medium Enterprises (SMEs) in global economic development, noting that they account for the majority of businesses worldwide and are significant contributors to job creation and GDP in emerging economies. SMEs' smaller scale can be advantageous for innovation as they are typically more nimble and can adapt more quickly to changing market conditions than larger firms (Machado, 2016). Business model innovation (BMI) in micro and small enterprises is driven by dynamic capabilities and the business owner's ability to reconfigure and exploit resources to create market value. This suggests that the innovative capacity of small businesses is not just about tangible resources but also hinges on intangible assets like the skills and capabilities of the owner or founder (ElNaggar & ElSayed, 2023).

An opinion piece on how technology has revolutionized small business highlights the transformative impact of digital innovations on small businesses, enabling them to compete with larger companies by advertising and marketing online, automating processes, and improving efficiencies. This digital revolution has opened up new opportunities for small businesses to innovate and grow (Gleed, 2023). There is a need for a supportive regulatory environment in developing economies that allows small businesses to innovate and scale up and this includes providing entrepreneurs with the knowledge and tools to navigate regulatory compliance and formalize their businesses, which can lead to better access to finance and markets (Brem & Wolfram, 2014). Small businesses in emerging economies are pivotal drivers of innovation and technological advancement. Their size and flexibility enable them to respond quickly to market demands and experiment with new technologies. The literature suggests that fostering an environment that supports the dynamic capabilities of small business owners and provides them with the necessary tools and knowledge is essential for maximizing their innovative potential (ElNagger & ElSayed, 2023; Anand et al., 2021). To sustain this innovation, it is crucial for policymakers to create regulatory frameworks that encourage and facilitate the growth and competitiveness of small businesses.

Financial Inclusion and Access to Finance

Access to finance remains a pivotal challenge for small businesses, particularly in emerging economies. These entities are crucial for promoting financial inclusion and ensuring that financial services reach underserved populations. However, their growth and sustainability are often hampered by limited access to financial resources. Small businesses encounter numerous obstacles in the form of operational, technical, and financial challenges, with access to finance being a significant hurdle. This is attributed to information asymmetry between banks and small businesses, inadequate institutional infrastructure for assessing these entities, and high transaction costs. Imperfect screening by lenders further exacerbates the difficulty in accessing finance, compounding other challenges faced by small businesses (Rao et al., 2023). Studies also emphasize the resource-constrained environments of SMEs, which limit their ability to respond to financial challenges. The advent of financial technology (FinTech) has begun to address some of these challenges by offering alternative financing models such as crowdfunding, peer-to-peer lending, and mobile payments. These FinTech-led business models are altering the ecosystem for small businesses, providing them with better and increased access to finance (Sharma, Ilavarasan, & Karanasios 2023).

In addition to it microfinance institutions and specialized lending programs have emerged as vital solutions to the financing gap faced by small businesses in emerging economies. These initiatives aim to provide small businesses with the necessary capital to grow and thrive. Developing new financing strategies, including microfinance, can reduce cases of inadequate funding and prevent bankruptcy among small businesses. These strategies are crucial for improving the profitability of small businesses and enabling them to maintain a competitive edge in their industries. The role of small businesses in promoting financial inclusion cannot be overstated. By providing access to finance for small businesses, microfinance and specialized lending programs not only support the growth of these entities but also ensure that financial services reach underserved populations. This, in turn, contributes to the overall economic development and social change within these communities. When small business leaders implement effective strategies for accessing capital, they can contribute to society by increasing the employment rate and enhancing the general management of their businesses (Agboh, 2021).

Local Community Development

Small businesses play a vital role in the social and economic fabric of their local communities. They contribute to the local economy, create job opportunities, and support community initiatives, thereby significantly impacting the well-being of the regions they operate in (Fiseha & Ovelana, 2015). Small businesses are a driving force behind the economic vitality of local communities. They generate revenue that circulates within the community, as owners and employees tend to shop locally and prefer local vendors for goods and services (Noreen, 2022). This revenue generation and circulation contribute to the overall economic growth and sustainability of the community. Job growth not only provides employment but also fosters economic self-sufficiency and helps reduce poverty within the community (Anigbogu et al., 2014). Small businesses are deeply rooted in their communities and are more likely to be involved in local initiatives and charitable activities. They contribute to local charities, sponsor events, and support local causes, thereby enhancing the social well-being of the community. Their involvement in community events and support for local charities not only fosters a sense of togetherness but also contributes to the overall vibrancy and liveliness of the community (Noreen, 2022; Suutari, Lähdesmäki & Kurki, 2023).

Small businesses often prioritize local sourcing, which contributes to the growth of other local businesses and industries. This practice not only stimulates the local economy but also lessens the environmental impact by reducing the need for long-distance transportation of goods. Furthermore, small businesses tend to set up shop in pre-existing buildings, thereby conserving green space and contributing to environmental sustainability (Ngida, 2023).

Export Potential

The role of small businesses in emerging economies as a gateway to the global market is a topic of significant interest and importance. Small and medium-sized enterprises (SMEs) in emerging economies can play a crucial role in enhancing a country's foreign exchange earnings and improving trade balances by entering the global market (Rustamovna & Anvarovich, 2016). The potential of small businesses to become exporters and sell their products or services to international markets is a key factor in their role as a gateway to the global market. Many SMEs from emerging economies consider entry into developed markets as a way to promote home country performance. This indicates that small businesses in emerging economies are increasingly looking to expand their market reach beyond domestic borders, which can have a positive impact on foreign exchange earnings and trade balances (Morkovina et al., 2018).

While the potential benefits of small businesses entering the global market are significant, there are also challenges that need to be addressed. The literature emphasizes the operational, technical, and financial challenges faced by small businesses, including limited access to finance, information asymmetry problems, and inadequate institutional infrastructure. Overcoming these challenges is crucial for small businesses to effectively serve as a gateway to the global market and realize their potential as exporters. To succeed in the global market, small businesses in emerging economies need to adopt effective marketing strategies (Chea, 2023).

Key Drivers of Small Businesses in Emerging Economies

Small businesses are integral catalysts for growth and development. Their success and resilience are influenced by a complex interplay of drivers that significantly mold their path. These drivers encompass a wide array of factors, including entrepreneurship, market demand, financial acumen, innovation, human resources, networking, marketing, regulatory adherence, technology integration, risk mitigation, community involvement, government assistance, global market reach, infrastructure, cultural nuances, educational interactions, sustainability commitments, and macroeconomic stability (Fiesha & Oyelana, 2015). Gaining a deep understanding of these crucial drivers is indispensable for both policymakers and small business owners as they navigate the distinct challenges and opportunities presented by emerging economies (Quatraro & 2015).

Government policies wield substantial influence over the growth of small businesses within emerging economies. The presence of supportive policies can create a fertile ground for these enterprises to thrive. For instance, policies that offer tax incentives, streamline bureaucratic procedures, and facilitate access to credit have been observed to enhance the business environment, encouraging small businesses to flourish (Eniola & Entebang, 2015).

Furthermore, government initiatives encompassing training programs, mentorship opportunities, and grant provisions have demonstrated a significant impact on fostering entrepreneurship and nurturing business development. These programs serve as essential instruments for equipping small business owners and aspiring entrepreneurs with the knowledge, skills, and resources necessary to navigate the intricacies of the business landscape in emerging economies (Perks & Smith, 2008). By fostering a supportive ecosystem through these policies, governments can contribute significantly to the resilience and growth of small businesses, thereby facilitating broader economic development (Khaskar, 2011).

Other than it the quality of local infrastructure, encompassing transportation, utilities, and communication networks, assumes a pivotal role in shaping the fortunes of small businesses. Robust and well-maintained infrastructure acts as a linchpin, streamlining business operations and catalyzing success (Mottaeva & Gritsuk, 2017). Effective transportation systems expedite the movement of goods, minimizing logistical bottlenecks and reducing operational costs. Furthermore, improved communication networks empower small businesses to reach a broader audience and coordinate activities efficiently (Ponmani, 2011). Small businesses that integrate into global supply chains also reap substantial benefits. This integration affords them access to valuable resources, a wider customer base, and cutting-edge technologies. By becoming part of these larger networks, small businesses can enhance their competitiveness and diversify their product offerings (Giovannetti, Marvasi & Sanfilippo, 2015). In essence, the state of local infrastructure acts as an essential driver for small businesses, determining their ability to function optimally, reach new markets, and forge connections within global supply chains. It is through the synergy of infrastructure quality and global integration that small businesses in emerging economies can chart a course toward growth and sustainability (Mottaeva & Gritsuk, 2017).

Market access holds paramount importance for small businesses, and the advent of globalization has ushered in a wealth of opportunities for these enterprises in emerging economies. The ability to access international markets has been significantly broadened, primarily through the facilitation of trade agreements and the proliferation of digital platforms, offering small businesses a gateway to a global consumer base (Romanovich et al., 2014).

Emerging technologies, particularly the rise of e-commerce, have played a transformative role in empowering small businesses to connect with a global audience with unprecedented ease. These digital platforms enable small businesses to transcend geographical boundaries and establish a robust online presence. As a result, they can showcase their products or services to a vast and diverse international clientele (Duncombe et al., 2006). In this contemporary landscape, globalization acts as a catalyst, enabling small businesses to expand beyond their domestic markets and embark on a journey of international growth. Through trade agreements and the digital realm, these enterprises can explore fresh avenues for development, tapping into a global audience and harnessing the opportunities presented by an interconnected world (Hirasawa, 2019).

Innovation and adaptability stand out as essential driving forces for small businesses. Small enterprises must maintain a continuous cycle of innovation, not only in their product and service offerings but also in the optimization of their internal processes to sustain competitiveness. This ongoing pursuit of innovative solutions allows small businesses to differentiate themselves in a crowded market and meet evolving customer needs effectively (Sahut & Peris Ortiz, 2014).

Moreover, adaptability plays a pivotal role in securing resilience when confronted with the dynamic fluctuations of markets and the inherent uncertainties of the economy. The ability to swiftly respond to changes in consumer preferences, technological advancements, and unforeseen economic challenges is a hallmark of successful small businesses. This adaptability ensures that these enterprises remain not only relevant but also well-prepared to navigate uncharted territory, subsequently enhancing their long-term viability in an ever-shifting business landscape (Pradhan et al., 2020).

Small Businesses and Sustainability Issues

Sustainability has evolved as a predominant global priority that includes environmental, social, and economic dimensions. In developing countries there is a growing awareness of the significance of sustainability. People are realizing that economic growth should be balanced with protecting the environment and promoting progress. The complex network of practices is crucial, for tackling challenges, like mitigating climate change responsibly managing natural resources and striving for social equality (Loucks, Martens & Cho 2010).

The imperative of sustainability is rooted in the acknowledgment that human activities, especially economic development, are intrinsically linked to environmental impacts. Emerging economies, often characterized by rapid industrialization and urbanization, face a delicate equilibrium between propelling economic progress and safeguarding their environment and society. The interplay between these dimensions calls for sustainable practices that not only reduce environmental footprints but also strengthen the well-being of communities (Revels, Stokes & Chen, 2010). In this context, sustainability emerges as a guiding spirit, prompting emerging economies to reassess their developmental models. It underscores the significance of responsible resource management, green technologies, community engagement, and inclusive labor practices. The evolving narrative of sustainability in these economies reflects a commitment to a balanced and sustainable future that addresses the global challenges and transcends the national boundaries (Miller, 2010).

Small businesses in emerging economies confront unique sustainability challenges and opportunities. Small businesses frequently encounter limitations when it comes to resources. This situation calls for creative and efficient methods of managing resources to minimize waste and safeguard valuable materials (Tien et al., 2020). The financial well-being of small businesses is intricately connected to their ability to make profits and maintain a stable financial position. In simple terms, it's about ensuring that a business can make money and not run into financial troubles which otherwise make it difficult to look at sustainable ways (López, Contreras & Espinosa, 2012). Limited access to credit can be a barrier to economic sustainability; thus, financial inclusion and microfinance programs are essential. Small businesses often play a significant role in community development, and their engagement in social initiatives can have a substantial impact on local well-being. Ensuring fair labor practices and promoting employee well-being is crucial for social sustainability (Konieczny et al., 2023).

Government policies and support systems have a considerable impact on how small businesses in emerging economies embrace sustainability practices. These policies can serve as a powerful catalyst for encouraging businesses to adopt sustainable approaches. Supportive policies often provide incentives, such as tax breaks, financial grants, and programs that help businesses build their capacity in sustainable practices. These incentives make it more attractive and financially feasible for small businesses to engage in sustainable activities. They essentially reward companies for making responsible choices in their operations. Other than it, the process of globalization, which connects businesses with the global marketplace, has opened up new opportunities for small businesses to embrace sustainability. The ever-expanding international market offers a fertile ground for businesses to engage in sustainable practices, often driven by consumer demand for environmentally friendly products. With an interconnected world, businesses are increasingly responsive to the global trend toward sustainability. Raising awareness and educating small business owners about sustainability issues is of paramount importance. Many businesses may not be aware of the benefits of sustainability or how to incorporate it into their operations. Educational initiatives, training programs, and efforts to spread information are vital components of this process. These programs equip business owners with the knowledge and tools they need to adopt sustainable practices (Loucks, Martens & Cho 2010).

Small businesses should adopt sustainable technologies, implement green supply chain practices, and engage in social and environmental responsibility. Sustainable technologies, such as renewable energy and energy-efficient products, can help small businesses reduce their environmental impact and save money on energy costs. Green supply chain practices, such as reducing waste and emissions, can also help small businesses reduce costs and improve their reputation. Engaging in social and environmental responsibility can also benefit small businesses by improving their reputation and attracting customers who value sustainability (Berniak et al., 2023).

Challenges and Bottlenecks

Small businesses in emerging economies encounter a spectrum of challenges and bottlenecks that impact their growth and sustainability. These issues encompass finance, regulation, infrastructure, technology, labor, competition, compliance, networks, and sustainability. Small businesses in emerging economies face a persistent and recurring hurdle in the form of scarcity of financial resources (Rao et al, 2023). These enterprises frequently struggle with the daunting task of procuring funds for a variety of purposes, be it launching their business, expanding their operations, or even sustaining day-to-day activities. The challenge becomes all the more daunting due to the inadequate accessibility of credit and financial services, ultimately putting a check on their potential for growth. This financial obstacle presents a multifaceted issue. When small businesses encounter difficulties in securing the necessary capital, it restricts their ability to take the crucial steps for growth and development. For startups, it can impede their very existence, hindering their entry into the market. Likewise, for established small businesses looking to expand or diversify, the absence of credit access can thwart their plans for progress. Even in the day-to-day operations, financial limitations can stifle their agility and innovative capacity, as they struggle to secure the funds required to seize opportunities or address unexpected challenges (Karlan & Morduch, 2010).

Another challenge lies in the form of complex and burdensome regulatory environments in many emerging economies. Excessive bureaucracy, lengthy permitting processes, and ambiguous legal frameworks can stifle entrepreneurship and limit business growth. Other than it inadequate infrastructure, encompassing transportation, energy, and telecommunications, presents a significant bottleneck for small businesses (Coad & Tamvada, 2012). Poor infrastructure can increase operational costs, reduce competitiveness, and constrain market reach. Many small businesses in emerging economies struggle to adopt modern technologies, hindering their efficiency and market competitiveness. The digital divide exacerbates this challenge, as it limits their ability to harness the benefits of technology (Akpan, Udoh & Adebisi, 2022).

Access to skilled labors is another problem faced by small businesses as finding and retaining skilled employees can be a substantial challenge for small businesses. Inadequate access to a qualified workforce can hinder productivity and business growth. Moreover, small businesses frequently encounter obstacles when it comes to entering markets and vying against bigger corporations. Unjust practices in the market, trade barriers, and unequal competition can all act as shackles that restrict their potential for growth (Maheshkar & Soni, 2021).

Access to valuable networks and resources can be a substantial bottleneck. Small businesses often find it challenging to access the mentorship, partnerships, and resources that are essential for growth and innovation. The limited connections can curtail their ability to expand and harness opportunities for development (Moyi, 2003). Finally, the incorporation of sustainability practices is frequently a formidable challenge. Small businesses face the dual dilemma of resource limitations and limited awareness regarding sustainability issues. Adhering to environmental regulations and adopting sustainable practices can necessitate significant adjustments in their operations, adding complexity to their entrepreneurial journey. These challenges underscore the need for comprehensive support mechanisms and initiatives that streamline regulatory processes, enhance access to networks, resources, and bolster sustainability education (Berniak et al., 2023).

Envisioning Future Goals

Small businesses are the lifeblood of emerging economies, playing a vital role in economic growth, employment generation, and poverty reduction. These enterprises are agile, innovative, and often deeply ingrained in the local communities, making them essential drivers of development (Storey,2016). However small businesses, in emerging economies also encounter obstacles. These include access to resources, regulatory hurdles and technological constraints. As we look ahead it becomes crucial to envision how the landscape for these businesses will evolve. We must anticipate the trends and strategies that can shape their trajectory. Envisioning the future of businesses in emerging economies requires an approach. This approach should incorporate financing methods, digital transformation, regulatory reforms, infrastructure development, sustainability initiatives improved access, to networks and resources global market opportunities, education and training programs well as supportive government policies (Shields & Shellman, 2015).

To overcome the challenge of limited access to financial resources, emerging economies should foster innovative financing solutions. Microfinance institutions, digital lending platforms, and peer-to-peer lending networks can bridge the gap and provide small businesses with the capital they need for startup and expansion. Governments and financial institutions should collaborate to create an ecosystem that promotes financial inclusion for small businesses, offering tailored financial products and support (Karlan & Morduch, 2010; Rao et al., 2023).

Digital transformation is crucial for the growth and development of small businesses in emerging economies. The COVID-19 pandemic has accelerated the adoption of digital tools by small and medium-sized enterprises (SMEs) in India (Kumar et al., 2023). China's SMEs contribute 70% of the country's GDP, and the smallest enterprises could generate even more dynamic growth from its small and micro-businesses (Woetzel et al., 2014). Brazilian micro and small businesses are mostly in the initial stages of digital transformation, but these companies are increasingly open to technology innovation (da Costa, 2022). Nigeria's proactive investment in telecom infrastructure has paved the way for the widespread adoption of 4G technology, and the nation is stepping into the 5G era (Olawinka & Wynn, 2022).

India's digital architecture could revolutionize the national credit landscape, and small businesses in India have long struggled to gain access to formal credit. Governments and industry stakeholders should invest in digital literacy programs and technology infrastructure to ensure that small businesses can leverage digital tools effectively. E-commerce, mobile payment solutions, and cloud-based software can empower small businesses to expand their market reach and streamline operations. The development of MSMEs is closely linked to economic growth, and digital transformation could turbocharge that process (Dixit, 2023).

The future of small businesses in emerging economies hinges on embracing digital transformation. Governments and industry stakeholders should invest in digital literacy programs and technology infrastructure to ensure that small businesses can leverage digital tools effectively (Popovic et al., 2022). E-commerce, mobile payment solutions, and cloud-based software can empower small businesses to expand their market reach and streamline operations (Baimukhamedova & Baimukhamedova, 2023).

Regulatory simplification is essential for the growth of small businesses. Governments in emerging economies should embark on regulatory reforms to streamline compliance processes and reduce bureaucratic hurdles. E-governance and digital platforms can facilitate easier and more efficient compliance. Business-friendly regulations that support entrepreneurship and innovation will stimulate small business growth (Thanetsunthorn & Wuthisatian, 2023).

Improving infrastructure is crucial for small businesses to remain competitive and grow in today's fast-paced market. By investing in better procurement systems, technology, transportation, and communication networks, small businesses can streamline their operations, reduce costs, increase efficiency and productivity (Oduyoye, Adebola & Binuyo, 2013). The McKinsey Global Institute (MGI) forecasts that the world will need to invest an average of $3.7 trillion in roads, railways, ports, airports, power, water, and telecoms every year through 2035 to keep pace with projected GDP growth and emerging economies will account for nearly two-thirds of that investment need (Hussain et al., 2019).

While robust infrastructure is crucial for all economies, the specific needs of emerging market economies like China or India differ from those of more advanced economies like the United States or Germany. Many emerging economies must substantially expand their energy and transportation networks, or build them from scratch, to accommodate rapid economic growth (Mauro, 2017). Infrastructure investing in emerging markets often faces challenges, but it also presents significant opportunities for private investors and developers. Private partnerships (PPPs) can be potent tools for infrastructure development in emerging economies. They leverage private-sector efficiency and expertise, potentially leading to quicker project completion, cost savings, and improved service quality. However, their success hinges on a delicate balance between attracting private investment **and** ensuring the public interest. The impact of investment in infrastructure in emerging markets is significant, and it is essential to identify key trends in infrastructure spending in these regions to unlock the potential for economic growth and development (Kateja, 2012).

Small businesses should increasingly focus on sustainability and corporate responsibility. Governments can incentivize sustainable practices through tax breaks, grants, and capacity-building programs. Moreover, public awareness campaigns can promote responsible consumer behavior, driving the demand for eco-friendly products and services. Small businesses should adopt sustainable technologies, implement green supply chain practices, and engage in social and environmental responsibility (Rao et al., 2023).

Governments, industry associations, and non-governmental organizations should establish networks, mentorship programs, and resources dedicated to small businesses. Business incubators, innovation hubs, and collaborative platforms can facilitate networking and knowledge exchange. These initiatives will provide small businesses with valuable support, mentorship, and resources for growth and innovation (Dourado et al., 2023).

The digital age presents unprecedented opportunities for global market access. Small businesses in emerging economies should leverage e-commerce platforms and digital marketing to expand their reach beyond borders. Governments can support export promotion initiatives and simplify trade regulations to enable small businesses to tap into international markets (Duncombe et al., 2006).

To enhance the knowledge and awareness of small business owners, governments and educational institutions should offer tailored education and training programs. These programs should cover sustainability, technological advancements, and modern business practices. They will empower entrepreneurs with the skills and knowledge needed to navigate a rapidly evolving business landscape (Tu & Akhter, 2023).

Governments play a pivotal role in shaping the future of small businesses. Supportive policies, such as tax incentives, grants, and capacity-building programs, can create an environment conducive to small business growth. Governments should simplify regulations; improve access to finance, and foster entrepreneurship. Public-private partnerships can be instrumental in implementing policies that provide small businesses with the support they need to thrive (Acs & Szerb, 2007).

CONCLUSION

Small businesses serve as the lifeblood of emerging economies, catalyzing economic growth, promoting sustainability, and driving social well-being. Their contributions are multi-faceted, encompassing employment generation, innovation, community development, and the potential for international expansion. Small businesses are pivotal agents in reducing income disparities, fostering entrepreneurship, and enhancing overall economic development in the context of emerging economies. These enterprises confront unique challenges, including limited access to financial resources, regulatory complexities, inadequate infrastructure, and the imperative of adopting sustainability practices. Overcoming these challenges necessitates innovative financing, digital transformation, regulatory reforms, infrastructure development, and the promotion of sustainability initiatives. Access to networks, resources, global markets, and education and training is essential for their future growth.

To realize the full potential of small businesses in emerging economies, governments, financial institutions, and industry stakeholders must collaborate. Supportive policies, inclusive infrastructure, and a focus on sustainability will create an environment where these enterprises can thrive. By embracing the use of tools streamlining processes and fostering a culture that encourages innovation small businesses can thrive and adapt in an ever evolving global environment. The future looks promising for businesses, in emerging economies when there is a shared dedication to addressing their challenges nurturing their growth and harnessing their potential as drivers of sustainability and prosperity. With strategies and support in place small businesses will continue to play a role, in the economy of self-reliant nations contributing to a balanced and prosperous future.

REFERENCES

Acs, Z. J., & Szerb, L. (2007). Entrepreneurship, economic growth and public policy. *Small Business Economics*, *28*(2-3), 109–122. doi:10.1007/s11187-006-9012-3

Agboh, Y. P. (2021). *Small Business Owners' Strategies for Accessing Capital and Improving Financial Performance* [Doctoral dissertation, Walden University].

Agyapong, D. (2010). Micro, small and medium enterprises' activities, income level and poverty reduction in ghana-A synthesis of related literature. *International Journal of Business and Management*, *5*(12), 196. doi:10.5539/ijbm.v5n12p196

Akpan, I. J., Udoh, E. A. P., & Adebisi, B. (2022). Small business awareness and adoption of state-of-the-art technologies in emerging and developing markets, and lessons from the COVID-19 pandemic. *Journal of Small Business and Entrepreneurship*, *34*(2), 123–140. doi:10.1080/08276331.2020.1820185

Anand, J., McDermott, G., Mudambi, R., & Narula, R. (2021). Innovation in and from emerging economies: New insights and lessons for international business research. *Journal of International Business Studies*, *52*(4), 545–559. doi:10.1057/s41267-021-00426-1

Anigbogu, T. U., Onwuteaka, C. I., Edoko, T. D., & Okoli, M. I. (2014). Roles of small and medium scale enterprises in community development: Evidence from Anambra south senatorial zone, Anambra State. *International Journal of Academic Research in Business & Social Sciences*, *4*(8), 302. doi:10.6007/IJARBSS/v4-i8/1099

Arofatkhan, K. (2023). The Impact of Small Business on Economic Growth in Developing Countries. *EPRA International Journal of Economics* [EBMS]. *Business and Management Studies*, *10*(8), 12–14.

Audretsch, D. B., & Keilbach, M. (2004). Does entrepreneurship capital matter? *Entrepreneurship Theory and Practice*, *28*(5), 419–430. doi:10.1111/j.1540-6520.2004.00055.x

Ayyagari, M., Demirgüç-Kunt, A., & Maksimovic, V. (2011). Small vs. young firms across the world: contribution to employment, job creation, and growth. *World Bank Policy Research Working Paper*, (5631).

Baimukhamedova, A., & Baimukhamedov, M. (2023). Digital Transformation of Small and Medium Businesses. In *Advancing SMEs Toward E-Commerce Policies for Sustainability* (pp. 19–43). IGI Global.

Beck, T., Demirguc-Kunt, A., & Levine, R. (2005). SMEs, growth, and poverty: Cross-country evidence. *Journal of Economic Growth*, *10*(3), 199–229. doi:10.1007/s10887-005-3533-5

Berniak-Woźny, J., Kwasek, A., Gąsiński, H., Maciaszczyk, M., & Kocot, M. (2023). Business Case for Corporate Social Responsibility in Small and Medium Enterprises—Employees' Perspective. *Sustainability (Basel)*, *15*(2), 1660. doi:10.3390/su15021660

Billen, A. (2023). *News and Events.* Maastrichit School of Management. https://www.msm.nl/news-events-and-blogs/blog/the-crucial-role-of-smes-in-emerging-markets

Brem, A., & Wolfram, P. (2014). Research and development from the bottom up-introduction of terminologies for new product development in emerging markets. *Journal of Innovation and Entrepreneurship, 3*(1), 1–22. doi:10.1186/2192-5372-3-9

Chea, A. C. (2023). Global Marketing: Emerging Market Economies' Challenges, Opportunities and Effective Marketing Strategy for Success. *Business and Economic Review, 13*(4), 103–122. doi:10.5296/ber.v13i4.21482

Coad, A., & Tamvada, J. P. (2012). Firm growth and barriers to growth among small firms in India. *Small Business Economics, 39*(2), 383–400. doi:10.1007/s11187-011-9318-7

da Costa, L. S., Munhoz, I. P., Pereira, L., & Akkari, A. C. S. (2022). Assessing the digital maturity of micro and small enterprises: A focus on an emerging market. *Procedia Computer Science, 200*, 175–184. doi:10.1016/j.procs.2022.01.216

Danaan, V. V. (2018). Analysing poverty in Nigeria through theoretical lenses. *Journal of Sustainable Development, 11*(1), 20. doi:10.5539/jsd.v11n1p20

Dixit, S. (2023, June 20). India's digital transformation could be a game-changer for economic development. *World Bank Blogs.* World Bank. https://blogs.worldbank.org/developmenttalk/indias-digital-transformation-could-be-game-changer-economic-development

Dourado Freire, C., Sacomano Neto, M., Moralles, H. F., & Rodrigues Antunes, L. G. (2023). Technology-based business incubators: The impacts on resources of startups in Brazil. *International Journal of Emerging Markets, 18*(12), 5778–5797. doi:10.1108/IJOEM-08-2020-0900

Duncombe, R., Heeks, R., Kintu, R., Nakangu, B., & Abraham, S. (2006). Ecommerce for small enterprise development. *A Handbook for entrepreneurs in developing countries*, 7-22.

ElNaggar, R. A., & ElSayed, M. F. (2023). Drivers of business model innovation in micro and small enterprises: Evidence from Egypt as an emerging economy. *Future Business Journal, 9*(1), 4. doi:10.1186/s43093-022-00180-2

Eniola, A. A., & Entebang, H. (2015). Government policy and performance of small and medium business management. *International Journal of Academic Research in Business & Social Sciences, 5*(2), 237–248. doi:10.6007/IJARBSS/v5-i2/1481

Fiseha, G. G., & Oyelana, A. A. (2015). An assessment of the roles of small and medium enterprises (SMEs) in the local economic development (LED). *The South African Journal of Economics, 6*(3), 280–290.

Gereffi, G., Humphrey, J., & Sturgeon, T. (2005). The governance of global value chains. *Review of International Political Economy, 12*(1), 78–104. doi:10.1080/09692290500049805

Giovannetti, G., Marvasi, E., & Sanfilippo, M. (2015). Supply chains and the internationalization of small firms. *Small Business Economics, 44*(4), 845–865. doi:10.1007/s11187-014-9625-x

Gleed, S. (2023). Opinion: How Technology has revolutionized small business. *Deseret News*. https://www.deseret.com/opinion/2023/5/20/23727697/technology-revolution-small-business

Guo, H., Yang, Z., Huang, R., & Guo, A. (2020). The digitalization and public crisis responses of small and medium enterprises: Implications from a COVID-19 survey. *Frontiers of Business Research in China, 14*(1), 1–25. doi:10.1186/s11782-020-00087-1

Hirasawa, K. (2019). *Globalization and small businesses* (No. 2019-06). Ordnungspolitische Diskurse.

Hussain, A., Jeddi, S., Lakmeeharan, K., & Muzaffar, H. (2019, October 10). *Unlocking private sector financing in emerging markets infrastructure.* Mckinsey & Conpany. https://www.mckinsey.com/industries/private-equity-and-principal-investors/our-insights/unlocking-private-sector-financing-in-emerging-markets-infrastructure

International Monetary Fund. (2023). *World Economic Outlook: Navigating Global Divergences.* Washington, DC.

Karadag, H. (2015). The role and challenges of small and medium-sized enterprises (SMEs) in emerging economies: An analysis from Turkey. *Business and Management Studies, 1*(2), 179–188. doi:10.11114/bms.v1i2.1049

Karlan, D., & Morduch, J. (2010). Access to finance. In *Handbook of development economics* (Vol. 5, pp. 4703–4784). Elsevier. doi:10.1016/B978-0-444-52944-2.00009-4

Kateja, A. (2012). Building infrastructure: Private participation in emerging economies. *Procedia: Social and Behavioral Sciences, 37*, 368–378. doi:10.1016/j.sbspro.2012.03.302

Keskġn, H., Ġentürk, C., Sungur, O., & Kġrġġ, H. M. (2010). The importance of SMEs in developing economies. In *2nd international symposium on sustainable development* (pp. 183-192). IEEE.

Khaksar, S. (2011). The role of government policy and the growth of entrepreneurship in the micro, small (&) medium-sized enterprises in India: An overview. *Australian Journal of Basic and Applied Sciences, 5*(6), 1563–1571.

Konieczny, G., Kolisnichenko, P., Górska, M., & Górski, T. (2023). The role of well-being in sustainable corporate development of companies. *Economics. Finance and Management Review*, (3), 59–67.

Kumar, V., Verma, P., Mittal, A., Tuesta Panduro, J. A., Singh, S., Paliwal, M., & Sharma, N. K. (2023). Adoption of ICTs as an emergent business strategy during and following COVID-19 crisis: Evidence from Indian MSMEs. *Benchmarking, 30*(6), 1850–1883. doi:10.1108/BIJ-11-2021-0685

López Salazar, A., Contreras Soto, R., & Espinosa Mosqueda, R. (2012). The impact of financial decisions and strategy on small business competitiveness. *Global. Journal of Business Research, 6*(2), 93–103.

Loucks, E. S., Martens, M. L., & Cho, C. H. (2010). Engaging small-and medium-sized businesses in sustainability. *Sustainability Accounting. Management and Policy Journal, 1*(2), 178–200.

Machado, H. P. V. (2016). Growth of small businesses: A literature review and perspectives of studies. *Gestão & Produção, 23*, 419–432. doi:10.1590/0104-530x1759-14

Maheshkar, C., & Soni, N. (2021). Problems Faced by Indian Micro, Small and Medium Enterprises (MSMEs). *SEDME (Small Enterprises Development, Management & Extension Journal), 48*(2), 142-159.

Masarira, S., & Msweli, P. (2013). The role of SMEs in national economies: the case of South Africa. *Economic and Social Development: Book of Proceedings*, 1484.

Mauro, P. (2017, May 04). Emerging economy consumers drive infrastructure needs. *IMF Blog*. IMF. https://www.imf.org/en/Blogs/Articles/2017/05/04/emerging-economy-consumers-drive-infrastructure-needs

Miller, J. L. (2010). Sustainability: Is It a Good Choice for Small Companies?. *Inquiries Journal, 2*(10).

Morkovina, S. S., Malitskaya, V., Panyavina, E. A., & Sibiryatkina, I. (2018). *Export potential and measures to support small and medium-sized enterprises*. Research Gate.

Mottaeva, A., & Gritsuk, N. (2017). Development of infrastructure of support of small and medium business. In *MATEC Web of Conferences (Vol. 106*, p. 08083). EDP Sciences. 10.1051/matecconf/201710608083

Moyi, E. D. (2003). Networks, information and small enterprises: New technologies and the ambiguity of empowerment. *Information Technology for Development, 10*(4), 221–232. doi:10.1002/itdj.1590100402

Muske, G., & Woods, M. (2004). Micro businesses as an economic development tool: What they bring and what they need. *Community Development (Columbus, Ohio), 35*(1), 97–116.

Ngida, S. (2023). *Community Engagement: How Businesses can foster Local Impact*. LinkedIn. https://www.linkedin.com/pulse/community-engagement-how-businesses-can-foster-positive-ngida/

Noreen, A. (2022). *6 Benefits of small businesses in community development*. Read Write. https://readwrite.com/benefits-of-small-businesses-in-a-community/

Oduyoye, O. O., Adebola, S. A., & Binuyo, A. O. (2013). Empirical study of infrastructure support and small business growth in Ogun state, Nigeria. *Journal of Research and Development (Srinagar), 1*(1), 14–22.

Olayinka, O., & Wynn, M. G. (2022). Digital transformation in the Nigerian small business sector. In Handbook of Research on Digital Transformation, Industry Use Cases, and the Impact of Disruptive Technologies (pp. 359-382). IGI Global. doi:10.4018/978-1-7998-7712-7.ch019

Pandya, V. M. (2012, September). Comparative analysis of development of SMEs in developed and developing countries. In *The 2012 International Conference on Business and Management (Vol. 6*, No. 7, pp. 1-20).

Pendleton, E. (2013). *The advantages of doing business in an emerging market*. Chron. https://smallbusiness.chron.com/advantages-doingbusiness-emerging-market-22717.html

Perks, S., & Smith, E. E. (2008). Focused training programmes for solving growth problems of very small businesses. *Acta Commercii, 8*(1), 145–159. doi:10.4102/ac.v8i1.77

Ponmani, R. (2011). Infrastructure and SMEs development in selected Asian countries. *Asian Journal of Research in Social Sciences and Humanities, 1*(4), 465–473.

Popović, J., Dudas, I., Milošević, D., & Luković, J. (2022). Digital Transformation as a chance for Small Business Development. *International Journal of Management Trends: Key Concepts and Research, 1*(1), 29–38. doi:10.58898/ijmt.v1i1.29-38

Pradhan, R. P., Arvin, M. B., Nair, M., & Bennett, S. E. (2020). The dynamics among entrepreneurship, innovation, and economic growth in the Eurozone countries. *Journal of Policy Modeling, 42*(5), 1106–1122. doi:10.1016/j.jpolmod.2020.01.004

Quatraro, F., & Vivarelli, M. (2015). Drivers of entrepreneurship and post-entry performance of newborn firms in developing countries. *The World Bank Research Observer, 30*(2), 277–305. doi:10.1093/wbro/lku012

Rao, P., Kumar, S., Chavan, M., & Lim, W. M. (2023). A systematic literature review on SME financing: Trends and future directions. *Journal of Small Business Management, 61*(3), 1247–1277. doi:10.1080/00472778.2021.1955123

Revell, A., Stokes, D., & Chen, H. (2010). Small businesses and the environment: Turning over a new leaf? *Business Strategy and the Environment, 19*(5), 273–288. doi:10.1002/bse.628

Robinson, K. L., Dassie, W., & Christy, R. D. (2004). Entrepreneurship and small business development as a rural development strategy. *Journal of Rural Social Sciences, 20*(2), 1.

Romanovich, G. L., Romanovich, A. M., Vybornova, V. V., & Nikolayevna, R. V. (2014). Small businesses is a sphere of innovation in the age of globalization. *Journal of Applied Engineering Science, 12*(4), 297–301. doi:10.5937/jaes12-7155

Rowinski, M. (2022). How Small Businesses Drive The American Economy. *Contribution to the Forbes Business Council*. https://www.forbes.com/sites/forbesbusinesscouncil/2022/03/25/how-small-businesses-drive-the-american-economy/?sh=460a8daa4169

Rustamovna, T. H., & Anvarovich, K. A. (2016). The role of small businesses to improve the export potential. *Academy*, (12 (15)), 21–23.

Saah, P. (2021). The impact of small and medium-sized enterprises on the economic development of South Africa. *Technium Soc. Sci. J., 24*, 549.

Sahut, J. M., & Peris-Ortiz, M. (2014). Small business, innovation, and entrepreneurship. *Small Business Economics, 42*(4), 663–668. doi:10.1007/s11187-013-9521-9

Sharafat, A. L. I., Rashid, H., & Khan, M. A. (2014). The role of small and medium enterprises and poverty in Pakistan: An empirical analysis. *Theoretical and Applied Economics, 18*(4), 593.

Sharma, S. K., Ilavarasan, P. V., & Karanasios, S. (2023). Small businesses and FinTech: A systematic review and future directions. *Electronic Commerce Research*, 1–41. doi:10.1007/s10660-023-09705-5

Shields, J., & Shelleman, J. M. (2015). Integrating sustainability into SME strategy. [archive only]. *Journal of Small Business Strategy, 25*(2), 59–78.

Storey, D. J. (2016). *Understanding the small business sector*. Routledge. doi:10.4324/9781315544335

Suutari, T., Lähdesmäki, M., & Kurki, S. (2023). Doing well and doing good? Small rural businesses' performance and responsibility towards local communities. *Journal of Rural Studies*, *102*, 103097. doi:10.1016/j.jrurstud.2023.103097

Thanetsunthorn, N., & Wuthisatian, R. (2023). Do business-friendly regulations foster corporate social performance? Evidence from 20 emerging market countries. *International Journal of Business and Globalisation*, *34*(2), 219–236. doi:10.1504/IJBG.2023.132801

The World Bank. (2023). *Small and Medium Enterprises Finance*. The World Bank. https://www.world-bank.org/en/topic/smefinance

Tien, N. H., Hiep, P. M., Dai, N. Q., Duc, N. M., & Hong, T. T. K. (2020). Green entrepreneurship understanding in Vietnam. *International Journal of Entrepreneurship*, *24*(2), 1–14.

Tu, J. J., & Akhter, S. (2023). Exploring the role of entrepreneurial education, technology and teachers' creativity in excelling sustainable business competencies. *Ekonomska Istrazivanja*, *36*(1), 2119429. doi:10.1080/1331677X.2022.2119429

Wagner, J. (2007). Exports and productivity: A survey of the evidence from firm-level data. *World Economy*, *30*(1), 60–82. doi:10.1111/j.1467-9701.2007.00872.x

Wennekers, S., Van Wennekers, A., Thurik, R., & Reynolds, P. (2005). Nascent entrepreneurship and the level of economic development. *Small Business Economics*, *24*(3), 293–309. doi:10.1007/s11187-005-1994-8

Woetzel, J., Orr, G., Lau, A., Yougang, C., Chang, E., Seong, J., Chui, M., & Qiu, A. (2014). *China's digital transformation: The Internet's impact on productivity and growth*. Mckinsey Global Institute.

Chapter 5
Scaling Up SMEs in China:
Overcoming Challenges and Embracing Opportunities for Sustainable Growth

Mohamad Zreik

https://orcid.org/0000-0002-6812-6529

Sun Yat-sen University, China

ABSTRACT

This chapter provides an in-depth examination of the advantages and disadvantages that China's SMEs confront in the country's dynamic economic climate. It begins by outlining the challenges small enterprises confront, including little money, complicated regulations, and the need to update outdated technology. It then examines the methods used by Chinese SMEs, such as the adoption of digital technologies, the creation of novel business models, and the development of non-traditional sources of funding, to achieve scalable growth. Several examples are given, primarily from the fields of agriculture and tourism, to illustrate the usefulness of these methods. SME capacity building and policy recommendations for an enabling environment round out the chapter. Those curious about the factors driving the expansion of China's small and medium-sized enterprises (SMEs) will find this book chapter essential.

INTRODUCTION

In terms of employment creation, GDP growth, and new product development, small and medium-sized enterprises (SMEs) in China are crucial. They are the backbone of China's dynamic economic structure, with millions of firms dispersed throughout a wide range of fields, from manufacturing to technology to services.

In China, as elsewhere, SMEs are often understood to be companies with fewer than 500 employees (Jeong, McLean, & Park, 2018). Small firms, especially in rural and underdeveloped areas, contribute to local economies and show remarkable agility and adaptability compared to larger enterprises. As a result, they foster innovation and economic diversification by swiftly reacting to market shifts and seizing new opportunities.

DOI: 10.4018/979-8-3693-0111-1.ch005

There are, nevertheless, distinctive features of China's SME landscape. Unlike publicly traded companies, many of these firms are privately held and run by members of the same family. The provinces of Zhejiang and Jiangsu, for example, are known for their thriving entrepreneurial culture and are home to many specialized SME clusters (Mei et al., 2020).

Despite the favorable environment created by China's economic growth and the government's supportive policies, SMEs nevertheless face several obstacles. Significant obstacles include the difficulty of gaining access to finance, technology, and skilled personnel, as well as the challenges of regulatory compliance. China's SMEs have shown remarkable fortitude and creativity in the face of adversity, and they continue to expand and contribute to the country's economic development (Agarwal, He, & Yeung, 2020).

Several key economic indicators in China can be traced back to the contributions made by China's SMEs. Without a shadow of a question, they are a huge employer in China, employing well over half of the country's urban workforce (Wang & Klugman, 2020). SMEs' ability to create new jobs is especially important in a country as populous as China, where finding productive ways to put people to work is essential to maintaining economic and social stability (Zreik, 2021).

SMEs also make significant contributions to China's GDP. Their aggregate economic output is enormous despite their modest individual size, as they make up the vast majority of China's businesses. The fact that many SMEs are involved in fast-growing industries like tech, services, and e-commerce highlights the importance of their contributions even further.

SMEs in China are vital to the promotion of innovation beyond mere quantitative considerations. SMEs are generally more innovative than larger, more bureaucratic companies because of their inherent flexibility and adaptability (Varga, 2021). Particularly in the technology and manufacturing industries, Chinese SMEs have achieved great achievements in product development, process improvement, and digital transformation, demonstrating their propensity for innovation (Wang et al., 2023).

SMEs are vital to fostering economic growth and addressing economic inequities on a global scale. In China's underdeveloped areas, they are typically the driving force behind the economy, creating jobs, inspiring new business owners, and allowing the transfer of wealth (Hasan, Yajuan, & Mahmud, 2020). SMEs play a crucial role in their communities by contributing to economic growth and so helping to alleviate poverty.

The goal of this chapter is to look into the difficulties of expanding Chinese SMEs, a task made crucial by the country's dynamic economy but fraught with difficulties. Due to China's prominent role in the global economy and the relevance of SMEs to the country's development, it is vital to comprehend the challenges and prospects faced by SMEs. This chapter aims to shed light on these aspects in order to better inform the budding SME scene in China, which includes entrepreneurs, business owners, managers, policymakers, academics, and students.

First, it looks at the specific challenges that Chinese SMEs confront and how these affect the company's capacity to expand and remain profitable. It will go deeply into issues like capital availability, technological progress, the complexity of regulations, and the demands of competition. These difficulties have far-reaching effects on SMEs, influencing everything from business tactics to productivity.

Next, it delves into the methods by which Chinese SMEs are attempting to overcome these obstacles and achieve scalable, long-term expansion. The emphasis is on making the most of opportunities afforded by digitization, new business models, non-traditional funding sources, and government subsidies.

It also dives at the disruptive and transformative influence that AI and digital entrepreneurs have had in the evolution of business. In order to illustrate these points, examples from real-world SMEs are provided, focusing on those operating in the agricultural and tourism industries.

The chapter finishes with a discussion of capacity development and policy proposals, with an emphasis on the importance of helping SMEs improve their entrepreneurial abilities and strategic processes and on proposing measures to foster a more growth-friendly atmosphere. This chapter as a whole provides a holistic view of the Chinese SME scene, illuminating how to succeed in the country's fast-paced, difficult, yet potentially fruitful business environment.

CHALLENGES FACED BY SMES IN CHINA

Access to Capital

Lack of access to financing is a major problem for China's SMEs. Obtaining sufficient capital remains a significant challenge for Chinese SMEs, despite the fact that it is essential for growth, expansion, and innovation. The absence of collateral, the high-risk reputation of SMEs, and the strict lending standards of traditional banks all contribute to this difficulty (Zhang et al., 2020).

The lower risk profile of large, established enterprises makes them a preferred clientele of traditional banks, the key source of capital for many businesses. The inability of many SMEs to provide adequate collateral compounds this risk aversion. Thus, SMEs are frequently underserved by the traditional banking sector.

In addition, potential investors are wary of SMEs because of the perceived high risk associated with them. This is due to factors such as the companies' short track records, inconsistent cash flows, and susceptibility to market swings (Giunipero, Denslow, & Rynarzewska, 2022). Venture capitalists and other private investors may be put off by this and instead seek 'safer' investment options with larger, more established companies.

Financial illiteracy and unfamiliarity with available funding choices are further barriers for Chinese SMEs. Many business owners of SMEs either don't know about or don't completely comprehend the various alternatives to traditional bank loans, such as equity financing, crowdsourcing, and government-backed lending programs.

Technological Modernization

Another significant problem for China's SMEs is keeping up with technological advancements. Failure to accept and integrate new technologies can seriously hamper a small or medium-sized enterprise's growth and survival in today's information-based economy.

The high price of adopting and upgrading technology is a major problem. The initial investment needed to purchase cutting-edge hardware, software, or machinery can be prohibitive for some SMEs. Maintenance, employee training, and periodic improvements are all continuous costs that can put a strain on a small or medium-sized business's budget (Gunningham & Sinclair, 2017).

In addition, SMEs typically lack the technical competence necessary to make the most of technology. This deficiency results from the company's inability to employ enough technically savvy workers, as well as the difficulties it faces in attracting and maintaining such workers due to resource restrictions and competition from larger firms. Without the proper knowledge, SMEs may not be able to make the most of their technology expenditures.

In addition, the ever-changing character of technology can be a challenge for SMEs. SMEs often lack the resources to keep up with the rapid rate at which new technologies emerge and older ones become obsolete (Ates & Acur, 2022). Due to the quick pace of technological advancement, SMEs may realize that the technology they have just adopted is already obsolete.

SMEs may also struggle to understand and comply with data privacy and cybersecurity regulations (Saban, Rau, & Wood, 2021). These bureaucratic roadblocks can make technological progress more difficult and expensive. Financial aid, skill-building, and streamlining of regulations are only some of the ways in which these obstacles to technological modernization might be overcome. SMEs in China cannot afford to neglect technological upgrading despite the difficulties they may encounter.

Regulatory Complexities

For China's SMEs, the country's complex regulatory environment is a major obstacle. These companies may feel overwhelmed by the sheer volume of laws, regulations, and compliance obligations with which they must comply. Understanding and adhering to these regulations becomes much more important given the country's distinct legal and political context.

Due to their complexity and frequent changes, laws can be challenging for SMEs to understand and comply with. Taxation, labor, the environment, and even individual industries all have their own sets of rules and laws. Many SMEs lack the manpower, finances, and knowledge to keep up with the ever-changing world of regulations (Economy & Levi, 2014).

Small and medium-sized enterprises in China have it tough due to the country's complex tax system. As it is, small enterprises may already be struggling to make ends meet due to the high tax burden and the frequently convoluted tax regulations (Owen, Sun, & Zheng, 2008). Complying with tax laws can be difficult because of variations in how they are interpreted and enforced from one location to the next.

Significant difficulties also exist in complying with labor rules and environmental standards. Understanding wage, hour, social security, and workplace safety standards is essential for compliance with labor laws. China's efforts to lessen its carbon footprint and advance sustainable development have resulted in strict environmental laws that SMEs must follow. But these rules often come with significant expenses and duties for SMEs to bear.

Depending on the field in which they operate, SMEs may be subject to additional rules and regulations. Manufacturing health and safety regulations and information technology privacy policies are two examples (Roberts et al., 2021).

Competitive Pressures

SMEs in China face a considerable challenge from competitive pressures. SMEs are feeling the heat as competition heats up in today's more varied and dynamic economy, yet they lack the resources of their larger counterparts to weather the storm.

Domestic market competition is one source of the issue. Since there are now more SMEs on the market than ever before, competition is fierce for customers' dollars. Additionally, large, established firms can be strong competitors, offering products or services at lower rates or with greater features, posing a substantial threat to SMEs due to their size, stability, and access to resources and economies of scale.

Chinese SMEs are under increasing pressure from foreign competitors as well as those at home. Foreign competitors enter the Chinese market with superior technology, branding, and operational efficiency as China continues to open its economy and participate with global markets (Yip & McKern, 2016). As a result, small and medium-sized enterprises in the area have to compete not just on price, but also on quality, innovation, and service to customers.

In addition, competitive pressures are being amplified by the rapid development of new technologies. SMEs must invest in technology and innovation or risk becoming outmoded or less competitive. As we've already established, though, this can be a huge obstacle for SMEs due to their limited resources and technology.

The proliferation of digital marketplaces and shopping options also raises the bar for success. These platforms may open up new possibilities, but they also make it easier for more rivals to enter the market (Parker, Van Alstyne, & Choudary, 2016). Small and medium-sized manufacturers (SMMs) must now find ways to set themselves apart from the competition in order to survive in the current economic climate.

Implications of These Challenges on SMEs Growth and Sustainability

Access to money, the need to modernize technology, regulatory complexity, and competitive pressures are just a few of the obstacles hindering the growth and sustainability of China's small and medium-sized businesses. Together, these challenges impede SMEs' capacity for growth, innovation, and survival in today's competitive market.

First, a shortage of money severely hampers SMEs' ability to expand and innovate. Lacking adequate capital, SMEs may be unable to make investments in company growth, purchase new technologies, engage qualified staff, or introduce new products (Stubblefield Loucks, Martens, & Cho, 2010). SMEs may not have the capital to invest in technical modernization or research and development, or even to upgrade equipment.

The growth possibilities of a small or medium-sized enterprise might be severely hampered by its lack of technological advancement. SMEs that are unable to adapt to the changing demands of their customers as a result of technological advancements run the risk of seeing their market share eroded by more technologically advanced competitors. It's also possible they'll pass up chances to enhance productivity and develop novel goods and services.

SME expansion can be impeded by overly complicated regulations. For SMEs, navigating complex rules and ensuring compliance may be a distraction that eats into their time, resources, and expertise that could be better spent on growing the firm. Furthermore, penalties or legal concerns resulting from noncompliance can have a devastating effect on a company's brand and financial viability.

Threatening to SMEs is the highly competitive pressures in the market. SMEs must constantly innovate, enhance operational efficiency, and differentiate themselves in order to succeed in today's cutthroat business climate (Yadava et al., 2022). However, these initiatives typically necessitate substantial expenditure, which creates additional difficulties for SMEs with limited resources.

OPPORTUNITIES AND STRATEGIES FOR SMES IN CHINA

Digital Technology and IoT

When it comes to overcoming obstacles and driving sustainable growth, China's SMEs have a huge potential in the widespread use of digital technology and the Internet of Things (IoT). China is at the vanguard of the digitalization revolution that is transforming business operations worldwide, providing countless chances for SMEs to become more productive, innovative, and competitive (Zreik, 2023).

SMEs can benefit from a variety of digital solutions that can increase efficiency, lower costs, and enhance customer service. For instance, cloud computing can give SMEs low- or no-upfront-cost entry to high-end information technology infrastructure. Similarly, data analytics technologies can improve SMEs' operational efficiency and market responsiveness by allowing them to make data-driven decisions (Khanna, 2016).

There is a lot of opportunity for China's SMEs in the IoT sector as well. The IoT allows for the communication and sharing of data between devices, which can help SMEs enhance their product lines, streamline their operations, and create more customized experiences for their customers (Mercan et al., 2021). With IoT, manufacturers, for instance, can keep tabs on machinery in real time, plan for repairs in advance, and boost output capacity.

Additionally, SMEs can take advantage of digital technologies to access new markets and expand their customer base. SMEs can benefit from e-commerce sites, social media, and digital marketing tools by reaching a wider audience outside of their immediate area (Abed, Dwivedi, & Williams, 2015).

The long-term benefits make the investment in digital technology and the Internet of Things worthwhile despite the high upfront price and technical complexity of doing so. It not only helps SMEs become more competitive and efficient in their operations, but it also opens up new doors for growth and development. Consequently, SMEs in China should make the adoption of digital technologies and IoT a top priority.

Innovative Business Models

One way that Chinese SMEs are striving to overcome obstacles and fuel long-term growth is through the implementation of novel business models. Innovative business models can help SMEs differentiate themselves, provide value, and increase competitiveness in today's increasingly digital business world and ever-changing consumer expectations (Gavrila & de Lucas Ancillo, 2021).

The concept of the "sharing economy" is an example of a novel approach to doing business. This concept can assist SMEs in making better use of underutilized resources, cutting expenses, and generating new revenue streams through the sharing of goods and services among users via digital platforms (Govindan, Shankar, & Kannan, 2020). Bike-sharing programs and co-working spaces are two Chinese examples that have upended established corporate norms (Mont, Curtis, & Palgan, 2021).

The platform business model is another example of a novel approach to doing business in which corporations use digital platforms to facilitate transactions between diverse communities of people. This allows them to scale quickly, expand their customer base, and make money without investing in expensive infrastructure. Electronic markets and shopping carts are two such examples (Van Alstyne, Parker, & Choudary, 2016).

Another form of innovation is subscription models, where users pay a regular price to gain ongoing access to a service or good (Ho et al., 2018). This model has the potential to increase customer retention rates while also providing SMEs with stable, recurring revenue. Small and medium-sized enterprises that sell software, digital material, or online courses may find it especially useful.

The servitization model is also gaining popularity, when businesses expand their product offerings to include complementary services alongside their core offerings. This framework can help SMEs stand out from the competition, improve the value of their products and services, and forge stronger bonds with their patrons (Opazo-Basáez, Vendrell-Herrero, & Bustinza, 2022).

Alternative Financing Mechanisms

Access to cash is a major problem for China's SMEs but crowdfunding and microfinancing offer viable alternatives. The term "crowdfunding" refers to a relatively new type of financing in which a large number of people (usually through the Internet) contribute to a project or commercial venture. Crowdfunding can take several forms, such as those focused on offering rewards, selling equity, or issuing debt (Macht & Weatherston, 2014). This approach can give a convenient and speedy alternative to conventional finance for small and medium-sized enterprises. It may also help with things like establishing credibility in the industry, expanding your network, and raising your company's profile. The fast expansion of crowdfunding platforms in China has given SMEs a new way to raise capital (Troise et al., 2023). But before SMEs can successfully raise cash through crowdfunding, they must be aware of the legal implications, potential hazards, and significance of transparency and accountability.

Microfinancing is the practice of lending small amounts of money to firms and individuals who might not otherwise have access to credit. Microfinance services are provided in China through a wide variety of banks, rural cooperatives, and online lending marketplaces (Yeung, He, & Zhang, 2017). Microfinance can help SMEs get off the ground, expand, or cover overhead costs. There are typically fewer requirements for qualification and the terms of repayment are more forgiving, making these loans ideal for start-ups and smaller firms (Malhotra, 2007). However, SMEs must be cautious of the dangers that may arise, such as excessive debt and exorbitant interest rates.

Crowdfunding and microfinancing both hold great promise for increasing access to capital for SMEs in China. There are risks and difficulties associated with using them, but with proper precautions and application, they may help small and medium-sized enterprises expand and thrive. SMEs can diversify their funding sources and decrease their dependency on traditional banking services by investigating these alternative financing alternatives.

Government Procurement and Support Schemes

In China, SMEs rely heavily on government procurement and support schemes to help them expand and thrive. They aid SMEs in two ways: directly and indirectly, helping them overcome obstacles and flourishing in a favorable setting.

SMEs can benefit greatly from government contracts. In many nations, like China, the government is one of the main purchasers of products and services, and the policies it implements in this area can have a major impact on the economy. The Chinese government has instituted preferential procurement regulations to encourage government agencies to make purchases from small and medium-sized enterprises (Luo, Xue, & Han, 2010). The result is a strong and consistent demand stream for SMEs, which in turn improves their standing in the market. However, SMEs may find it difficult to obtain government procurement opportunities due to the frequently convoluted procedures and stringent requirements that must be met (Zreik, Iqbal, & Rahman, 2022).

The Chinese government has launched a number of programs beyond procurement to help small and medium-sized businesses thrive. Subsidized loans, tax incentives, and grant programs are examples of such initiatives that help reduce the financial burdens small and medium-sized businesses experience (Liu et al., 2022). SMEs can also benefit from non-financial forms of support like business training programs, consultancy services, and R&D funding.

For SMEs, the Chinese government has created special economic zones, technology parks, and incubators. Many SMEs benefit from the accessibility of the facility's infrastructure, resources, and networks (Banwo, A. O., Du, J., & Onokala, 2017). While the Chinese government's procurement and support programs have helped small and medium-sized enterprises expand, they could do more. It is possible to increase the effectiveness of support measures by streamlining processes, increasing transparency, and directing resources to the SMEs that need them most.

In evaluating the effectiveness of existing government support schemes for SMEs in China, it becomes evident that while these initiatives have provided a foundational level of support, there is room for significant enhancement to more effectively meet the needs of SMEs. Current policies could be adjusted to offer more targeted financial assistance, reducing the bureaucratic hurdles that often impede SME access to funds and government contracts. Additionally, new initiatives could focus on digital literacy and technology adoption, areas crucial for SME competitiveness in the digital age. For instance, implementing more comprehensive digital transformation support programs, including subsidies for technology acquisition and training for digital skills, could catalyze SME innovation and growth. Furthermore, establishing a more streamlined regulatory framework could alleviate the compliance burden on SMEs, enabling them to focus more on growth and less on navigating red tape. Finally, fostering a more robust ecosystem of venture capital and angel investment specifically earmarked for SMEs could address the significant gap in early-stage funding. By adjusting existing policies and introducing these new initiatives, the government could significantly bolster the development of SMEs, ensuring their role as a cornerstone of China's economic vitality and innovation landscape.

ROLE OF AI AND DIGITAL ENTREPRENEURS IN SMES

Disruption of Traditional Business Practices

SMEs in China are undergoing radical change as a result of the advent of Artificial intelligence (AI) and the emergence of digital entrepreneurs. These factors are altering the business landscape and encouraging an atmosphere of innovation and adaptability by opening up new growth avenues (Perifanis & Kitsios, 2023).

AI is disrupting conventional methods of doing business in several sectors. AI is allowing SMEs to increase operational efficiency, improve decision-making, and provide individualized customer experiences due to its capacity to analyze large volumes of data, generate predictions, and automate complicated activities (Boddu et al., 2022). Algorithms powered by artificial intelligence can aid SMEs in the retail industry in a number of ways. Production planning, quality control, and predictive maintenance are all areas where manufacturing businesses might benefit from AI use (Hansen & Bøgh, 2021).

The automation of mundane chores is another area where AI is helping SMEs reclaim time and resources for more strategic endeavors. Chatbots powered by AI can manage consumer enquiries, HR operations can be streamlined, and accounting duties can be automated (Ng et al., 2021).

The emergence of online business owners is also having a profound effect on the status quo of doing business. These entrepreneurs are using digital tools to develop disruptive business models, transform entire sectors, and open up entirely new consumer markets (Kraus et al., 2019). They are quicker to adapt to shifting market conditions and changing client preferences because they are nimble and customer-focused than conventional enterprises.

Entrepreneurs in the digital realm are also taking advantage of digital channels to broaden their customer base, expand their networks, and tap into previously unavailable resources and opportunities. They use online marketplaces to reach clients all over the world, social media to build relationships with those customers, and cloud-based collaboration apps to get their work done.

Creation of New Pathways for Growth

SMEs in China are benefiting from the combination of AI and digital entrepreneurs, who are not only shaking up the status quo but also opening up new growth opportunities. SMEs can benefit from AI in a number of different ways. To begin, SMEs can use AI to develop previously impossible goods or services. AI can help SMEs in the healthcare industry create predictive diagnosis tools, individualized treatment plans, and telemedicine services, for example. AI can help retailers improve their supply chains, customer service, and the shopping experience overall (Kumar, Pujari, & Gupta, 2021).

SMEs can benefit from AI by opening doors to new markets and client bases. With the help of AI, SMEs may evaluate customer data and market trends to find new revenue streams, refine their marketing approaches, and better serve their niche markets (Gilmore & Carson, 2018). However, digital entrepreneurs are also blazing new growth trails through the introduction of novel business models and the strategic use of digital technologies. Examples of industries that have been revolutionized by digital entrepreneurs include e-commerce, fintech, edtech, and healthtech. They are using the internet to expand their businesses globally, make new connections, and grow quickly (Alvarez-Salazar, 2020).

In addition, digital entrepreneurs are leading the charge toward more ethical and environmentally friendly methods of doing business. Business models that help society, advance sustainable development, and create mutually beneficial outcomes are being developed with the help of digital technologies. Entrepreneurs in the digital realm, for instance, are building platforms to further the sharing economy, popularize circular economy principles, and broaden access to financial services.

CASE STUDIES OF SUCCESSFUL SMES IN CHINA

Agriculture Sector

Many Chinese agricultural SMEs have found success thanks to the implementation of cutting-edge tactics and technologies. These businesses are enhancing their competitiveness and sustainability by using digital technologies, AI, and other innovations.

Pinduoduo is a well-known example of a Chinese e-commerce platform that bridges the gap between farmers and consumers. By eliminating middlemen and shortening the distance goods travel from farm to table, this platform helps farmers maximize the value of their produce while minimizing costs. In addition, Pinduoduo has introduced a program dubbed "Duo Duo Farming," which employs AI and big data to educate farmers on how to better cater to their customers. Farmers can adjust output to meet changing market demands, cutting costs while maximizing profits (Zhao, Wang, & Chen, 2019).

XAG, a pioneer in agricultural technology, is another thriving small and medium-sized enterprise. XAG creates drones and other intelligent devices for use in precision agriculture using AI and IoT technology. Their wares aid farmers in a number of ways, including keeping tabs on crop vitals, applying just the right quantity of fertilizer or pesticide, and saving time and money. The solutions provided by XAG have greatly enhanced agricultural productivity while decreasing their negative effects on the environment (Wang, 2020).

Successful Chinese agricultural SME Jingold is just one more. This firm's main focus is on growing and selling kiwifruits. Jingold has implemented a cutting-edge business approach that incorporates R&D, farming, post-harvest processing, and sales and marketing. It has also used cutting-edge breeding procedures to create its own unique strains of kiwifruit. Jingold's development, reputation, and product quality have all improved because to these measures (Marzuki et al., 2021).

These examples show how small and medium-sized enterprises in the agricultural industry can benefit greatly from the convergence of digital technology, artificial intelligence, and novel business strategies. Small and medium-sized enterprises can boost their competitiveness, increase their sustainability, and aid in the modernization of China's agricultural industry by implementing the aforementioned tactics.

Tourism Sector

Chinese SMEs in the tourist industry are using cutting-edge methods and tools to develop distinctive selling points and distinguish themselves from the competition. Here are some examples of where this has worked well.

One such small and medium-sized enterprise is Mafengwo, which began as a place for tourists to talk about their trips but is now one of China's most prominent tour operators. Through the use of AI and large amounts of data, it recommends trips to its users based on their individual tastes. Its community-based strategy encourages users to share their own travel experiences, which improves the quality of the service for everyone and gives companies new insights (Leng, Yu, & Niu, 2022).

Another case in point is Tujia, China's most popular website for renting out short-term lodgings (think of it as the "Airbnb" of China). Tujia has adapted its business model to meet the needs of Chinese consumers by providing them with services such as expert property management and offline maintenance (Qiu et al., 2020). With this strategy, it has been able to corner a sizable piece of China's booming short-term rental industry.

Finally, a digital firm in the tourism industry called Yitu8 has found great success by employing AI to offer something no one else does. Yitu8's AI algorithm creates customized itineraries based on customer input on desired destinations, desired length of trip, and other criteria. Because of this ground-breaking strategy, Yitu8 stands apart from other travel firms and is rapidly expanding (Zuboff, 2022).

These examples illustrate how China's dynamic and ever-evolving tourism industry can benefit from the combination of novel business models and cutting-edge technologies like AI. These efforts are helping China's SMEs provide travelers better service, more options, and more personalization, all of which contribute to the sector's expansion and increased global competitiveness.

In the manufacturing sector, for example, Zhejiang Huayou Cobalt Co., Ltd has made significant strides by focusing on sustainable mining practices and investing in R&D to improve the efficiency of cobalt extraction, essential for battery production. This approach not only minimized environmental impact but also positioned Huayou as a leader in the global supply chain for electric vehicle batteries.

In the technology sector, Shenzhen Transsion Holdings Co., Ltd, the maker of Tecno mobile phones, has achieved remarkable success by tailoring its products to meet the specific needs of consumers in emerging markets. By focusing on affordable smartphones with features designed for African users, such as cameras optimized for darker skin tones, Transsion has outpaced many global competitors in these regions.

Furthermore, in the service industry, New Oriental Education & Technology Group has transformed the educational landscape by leveraging digital platforms to provide online learning. Their innovative approach to education, which combines quality teaching with technology-driven delivery methods, has not only expanded access to education across China but also demonstrated the scalability and adaptability of SMEs in the face of digital transformation challenges.

These examples underscore the diversity and resilience of SMEs in China across various sectors. They illustrate the importance of innovation, market understanding, and sustainability in achieving growth. By embracing best practices such as investing in technology, focusing on niche markets, and prioritizing sustainable operations, SMEs can navigate challenges and contribute significantly to China's economic dynamism.

CAPACITY BUILDING FOR SMES IN CHINA

Strengthening Entrepreneurial Skills

Sustainable growth and competitiveness for China's SMEs depend on their ability to build capacity. Enhancing entrepreneurial abilities is an essential part of this process of capacity growth. Successful SMEs rely heavily on entrepreneurial abilities such strategic planning, risk management, innovation, leadership, and financial management (Schoemaker, Heaton, & Teece, 2018). These abilities allow company owners to spot profitable opportunities, mitigate threats, create new ones, guide their people toward success, and keep their businesses afloat financially.

Entrepreneurs can take part in a wide range of training and education programs to hone these abilities. Business schools, trade groups, and government organizations often host seminars, workshops, and other forms of professional development for their students and employees. Business planning, marketing, money management, leadership, and innovation are just some of the topics that these programs address. They teach business owners how to run their companies efficiently and expand their operations.

The significance of mentorship programs in developing business acumen is equally critical. SME owners can improve their ability to make decisions and solve problems by forming strategic alliances with more seasoned entrepreneurs and business professionals. In addition, mentors can introduce entrepreneurs to others who could become valuable contacts, such as consumers, business partners, or investors (Leach & Melicher, 2020).

To further their development, business owners can take advantage of online education resources. These sites provide businesses with easy, on-demand access to a wealth of educational materials, like as webinars, videos, and e-books (Oda Abunamous et al., 2022). From business management and analytics to leadership and entrepreneurship, they have you covered.

Improving Strategic Processes

Enhancing strategic processes is another critical part of enhancing the capabilities of China's SMEs. An organization's strategic processes are the means through which it determines its future course of action, makes key choices, and coordinates its operations to achieve its goals.

Improving strategic processes requires a number of important actions. The first stage is strategic planning, which entails deciding on specific, attainable objectives, figuring out how to get there, and listing the means at one's disposal. A well-thought-out strategic plan can serve as a road map for SMEs, directing their choices and activities in the direction of their goals (Hammond, Keeney, & Raiffa, 2015).

Decision-making is also an important part of any successful strategic plan. Enhancing the use of data and analytics, encouraging critical thinking, and encouraging cooperation and diversity in decision-making are all ways to boost decision quality (Gregory et al., 2012). Decisions made by SMEs can be more informed, more efficient, and made faster if their decision-making processes are enhanced.

Strategic processes including innovation are another area where SMEs might stand to improve. This necessitates the establishment of systems for the discovery of novel possibilities, the analysis and refinement of novel ideas, and the introduction of novel solutions. SMEs must create an environment conducive to innovation, promote experimentation, and control the risks that come with new ideas.

One final point, SMEs should refine their methods of monitoring and evaluation. Indicators of success must be established, tracked on a regular basis, and results-driven course corrections must be made. Small and medium-sized enterprises can stay on course, spot problem areas, and correct course with regular monitoring and review.

Given their smaller size and limited resources, SMEs often struggle to improve their strategic processes. With the appropriate help, however, SMEs may improve their strategic processes, increase their performance, and develop sustainably. In order to enhance strategic procedures, it may be required to bring in outside help in the form of consulting services, training programs, or digital tools.

CONCLUSION

The role of SMEs in China's economy is crucial, as they are responsible for a large portion of the country's new jobs and economic expansion. Despite their potential, Chinese SMEs confront a number of obstacles, such as the difficulty of gaining access to financing, the cost of keeping up with technical advances, the complexity of relevant regulations, and the pressures of the global marketplace. The expansion and viability of these organizations is threatened by these factors, which also pose serious threats to their success.

SMEs are using a variety of tactics to face these difficulties and take advantage of the potential for long-term growth. They're taking advantage of the Internet of Things and other digital technologies, creating novel business models, using non-traditional sources of funding, and making the most of government contracts and grants. They are using AI and digital entrepreneurship to shake up established industries and pave the way for new methods of doing business and economic growth. Successful SMEs in the agriculture and tourist industries give case studies that illustrate how these tactics are being put to use in the real world.

For SMEs to develop their strategic thinking and entrepreneurial abilities, capacity building is crucial. SMEs can improve their capacity to make decisions, creativity, and strategic orientation by focusing on these areas. There is an urgent need for supportive policies because of the crucial role SMEs play in China's economy and the difficulties they encounter. Policies that increase access to financing, encourage technology modernization, streamline regulatory processes, and reduce competitive pressures can all have a substantial impact on a small business's capacity to grow and thrive. Simplifying administrative procedures, implementing fair competition regulations, easing SMEs' access to public equity markets, and so on are all examples of possible policy actions.

Policymakers should also encourage small and medium-sized enterprises to increase their capabilities. In order to accomplish this, it would be helpful to provide access to advisory services and digital technologies while also supporting training and development activities for entrepreneurs. SMEs can succeed in today's competitive market by honing their abilities to adapt to change, grasp opportunities, and grow sustainably.

Several potential avenues for further study and application are suggested in this chapter as well. More research is needed to better understand the dynamics of SME growth in China, the efficacy of diverse growth strategies, and the influence of policy interventions. The dynamics of SME expansion in China and other countries could be compared and contrasted through comparative research.

Business advisory services, digital platforms, and innovation hubs are just some of the services that could help small and medium-sized enterprises succeed. Services like this can help small and medium-sized enterprises get over their hurdles, develop their skills, and eventually grow sustainably.

REFERENCES

Abed, S. S., Dwivedi, Y. K., & Williams, M. D. (2015). Social media as a bridge to e-commerce adoption in SMEs: A systematic literature review. *The Marketing Review*, *15*(1), 39–57. doi:10.1362/14693 4715X14267608178686

Agarwal, S., He, Z., & Yeung, B. (Eds.). (2020). *Impact of COVID-19 on Asian economies and policy responses*. World Scientific.

Alvarez-Salazar, J. (2020). The fuzzy boundaries in start-up firms industries. a social network analysis. *Journal of Technology Management & Innovation*, *15*(4), 30–42. doi:10.4067/S0718-27242020000400030

Ates, A., & Acur, N. (2022). Making obsolescence obsolete: Execution of digital transformation in a high-tech manufacturing SME. *Journal of Business Research*, *152*, 336–348. doi:10.1016/j.jbusres.2022.07.052

Banwo, A. O., Du, J., & Onokala, U. (2017). The determinants of location specific choice: Small and medium-sized enterprises in developing countries. *Journal of Global Entrepreneurship Research*, *7*(1), 1–17. doi:10.1186/s40497-017-0074-2

Boddu, R. S. K., Santoki, A. A., Khurana, S., Koli, P. V., Rai, R., & Agrawal, A. (2022). An analysis to understand the role of machine learning, robotics and artificial intelligence in digital marketing. *Materials Today: Proceedings*, *56*, 2288–2292. doi:10.1016/j.matpr.2021.11.637

Economy, E., & Levi, M. (2014). *By all means necessary: How China's resource quest is changing the world*. Oxford University Press.

Gavrila, S. G., & de Lucas Ancillo, A. (2021). Spanish SMEs' digitalization enablers: E-Receipt applications to the offline retail market. *Technological Forecasting and Social Change, 162*, 120381. doi:10.1016/j.techfore.2020.120381 PMID:33082601

Gilmore, A., & Carson, D. (2018). SME marketing: Efficiency in practice. *Small Enterprise Research, 25*(3), 213–226. doi:10.1080/13215906.2018.1521740

Giunipero, L. C., Denslow, D., & Rynarzewska, A. I. (2022). Small business survival and COVID-19-An exploratory analysis of carriers. *Research in Transportation Economics, 93*, 101087. doi:10.1016/j.retrec.2021.101087

Govindan, K., Shankar, K. M., & Kannan, D. (2020). Achieving sustainable development goals through identifying and analyzing barriers to industrial sharing economy: A framework development. *International Journal of Production Economics, 227*, 107575. doi:10.1016/j.ijpe.2019.107575

Gregory, R., Failing, L., Harstone, M., Long, G., McDaniels, T., & Ohlson, D. (2012). *Structured decision making: a practical guide to environmental management choices*. John Wiley & Sons. doi:10.1002/9781444398557

Gunningham, N., & Sinclair, D. (2017). *Leaders and laggards: next-generation environmental regulation*. Routledge. doi:10.4324/9781351282000

Hammond, J. S., Keeney, R. L., & Raiffa, H. (2015). *Smart choices: A practical guide to making better decisions*. Harvard Business Review Press.

Hansen, E. B., & Bøgh, S. (2021). Artificial intelligence and internet of things in small and medium-sized enterprises: A survey. *Journal of Manufacturing Systems, 58*, 362–372. doi:10.1016/j.jmsy.2020.08.009

Hasan, M. M., Yajuan, L., & Mahmud, A. (2020). Regional development of China's inclusive finance through financial technology. *SAGE Open, 10*(1), 2158244019901252. doi:10.1177/2158244019901252

Ho, C. Q., Hensher, D. A., Mulley, C., & Wong, Y. Z. (2018). Potential uptake and willingness-to-pay for Mobility as a Service (MaaS): A stated choice study. *Transportation Research Part A, Policy and Practice, 117*, 302–318. doi:10.1016/j.tra.2018.08.025

Jeong, S., McLean, G. N., & Park, S. (2018). Understanding informal learning in small-and medium-sized enterprises in South Korea. *Journal of Workplace Learning, 30*(2), 89–107. doi:10.1108/JWL-03-2017-0028

Khanna, G. (2016). *How companies can transform from product to platform ecosystem* [Doctoral dissertation, Massachusetts Institute of Technology].

Kraus, S., Palmer, C., Kailer, N., Kallinger, F. L., & Spitzer, J. (2019). Digital entrepreneurship: A research agenda on new business models for the twenty-first century. *International Journal of Entrepreneurial Behaviour & Research, 25*(2), 353–375.

Kumar, A., Pujari, P., & Gupta, N. (2021). Artificial Intelligence: Technology 4.0 as a solution for healthcare workers during COVID-19 pandemic. *Acta Universitatis Bohemiae Meridionales*, *24*(1), 19–35. doi:10.32725/acta.2021.002

Leach, J. C., & Melicher, R. W. (2020). *Entrepreneurial finance*. Cengage Learning.

Leng, Y., Yu, L., & Niu, X. (2022). Dynamically aggregating individuals' social influence and interest evolution for group recommendations. *Information Sciences*, *614*, 223–239. doi:10.1016/j.ins.2022.09.058

Liu, Y., Dilanchiev, A., Xu, K., & Hajiyeva, A. M. (2022). Financing SMEs and business development as new post Covid-19 economic recovery determinants. *Economic Analysis and Policy*, *76*, 554–567. doi:10.1016/j.eap.2022.09.006

Luo, Y., Xue, Q., & Han, B. (2010). How emerging market governments promote outward FDI: Experience from China. *Journal of World Business*, *45*(1), 68–79. doi:10.1016/j.jwb.2009.04.003

Macht, S. A., & Weatherston, J. (2014). The benefits of online crowdfunding for fund-seeking business ventures. *Strategic Change*, *23*(1-2), 1–14. doi:10.1002/jsc.1955

Malhotra, M. (2007). *Expanding access to finance: Good practices and policies for micro, small, and medium enterprises*. World Bank Publications. doi:10.1596/978-0-8213-7177-0

Marzuki, S. Z. S., Osman, C. A., Buyong, S. Z., & Zreik, M. (2021). Design Thinking Mini Project Approach Using Factor Analysis. *Environment-Behaviour Proceedings Journal*, *6*(17), 93–98. doi:10.21834/ebpj.v6i17.2797

Mei, Y., Mao, D., Lu, Y., & Chu, W. (2020). Effects and mechanisms of rural E-commerce clusters on households' entrepreneurship behavior in China. *Growth and Change*, *51*(4), 1588–1610. doi:10.1111/grow.12424

Mercan, S., Cain, L., Akkaya, K., Cebe, M., Uluagac, S., Alonso, M., & Cobanoglu, C. (2021). Improving the service industry with hyper-connectivity: IoT in hospitality. *International Journal of Contemporary Hospitality Management*, *33*(1), 243–262. doi:10.1108/IJCHM-06-2020-0621

Mont, O., Curtis, S. K., & Palgan, Y. V. (2021). Organisational response strategies to COVID-19 in the sharing economy. *Sustainable Production and Consumption*, *28*, 52–70. doi:10.1016/j.spc.2021.03.025 PMID:34786447

Ng, K. K., Chen, C. H., Lee, C. K., Jiao, J. R., & Yang, Z. X. (2021). A systematic literature review on intelligent automation: Aligning concepts from theory, practice, and future perspectives. *Advanced Engineering Informatics*, *47*, 101246. doi:10.1016/j.aei.2021.101246

Oda Abunamous, M., Boudouaia, A., Jebril, M., Diafi, S., & Zreik, M. (2022). The decay of traditional education: A case study under covid-19. *Cogent Education*, *9*(1), 2082116. doi:10.1080/2331186X.2022.2082116

Opazo-Basáez, M., Vendrell-Herrero, F., & Bustinza, O. F. (2022). Digital service innovation: A paradigm shift in technological innovation. *Journal of Service Management*, *33*(1), 97–120. doi:10.1108/JOSM-11-2020-0427

Owen, B. M., Sun, S., & Zheng, W. (2008). China's competition policy reforms: The anti-monopoly law and beyond. *Antitrust Law Journal*, *75*(1), 231–265.

Parker, G. G., Van Alstyne, M. W., & Choudary, S. P. (2016). *Platform revolution: How networked markets are transforming the economy and how to make them work for you.* WW Norton & Company.

Perifanis, N. A., & Kitsios, F. (2023). Investigating the influence of artificial intelligence on business value in the digital era of strategy: A literature review. *Information (Basel)*, *14*(2), 85. doi:10.3390/info14020085

Qiu, D., Lin, P. M., Feng, S. Y., Peng, K. L., & Fan, D. (2020). The future of Airbnb in China: Industry perspective from hospitality leaders. *Tourism Review*, *75*(4), 609–624. doi:10.1108/TR-02-2019-0064

Roberts, H., Cowls, J., Morley, J., Taddeo, M., Wang, V., & Floridi, L. (2021). The Chinese approach to artificial intelligence: An analysis of policy, ethics, and regulation. *AI & Society*, *36*(1), 59–77. doi:10.1007/s00146-020-00992-2

Saban, K. A., Rau, S., & Wood, C. A. (2021). SME executives' perceptions and the information security preparedness model. *Information and Computer Security*, *29*(2), 263–282. doi:10.1108/ICS-01-2020-0014

Schoemaker, P. J., Heaton, S., & Teece, D. (2018). Innovation, dynamic capabilities, and leadership. *California Management Review*, *61*(1), 15–42. doi:10.1177/0008125618790246

Stubblefield Loucks, E., Martens, M. L., & Cho, C. H. (2010). Engaging small-and medium-sized businesses in sustainability. *Sustainability Accounting. Management and Policy Journal*, *1*(2), 178–200.

Troise, C., Battisti, E., Christofi, M., van Vulpen, N. J., & Tarba, S. (2023). How can SMEs use crowdfunding platforms to internationalize? The role of equity and reward crowdfunding. *Management International Review*, *63*(1), 117–159. doi:10.1007/s11575-022-00493-y PMID:36465887

Van Alstyne, M. W., Parker, G. G., & Choudary, S. P. (2016). Pipelines, platforms, and the new rules of strategy. *Harvard Business Review*, *94*(4), 54–62.

Varga, J. (2021). Defining the economic role and benefits of micro small and medium-sized enterprises in the 21st century with a systematic review of the literature. *Acta Polytechnica Hungarica*, *18*(11), 209–228. doi:10.12700/APH.18.11.2021.11.12

Wang, L., & Klugman, J. (2020). How women have fared in the labour market with China's rise as a global economic power. *Asia & the Pacific Policy Studies*, *7*(1), 43–64. doi:10.1002/app5.293

Wang, X. (2020). *Blockchain chicken farm: And other stories of tech in China's countryside.* FSG Originals.

Wang, Y., Ali, Z., Mehreen, A., & Hussain, K. (2023). The trickle-down effect of big data use to predict organization innovation: The roles of business strategy alignment and information sharing. *Journal of Enterprise Information Management*, *36*(1), 323–346. doi:10.1108/JEIM-10-2021-0439

Yadava, A. K., Khan, I. A., Pandey, P., Aarif, M., Khanna, G., & Garg, S. (2022). Impact of marketing communication and information sharing on the productivity of India's small and medium-sized businesses (SMEs). *International Journal of Health Sciences*, *6*, 12745–12755. doi:10.53730/ijhs.v6nS2.8352

Yeung, G., He, C., & Zhang, P. (2017). Rural banking in China: Geographically accessible but still financially excluded. *Regional Studies*, *51*(2), 297–312. doi:10.1080/00343404.2015.1100283

Yip, G. S., & McKern, B. (2016). *China's next strategic advantage: From imitation to innovation*. MIT press.

Zhang, M., Lian, Y., Zhao, H., & Xia-Bauer, C. (2020). Unlocking green financing for building energy retrofit: A survey in the western China. *Energy Strategy Reviews*, *30*, 100520. doi:10.1016/j.esr.2020.100520

Zhao, W., Wang, A., & Chen, Y. (2019). How to maintain the sustainable development of a business platform: A case study of Pinduoduo social commerce platform in China. *Sustainability (Basel)*, *11*(22), 6337. doi:10.3390/su11226337

Zreik, M. (2021). The Regional Comprehensive Economic Partnership and Its Impact on the US-China Trade War. *Journal of Asia Pacific Studies*, *6*(3), 339–348.

Zreik, M. (2023). From Boom to Bust: A Study of China's Economy in the Wake of COVID-19 Outbreak in H1 2020. *BRICS Journal of Economics*, *4*(1), 147–171. doi:10.3897/brics-econ.4.e101050

Zreik, M., Iqbal, B. A., & Rahman, M. N. (2022). Outward FDI: determinants and flows in emerging economies: evidence from China. *China and WTO Review*, *8*(2), 385–402. doi:10.14330/cwr.2022.8.2.07

Zuboff, S. (2022). Surveillance capitalism or democracy? The death match of institutional orders and the politics of knowledge in our information civilization. *Organization Theory*, *3*(3), 26317877221129290. doi:10.1177/26317877221129290

Chapter 6
From Power Outages to Business Shutdowns:
Exploring the Fate of Small and Medium-Sized Enterprises SMEs in South Africa's Electricity Crises

Phathutshedzo Madumi
University of Stellenbosch, South Africa

ABSTRACT

This chapter reveals that SMEs in South Africa are highly vulnerable to electricity crises, with many experiencing significant financial losses and business closures. The impact of power outages and load shedding varies across sectors, with manufacturing and retail businesses particularly affected. SMEs also face challenges in accessing alternative energy sources, such as solar power, due to high costs and limited availability. Factors contributing to SMEs' vulnerability include their reliance on the national electricity grid, limited access to finance for alternative energy solutions, and inadequate government support. Many SMEs are also struggling to compete with larger firms that have the resources to invest in backup power solutions and other resilience measures. Further, the chapter identifies several policy interventions that could support SMEs in mitigating the impact of electricity crises, including incentives for renewable energy, increased access to finance for energy-saving solutions, and targeted business support programs.

INTRODUCTION

Small and medium-sized enterprises (SMEs) play a vital role in the economic progress and advancement of a country. They have a substantial impact on economic growth by generating employment opportunities, reducing poverty, inequality, and promoting innovation. Typically, they represent the primary source of employment in most countries. Despite their contribution to the economy, ensuring their continued success over time is a major obstacle. SMEs are currently experiencing a slower growth rate, falling short

DOI: 10.4018/979-8-3693-0111-1.ch006

of the National Development Plan (NDP) objectives. The NDP aimed for this sector to contribute up to 80% of Gross Domestic Product (GDP) growth and create 90% of approximately 11 million new jobs by 2030. The decline in the expansion of small businesses and their high failure rates in South Africa have been attributed to several things. These include poor electricity supply, inadequate financial support, lack of information technology, high transport costs, high taxes, recession in the economy, high-interest rates, lack of business skills, shortage of skilled labour, poor infrastructure, crime, and corruption among other things. Additional shocks from COVID-19 are putting further pressure on their operations. Imposed lockdown measures have resulted in a drastic decline in revenues for numerous SMEs, compelling most of them to implement cost-cutting measures to sustain their operations.

Generally, the global economy experienced significant disruptions due to the COVID-19 crisis, inflicting severe hardships on SMEs and entrepreneurs. However, in certain circumstances timely actions taken by governments and public financial institutions serve as a vital support system for cash-strapped SMEs, providing them with much-needed liquidity assistance. The significance of SMEs is well recognized by the South African government, which has established frameworks to foster their development and provide support. However, South Africa's electricity crisis has had a severely detrimental effect on small and medium-sized enterprises (SMEs), as frequent power outages and load shedding have led to substantial financial losses and the closure of businesses. This chapter aims to explore the fate of SMEs in the electricity crisis and identify the factors contributing to their vulnerability. The objectives of this chapter are to:

1. Analyse the impact of the electricity crisis on SMEs in South Africa.
2. Explore the factors contributing to SMEs' vulnerability to power outages and load shedding.
3. Identify potential solutions to address these challenges.

Certainly, SMEs are a crucial driver of economic growth and employment in South Africa, but they face significant challenges in accessing finance, skills, and markets. The electricity crisis has added to these challenges, with power outages disrupting business operations, reducing productivity, and increasing costs. This chapter aims to uncover the growth traps of SMEs in South Africa, with a focus on the electricity crises and identifying the factors contributing to their vulnerability. This chapter will utilize a qualitative literature assessment drawing largely from key secondary sources, and analysis of relevant data from government and industry sources.

The Indispensable Contribution of SMEs to the Economy

According to the South African Small Business Act (South Africa, 1996), a small-scale business in South Africa is characterized as having a workforce of fewer than 50 employees, while a medium-sized enterprise is identified as employing fewer than 200 individuals. Based on the estimates by the World Bank (2017), small and medium-sized enterprises (SMEs) constitute approximately 95% of businesses globally and contribute to 50% of total employment. In emerging markets, formal SMEs alone contribute up to 40% of the gross domestic product (GDP), and when considering the informal economy, this figure increases significantly. Moreover, SMEs play a crucial role by providing around 70% of employment opportunities. in the same vein, the OECD (2017), affirms that small SMEs have a significant presence in all OECD economies. They constitute more than 95% of all enterprises and contribute to approximately 60% to 70% of total employment in most OECD countries.

Bruwer (2020) highlights the crucial role of South African SMEs in the economy, emphasizing their substantial contributions towards socio-economic objectives and their potential as key drivers of economic growth, innovation, and job creation. The South African government recognizes the significance of SMEs, as evidenced by the establishment of a dedicated Ministry of Small Business Development in early 2014. The primary goal of the Ministry is to promote and support the progress of SMEs, intending to create a favorable environment that enables their success and long-term viability. This includes the promotion and development of small businesses in South Africa, as outlined by the Department of Small Business Development in 2019. South Africa is grappling with a concerning unemployment rate of 32.9%, which is further compounded by a persistent scarcity of skilled workforce (Stats SA, 2023). Considering this situation, the government is actively working towards implementing policies, strategies, and programs to create an enabling environment for SMEs (SEDA, 2018). The objective is to establish a supportive framework that empowers SMEs and addresses the challenges of unemployment and skills shortages in the country.

SMEs play a pivotal role in fostering innovation, creating employment opportunities, and making a substantial contribution to the GDP (Viljoen, Blaauw, and Schenck, 2019). According to Smit (2017), South Africa currently hosts around 5.6 million SMEs, representing a significant portion of the country's labour force, estimated to be approximately 70% to 80%. Furthermore, these SMEs make a notable contribution to the South African GDP, accounting for approximately 36% of the total GDP. According to Bhorat, Asmal, Lilenstein, and Van Der Zee (2018), small businesses play a vital role in achieving "inclusive development and growth" in South Africa. According to the Small Enterprise Development Agency (SEDA) (2019) report, small businesses in South Africa were predominantly located in Gauteng, accounting for 35% of all businesses in the first quarter of 2019. This was followed by KwaZulu-Natal at 15% and Limpopo at approximately 12%. Other provinces included the Western Cape 11.3%, Eastern Cape 7.1%, Northern Cape 1.0%, Free State 4.1%, North-West 5.0%, and Mpumalanga 8.6% (SEDA, 2019).

Regarding the profitability of SMEs, the first quarter of 2019 saw a mere 0.4% year-on-year increase in the nominal turnover of SMEs. This limited growth in turnover prompted small and medium-sized businesses to carefully manage their expenditures by reducing operational costs, excluding labour and capital expenses. Consequently, the profitability level of SMEs remained relatively stable during this period (SEDA, 2019). According to a report from the International Monetary Fund (IMF) (2019), SMEs make up over 90% of all formal businesses in the country, employing 50-60% of the workforce and contributing 34% to the GDP. Despite their significant presence, the MSME sector has experienced stagnation. The IMF's findings reveal that the sector grew from 2.019 million businesses in 2008 to just 2.309 million in 2017, representing a meagre 14.3% growth over a span of nine years. Moreover, South Africa's early-stage entrepreneurship rate is three times lower than it should be when considering the GDP per capita, and it significantly lags behind other African nations. On the other, the current estimates suggest that while SMEs make up 98.5% of the economy, they only account for 28% of job creation (Langa and Govender, 2019).

Since 2005, South Africa has encountered ongoing challenges within its electricity supply industry, which have had adverse effects on SMEs operating in the country. Primarily, these issues have been characterized by problems related to energy supply, notably the failure of switchgear and a series of subsequent incidents that compounded the situation. These incidents include a fire under a power line, a tripped transformer, and a damaged generator caused by a misplaced bolt. Concurrently, the country has also grappled with a load-shedding crisis that commenced in 2008, while the significant increase in electricity prices has further exacerbated the difficulties. Considering these circumstances, improving energy efficiency and transitioning towards the utilization of clean, renewable sources of energy become paramount objectives.

Barriers to SMEs' Sustainable Growth

Many SMEs in emerging economies might considerably benefit from programs that promote sustainable growth. However, certain business decisions made by SME owners can have an impact on their firms' growth potential and, in some cases, lead to failure. In other words, efficient governance is critical for the long-term success of any business, regardless of its size. Owners face several hurdles in achieving profitability and ensuring the survival of their businesses. For example, inadequate infrastructure, such as unreliable electricity or transportation systems, can impede the adoption of environmentally friendly technology and practices. High-quality, easily accessible infrastructure promotes productivity, corporate growth, and investment. Escribano et al. (2009) revealed that inadequate infrastructure quality significantly reduces total factor productivity, with low-quality electricity supply having the most negative impact on firm productivity, particularly in impoverished African countries.

However, inferior and unreliable infrastructure hurts corporate productivity and growth. Aterido et al. (2009) revealed that infrastructure bottlenecks typically impede the growth of medium and large firms. However, these bottlenecks have a positive impact on micro-enterprises, which are often less capital and energy-intensive and can capitalize on opportunities arising from challenges faced by larger firms. Insufficient power services might impede business operations owing to a lack of electricity. Even when electricity is available, establishing a connection might be difficult, and the supply itself may be intermittent. Rud (2012) suggests that electrical infrastructure and consumption are positively related to productivity and economic growth. Along the same lines, Osabohien et al. (2023) noted that the level of ICT adoption among entrepreneurs is notably low, especially within emerging economies. All of these factors can have an impact on businesses, even before we consider the associated costs.

The Impact of South Africa's Electricity Crisis on Small Businesses

The prospects for resolving Eskom, the state-owned electricity utility, and South Africa's energy crises appear bleak. Load-shedding commenced over 15 years ago, and instead of improving, the problem has worsened over time. According to Oseni (2012), electricity provision in Africa has been plagued by inadequate generation, unreliable supply, and frequent occurrences of power outages. In the 21st century, electricity has become an essential resource that impacts both residential and industrial consumers when it is unavailable. The significance of this issue lies in the fact that energy serves as a crucial catalyst and essential input for economic growth in any society or nation. The absence of a dependable electricity supply in South Africa has a devastating impact on the productivity of individuals and businesses throughout the country. This situation particularly affects SMEs and self-employed individuals, who bear the brunt of the consequences.

Generally, an electricity shortage occurs when the desired quantity of electricity by all users surpasses the available supply. In such situations, measures must be taken to align the demand and supply, as the economy cannot consume more electricity than what is available. Unfortunately, there is a likelihood of electricity demand surpassing supply in the foreseeable future. Eskom is already encountering challenges in meeting the power requirements during peak times, particularly on cold days, in the mornings, and evenings when significant amounts of electricity are consumed. This issue is expected to worsen as urbanization and economic growth continue to escalate.

The electricity crisis in South Africa resulted in a series of power outages, causing significant operational challenges for SMEs in the country. Power outages are a global occurrence, and the causes of these outages vary across different countries. For example, in Sweden, the supply of electricity has often faced challenges due to nature, which has emerged as the primary adversary to ensuring a secure electricity supply (Gündüz, Küfeoğly & Lehtonen, 2017). Arguably, crises such as power outages may be an effective driver of change in organizations, whether internal or external. Crises have been known to prompt organizations to critically assess their business strategy, leading them to reevaluate their mission, structure, systems, and procedures (Bartlett, 1983; Tushman et al., 1986). The electricity crisis had a significant and widespread impact on these businesses, with many of them experiencing a loss of trade or reduced productivity. This was primarily due to the burden of bearing overhead costs without being able to engage in normal trading activities.

Unfortunately, over three years later, the situation at Eskom, the South African electricity utility, has deteriorated further. Despite government support, the company's debt remains at an unsustainable level of approximately R423 billion. The energy availability factor, which measures the reliability of electricity supply, has decreased from 66% to 58% in 2022. Figure 1, reflects that the frequency of load-shedding has significantly multiplied, reaching 22,529 gigawatt-hours (GWh) or the equivalent of 157 full days of power cuts in 2022 (Godinho, 2023). Godinho further stated that load-shedding is affecting customers for up to ten hours per day. Additionally, tariffs have increased by 34%, reaching R1.40 per kilowatt-hour (kWh) in 2023. These alarming figures reflect the worsening state of the energy crisis, with severe consequences for both consumers and businesses in South Africa.

As per the findings of South Africa's Council for Scientific and Industrial Research (CSIR), Eskom, the state-owned electricity utility in South Africa, implemented significant electricity cuts in the first half of 2022 (Writer, 2022). Writer, (2022) further reported that the figure indicates that Eskom curtailed approximately 2,276 gigawatt-hours (GWh) of electricity during this period. This amount exceeded 90% of the total 2,521 GWh of load shedding experienced throughout the entirety of 2021. These statistics highlight the substantial increase in electricity cuts implemented by Eskom in the given timeframe, signifying the severity of the energy crisis and its impact on the availability and reliability of electricity supply in South Africa.

In a study conducted by Cole, Elliot, Occhiali, & Strobl (2018) on power outages and firm performance in Sub-Saharan Africa, it was found that the electricity network in many major African cities is relatively inadequate, leading to significant disruptions in power supply. The research highlighted that frequent and unplanned power outages pose a substantial burden on African firms, particularly small businesses with lower total sales compared to medium-sized firms during such outages. Estimates indicate that if the average duration of power outages can be reduced to the level observed in South Africa, firms without generators could experience a remarkable increase in sales, reaching up to 83 percent (Cole et al.,2018).

As per the report African Energy Chamber (AEC) (2023), even though South Africa has a relatively high level of electricity access compared to other sub-Saharan African countries, with an electrification rate of approximately 84%, there has been a significant increase of over 30% in outage hours from 2021 to 2022. This rise in outage hours is a consequence of insufficient investments in electricity generation, leading to an unreliable power supply that adversely affects the country's industries and economic growth. Currently, South Africa is facing a situation where it has to implement regular scheduled rolling blackouts, commonly known as load shedding, lasting between 4.5 and 6 hours per day. The AEC further states that load-shedding costs South Africa over R4 billion a day. Most small businesses are highly reliant on electricity for operations, and load shedding is forcing them to cut production time and drive-up business operating costs, thereby impacting profitability.

The consequences of these power interruptions extend beyond the immediate loss of production or inconvenience experienced by households. Power outages have a significant impact on the production levels of many businesses, leading to a subsequent effect on their financial performance. Small businesses continue to play a crucial role in the economy by driving economic activity and generating employment within local communities. However, to sustain their operations, many small businesses must find alternative ways to continue functioning amidst challenges such as load-shedding. This often entails implementing workforce reduction measures within the business and investing in alternative energy sources, which results in additional operational costs. Load-shedding forces numerous small businesses to temporarily close their doors for a significant portion of the day, leading to adverse effects on their revenue and profits. These challenges are particularly pronounced for small businesses located in townships and rural communities, where access to information, alternative energy solutions, and affordability constraints are often limited.

In other words, power outages have long-term implications for business confidence within an economy and can greatly influence investment decisions. When power interruptions become a frequent and recurring issue, they cannot be treated as isolated anomalies in the regular operations of businesses. Such regular interruptions fundamentally alter the profitability of industries and have a detrimental effect on a country's economic growth. Most productive sectors have been witnessing a significant decline in growth, primarily due to the severe constraints imposed by an unsustainable electricity supply for operations in the South African business environment (Von Ketelhodt and Wöcke, 2008).

Unimaginable, in a country grappling with an unmanageably high unemployment rate, poverty, and income inequality, small businesses in townships have been compelled to reduce their workforce due to load-shedding. Regrettably, South Africa currently holds the unenviable position of having the highest unemployment rate globally, largely attributed to the unsustainability of SMEs (Ranchhod, 2019). As frequent power outages persist, operating costs escalate across various sectors, forcing small business owners to invest in alternative solutions to mitigate the impact. Consequently, these businesses experience decreased production levels, resulting in tighter profit margins and reduced profitability. Clearly, there is a notable correlation exists between electricity and economic growth in South Africa, as highlighted in the study conducted by Bah and Azam in 2017. The economy is facing significant constraints due to the adverse effects of inadequate and unreliable electricity supply (Industrial Development Corporation, 2015).

Challenges and Issues Concerning Power Outages That Lead to the Closure of SMEs

As mentioned before, small businesses are integral to the economy, driving economic activity and job creation. However, they are particularly susceptible to the challenges posed by electricity-related issues. Almeshqaba and Ustunb (2019) highlight that a staggering 1.1 billion people worldwide still lack access to electricity, predominantly in rural areas of developing countries. The provision of reliable electricity can play a crucial role in addressing various challenges related to healthcare, education, social well-being, economic development, and environmental sustainability. Moreover, it has the potential to uplift the income levels of underserved communities, contributing to their overall advancement. A reliable and uninterrupted supply of electricity is essential for small businesses to operate smoothly and maintain their competitiveness. Yet, many small businesses face vulnerabilities and disruptions caused by electricity woes, such as power outages, Limited access to finance, and inadequate infrastructure. These factors significantly impact their ability to sustain operations, meet customer demands, and ensure financial stability. In this context, it is crucial to explore and understand the various factors that contribute to the vulnerability of small businesses to electricity woes.

- Reliance on the national electricity grid

The national electricity grid serves as a vital lifeline for countless industries, businesses, and households around the world. It provides the necessary power to keep economies running, ensuring the smooth functioning of essential services and daily activities. However, the heavy reliance on the national electricity grid also exposes businesses to certain vulnerabilities, particularly when disruptions occur. However, the reliability and capacity of the national electricity grid can be a significant challenge in many countries, including South Africa. Small businesses heavily depend on the national electricity grid to power their operations. From lighting and heating to machinery and equipment, electricity is an indispensable resource that enables these businesses to function effectively. The grid's ability to deliver a consistent and reliable supply of electricity directly impacts the productivity, profitability, and overall sustainability of small enterprises. It can be argued that a significant proportion of SMEs, approximately 90%, rely heavily on a consistent and uninterrupted electricity supply. Furthermore, a substantial number of these businesses, around 70%, reported being significantly affected by power outages.

Certainly, reliance on the national electricity grid comes with its challenges. Infrastructure limitations, aging power plants, transmission bottlenecks, and increasing demand for energy strain the capacity and reliability of the grid. As a result, power outages, voltage fluctuations, and load-shedding become recurrent issues that disrupt business operations, leading to significant economic losses. When the grid experiences disruptions, small businesses bear the immediate consequences. Production processes come to a halt, causing delays in order fulfillment and missed deadlines. Moreover, perishable goods may spoil, further exacerbating financial losses. Customer dissatisfaction and reputational damage can ensue, as businesses struggle to meet commitments and maintain service standards. Additionally, the reliance on the national electricity grid exposes businesses to electricity price fluctuations, which can impact their cost structure and profit margins. South African businesses must reduce their dependence on the national electricity grid and take proactive steps to invest in alternative power systems that offer consistent and reliable energy supply. By doing so, not only will they enhance business continuity, but they will also move closer to achieving their sustainability objectives.

- Limited access to finance for alternative energy solutions

In South Africa, the small business landscape is facing significant challenges, with a concerning rate of failure reaching 75 percent, which is the highest in the world (Lekhanya, 2016). Additionally, the growth rate of small businesses in the country remains stagnant, posing further obstacles to their success and sustainability. According to Kgosana (2013), a significant number of small businesses in South Africa face a challenging start, with a high failure rate within the first year of operation. This trend results in only two out of seven businesses successfully continuing beyond their initial year. Furthermore, even for those businesses that manage to survive this critical period, there are ongoing risks to their financial sustainability (Ortiz-de-Mandojana and Bansal, 2016). Access to reliable and affordable energy is crucial for businesses to thrive and contribute to economic growth. However, many businesses, especially SMEs, face challenges in securing financing for alternative energy solutions. Unsurprisingly, access to finance has been identified as a key limitation for the long-term viability of SMEs (Ye and Kulathunga, 2019). This section explores the implications of limited access to finance for alternative energy solutions on businesses, including its impact on operations, sustainability, and overall economic development.

Limited access to finance for alternative energy solutions can be attributed to several barriers faced by businesses. These barriers include high initial costs, lack of collateral, and risk Perception. Implementing alternative energy solutions, such as solar panels or wind turbines, often requires a significant upfront investment. SMEs may struggle to secure the necessary capital to cover these initial costs. Traditional financial institutions typically require collateral when providing loans to businesses. SMEs, particularly those in their early stages or with limited assets, may lack the necessary collateral to secure financing for alternative energy projects. In certain circumstances, some financial institutions may perceive renewable energy projects as high-risk investments, leading to reluctance in providing loans or imposing high-interest rates.

Likewise, the limited access to finance for alternative energy solutions has various implications for businesses such as higher operating costs, sustainability challenges, and missed opportunities among others. Firstly, businesses relying on traditional energy sources face rising electricity prices and are vulnerable to supply disruptions. Alternative energy solutions offer cost savings in the long run but require upfront investment. Without access to finance, businesses continue to bear high operating costs, impacting their competitiveness and profitability. Secondly, SMEs striving to embrace sustainable practices and reduce their carbon footprint may face hurdles in adopting alternative energy solutions. Limited access to finance hampers their ability to invest in renewable technologies, hindering progress toward environmental sustainability. Lastly, the inability to access finance for alternative energy solutions limits innovation and hampers business growth. Businesses that could benefit from transitioning to renewable energy may miss out on opportunities to enhance efficiency, attract environmentally conscious customers, and tap into emerging markets.

The limited adoption of alternative energy solutions due to financing constraints has broader economic implications including energy security risks, environmental impact, and missed job creation opportunities. Reliance on traditional energy sources can lead to energy supply shortages and vulnerabilities. This affects overall economic stability and hinders long-term economic development. Inadequate adoption of renewable energy sources contributes to increased greenhouse gas emissions and environmental degradation, exacerbating climate change challenges. The renewable energy sector offers significant potential for job creation. According to Mzini and Muhiya (2014), energy plays a central role in the achievement of the United Nations (UN) Sustainable Development Goals (SDGs). However, limited financing for alternative energy solutions hampers the growth of this sector and its associated employment opportunities. In general, limited access to finance for alternative energy solutions poses significant challenges for businesses, particularly SMEs, and has broader implications for economic development and environmental sustainability. To address these issues, collaborative efforts between financial institutions, government agencies, and business support organizations are crucial. Facilitating access to affordable financing options, providing incentives for renewable energy investments, and raising awareness about the benefits of alternative energy solutions are essential steps toward a more sustainable and resilient business environment.

- Inadequate government support for small businesses

Insufficient government support for small businesses is a pressing concern that hinders their growth and development. Small businesses play a crucial role in driving economic activity and job creation, yet they often face numerous challenges and barriers that can impede their success. the lack of adequate government support programs and initiatives tailored specifically to the needs of small businesses. These enterprises require targeted assistance in various areas, such as access to finance, business training and mentorship, market development, and regulatory compliance. However, the existing support mechanisms often fall short of providing comprehensive and sustained assistance.

Moreover, bureaucratic hurdles and complex regulatory frameworks can create additional burdens for small businesses. Excessive red tape, licensing requirements, and cumbersome administrative procedures can discourage entrepreneurship and hinder the growth potential of small enterprises. Simplifying and streamlining these processes would greatly benefit small businesses and encourage their growth. Additionally, the availability of affordable financing options remains a significant challenge for small businesses. Limited access to capital restricts their ability to invest in technology, equipment, and talent, hindering their competitiveness and growth potential.

The government could play a pivotal role in addressing this issue by implementing policies that facilitate easier access to credit and financial support for small businesses. van Rhyn (2023) suggests that Government support programs, industry associations, and networks play a vital role in aiding, guiding, and resources to small businesses. These initiatives can offer funding opportunities, mentorship programs, and access to business development services. Furthermore, the government's role in creating an enabling business environment cannot be overstated. According to van Rhyn (2023), small business owners frequently encounter difficulties when attempting to access markets beyond their immediate communities. The lack of resources and networks poses a significant challenge for them to expand their customer base and tap into new markets.

Clear and consistent policies, coupled with a favorable regulatory framework, can foster an atmosphere conducive to small business growth. This includes measures such as tax incentives, streamlined licensing procedures, and support for innovation and research and development. To address the issue of inadequate government support, policymakers should prioritize the needs of small businesses and work closely with industry stakeholders to develop comprehensive strategies. This entails allocating sufficient resources to support programs, enhancing coordination among relevant government agencies, and actively engaging with the small business community to identify their specific needs and challenges. By strengthening government support for small businesses, we can unlock their full potential as engines of economic growth, job creation, and innovation. A supportive and nurturing environment will enable small businesses to thrive, contribute to the economy, and ultimately foster sustainable development for the nation.

The Challenges Faced by Different Sectors of Small Businesses

Power outages pose significant challenges for small businesses across various sectors. The lack of a reliable electricity supply can disrupt operations, impact productivity, and lead to financial losses. It is evident that the absence of affordable electricity access is associated with a range of issues, including persistent poverty, unemployment, low living standards, food insecurity, and gender disparities, especially in underserved communities, particularly in rural areas (McPeak et al., 2011). O'Flynn (2020) states that South Africa is currently facing a growing demand for energy, particularly electricity, across all sectors of human activities, the economy, and businesses. The increasing reliance on electricity as a vital resource is evident as it plays a crucial role in powering various industries, supporting economic growth, and facilitating the smooth functioning of businesses. Meeting this rising energy demand has become a pressing need for the country in order to sustain and enhance its overall development and ensure the continued success of its businesses. This section briefly explores the specific power outage challenges faced by different sectors of small businesses and their implications.

Retail Sector: Power outages in the retail sector can result in interrupted sales transactions, inability to operate electronic payment systems, and spoilage of perishable goods. Small retail businesses heavily rely on electricity for lighting, refrigeration, and electronic equipment, making power disruptions particularly detrimental to their daily operations and customer experience.

Manufacturing Sector: Power outages can significantly affect small manufacturing businesses by causing production delays, equipment downtime, and potential damage to machinery. These disruptions can lead to decreased output, increased production costs, and missed delivery deadlines, impacting customer satisfaction and overall profitability.

Service Sector: Service-oriented small businesses, such as salons, spas, and restaurants, heavily depend on electricity for lighting, heating, cooling, and equipment operation. Power outages can disrupt scheduled appointments, impact customer service quality, and lead to financial losses. In some cases, businesses may need to reschedule or compensate clients, affecting their reputation and customer loyalty.

Healthcare Sector: Power outages in the healthcare sector can have severe consequences. Small healthcare facilities, clinics, and pharmacies require an uninterrupted power supply to maintain critical equipment, refrigerate medications, and provide life-saving treatments. Power disruptions can compromise patient care, lead to medication spoilage, and pose risks to individuals who rely on medical devices.

Information Technology Sector: Small businesses in the information technology sector heavily rely on electricity to power servers, computer systems, and data centers. Power outages can result in service disruptions, data loss, and potential damage to equipment. These challenges can impact the delivery of digital services, compromise data security, and result in financial losses.

Food and Hospitality Sector: Restaurants, cafes, and food service businesses face significant challenges during power outages. The loss of electricity can affect food storage, food preparation, and cooking equipment, leading to temporary closures, loss of inventory, and dissatisfied customers. In addition, power outages can impact food safety standards and compliance regulations.

The load shedding has had a significant negative impact on the poultry industry, leading to a potential shortage of chicken in the market. Poultry suppliers across the country are facing challenges such as high mortality rates among chickens, difficulties in timely slaughter, and increased costs of feeds and fuel. These challenges arise from power outages, which disrupt the necessary operations and conditions for maintaining poultry production. Without a stable electricity supply, suppliers struggle to provide the appropriate environment and care for the chickens, resulting in higher mortality rates. Additionally, the inability to slaughter chickens on time further exacerbates the situation, as it disrupts the supply chain and reduces the availability of chicken products. Moreover, the rising costs of feeds and fuel, which are needed to generate power during outages, add to the financial burden faced by poultry suppliers. These combined factors create a significant challenge for the poultry industry, leading to concerns about potential shortages of chicken and eggs in the market.

Ultimately, power outage challenges affect small businesses across various sectors, posing significant disruptions to their operations, customer service, and financial stability. To mitigate these challenges, small businesses should consider investing in backup power solutions, such as generators or uninterrupted power supply (UPS) systems. Governments and utility providers should prioritize infrastructure improvements, invest in renewable energy sources, and implement measures to minimize power outages. Additionally, support programs and resources should be available to assist small businesses in preparing for and managing power outage situations. By addressing these challenges, small businesses can enhance their resilience, maintain productivity, and continue contributing to economic growth.

Effective Strategies for Addressing Power Shortages and Supporting SME Growth in Emerging Markets

A reliable supply of electricity is crucial for the smooth functioning and productivity of small businesses. However, in many countries, including South Africa, electricity woes such as power outages and unreliable service pose significant challenges to the operations and growth of small businesses. According to Gosa (2012), sustainable renewable energy sources and energy efficiency measures are highly regarded for their inherent advantages, such as their limitless availability, long-term viability, and the potential to provide hot water access to previously underserved populations. These sustainable energy solutions not only contribute to reducing electricity consumption but also play a crucial role in mitigating CO_2 emissions, thus promoting environmental sustainability. By embracing renewable energy and energy-efficient technologies, societies can enhance their energy security, reduce reliance on finite resources, and foster a cleaner and more sustainable future. This section briefly discusses effective strategies and measures that can be undertaken to mitigate the impact of electricity woes on small businesses.

Investing in Alternative Energy Solutions: One of the key approaches to reducing the impact of electricity woes is for small businesses to invest in alternative energy solutions. This includes installing solar panels, utilizing battery storage systems, or exploring other renewable energy sources. By diversifying their energy sources, businesses can maintain operations during power outages and ensure a consistent power supply, reducing disruptions and potential losses.

Energy Efficiency and Conservation: Small businesses can mitigate the impact of electricity woes by adopting energy-efficient practices. This includes using energy-efficient appliances and equipment, implementing lighting controls, and optimizing energy usage. By reducing energy consumption, businesses can lower their reliance on the grid and minimize the impact of power outages. Moreover, energy conservation efforts contribute to cost savings and environmental sustainability.

Business Continuity Planning: Developing robust business continuity plans is essential for small businesses to navigate electricity-related challenges effectively. These plans should outline alternative power sources, backup systems, and protocols to follow during power outages. By having contingency measures in place, businesses can minimize disruptions, ensure customer satisfaction, and maintain productivity.

Collaborations and Partnerships: Small businesses can consider forming collaborations and partnerships to address electricity woes collectively. This can involve sharing resources, such as backup power generators, with neighboring businesses or pooling funds to invest in alternative energy solutions. Collaborative efforts strengthen resilience and create a support network to tackle shared challenges.

Government Support and Policy: Government support and favorable policies play a crucial role in mitigating the impact of electricity woes on small businesses. Governments can provide financial incentives, subsidies, or tax breaks for businesses investing in alternative energy solutions. Additionally, policy reforms can be enacted to improve the reliability of the national grid and address infrastructure shortcomings. Engaging with government bodies and advocating for supportive policies can greatly benefit small businesses.

Education and Training: Providing education and training programs on energy management and conservation can empower small business owners and employees to adopt sustainable practices. By raising awareness about energy efficiency and the benefits of alternative energy sources, businesses can become more proactive in mitigating the impact of electricity woes. Government agencies, industry associations, and energy service providers can play a pivotal role in delivering such training initiatives.

The challenges posed by electricity woes on small businesses require proactive measures and collaborative efforts to mitigate their impact. By investing in alternative energy solutions, adopting energy-efficient practices, developing business continuity plans, forming collaborations, and advocating for government support, small businesses can enhance their resilience and reduce vulnerabilities. Additionally, education and training initiatives play a crucial role in promoting energy management practices. By implementing these strategies, small businesses can navigate electricity woes more effectively and sustain their operations even in challenging circumstances.

CONCLUSION

In conclusion, the electricity crises in South Africa have had a detrimental impact on small and medium-sized enterprises (SMEs) across the country. Power outages and unreliable electricity supply have led to decreased productivity, increased operational costs, and even business shutdowns. The vulnerability of SMEs to these electricity woes is evident, with high failure rates and limited access to alternative energy solutions. The occurrence of load shedding has resulted in a decrease in the operational assets of numerous businesses, compelling them to operate at diminished capacity. This decline in operational capacity has had a direct negative impact on productivity, causing repercussions throughout South Africa's economy. Furthermore, the energy crisis has had a deterrent effect on potential foreign investors, impeding investments in the country. This reduced level of investment further exacerbates the challenges faced by the economy, hindering economic growth and impeding job creation. The combined effect of decreased productivity and limited investments intensifies the gravity of the situation, necessitating urgent measures to address and overcome the energy crisis for the betterment of the economy and the welfare of its citizens.

To mitigate the impact, SMEs need to explore ways to reduce their reliance on the national grid and invest in sustainable energy sources. Moreover, government support and access to finance for alternative energy solutions are crucial for the long-term sustainability of SMEs. Addressing these challenges and finding solutions will be vital for the survival and growth of SMEs in South Africa, ultimately contributing to the overall economic development of the nation. By supporting SMEs, South Africa can build a more resilient and inclusive economy that benefits all sectors of society. On the other hand, companies must think of new ways to improve their businesses to create a competitive advantage.

REFERENCES

African Energy Chamber (AEC). (2023). *The State of African Energy 2023*. AEC. https://africa-energy-portal.org/sites/default/files/2023-01/AEC-Outlook-2023_b.pdf

Almeshqaba, F., & Ustunb, T. S. (2019). Lessons learned from rural electrification initiatives in developing countries: Insights for technical, social, financial and public policy aspects. *Renewable & Sustainable Energy Reviews, 102*, 35–53. doi:10.1016/j.rser.2018.11.035

Aterido, R., Hallward-Driemeier, M., & Pages, C. (2009). *Big constraints to small firms' growth? business environment and employment growth across firms.* (Policy Research Working Paper Series 5032) The World Bank.

Bartlett, C. (1983). MNCs: Get off the reorganizational merry-go-round. *Harvard Business Review,* (March-April), 138–145.

Bhorat, H., Asmal, Z., & Lilenstein, K. & Van der zee K. (2018). *SMMEs in South Africa: Understanding the constraints on growth and performance.* (Development Policy Research Unit (DPRU) Working Paper 201802).University of Cape Town

Bruwer, J. (2020). Fortifying South African small medium and micro-enterprise sustainability through a proposed internal control framework: The sustenance framework. *Expert Journal of Business and Management, 8*(2), 147–158.

Cole, M. A., Elliot, R. J. R., Occhiali, G., & Strobl, E. (2018, September). Power outages and firm performance in Sub-Saharan Africa, ‖. *Journal of Development Economics, 134*, 150–159. Advance online publication. doi:10.1016/j.jdeveco.2018.05.003

Department of Minerals and Energy. (2008). *National Response to South Africa's Electricity Shortage.* DME. http://www.dme.gov.za/energy/efficiency_sectors.stm

Escribano, A., Guasch, J. L., & Pena, J. (2009). *Assessing the Impact of Infrastructure Constraints on Firm Productivity in Africa.* (Working Paper 9). Africa Infrastructure Sector Diagnostic, World Bank. Washington D.C.

Falkena, H., Abedian, I., von Blottnitz, M., Coovadia, C., Davel, G., Madungandaba, J., Masilela, E., & Rees, S. (2001). *SMEs access to finance in South Africa – supply side regulatory review.* Policy Board for Financial Services and Regulation, South Africa: Pretoria. www.treasury.gov.za/documents/me/p1 24.pdf

Godinho, C. (2023). The Eskom crisis update: Where we are now. *Energy for Growth.* https://energyforgrowth.org/article/the-eskom-crisis-update-where-we-are-now/

Gosa, T. (2012). *Sustainable energy and policy design on the energy transition to renewable energy systems in Stellenbosch, case study: Stellenbosch solar water heater bylaw.* https://scholar.sun.ac.za/handle/10019.1/71957

Gündüz, N., Küfeoğly, S., & Lehtonen, M. (2017). Impacts of natural disasters on Swedish electric power policy: A case study. *Sustainability (Basel), 9*(2), 230. doi:10.3390/su9020230

IMF. (2019). *Enhancing the Role of SMEs in the Arab World—Some Key Considerations.* IMF. https://www.imf.org/en/Publications/Policy-Papers/Issues/2019/12/13/Enhancing-the-Role-of-SMEs-in-the-Arab-World-Some-Key-Considerations-48873

Industrial Development Corporation. (2015). *Economic Overview of the Department of Research and Information: Recent developments in the global and South African economies.* IDC. www.idc.co.za/images/downloadfiles/economicoverviews/economic_overview_jun_2015.pdf

Kgosana, C. (2013). *Small businesses failure rate high.* Sowetanlive. https://www.sowetanlive.co.za/news/businessnews/2013/05/16/small-businesses-failure-rate-high

Langa, M. T., & Govender, K. K. (2019). The need for agile relationship lending between small business and banks, towards a more engaged relationship: A case study in Khayelitsha, South Africa. *Asian Business Research Journal, 4*(1), 29–34. doi:10.20448/journal.518.2019.41.29.34

Lekhanya, L. M. (2016). *Determinants of Survival and Growth of Small and Medium Enterprises in Rural KwaZulu-Natal* [Ph.D. Thesis, Cape Town: University of the Western Cape].

McKinsey. (2016). *Why customer analytics matter.* McKinsey Global Institute.

McPeak, J. G., Little, P. D., & Doss, C. R. (2011). *Risk and social change in an African rural economy: livelihoods in pastoralist communities.* Routledge Taylor & Francis. doi:10.4324/9780203805824

Mzini, L., & Lukamba-Muhiya, T. (2014). An assessment of electricity supply and demand at Emfuleni Local Municipality. *Journal of Energy in Southern Africa, 25*(3), 20–26. doi:10.17159/2413-3051/2014/v25i3a2654

O'Flynn, J. (2020). Confronting the big challenges of our time: Making a difference during and after. *COVID, 19.* https://www.tandfonline.com/doi/full/10.1080/14719037.2020.1820273

OECD. (2017). *Enhancing the Contributions of SMEs in a Global and Digitalised Economy.* OECD. https://www.oecd.org/industry/C-MIN-2017-8-EN.pdf

Ortiz-de-Mandojana, N., & Bansal, P. (2016). The long-term benefits of organizational resilience through sustainable business practices. *Strategic Management Journal, 37*(8), 1615–1631. doi:10.1002/smj.2410

Osabohien, R., Worgwu, H., & al-Faryan, M. A. S. (2023). Social entrepreneurship, technology diffusion and future employment in Nigeria. *Social Enterprise Journal, 19*(1), 40–50. doi:10.1108/SEJ-03-2022-0032

Oseni, M. O. (2012). Power Outages and the Costs of Unsupplied Electricity: Evidence from Backup Generation among Firms in Africa. *Proceedings of the USAEE 2012.* Austin: Internation Association of Energy Economics. USAEE. https://www.usaee.org/usaee2012/submissions/OnlineProceedings/IEE%20PAPER%20FRST%20YEAR%20EDITED%20LAST%201%20LATEST.pdf

Ranchhod, V. (2019). *Why is South Africa's unemployment rate so high?* Ground Up. https://www.groundup.org.za/article/why-south-africas-unemployment-rate-so-high/.

Rud, J. P. (2012). Electricity Provision and Industrial development: Evidence from India. *Journal of Development Economics, 97*(2), 352–367. doi:10.1016/j.jdeveco.2011.06.010

SEDA (Small Enterprise Development Agency). (2018). *Annual report 2017/2018.* Unpublished Report, RP368/2018, Pretoria.

SEDA (Small Enterprise Development Agency). (2019). *SMME Quarterly Update 3rd Quarter 2018.* SEDA. http://www.seda.org.za/Publications/Publications/SMME%20Quarterly,%202018-Q3.pdf

Smit, W. (2017). *SMMEs contribute 36% to economy.* IOL. https://www.iol.co.za/business-report/entrepreneurs/smmes-contribute-36-to-economy-8269623

South Africa. (1996). Small Business Act, No, 102 of 1966. South Africa: Pretoria.

Stats, S. A. (2023). Bey*ond unemployment – Time-Related Underemployment in the SA labour market.* https://www.statssa.gov.za/?p=16312#:~:text=Quarter%2Dto%2Dquarter%20changes%20indicate,9%25%20in%20Q1%3A2023

Tushman, M., Newman, W., & Romanelli, E. (1986). Managing the unsteady pace of organizational evolution. *California Management Review, 29*(Fall), 29–44. doi:10.2307/41165225

van Rhyn, L. (2023). *Challenges Faced by Small Business Corporations in South Africa.* Thrive CFO. https://thrivecfo.cloud/challenges-faced-by-small-business-corporations-in-southafrica/#Government_Support_Programs_for_Small_Businesses.

Viljoen, J., Blaauw, D., & Schenck, C. (2019). The opportunities and value-adding activities of buy-back centres in South Africa's recycling industry: A value chain analysis. Local Economy, London South Bank University.

Von ketelhodt, A. & Wocke, A. (2008). The impact of electricity crises on the consumption behaviour of small and medium enterprises. *J. energy South Africa, 19*(1), 4-12.

World Bank. (2017). *What's Happening in the Missing Middle? Lessons from Financing.* World Bank. https://www.worldbank.org/en/topic/financialsector/publication/whats-happening-in-the-missing-middle-lessons-from-financing-smes

Writer, S. (2022). *South Africa's horror year of load shedding – here's how it compares.* Business Tech. https://businesstech.co.za/news/energy/630667/south-africas-horror-year-of-load-shedding-heres-how-it-compares/

Ye, J., & Kulathunga, K. M. M. C. B. (2019). How does financial literacy promote sustainability in SMEs? A developing country perspective. *Sustainability (Basel), 11*(10), 2990. doi:10.3390/su11102990

Zwane, S. (2023). *Poultry sector suffering as loadshedding persists.* Zimoja. https://www.zimoja.co.za/articles/poultry-sector-suffering-as-load-shedding-persist

Chapter 7
A Study on the Impact of Digitalization on SME Growth

Gargi Malhotra
https://orcid.org/0009-0008-8105-8293
Lovely Professional University, India

Mridula Mishra
https://orcid.org/0000-0002-5585-4236
Lovely Professional University, India

ABSTRACT

Small and medium-sized enterprises are a critical component of the global economy, contributing significantly to job creation, innovation, and economic growth. The emergence of digitalization has significantly changed the business landscape leading to both challenges and opportunities for SMEs. The study provides new insights into how digital platform service providers may assist SMEs in their transformation and competitiveness. This chapter aims to provide a comprehensive review and analysis of the impact of digitalization on SMEs growth. The study explores the various aspects of digitalization, its effects on SMEs, and strategies that SMEs may use to take advantage of digital technologies to enhance growth and competitiveness. A total of fifteen papers are reviewed; their methodology and findings are summarized. It shows that digital transformation ensures easy accessibility of the business significantly affects customer relationships. The results further indicate online selling and digital marketing as the leading digital platforms successfully implemented by most SMEs.

INTRODUCTION

Digitalization is the incorporation of digital technology into daily life, which includes the computerization of systems and employment for greater convenience and accessibility. Small and medium-sized enterprises (SMEs) have unique qualities that set them apart from bigger corporations. For example, more adaptability and agility in responding to changing situations, limited resources, and specialisation capacities (Kraft et al., 2022). To achieve improved operational efficiency and a stronger emphasis on the customer, SMEs

DOI: 10.4018/979-8-3693-0111-1.ch007

are exploring digitalization initiatives to replace their ageing infrastructure with IIoT-ready networks. (Lee et al., 2017). This includes implementing certain digital technology in all aspects of production, planning, and design processes. With real-time data gathered from production and quality equipment available on the shop floor, quality iterations involving the phases of develop-test-analyse-implement can be simulated and hence validated in a digital environment. (Buer et al., 2018) Although it is critical to establish methods for systematically monitoring SMEs' performance in numerous elements of the digitalization, ensuring their survival and competitiveness, these traits are reflected in the digitalization process. SMEs could improve their business processes by utilising new digital technology as an effective method of disseminating information to a target audience at the point of request, without significantly increasing costs. Furthermore, one of the most significant shifts in human contact is the spread of online social networks. Along with its economic significance, digitalization of SMEs directly incorporates the social and environmental pillars of sustainability. Small and Medium Enterprises (SMEs) in the growth process mall and medium-sized businesses (SMEs) are considered as an important component of economic growth in India. It is crucial that SMEs adapt to this new technology to take advantage of its benefits, gain access to the market, and identify new business opportunities. Small and medium-sized businesses (SMEs) are thought to be responsible for 80 percent of global economic growth and make significant contributions to national economies. It was discovered in countries like Germany, China, India, and Brazil 4000 SMEs that had previously used digital technology produced jobs nearly twice as quickly as other SMEs. Furthermore, SMEs that trade globally are more optimistic in the present and future business climate and have better job generation potential. From it was observed that digitalization favourably improves the worldwide performance of SMEs. Digitalisation has changed the orientation of doing business. The entire process, from the acquisition of raw materials to production to delivery and consumption, has changed It has not only created buzz but has also brought about a significant change in how business is conducted. SMES are the engine of the Indian economy, yet they are up against fierce competition from international corporations. They experience themselves as small fish in a vast ocean, where their continued survival is in doubt. Also, SMEs are now struggling to survive in this cutthroat marketplace, they must alter their strategies as well as the way they sell their goods and services to consumers. Organisations have taken the first steps towards this revolution by focusing on the advantages such as an increase in sales and profitability due to increased reach, an increase in market share, the creation and building of brand awareness at a lower cost, quick feedback that allows companies to incorporate requested changes by customers, assistance with environment analysis and decision-making, and more satisfied customers as well as a more valuable customer insight. (Bouwman, et al., 2019).

But several difficulties are making the adoption of digitalization extremely difficult. Organisations aren't prepared to make the investment because the setup and reengineering costs are quite high and the returns aren't entirely quantified. Although the long-term benefits of digitalization are difficult to quantify, their impact on productivity and efficiency can be recognised to some extent. But even so, by altering the paradigms of supply chain management and integrated marketing communication, digitalization can expand the range and size of production. The largest obstacle to integrating any new technology is the lack of skill and information, lack of awareness or limited awareness among the target beneficiaries about the various support tools, slow decision-making, and aversion to risk. Employees are also quite resistant to change and prefer the way things are set up; this may be due to a fear of losing their jobs. Companies should provide appropriate training and good communication throughout the channel to win the trust of the workforce to solve these types of problems. As a result of the foregoing, we can conclude that digitalization is necessary for the present and has given rise to new rivals. To succeed in this changing environment, organisations must take aggressive measures to obtain this new technology (Venkatesh & Kumari, 2015).

This chapter explorers various digitalization strategies that SMEs have employed in different industries and the impact of digitalization on the growth of SMEs.

Literature Review

The term "digitalization" refers to the organisation of a wide range of social life areas around digital media and communication infrastructures. In this paper it is discussed that how digitalization has affected business performance.

Digital technologies have a substantial impact on practically every organisation and have made it possible for businesses to collaborate, store and analyse information, and provide better customer service. They have greatly improved the ability to achieve service convenience and have had a significant impact on customer service performance (Setia et al., 2013). According to (Mazzarol, 2015) Digital technology, and their application to e-commerce, e-business and digital marketing have a significant impact on business at a global level. The expansion of digital technology represents both a tremendous opportunity and a potentially serious threat to SMEs. The opportunity comes from SMEs' capacity to gain access to digital technology earlier only available to large organizations and to use these to compete in domestic and international markets. However, the concern arises from SMEs losing business by not embracing the opportunities and becoming inefficient in increasingly digital and online marketplaces. Digitalization offers many advantages, including improved delivery, improved control over operational activities and their effects, quicker response times, and better customer service when interacting with external stakeholders (Mazurek, 2019). Digitization also influences the effectiveness, quality, and stability of implemented processes, resulting in a higher level of delivery. Although the digitalization of enterprises is technology based, the concept of digital transformation is not so much about technology as it is about people. Infrastructure, the business environment, and the digital skills of business owners and staff all needed to alter for the Polish SMEs to successfully embrace the digital revolution. (Sledziewska et al., 2015). Enterprises are currently undergoing a digital transformation that is all about remote work opportunities (employee mobility), online activities (e-business, e-commerce), low transaction costs, and coordinated activities. These are all made possible by the digitization of the information sent and the ability to provide services by electronic means (e-payments), as well as the ability to confirm the validity of documents. (Vásquez et al., 2018). According to Autio et al. (2018), The process of digitization is socio-technical, and it calls for complementary knowledge-based assets, such as organisational and human capital" for SMEs to successfully adopt information and communication technology (ICT). These resources give SMEs more power, reducing the likelihood that they would become overly reliant on any one technology or platform. Additionally, it is suggested that "the lack of investment in complementary knowledge may have slowed the diffusion of technology to smaller and younger firms." The statement "is fundamentally not about technology, but about strategy" in regards to digital transformation. agreeing that "digital transformation is multidisciplinary by nature, as it involves changes in strategy, organisation, information technology, supply chains, and marketing. Digital transformation is the integration of digital technology throughout all functional areas of the business, completely changing how work is done and how consumers are served. The process of digital transformation is followed by the full business model change, and it need a focused digital strategy, a supportive ecosystem, and digital talents. Additionally, because of the cultural shift, businesses must constantly question the status quo. As is, try new things and learn to be okay with failure.

Findings

Table 1 below summarises a main finding from the diverse literature review.

Table 1. Literature on digital transformation and SMEs

Study	Design	Methods	Findings
Kraft et al. (2022)	A study looked at Swiss SMEs' digital transformation.	Multiple case study.	Digital transformation demandes change in SME management policiers.
Isensee et al. (2020)	This study aimed to integrate SME organizational culture, environmental sustainability, and digitization.	Systematic literature review and meta-analysis.	According to the authors, there is a two-way relationship between organizational agility and digitization.
Li et al. (2017)	This study examines how small and medium-sized business owners with limited resources promotes digital transformation.	Qualitative research.	It provides information on how digital platform service providers can help SMEs to transform and compete.
Eller et al. (2020) Scuotto et al. (2021) Garzoni et al. (2020) Starkov, (2023) Mazzaro (2020)	The study examines three SME resources: IT, personnel skills, and digital strategy on digitalization. This study provides distinct contributions to the existing SME literature on labor-intensive SMEs operating in Europe. This study analyses how digital technologies trigger changes in the business process of manufacturing SMEs in the Apulia Region (South Italy). The study focused on the issue of digital transformation of business models. The study shows the impact of digital technology on small to medium enterprises (SMEs), in particular e-commerce, e-marketing and e-business implementation and strategy.	Survey analysis on 193 SMEs. Regression analysis. Qualitative approach based on the case study. Qualitative research. Literature review	The study shows that Digitalization affects performance, mediated through IT. This study shows the relevance of individual digital capabilities for SMEs' growth and innovation performance. The study identifies a four levels approach for the understanding of digital transformation of SMEs. The study also correlates he level of digitalization with SMEs' engagement through a four levels model. The study shows that there is a need for digitization process of the entire value chain in the structure of the main value-creating processes and supporting processes. The study shows that despite many potential costs and risks, it is feasible for even the smallest of firms to engage successfully with digital technologies.

Continued on following page

Table 1. Continued

Study	Design	Methods	Findings
Mubarak et al (2019) Xiaoyan et al. (2022). North et al. (2019) Tarute & Gatautis (2013) Foroudi et al. (2017) Denicolai et al, (2021) Ritala et al. (2021) B. Ramdani et al, (2021) Pham & Vu, (2022) A. Lutfi et al, (2022) A. Mechman et al, (2022) Pardiman et al (2022) N. Omrani et al ; (2022) I.Melo et al, (2023) Angela& Diana (2022) X.Zhang et.al (2022) N. Zahoor et.al (2023) D. Vrontis et al, (2022) N. Hasan et al (2022) S. Frimpong et. Al (2022) S. Philbina et al, (2022) X. Teng et al (2022) A. Telukdarie et al (2022) Brodny& Tutak (2022)	This study investigated the impact of industry 4.0 technologies including big data, CPS, IoT, and interoperability on the performance of SMEs. This study attempts to identify the influencing factors that determine their sustainable development to provide reference for academic researchers and industrial decision makers. The purpose of this paper is to provide guidance to SMEs to sense and seize digitally enabled growth opportunities. The aim of this study is to analyze the literature on potential direct and indirect effects of ICT on SMEs performance and to identify those that could determine a business success. This study examines to what extent does digital technology influence marketing capability which leads to companies' growth. The study explores whether the relationship between digitalization and internationalization is affected by sustainability readiness. This study examines the role of employees' individual-level entrepreneurial orientation (IEO) in terms of proactiveness, risk-taking, and innovativeness, and their relational capital within the organization, on their performance in achieving organizations' digital strategy goals. The study developed a theoretical framework which shows digital innovation in SMEs is driven by a configuration of antecedents, goes through different stages of innovation process, and leads to organizational and business performance outcomes. The study aims to dispense a concrete and coherent picture on the role of digitalization of accounting information (DOAI) among the small and medium-sized enterprises (SMEs). The study examines the Influence of Digital Accounting System Usage on SMEs Performance. The study describes the Relationship of digital marketing and e-commerce in enhancing SMEs performance. The study analyzes the impact of financial capital, social capital, and business digitalization in improving business sustainability in SMEs. The study aims to identify and analyze factors determining the adoption of digital technologies in SMEs. The study aims to describe and analyze the state-of-art performance evaluations of digital transformation in SMEs, mainly focusing on performance measurement. The study examines the extent to which the use of various forms of digital technology could stimulate the growth of SME performance. The purpose of this study is to discover the key factors of the digital transformation in SMEs and explore their interaction mechanisms. The study illustrates the importance of digital transformation for small and medium-sized enterprises (SMEs), and how digital literacy and technology interact with managerial attributes. The study determine how adopting different modern digital technologies can create value for small and medium enterprises (SMEs). This study examines the importance of embedding digital technology into business models among SMEs. The study analyses SMEs' digital platform knowledge and utilization. It also examines the relationship between financial literacy, access to digital finance, and SME performance. The study examines how digital transformation can enable SMEs to achieve sustainable development. The study examines impact of digital transformation on SMEs performance. The study tries to find. out the opportunities and challenges of digitalization for SME's The aim of the study was to determine the level of digital maturity of SMEs.	Multiple regression Structural equation model Descriptive Analysis Systematic, logic and comparative analysis Qualitative data analysis Empirical analysis Empirical Analysis Systematic literature review A three-pronged methodology was used in this research, namely, literature review, expert interviews and self-administered survey. Self-administered survey questionnaire Quantitative data analysais Survey technique using Structured questionnaire Empirical analysis Systematic literature review Empirical data analysis Structural equation modeling Moderated mediation model was tested survey data. Resource-based view (RBV) and dynamic capability view (DCV) theories Resource-Based View Theory (RBV) Quantitative research approach Systematic literature review Empirical analysis Quantitative research Principal Component Analysis	The study shows that big data, cyber physical systems, and interoperability have a significant positive impact to improve business performance, while the insignificant effect of internet of things was revealed. It found that for SMEs, focusing on investing in digital technologies, employee digital skills, and digital transformation strategies are three key factors that are beneficial for digital transformation, thus helping to improve performance and maintain their sustainable development. The study shows that the DIGROW framework is well understood by SME owners or managers and contributes to a comprehensive perception of digitalization challenges and potentials. The study shows that ICT has impact on the improvement of external and internal communication and that for best performances. Digital technology has an enormous impact on marketing capabilities, which leads to the development of core competences in UK firms. Artificial Intelligence readiness positively influences the international performance of SMEs. Moreover, it is found that digitalization and sustainability are positively related, but they turn to be competing growth paths when the firm internationalizes. It is found that individual proactiveness and risk-taking orientations (which load empirically as one construct) positively affected employee performance for three of the four digital strategy goals. The study shows that digital innovation in SMEs has several outcomes including profitability, competitiveness and internationalization. The outcomes analysis highlighted that there were significant positive associations between the hypothesized constructs. The study reveals that compatibility, organizational readiness, top management support and government support all had significant effects on Digital accounting system usage, which, in turn, had a positive and significant effect on SMEs performance. The study finds that there is positive effect of digital marketing and e-commerce variables on SME's performance. The study found that business digitization which can improve business sustainability for SMEs. The study shows that the technology context (IT infrastructure and digital tools) along with the existing level of innovation are the main drivers that act as steppingstones in digital technology adoption in SMEs. A conceptual framework is proposed by using literature review based on evaluations of digital transformation in SMEs. The result of this study shows that the level of digitalization of SMEs has increased, especially in recent years. Also, digitization of SMEs can increase their performance. The study shows that technological and environmental factors have a positive impact on organizational capabilities, and then promote the success of digital transformation of SMEs. The study conclude that managers' digital literacy (MDL) impacts digital transformation through the usage of digital technologies in SMEs. The study shows that adopting digital technologies has a significant impact on the creation of economic sustainability and social value for SMEs. Also, the study found a significant moderating impact of entrepreneurial orientation on the relationship between social and economic value creation and SME performance. The study shows that SMEs investment in digital technology improves their performance. The result of the study shows that SMEs in the study areas use Mobile Money more than any other digital platform. The study concludes that marketing execution capability, digital product display capabilities, IT skills, project operational capabilities and managerial capabilities with qualifications and training are found to have positive influence in attaining economic overall sustainability. The study Conclude that those SMEs, who focus on investing in digital technologies, employee digital skills, and digital transformation can improve their performance and maintain their sustainable development. The result of the study shows constraints such as time, costs and resources as great obstacles for SMEs to adopt digital technologies. The study explains that to remain competitive and attractive on the open market, SMEs need to implement innovative digital technologies. For these processes to be successful, they need to apply open business models and cooperate extensively with external partners.

The use of digital transformation a phenomenon that has multiple dimensions and necessitates the employment of numerous tools and techniques Various technologies used for various objectives. The three primary ways to studying the digital transformation process are: addressing the drivers and objectives that start the digital journey, elements of success and implications. (Osmundsen et. Al., 2018). Effective use of digitalization through digital transformations can speed up and simplify a variety of commercial operations, including the selling, buying, distributing, and marketing of goods. This consequently has a favourable effect on businesses' financial performance. As a result, it is crucial for all SMEs' stakeholders to have the necessary skills and expertise to successfully apply digitization to both their operational and non-operational areas of their organisation. Such strategic digitalization adoption aims to promote product innovation within SMEs. (Kovalevska et. al. 2022) Adopting digital technology enables companies to compete globally, increase efficiency, and develop stronger relationships with clients and suppliers. SMEs must create new business strategies and procedures that employ digital technologies if they want to compete. (Quinton et al., 2017) argued that SMEs could excel in the digitalized organization environment because digital technology supports intelligence gathering, cost reduction and audience extension. As smaller business partners, SMEs often find themselves compelled to adapt to the needs of others. Their competitiveness will depend strongly on their capacity to better connect to an integrated business network. Literature analysis by (Tarutėa & Gatautisa, 2014) showed that the adoption of information and communications technology (ICT) has an impact on SMEs' performance dimensions, such as profitability, growth, market value, social and environmental performance and satisfaction. ICT's extremely rapid growth in the digital age influences many facets of society, including shifts in consumer shopping behaviour. To effectively target the right consumers, businesspeople need to understand how to use digital marketing properly. Digital marketing is defined as achieving marketing objectives through applying digital technologies. According to Pradhan et al. (2018), "digital marketing" is the use of technology in marketing campaigns and business practises to promote products, services, information, and ideas through the internet, mobile devices, display adverts, and other electronic media. A range of strategies to approach, attract, revive, delight, and drive clients to online marketing are discovered by data-driven marketing. Due to the high level of connectivity, digital marketing makes it possible to communicate with many people at once. It is typically used to offer goods and services in a timely, relevant more individualised, and economical way (Thaha et al., 2021). Digital media has a significant role in marketing activities, from promotions or product offers through product sales. Business owners may easily track and fulfil all the demands and wishes of potential customers due to digital marketing (Bala & Verma, 2018).

In online survey of SMEs, (Harrigan et al., 2011) found that SMEs are adopting relatively simple internet-based technologies to improve their customer communication and information management capabilities and thus create competitive advantage in their own strategic way. External support from digital platform service providers often paves the way to digitalization. According to studies on the digitalization of SMEs, (North et al., 2019) during this initial phase of digitisation, SMEs take rapid impact measures, experiment with new solutions, monitor their peers and move carefully forward, most often without having a clear picture of what digitisation means for the organisation. However, there is currently a dearth of comprehensive data covering SMEs in general and the learning curve for advancing digitization capabilities in particular. The US, Germany, China, and other nations have all incorporated digitalization of the manufacturing sector into their national development strategies. The world has paid close attention to its advancements in the digitalization of the manufacturing industry. The adoption and application of digital technologies in SMEs will be essential to the success of the digital transformation because

SMEs typically serve as the foundation of most economies. (Andulkar et al., 2018). The globalisation of associated economies and the development of digital technologies are accelerating innovation cycles for goods and services, creating new business models, and altering the operational and organisational environments for both businesses and consumers. (Lucas et al. 2013). As a result, businesses from all industries are experimenting and exploring new ways to use digital tools and technology within their own organisations. All areas of activity, including many conventional businesses, are adopting new digital technologies, such as data analysis, digital communication, connected items, intelligent systems, and user experience through digital technology (Pagani et al., 2016).

SMEs digitalization adoption has the potential to significantly and favourably affect productivity. This is only true, though, if adopting such technology coincides with significant organisational or strategic changes. The key areas where enterprise participation in digital transformation benefits them are as follows:

i. Efficiency and process optimization—Due to networking and cross-linking of production, businesses can produce more affordably and respond to individual customer needs more quickly due to increased automation and robotics, fast data exchange enabling almost immediate decision-making, improved productivity, and cost reduction (optimised manufacturing process, fast information about potential and real breakdowns, customer expectations, wider variety of deliverers, robotics and auto).

ii. Innovation —As a result of digitalization, investments in cutting-edge technology are forced, and both fundamental and applied research are more successful than before. This leads to new technologies, operating models, consumer communication channels, a quicker reaction to customer expectations and change, and a quicker adaptability to market conditions.

iii. Access to a larger market—The digitalization of goods and services, along with more extensive marketing possibilities, presents a chance to venture outside of regional and national markets.

iv. Employment – Remote working is an alternative made available by digitalization. With a broad range of specialisation and the capacity to hire remote workers from distant countries guarantee a lot more HRM alternatives.

Trends in SMEs in Digitalization of SMEs

The digitalization of small and medium-sized firms (SMEs) has been a significant trend that is expected to persist in its evolution. The following are some major trends:

1. *Cloud Adoption:* To improve scalability, flexibility, and cost-effectiveness, SMEs are moving more and more of their operations to cloud-based platforms. Cloud services eliminate the need for significant upfront infrastructure investments by providing simple access to software, storage, and processing power.

2. *E-commerce Expansion:* To reach a larger audience and enter new markets, SMEs are making use of e-commerce platforms. The rise in online purchasing and the movement in consumer behaviour towards digital platforms have both contributed to this trend.

3. *Automation and AI:* SMEs may improve operational efficiency, decrease manual labour, and streamline workflows with the use of automation technology and artificial intelligence (AI). Supply chain management is being optimised, repetitive processes are being automated, and chatbots, robotic process automation (RPA), and AI-driven analytics are being used.

4. *Cybersecurity Measures:* As the amount of digital information grows, similarly the risk of cyber-attacks also rises. To protect sensitive data and prevent cyberattacks, SMEs are giving priority to cybersecurity solutions like encryption, multi-factor authentication, and employee training.

5. *Remote Work Tools:* SMEs adopted remote work tools more quickly after pandemic. Virtual private networks (VPNs), project management software, video conferencing, and collaboration technologies are becoming essential for preserving connectivity and productivity in distant work environments.

6. *Flexible Payment Options:* Due to their ease of use, quickness, and security features, digital payment options like peer-to-peer (P2P) platforms, mobile wallets, and contactless payments are growing in popularity among SMEs and their clients.

7. *Sustainability Initiatives:* Using digitization to help with sustainability initiatives is becoming more and more important. This entails using technology to track and maximise energy use, lower carbon emissions, and integrate environmentally friendly procedures into all aspects of company operations.

8. *Blockchain Integration:* Though still in its early phases, blockchain technology has begun to catch on with small and medium-sized enterprises (SMEs) due to its potential to enhance security, traceability, and transparency in a range of business processes, including financial transactions, supply chain management, and intellectual property rights.

9. *Data analytics:* SMEs are realising the benefits of making decisions based on data. Businesses can make well-informed strategic decisions by utilising data analytics tools and technology to obtain insights into customer preferences, market trends, and operational efficiencies.

10. *Digital Marketing:* Small and medium-sized businesses (SMEs) are refocusing their marketing efforts on digital platforms like email campaigns, social media, search engine optimisation (SEO), and content marketing. When compared to traditional approaches, digital marketing offers cost-effective advertising possibilities, real-time feedback, and targeted reach.

Strategies of Transforming an SME Through Digitalization

Transforming small and medium-sized enterprises (SMEs) through digitalization involves several stages, each requiring specific strategies to navigate successfully. Following are the strategies:

1. Assessment and Planning:
    - Evaluate the SME's present technological infrastructure, procedures, and staff skills.
    - Determine digitalization goals and priorities based on company objectives.
    - Create a digitization plan with specific milestones and dates.
2. Awareness and Education:
    - Raise awareness and educate stakeholders on the benefits of digitization for SMEs.
    - Train personnel on digital tools and technology.
    - Encourage a culture of innovation and willingness to change within the organisation.
3. Digitalization of processes:
    - Identify and digitalize important business operations to improve efficiency and save costs.
    - Use digital tools like ERP systems, CRM software, and project management platforms.
    - Automate repetitive procedures to improve efficiency and minimise manual mistakes.
4. Data Management and Analytics:
    - Implement data governance policies to assure quality, security, and compliance.

- ◦ Use data analytics technologies to understand customer behaviour, market trends, and operational performance.
- ◦ Utilise predictive analytics to forecast future trends and make data-driven decisions.
5. Improve Customer Engagement and Experience:
   - ◦ Establish your online presence through website creation, e-commerce, and social media outlets.
   - ◦ Implement CRM technologies to personalise interactions and enhance client satisfaction.
   - ◦ Use digital marketing tactics like content marketing, email campaigns, and SEO to reach and engage customers.
6. Supply Chain Integration:
   - ◦ Collaborate with suppliers and partners to digitise supply chain operations for greater transparency and efficiency.
   - ◦ Use inventory management tools and supply chain analytics to optimise inventory levels and shorten lead times.
   - ◦ Use blockchain technology to provide safe and transparent supply chain transactions.
7. Innovation and Adaption:
   - ◦ Fostering a culture of experimentation and risk-taking can promote organisational innovation and adaptation.
   - ◦ Stay up to date on emerging technology and market trends to drive growth and distinction.
   - ◦ Monitor and assess digitalization strategy to adapt changing market circumstances and business requirements.
8. Scaling and Expansion:
   - ◦ Use digital tools and platforms to grow operations and enter new markets.
   - ◦ Collaborate with other SMEs or major enterprises to gain access to new resources and markets.
   - ◦ Invest in scalable infrastructure and technology to enable growth and scalability.

Process of Transforming an SME Through Digitalization

To effectively incorporate digital technology into operations, a small or medium-sized firm (SME) must go through multiple stages of digitalization. Here's a general outline of the process:

1. Assessment and Planning:
   - ◦ Evaluate existing processes, systems, and technology.
   - ◦ Identify pain spots, inefficiencies, and opportunities for change.
   - ◦ Create explicit goals and objectives for digital transformation.
   - ◦ Create a plan describing actions to attain desired results.
2. Leadership Commitment and Culture Change:
   - ◦ Obtain buy-in from senior management for digital transformation programme.
   - ◦ Create a culture of innovation and constant development.
   - ◦ Ensure stakeholders recognise the relevance of digitization and are willing to adapt to changes.
3. Technology Selection:

- Research and choose relevant digital tools and technology for the organization's goals and budget.
- Think about scalability, integration, security, and compatibility with current systems.

4. Implementation:
   - Introduce digital solutions gradually, starting with pilot projects or small-scale efforts.
   - Train and enable personnel to adapt to new technology and practices.
   - Monitor progress and make modifications as needed.

5. Data Management and Analysis:
   - Set up processes to gather, store, and analyse data to get insights into business operations.
   - Analyse data to find trends, patterns, and possibilities for optimisation.
   - Ensure adherence to data protection rules and security best practices.

6. Process Optimization:
   - Utilize digital technologies and automation to streamline operations and remove unnecessary procedures.
   - Identify bottlenecks and areas for improvement, then implement changes to increase efficiency and productivity.

7. Improve consumer Experience:
   - Utilize digital channels to enhance consumer engagement and create personalised experiences.
   - Implement CRM technologies to track interactions and strengthen connections.
   - Use social media, websites, and mobile apps for better communication and accessibility.

8. Monitoring and Continuous Improvement:
   - Establish key performance indicators (KPIs) to assess digitization progress.
   - Monitor progress towards targets and make modifications as required.
   - Seek input from staff and customers to discover areas for improvement.

9. Cybersecurity and Risk Management:
   - Implement strong cybersecurity measures to safeguard digital assets and sensitive information.
   - Conduct frequent risk assessments and fix any weaknesses or threats quickly.
   - To successfully manage possible threats, keep up with the newest security trends and changes.

10. Scaling and Growth:
    - Once initial digitalization efforts have proven successful, consider expanding digitalization activities throughout the organisation.
    - Identify chances for innovation and development into new markets or product/service offerings.
    - Adapt digital strategies to be competitive in a continuously changing corporate world.

Stages of Transforming an SME Through Digitalization

Transforming an SME (Small and Medium Enterprise) through digitalization typically involves several stages. These stages can vary depending on the specific needs, resources, and goals of the SME, here is a generalized outline of the common stages involved:

1. *Digital awareness:* This level focuses on understanding the impact of digital technology on small and medium-sized enterprises. At this step, stakeholders from all three industries engage in phone conversations and live meetings to learn about the initiative and sign up for subscriptions.

2. *Digital enquirement:* At this level, the technology solutions are presented in terms of functionality and potential to raise awareness among SMEs and stakeholders. SMEs are engaged in the digital transformation project through various methods such as working sessions, seminars, and focus groups, reflecting their strong enthusiasm.

3. *Digital collaboration*: It involves firms exploring the benefits of digitalization in their business operations and plans based on their interests. At this level, only a few organisations are authorised to utilise G Suite for administrative and communication purposes.

4. *Digital transformation:* Few SMEs are interested in digital transformation, despite its high degree of involvement. SMEs at this level are very interested in digitalization, which may play a crucial role in achieving project objectives. At this moment, accessible technologies primarily focus on digital production and distribution, with a significant influence on the company's strategic and organisational issues.

KPIs for Monitoring the Impact of Digitalization on the Growth of SMEs

The impact of digitalization on the growth of Small and Medium Enterprises (SMEs) can be assessed through various key performance indicators (KPIs) or key factor indicators. Some of them are as follows:

1. *Digital Adoption Rate:* Determine the extent to which SMEs use digital technology in their operations. This may involve the use of digital technologies for marketing, sales, operations, and customer support.

2. *Competitive edge:* Determine the extent to which digitization has provided SMEs with a competitive edge in the market. This might include indicators like market share growth, differentiation from rivals, and adaptability to changing market conditions.

3. *Customer Engagement:* Determine the extent of connection and engagement with customers via digital platforms. This might include data like social media engagements, online reviews, and customer feedback gathered via digital channels.

4. *Employee Skills & Satisfaction:* Determine the effect of digitalization on employee skill development and work satisfaction. Assess the amount of training for digital tools and technology, as well as employee satisfaction surveys. By following these key factor indicators, stakeholders may acquire insights into how digitalization affects the growth and competitiveness of SMEs. These metrics can also assist in identifying opportunities for future progress and investment in digital capabilities.

5. *Revenue Growth:* Monitor the impact of digitization on revenue growth in SMEs. Compare revenue growth rates before and after digitalization activities and evaluate the role of digital channels in overall revenue.

6. *Data Utilization*: Assess the efficacy of SMEs in using data for decision-making and plan building. Measure metrics such as data collection capabilities, analytics maturity, and the ability to derive insights from data.

7. *Innovation Rate:* Determine the rate of innovation in SMEs driven by digitalization. This might involve launching new products or services, implementing new business strategies, and integrating newer technology.

8. *Operational Efficiency*: Evaluate how digitalization has increased operational efficiency in small and medium-sized enterprises (SMEs). This might include indicators like reduced turnaround times, higher productivity, and cost savings achieved by process automation and digitalization.

9. *Online presence:* Evaluate the efficiency of SMEs' online presence, including websites, social media accounts, and e-commerce platforms. Track data like website traffic, social media participation, and online transactions.

10. *Market Reach:* Evaluate the extension of market reach facilitated by digitalization. Metrics like as geographic reach, market penetration, and online client acquisition are all important to measure.

According to the author (Paiola, 2017), customers and/or suppliers who frequently demanded that these SMEs embrace the technology as part of supply chain and customer management processes may have an impact on the productivity improvements for manufacturing enterprises. Multiple issues are also pointing to the size of enterprises and the issue of SMEs. SMEs, in contrast to huge organisations, are less convinced about the future direction of their company and how they will fit into these new situations. In fact, it can be particularly difficult for smaller businesses to experiment with new business models while still performing successfully in the present business environment.

KPIs For Monitoring the Digitalization Progress of SMEs

Following are the Key Performance Indicators (KPIs) are essential for monitoring the digitalization progress of Small and Medium Enterprises (SMEs).

1. *No. of visitors &duration of each visit:* Website Traffic: Track the number of visitors visiting the SMEs' website over time. Increased traffic could indicate good digital marketing and online visibility.

2. *Online revenue analysis:* Track online sales income from e-commerce platforms and SME websites. Increased online sales reflect an effective digitization of sales operations.

3. *ROI for Digital marketing:* Calculate the ROI for digital marketing campaigns. This may include measures like as cost per acquisition (CPA), conversion rates, and customer lifetime value (CLV).

4. *Social media engagement:* Social media engagement indicators include likes, shares, comments, and followers. An expanding and engaged audience reflects successful digital engagement techniques.

5. *Customer Feedback and Reviews:* Analyse consumer comments and reviews across online platforms and social media. Positive feedback and high ratings reflect client happiness and effective digital experiences.

6. *Cost Savings from digitalization:* Calculate the cost savings resulting from digitalization activities, such as decreased overhead costs, lower operational expenditures, and higher productivity.

7. *Time Spent on Administrative activities:* Determine how much time employees spend on administrative activities before and after digitalization initiatives. Reduced time spent on manual processes implies enhanced efficiency through digitalization.

8. *Digitalization Maturity Level:* Assess the SME's digitalization maturity using frameworks like the Digital Maturity Model. This gives a comprehensive perspective of digital transformation progress and opportunities for improvement.

9. *Technology Adoption Rate:* Monitor the adoption of digital tools and technology inside the SME, such as cloud computing services, Customer Relationship Management (CRM) systems, and collaborative tools.

10. *Cybersecurity Incident Rate:* Monitor the frequency of cybersecurity issues such as data breaches, spread of malware, and phishing attempts. A decrease in occurrences indicates better cybersecurity measures and awareness.

Factors Affecting Digitalisation in SMEs

The adoption of digital technology in SMEs is influenced by a variety of factors. These factors include both internal factors and external factors.

Internal Factors

Support of Owners/Managers: The CEO and senior management qualities are the most crucial aspects of technology adoption in SMEs. Some these include technical proficiency, a welcoming environment, passion, a leadership style, academic credentials, and technology, knowledge obtained through networking, etc. The adoption of digitalization is influenced by owner/manager characteristics. An innovative owner/manager is aware of the importance and benefit of these technologies for their SME, and as a result, they are more likely to adopt them than other members of the organisational team. (Tajudeen et.al, 2018)

Perceived Adoption Cost: Expenses associated with system adoption and maintenance are critical for SMEs since no company will use e-commerce or ICT unless the advantages outweigh the expenses. Due to financial restrictions, Malaysian SMEs frequently have doubts about the costs of system development and maintenance and see adoption costs as a major barrier. (Aalm & Noor2009)

Employee Technological Skills: Lack of technical expertise, ignorance of information technology, and high implementation costs are barriers to digitalization adoption. The speed at which organizations adopt new technologies is also influenced by the IT skills of the people who work there. (Bharati et.al. 2015)

Changes in the business model: Another internal factor related to the success of digital transformation is necessary changes in the current business model. As the core of business model is related to redefining the value proposition and enhancing customer collaboration and interaction through adjustments and changes in current and potential customer contact points are identified as the main changes to the business model that will influence the overall business model and the digital transformation process because these are related to the business model's value proposition and relationships with customers. (Berman, 2012).

External Factors

Government regulations: Government laws have been identified as one of the most significant external factors affecting the process of SMEs digital transformation. (Kruger & Teuteberg, 2016).

Industry related factor: Industry related factors such as industry maturity or specialised requirements and expectations are also significant in the context of affecting the process of SMEs digital transformation. (Biahmou et al., 2016).

External capabilities fit, and resources fit: External abilities like customization and collaboration are essential. Collaboration is a process in which two or more organisations cooperate to achieve a common objective. Moreover, an effect of synergy achieved from collaboration between various organisations can be seen as a promoter of digital transformation in SMEs. The ability to distinguish products or services based on market demands is the focus of customisation factors. As for the external resources fit, the historical path of the company (current strategic alternatives) and embedded trust (belief in the reliability of another organisation) may have an impact on the success of the digital transformation. (Tarutė et al., 2018).

Issues and Problems Faced by SMEs in Adoption of Digitalization

SMEs face several challenges in the digitalization process. First, they are uncertain about their position in the new scenarios and their future business. It can be especially difficult for smaller businesses to find a balance between experimenting new business models and the need to perform effectively in their current business. Furthermore, there should be attention because the profits from new experimental models are sometimes lower than those from existing ones. Additionally, SMEs struggle with a serious lack of knowledge in areas like big data analysis. The structure of distribution routes, distance from end users, and limited bargaining power in the value chain all contribute to the complexity of the digitalization process for SMEs. Rather than extending the services provided, the sales model, particularly for suppliers and OEMs selling through distributors, can necessitate working with distributors to reconfigure service operations.

In general, SMEs encounter difficulties in the process of digitalization because of uncertainties, scarce resources, gaps in skill, and the design of their value chain.

Opportunities SMEs Get After Adoption of Digitalization Are as Follows

- *Technological innovation*: Technological innovation refers to innovation in terms of inputs, activities, and outputs. Such corporate or company innovation is critical to a company's success. However, technical innovation is difficult to attain due to a variety of hurdles. (Bagheri et al. 2019).
- *Market competitiveness:* Integrating digital technology allows SMEs to significantly enhance all their processes, both operationally and in terms of customer experience. For SMEs it may be an effective strategy for preserving or even boosting competitiveness in both domestic and global markets. (Ahn, S.J., 2020).
- *Cost efficiency:* Digitalization aids in cost reduction by Increasing the amount of time spent on mechanical chores, Process improvement. Saving money on materials. Providing instant digital access to information from anywhere and at any time.
- *Increased production:* Digitalization helps SMEs in increasing their production capacity by enabling them to gather data on specific performance metrics.
- *Product differentiation:* Digitalization helps SMEs by improving product quality and promote product individuation It enable SME's to better personalize goods and services based on customer preference.
- *Increase in financial returns:* Digitalization assists SMEs by opening new market opportunities and enhancing financial returns; developing new services to fulfil unsatisfied consumer expectations; and better regulating industrial processes, allowing for cost-cutting measures. (Telukdarie et al., 2023)

Challenges and Barriers Faced by SMEs in Adoption of Digitalization Are as Follows

- *Technical Barriers*: Technical barriers are primarily related to human resources, namely, inadequate skills, low formal competencies and qualifications, and limited motivation to become involved in the innovation process. Also, the most significant obstacle to innovation is the inadequate quality of human resources in businesses. (Gazem et al., 2017).

- *Organizational barriers*: Organizational barriers such as lack of financial resources, managerial support, resistance to change, and lack of R&D infrastructure etc. The high cost of technical innovation is sometimes not proportionate to the inadequate financial commitment. In fact, it has always been the reason of difficulties in adopting technical innovation. (Capozza and Divella, 2019).
- *Technological Barriers*: Barriers to technology refers to the obstacles that can prevent the effective adoption and implementation of technology in the organization. SMEs are hesitant to implement advanced service technologies in Industry 4.0, which fosters innovation in manufacturing, logistics operations, and other activities due to a lack of understanding. (For instance, Enterprise Resource Planning (ERP) or Computer-Aided Design (CAD), Artificial Intelligence, or Industry 4.0 Applications such as BDA).
- *Legal Barriers*: Legal barriers are those which are related with the lack of cooperation and integration between management and departments, as well as privacy difficulties. (Telukdarie et al., 2023)
- *High training costs:* High training cost is also a big challenge for SMEs as there is lack of financial resources and due to low finance SMEs find it as a burden. (Telukdarie et al., 2023).
- *Rapid pace of technological change*: Another challenge for SMEs is Rapid pace of technological change. SMEs, who frequently lack the resources and expertise needed to keep up with the latest digital trends and innovations. (Telukdarie et al., 2023).

RESEARCH METHODOLOGY

A literature review is conducted to analyse the impact of digitalization on SMEs growth and to identify various opportunities and challenges SMEs face during the digitalization process. In this study thirty-two papers published in 2013–2023, are reviewed and their methodology, findings and implications for research, policy and practice are summarized. This review cover recently published research in the field of Digitalization in SMEs and its impact on SMEs growth. As digitalization in SMEs is need of the hour. In the current business environment, the effect of digitization on the growth of SMEs is significant. Adopting digital technologies increases competitiveness overall, increases market reach, and improves operational efficiency. It gives SMEs the flexibility to adjust to shifting customer preferences, optimise workflows, and obtain important information for well-informed decision-making. Digitalization has become essential for the market's sustainability and further expansion in the current dynamic environment. In this review those literature reviews are included which shows engagement of SMEs in the adoption of digital technologies, namely, digital awareness, digital acquirement, digital collaboration and digital transformation. Also, in this review those papers which deal with the importance of digital technology to the performance of SMEs and those that focus on SMEs engagement with e-commerce, e-business and e-marketing.

CONCLUSION

One of the most significant changes in the global economy since the end of the 1980s has been the increase in the adoption of digitalization. The analysis of the most recent academic research on how SMEs interact with digital technology conveys both a positive and a negative message. Positively, these studies demonstrate that even the smallest businesses may successfully use digital technologies despite many potential costs and risks. In comparison to what they might anticipate using more traditional off-line techniques, this might give SMEs access to a considerably wider range of market opportunities. It can also help them to retain customers and obtain information on customer and market trends at a much lower cost than had previously been thought possible. Most SMEs can now afford to join in the digital economy because of the reduction in digitalization costs. However, the attitude of its owner-managers will influence whether SMEs use digitalization. Most small business owners are limited by time and have short planning periods. They will need to understand the costs, risks, and advantages of investing in digitalization to fully appreciate its advantages. SMEs account for around 99 percent of all enterprises in the world's economies, employ at least half of the workforce, and generate more than half of the value contributed to GDP. It is crucial for government to make sure that their SME sector is not excluded from the digital economy to promote economic and employment growth. This study examines the complex relationship between digitalization and the expansion of small and medium-sized businesses (SMEs). The findings highlight how digital technology may transform SMEs by improving their operating efficiency, stimulating innovation, and expanding market reach for SMEs. It is essential for further development to embrace technological advancements as we navigate an increasingly digital landscape. To take full advantage of the benefits of digitization, though, issues like cybersecurity concerns and a lack of digital skills must be resolved. All things considered, this study adds insightful information to the ongoing discourse about how digitalization will significantly influence the direction that SMEs take in the future and emphasises the necessity of strategic adaptation for attaining success in the changing business environment. For the owner-managers of SMEs the decision to engage and invest in the digital economy is no longer an option. While some industries are more severely impacted by the development of digital technologies than others, the overall trend indicates that very few will be able to escape its influence. Even small firms may now adopt and employ online, digital, and mobile information and communications technologies solutions far more easily than in the past. With the help of such technologies, small businesses may link with global supply chains, reach millions of people, track customers efficiently, and improve internal processes. They should not be ignored because they are a crucial instrument in the toolbox of the business owner-manager.

REFERENCES

Alam, S. S., & Noor, M. K. M. (2009). ICT adoption in small and medium enterprises: An empirical evidence of service sectors in Malaysia. *International Journal of Business and Management*, 4(2), 112–125. doi:10.5539/ijbm.v4n2p112

Andulkar, M., Le, D. T., & Berger, U. (2018): A multi-case study on Industry 4.0 for SMEs in Branden-burg, Germany. In: *Proceedings of the Annual Hawaii International Conference on System Sciences*. IEEE. 10.24251/HICSS.2018.574

Angela, R. & Diana, R. (2022). DIGITAL TECHNOLOGIES AND THE PERFORMANCE OF SMALL AND MEDIUM ENTERPRISES. *Studies in Business and Economics, 17*(3).

Autio, E., Nambisan, S., Thomas, L. D. W., & Wright, M. (2018). Digital affordances, spatial affordances, and the genesis of entrepreneurial ecosystems. *Strategic Entrepreneurship Journal, 12*(1), 72–95. doi:10.1002/sej.1266

Bagheri, M., Mitchelmore, S., Bamiatzi, V., & Nikolopoulos, K. (2019). Internationalization orientation in SMEs: The mediating role of technological innovation. *Journal of International Management, 25*(1), 121–139. doi:10.1016/j.intman.2018.08.002

Bala, M., & Verma, D. (2018). A critical review of digital marketing. International Journal of Management. *IT & Engineering, 8*(10), 321–339.

Becker, W., & Schmid, O. (2020). The right digital strategy for your business: An empirical analysis of the design and implementation of digital strategies in SMEs and LSEs. *Business Research, 13*(3), 985–1005. doi:10.1007/s40685-020-00124-y

Berman, S. J. (2012). Digital transformation: Opportunities to create new business models. *Strategy and Leadership, 40*(2), 16–24. doi:10.1108/10878571211209314

Bharati, P., Zhang, W., & Chaudhury, A. (2015). Better knowledge with social media? Exploring the roles of social capital and organizational knowledge management. *Journal of Knowledge Management, 19*(3), 456–475. doi:10.1108/JKM-11-2014-0467

Biahmou, A., Emmer, C., Pfouga, A., & Stjepandić, J. (2016). Digital master as an enabler for industry 4.0. *Advances in Transdisciplinary Engineering, 4*, 672–681.

Bouwmana, H., Nikoub, S., & Reuver, M. D. (2019). Digitalization, business models, and SMEs: How do business model innovation practices improve performance of digitalizing SMEs? *Telecommunications Policy, 43*(9), 101828. doi:10.1016/j.telpol.2019.101828

Brodny, J., & Tutak, M. (2022). Digitalization of Small and Medium-Sized Enterprises and Economic Growth: Evidence for the EU-27 Countries. *Journal of Open Innovation, 8*(2), 67. doi:10.3390/joitmc8020067

Buer, S. V., Fragapane, G. I., & Strandhagen, J. O. (2018). The data driven process improvement cycle: Using digitalization for continuous improvement. *IFAC-PapersOnLine, 51*(11), 1035–1040. doi:10.1016/j.ifacol.2018.08.471

Capozza, C., & Divella, M. (2019). Human capital and firms' innovation: Evidence from emerging economies. *Economics of Innovation and New Technology, 28*(7), 741–757. doi:10.1080/10438599.2018.1557426

Denicolai, S., Zucchella, A., & Magnani, G. (2021). Internationalization, digitalization, and sustainability: Are SMEs ready? A survey on synergies and substituting effects among growth paths. *Technological Forecasting and Social Change, 166*, 120650. doi:10.1016/j.techfore.2021.120650

Eller, R., Alford, P., Kallmünzer, A., & Peters, M. (2020). Antecedents, consequences, and challenges of small and medium-sized enterprise digitalization. *Journal of Business Research, 112*, 119–127. doi:10.1016/j.jbusres.2020.03.004

Foroudi, P., Gupta, S., Nazarian, A., & Duda, M. (2017). Digital technology and marketing management capability: Achieving growth in SMEs. *Qualitative Market Research, 20*(2), 230–246. doi:10.1108/QMR-01-2017-0014

Frimpong, S., Agyapong, G., & Agyapong, D. (2022). Financial literacy, access to digital finance and performance of SMEs: Evidence From Central region of Ghana. *Cogent Economics & Finance, 10*(1), 2121356.

Garzoni, A., De Turi, I., Secundo, G., & Del Vecchio, P. (2020). Fostering digital transformation of SMEs: A four levels approach. *Management Decision, 58*(8), 1543–1562. doi:10.1108/MD-07-2019-0939

Gazem, N., Abdul Rahman, A., & Saeed, F. (2017). Using TRIZ systematic innovation methods for re-design services in small and medium enterprises [IJISSS]. *International Journal of Information Systems in the Service Sector, 9*(3), 78–92. doi:10.4018/IJISSS.2017070105

Harrigan, P., Ramsey, E., & Ibbotson, P. (2011). Critical factors underpinning the e-CRM activities of SMEs. *Journal of Marketing Management, 27*(5-6), 503–529. doi:10.1080/0267257X.2010.495284

Isensee, C., Teuteberg, F., Griese, K.-M., & Topi, C. (2020). The relationship between organizational culture, sustainability, and digitalization in SMEs: A systematic review. *Journal of Cleaner Production, 275*, 122944. doi:10.1016/j.jclepro.2020.122944

Kovalevska, N., Nesterenko, I., Lutsenko, O., Nesterenko, O., & Hlushach, Y. (2022). Problems of accounting digitalization in conditions of business processes digitalization. *Amazonia Investiga, 11*(56), 132–141. doi:10.34069/AI/2022.56.08.14

Kraft, C., Lindeque, J. P., & Peter, M. K. (2022). The digital transformation of Swiss small and medium-sized enterprises: Insights from digital tool adoption. *Journal of Strategy and Management, 15*(3), 468–494. doi:10.1108/JSMA-02-2021-0063

Kraft, C., Lindeque, J. P., & Peter, M. K. (2022). The digital transformation of Swiss small and medium-sized enterprises: Insights from digital tool adoption. [Emerald Publishing.]. *Journal of Strategy and Management, 15*(3), 468–494. doi:10.1108/JSMA-02-2021-0063

Krüger, N., & Teuteberg, F. (2016). IT consultants as change agents in digital transformation initiatives. In Multikonferenz Wirtschaftsinformatik (Vol. 2, pp. 1019-1030). Universitätsverlag Ilmenau, Ilmenau, Germany, March 9-11.

Lee, C. K. M., Zhang, S., & Ng, K. K. H. (2017). Development of an industrial Internet of things suite for smart factory towards re-industrialization. *Advances in Manufacturing, 5*(4), 335–343. doi:10.1007/s40436-017-0197-2

Li, L., Su, F., Zhang, W., & Mao, J.-Y. (2017). Digital transformation by SME entrepreneurs: A capability perspective (. Portico). *Information Systems Journal, 28*(6), 1129–1157. doi:10.1111/isj.12153

Lucas, H. Jr, Agarwal, R., Clemons, E. K., El Sawy, O. A., & Weber, B. (2013). Impactful Research on Transformational Information Technology: An Opportunity to Inform New Audiences. *Management Information Systems Quarterly, 37*(2), 371–382. https://www.jstor.org/stable/43825914. doi:10.25300/MISQ/2013/37.2.03

Lutfi, A., Alkelani, S. N., Al-Khasawneh, M. A., Alshira'h, A. F., Alshirah, M. H., Almaiah, M. A., Alrawad, M., Alsyouf, A., Saad, M., & Ibrahim, N. (2022). Influence of Digital Accounting System Usage on SMEs Performance: The Moderating Effect of COVID-19. *Sustainability (Basel), 14*(22), 15048. doi:10.3390/su142215048

Mazurek, G. (2019). *Transformacja cyfrowa. Perspektywa marketing (The Digital Transformation. A Marketing Outlook).* Warszawa PWN.

Mazzarol, T. (2015). SMEs engagement with e-commerce, e-business and e-marketing. *Small Enterprise Research, 22*(1), 79–90. doi:10.1080/13215906.2015.1018400

Mechman, A., Omar, S. S., Hamawandy, N. M., Abdullah, A. S., & Qader, A. N. (2022). The Effect of Digital Marketing, And E-Commence on SMEs performance of Baghdad. *Journal of Positive School Psychology, 6*(3), 4197–4212.

Melo, S. C., Queiroz, G. A., & Junior, P. A. (2023). Sustainable digital transformation in small and medium enterprises (SMEs): A review on performance. *Heliyon, 9*(3), e13908. doi:10.1016/j.heliyon.2023. e13908 PMID:36915489

Mubarak, M. F., Shaikh, F. A., Mubarik, M., Samo, K. A., & Mastoi, S. (2019). The Impact of Digital Transformation on Business Performance. Engineering, Technology &. *Applied Scientific Research, 9*(6), 5056–5061.

North, K., Aramburu, N., & Lorenzo, O. J. (2019). Promoting digitally enabled growth in SMEs: A framework proposal. *Journal of Enterprise Information Management, 33*(1), 238–262. doi:10.1108/JEIM-04-2019-0103

Omrani, N., Rejeb, N., Maalaoui, A., Dabi, M., & Kraus, S. (2022). Drivers of Digital Transformation in SMEs. *IEEE Transactions on Engineering Management.*

Osmundsen, K., Iden, J., & Bygstad, B. (2018). Digital transformation: Drivers, success factors, and implications. In *Proceedings of the MCIS 2018*, Corfu, Greece.

Pagani, M., & Pardo, C. (2017). The Impact of Digital Technology on Relationships in a Business Network. *Industrial Marketing Management, 67*(2), 185–192. doi:10.1016/j.indmarman.2017.08.009

Paiola, M. (2017). Digitalization and servitization: opportunities and challenges for Italian SMES. Sinergie italian journal of management, 36(107).

Pardiman, J. (2022), Impact of financial capital, social capital, and business digitalization on business sustainability of SMEs in Indonesia. Journal Manajemen dan Pemasaran Jasa, 15(1).

Pham, Q. H., & Vu, K. P. (2022). Digitalization in small and medium enterprise: A parsimonious model of digitalization of accounting information for sustainable innovation ecosystem value generation. *Asia Pacific Journal of Innovation and Entrepreneurship, 16*(1), 2–37. doi:10.1108/APJIE-02-2022-0013

Philbin, S., Viswanathan, R., & Telukdarie, A. (2022). Understanding how digital transformation can enable SMEs to achieve sustainable development: A systematic literature review. *Small Business International Review*, *6*(1), e473. doi:10.26784/sbir.v6i1.473

Pradhan, P., Nigam, D., & Ck, T. (2018). Digital marketing and SMES: An identification of research gap via archives of past research. *Journal of Internet Banking and Commerce*, *23*(1), 1–14.

Quinton, S., Canhoto, A., Molinillo, S., Pera, R., & Budhathoki, T. (2017). Conceptualising a digital orientation: Antecedents of supporting SME performance in the digital economy. *Journal of Strategic Marketing*, 1–13.

Ramdani, B., Raja, S., & Kryukova, M. (2021). Digital innovation in SMEs: A systematic review, synthesis and research agenda. *Information Technology for Development*.

Ritala, P., Baiyere, A., Hughes, M., & Kraus, S. (2021). Digital strategy implementation: The role of individual entrepreneurial orientation and relational capital [Published by Elsevier Inc.]. *Technological Forecasting and Social Change*, *171*, 171. doi:10.1016/j.techfore.2021.120961

Santos-Jaén, J. M., Gimeno-Arias, F., León-Gómez, A., & Palacios-Manzano, M. (2023, September 26). The Business Digitalization Process in SMEs from the Implementation of e-Commerce: An Empirical Analysis. *Journal of Theoretical and Applied Electronic Commerce Research*, *18*(4), 1700–1720. doi:10.3390/jtaer18040086

Scuotto, V., Nicotra, M., Del Giudice, M., Krueger, N., & Gregori, G. L. (2021). A micro foundational perspective on SMEs' growth in the digital transformation era. *Journal of Business Research*, *129*, 382–392. doi:10.1016/j.jbusres.2021.01.045

Setia, P., Venkatesh, V., & Joglekar, S. (2013). Leveraging digital technologies: How information quality leads to localized capabilities and customer service performance. *Management Information Systems Quarterly*, *37*(2), 565–590. doi:10.25300/MISQ/2013/37.2.11

Śledziewska, K., Gabryelczyk, R., & Włoch, R. (2015). *Go digital! Diagnoza luki w kompetencjach cyfrowych MŚP (Go Digital! Gap Analysis in Digital Competences of SMEs)* (Working paper delab UW, 38).

Straková, J., Talíř, M., & Váchal, J. (2022). Opportunities and threats of digital transformation of business models in SMEs. *Economics & Sociology (Ternopil)*, *15*(3), 159–171. doi:10.14254/2071-789X.2022/15-3/9

Tajudeen, F. P., Jaafar, N. I., & Ainin, S. (2018). The impact of social media usage among organizations. *Information & Management*, *55*(3), 308–321. doi:10.1016/j.im.2017.08.004

Tarutė, A., Duobienė, J., Klovienė, L., Vitkauskaitė, E., & Varaniūtė, V. (2018). Identifying factors affecting digital transformation of SMEs. In *Proceedings of The 18th International Conference on Electronic Business* (pp. 373- 381). ICEB.

Tarutėa, A., & Gatautisa, R. (2013). ICT impact on SMEs performance. Contemporary Issues in Business, Management and Education conference. *Procedia - Social and Behavioral Sciences 110* (2014) 1218 – 1225.

Telukdarie, A., Dube, T., Matjuta, P., & Philbin, S. (2023). The opportunities and challenges of digitalization for SME's. *Procedia Computer Science, 217*, 689–698. doi:10.1016/j.procs.2022.12.265

Telukdarie, T., Dube, T., Matjuta, P., & Philbin, S. (2023). Dube, P. Matjuta, S. Philbin (2023), The opportunities and challenges of digitalization for SME's. *Procedia Computer Science, 217*, 689–698. doi:10.1016/j.procs.2022.12.265

Teng, X., Wu, Z., & Yang, F. (2022). Research on the Relationship between Digital Transformation and Performance of SMEs. *Sustainability, 14*, 6012.

Teng, X., Wu, Z., & Yang, F. (2022). Research on the Relationship between Digital Transformation and Performance of SMEs. *Sustainability (Basel), 14*(10), 6012. doi:10.3390/su14106012

Thaha, A. R.; Maulina, E.; Muftiadi, R. A.; & Alexandri, M. B., (2021). Digital Marketing and SMEs: A Systematic Mapping Study. *Library Philosophy and Practice (e-journal), 5113.*

Vásquez, J., Bruno, G., Settineri, L., & Aguirre, S. (2018). Conceptual Framework for Evaluating the Environmental Awareness and Ecoefficiency of SMEs. *Procedia CIRP, 78*, 347–352. doi:10.1016/j.procir.2018.09.062

Venkatesh, J., & Kumari, R. L. (2015). Performance of Mudra Bank: A Study on Financial Assistance to MSME Sector. *International Journal of Research in Economics and Social Sciences, 5*, 185–191.

Vrontis, D., Chaudhuri, R., & Chatterjee, S. (2022). Adoption of Digital Technologies by SMEs for Sustainability and Value Creation: Moderating Role of Entrepreneurial Orientation. *Sustainability (Basel), 14*(13), 7949. doi:10.3390/su14137949

Zahoor, N., Zopiatis, A., Adomako, S., & Lamprinakos, G. (2023). The micro-foundations of digitally transforming SMEs: How digital literacy and technology interact with managerial attributes. *Journal of Business Research, 159*, 113755. doi:10.1016/j.jbusres.2023.113755

Zhang, X., Xu, Y., & Ma, L. (2022). Research on Successful Factors and Influencing Mechanism of the Digital Transformation in SMEs. *Sustainability (Basel), 14*(5), 2549. doi:10.3390/su14052549

KEY TERMS AND DEFINITIONS

Challenges: Challenges here refer to the obstacles and difficulties faced by SMEs in adoption of digitalization. Lack of finance, managerial support, resistance to change, and lack of R&D infrastructure, lack of cooperation and integration between management and departments, low formal competencies and qualifications, and limited motivation to become involved in the innovation process are some of the challenges that can prevent the effective adoption and implementation of technology in SMEs.

Digital transformation: Digital transformation is the process of using digital technologies to change traditional and non-digital business processes and services, or to develop new ones, to meet changing customer and market expectations. Thus, completely altering the way businesses are operated and managed, and how value is delivered to customers. It is also used as a method that alters an entity's characteristics significantly by utilising a combination of information, computing, communication, and connectivity technologies.

Digitalization: Digitalization is the process of using digital technologies to change a business model, produce new revenue streams, and value-producing opportunities. It involves incorporating digital tools and systems into a variety of corporate processes, including management, communication, production, and customer service.

Economic growth: Economic growth is an increase in national income per capita, and it involves analyses especially in quantitative terms, with a focus on the functional relationships between the endogenous variables. In a broader sense, it involves an increase in GDP, GNP, and NI, which results in an increase in national wealth, including the production capacity, expressed in both absolute and relative size, per capita, as well as structural changes to the economy.

Innovation: Innovation refers to the incorporation of new knowledge into processes, procedures, and services that boosts the national economy, increases employment, and generates pure profit for the innovative business firm. Innovation is never a one-time occurrence; rather, it is a continuous and cumulative process involving several organisational decision-making processes, from the ideation stage through the execution stage.

Opportunity: Opportunity is basically an idea or a situation that makes it possible to establish or develop a successful, long-lasting business. It is described as an entrepreneurially discovered or created situation in which new goods, services, raw materials, markets, and organising methods are conceived as having a potential for exploitation through entrepreneur-led action to form and transform them into new means, ends, or means-ends relationships.

SMEs: Small and medium size enterprises (SMEs) are businesses that fall below a specific threshold in terms of income, assets, or personnel count. Every country has its own definition of what small and medium businesses are. In India, small scale industries are those in which investment in plant and machinery or equipment is not more than 10 crores & annual turnover is not more than 50 crores and medium size industries re those in which investment in plant and machinery or equipment is not more than 50 crores and annual turnover is not more than 250 crores.

Chapter 8
Barriers Hindering Digital Transformation in SMEs

Siva Kumar Pujari
 https://orcid.org/0000-0002-9178-4220
Christ University, India

Saibal Kumar Saha
 https://orcid.org/0000-0002-7842-698X
Christ University, India

ABSTRACT

The chapter aims to find interdependencies between barriers that hinder adoption of digital transformation technologies in small and medium firms. Barriers were identified using an extensive literature review and finalized after consulting an expert panel. Next, a pairwise questionnaire was developed, and responses from essential stakeholders working with small and medium firms were collected. Data were analyzed using the DEMATEL technique. Salient challenges for implementing digital transformation technologies were identified, and the cause-and-effect relationship between the barriers was established. Lack of proper digital vision and strategy was identified as the most critical barrier that hinders adoption of digital transformation technologies in small and medium firms. Digital technologies help to improve the efficiency of the firms and improve resource utilization by facilitating timely and accurate decision making. Hence, overcoming the identified challenges in transformation will improve the operations of the production system and organizational process.

INTRODUCTION

Customers' faster changing needs create a complex working climate for SMEs. In this climate, only agile enterprises have a greater chance of surviving the current or upcoming crises. SMEs have been fighting to survive in the post-COVID-19 environment while being the backbone of many economies. Many SMEs have started realizing the importance of adopting digital technologies to improve their operations. Digitization can help improve operations and make organizations agile and resilient. Additionally, adoption

DOI: 10.4018/979-8-3693-0111-1.ch008

of digital technologies helps extend the potential customer base for SMEs. Firms appear to be competing for enormous opportunities and increasing market share, while digital transformation appears to be lagging among small businesses and enterprises (Nimawat and Gidwani, 2021). The application and usage of digital transformation technology by businesses in various industries for the creation of new digital value streams and help businesses use digital technologies to transition from old to new business models.

It has been established from previous literature that technology is the only futuristic solution for SMEs, as these transformation technologies improves all aspects of business which includes production process, customer relations, material management, financial management, marketing, supply chain management, product design innovation, skill or talent development, and employee engagement, among other things. Digital technologies are revolutionising the way systems and processes work around the world, and they are driving the present corporate landscape of SMEs. Therefore, the technology partnership can help for faster implementation of technology in small firms (Turkes et al., 2019; Ulas, 2019). The difficulty of getting a proper partner for technology implementation lags the adoption of digital transformation in existing and new business landscapes across the country.

As small companies and businesses adjust to technological advances, these micro and small businesses find themselves in various levels of the digital curve, forcing them to reassess their processes and systems. It wouldn't be inaccurate to claim that organisations would never be able to acquire a competitive advantage unless they embrace digitalisation today and oppress barriers to the adoption of technologies. For them to drive company efficiency, digital adoption is the important and primary factor for growth and survival. It is now a prerequisite for businesses to be digitally equipped to survive in the competitive environment.

The study aims to answer following research questions.

RQ. What are the critical challenges and interdependencies of barriers for implementing Digital Transformation Technologies in SMEs of developing countries?

To provide the solution for the question, the barriers to the adoption of transformation technologies are identified using detailed literature review. A pairwise questionnaire based on DEMATEL framework was sent to experts. The responses of the experts were analysed for identifying the relationships among the barriers and rank them in order of their influence.

The structure of the paper is as follows. Next section highlights the review of the previous literature and defines the barriers obtained during the review. The following sections describes the DEMATEL method and describes the data collection process. The fourth section provides the result of the analysis. The next sections discuss the findings and provides managerial implications. The last section includes the conclusions, relevance and future study.

LITERATURE REVIEW

The impact of innovations or improvements in digital technology and technical breakthroughs is huge on operations of small enterprises. Adoption of these technologies contribute to the nation's economic and societal development through prosperity as well as their global expansion. As the speed or rate of digital technological innovation continues to increase rapidly and exponentially Coad and Tamvada (2012), digital technology transformation is highly required and critical to survive in today's competitive market landscape.

The primary goal of digital technology research continues to be accelerating and acting as a catalyst for effective and efficient digital transformations of organizations (Zaoui and Souissi, 2020). The updating and verification of digital transformation technologies are connected with the current digital technology state of the process and technology in the company. As numerous studies have suggested and proposed, the evaluation of the adoption of technology should be multi-dimensional with the help of MCDM or DEMATEL techniques. It is critical to do the assessment of risks and barriers at various phases of digital transformation in order to evolve and reflect on the company's digital process maturity and raise concerns about the efficacy of the procedures used for implementation. This can facilitate sensitization of the various stakeholders and also help them understand the importance of a collaborative and agile approach to the digital technology transformation process.

Barriers to Digital Transformation in SMEs

IT Infrastructure and Facilities

Many products, applications and services in firms may face substantial barriers due to Information technology infrastructure in the country for effective communication and internet access (Rawat and Purohit, 2019). In some production facilities of operational firms (Norman et al., 2020), while implementation of digital technologies, a weak signal or network causes signal attenuation and failure.

Availability of Training/Trainers

Job displacement and De-industrialisation is an output of digital technology transformations (Parschau and Hauge, 2020). A skilled workforce is required to operate modern equipment. Machines can replace humans, and skills like problem-solving and decision making are important for the workforce. New job roles will appear in the firm and existing work profiles will be disappeared (Vaidya et al., 2018). The proper training by the professionals can help employees easily adapt to the changes in technology.

Organizational Culture and Mind-Set

Organizations must experience or feel in the market for a significant socio-technical transition to move towards digitalized business, which will affect the overall organization, organisational hierarchies, structures, strategy or goals, objectives, IT and cyber security systems, techniques, and business models (Legner et al., 2017). In order to survival in a dynamic, disruptive world, businesses must radically reform and restructure their business model and environment (Hartl and Hess, 2017). The willingness to learn, customer centricity, agility and trust between co-workers are a few keys for successful transformation. The mind-set of people differs, and it will be a barrier to digital transformation in most firms (Wiliandri, 2020).

Huge Investment and Finance

The small firms find it difficult to raise finance for upgrading new technologies and adopting digital transformations due to existing loans and debts. Additionally, fewer investors interested to invest in the performance and operation of the organization (Kiel et al., 2017). The digital technology in organizations is implemented as per the urgent needs to match the market needs and strategic planning and focus on customers. Financial requirements exist to build new infrastructure, training of resources, buy required resources for the firm, etc. (Shin et al., 2014). Digital technology is implemented due to the urgent needs and strategic planning and focus on customers and removing obstacles on their way to implementation (Norman et al., 2020).

Legal and Contractual Uncertainty

The law or enforcement institutions and governments of developing nations face a challenge as a result of sudden and dynamic changes made in digital technologies and the increased market competition brought on by the digitalization of small and large organizations (Türkeş et al., 2019). Data security and protection norms or laws, digitalization liability of new technology, and standardisation of technology should all be considered and are major challenges while implementing a digital strategy by SMEs.

Lack of Reference and Standards

The development of efficient and effective network architecture or transformation technologies is challenging without an existing document or reference materials (Cichosz et al., 2020). The value chains across different departments of small firms that involve objects or technological tools, networks, information, mobility and communication services, and applications without the proper set of standards or reference materials is considered as a significant obstacle to successful digital transformation technology adoption (Raj et al., 2020).

Security and Privacy

Organizations have substantial challenges in terms of approval, privacy protection, system access, applications, network, and information (Schroeder, 2016). The security software and antivirus installation and implementation for small firms are not viable and costly. SMEs continue to have a low level of involvement in environmental protection. Production practises that pollute the locality and environment, such as the use of hazardous chemicals and materials, and produce dangerous waste that is not effectively managed and disposed to sources like air, sea, etc., pose a threat to organization and environment on long-term sustainability (Hasan et al., 2021).

Lack of Digital Operations and Strategy

Successful digitalization involves the adoption, implementation, and absorption of technologies by the entrepreneur, employees or the firm management that help to break or minimize the challenges or barriers to digital technology transformation in small businesses or organizations (Ras et al., 2017). SME's digital transformation process necessitates multidisciplinary and holistic research and tools. As a result of engaging all relevant scientific methodologies, arts and technology fields in different departments of the organization, a more holistic knowledge with the total approach of why, how, and when digital transformation technologies might work or suit for the firm and is required needs to be analysed (Mintocoy et al., 2016).

Coordination and Integration

There are numerous impediments and challenges that may arise throughout when updating or integrating present machinery and equipment in order to transform technologies in businesses (Legner., et al, 2017). One of the major challenges involved with the digital transition is ensuring and coordinating consistent integration and compatibility between various emerging or dynamic digital technologies and existing equipment or machinery, human resources, and value systems.

Table 1. Barriers of adoption

Variable	Barriers	Source
B1	Lack of IT infrastructure & facilities	Rawat and Purohit (2019); Norman, F. (2020)
B2	Availability of training/ trainers	Vaidya, et al. (2018): Parschau and Hauge, J. (2020)
B3	Organizational culture & mind-set	Hartl and Hess (2017), Wiliandri, (2020)
B4	Huge Investment and finance	Kiel et al., (2017) ; Shin et al., (2014)
B5	Legal & contractual uncertainty	Türkeş et al., (2019); Norman (2020)
B6	Lack of reference and standards	Raj, et al., (2020),
B7	Security & privacy	Norman (2020); Schr€oder (2016); Kiel et al., (2017)
B8	Lack of digital operations & Strategy	Ras et al (2017); Nimawat and Gidwani (2021); Minto-Coy et al., (2016).
B9	Coordination and integration	Legner et al., (2017) ; Glass et al., (2018)
B10	Uncertain economic benefit	Rahmatullah et al., (2020); Nimawat and Gidwani (2021)
B11	Lack of technological partnership	Medic et al., 2020
B12	Skill gap	Parschau and Hauge (2020); Nimawat and Gidwani (2021)

Emerging-market enterprises are lagging behind in implementing the industry 4.0 digital technology transformation concept in the manufacturing and service environment (Glass., et al, 2018). Since developed and rich countries are driving this change, which involves digitalization and integration of manufacturing and operation processes across the entire market value chain, it could be the reason for change in the market. Because emerging-market enterprises have a low level of digital technological maturity, they should concentrate on adoption and implementing well-established and successful technologies.

Uncertain Economic Benefit

Overseeing the product demand in different market segments, poor inventory management due to flawed analysis, visual communication of products using advertisements through various media, usability and functionality or need of product or service should successfully reach to clients or customers in order to establish proper benefits (Rahmatullah et al., 2020) of releasing a new product. Businesses across different parts of the world will evolve with the increase in customer demand. The research and development for new products or services provided in small firms is considerably less, and the production focus is mostly on manufacturing existing products or satisfying the customer needs due to lack of analysis and evaluation of economic benefits of digital transformation technologies. Digital technologies help to focus on innovation, transformation and supporting or delighting the future needs of clients or customers are not in the interest of SMEs (Agrawal et al., 2019).

Lack of Technological Partnership

The enterprise systems or network for a smaller organization is not easy to implement without the help of technology or service companies. The firms need to invest a huge amount to have in house technology and many firms are not interested in spending a huge amount for these technologies due to this challenge. The technology partnership can help the smaller firms to grow faster with the help of technical skills from expert firms which supports in the analysis of the market or customer demand, supporting the technology infrastructure, etc. (Türkeş et al., 2019). Few firms are hesitant due to fear for partnership and continue with the existing technology, which run with inferior technology due to lack of confidence in partners as well as partnerships. Small firms perform and outgrow with the help of proper technology partnerships of required digital technologies for the organization (Medic et al., 2020).

Skill Gap

Digital technologies require specialist and skilled labours for running and operations in the organization like programming the numerically controlled machines, analysing the organizational data, etc. (Benešová & Tupa, 2017). The technologies require and need administration of a graduate or skilled technician for the operation of these advanced technologies (Gabriel & Pessl, 2016). Meanwhile, human resource constraints for transformation include employees' lack of environmental understanding, a lack of empowerment training, and a limited ability to adopt the technology. Operation knowledge of employees in digital transformation technologies is a factor of success in the implementation of these in the organization.

RESEARCH METHODOLOGY

Figure 1. Research methodology

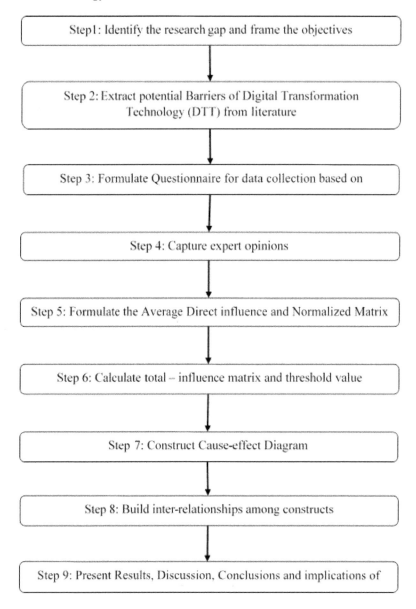

The research study focused on Indian MSME's digital technology transformation and to model the barriers of this transformation. The intention of the study is to inspire the smaller firms towards digitalization, help understand the entrepreneur or organization management the needs of digital transformation and to adopt the technologies such as cloud computing, automation, artificial intelligence, etc. The figure 1 depicts the systematic flow of research methodology adopted for conducting this research study.

The existing and new firms in the Indian ecosystem focus to boost their product and market profitability and optimize the efficiency to compete with global players which makes the implementation of digital technologies a necessity. The Government comes up with multiple schemes to enhance the growth of small firms (Machado et al., 2019). From the literature review twelve barriers that impede the adoption of digital technologies in small or medium firms in India have been found. The selected barriers for digital transformation technologies are analysed by decision making trial and error laboratory (DEMATEL) for finding relation, influence, and cause-effect between the barriers.

A questionnaire has been prepared and data has been collected from 15 experts who have experience in industry and digital transformation technologies from India.

The questionnaire provided to the experts includes the introduction of digital technologies, an explanation of studied barriers and a response matrix which reflects pairwise influence of the barriers with a scale ranging 0 – 4 where '0' refers to "No Impact" on the system, '1' refers "Low Influence", '2' refers "Medium Influence", '3' refers "High Influence and '4' refers to "Very High Influence".

The following steps of DEMATEL analysis are used to find inter-relationship between various barriers in the implementation of DTT.

Step1: The experts provide the impact of each barrier in the pairwise matrix columns on the respective barriers contained in the matrix rows. The matrix was developed so that the respondents can measure the direct relationship between each digital technology implementation barriers. The degree of influence through which digital technology barrier bi viewed by the respondent influences digital technology barrier bj is represented as bij.

Step2: The average direct influence matrix for digital implementation barrier that provide average value from different experts are obtained with the help of equation (1) and displayed in Table 8.1. A 12*12 (n*n) non-negative valued matrix is generated as $B_x = b^x_{ij}$ by individual respondent.

Average direct influence matrix of B = bij.

$$b_{ij} = \frac{1}{x} \sum_{i=1}^{x} bij \dots \dots \tag{1}$$

where x is the number of respondents participated and B1, B2,..,Bx are matrices of different experts.

Table 2. Aérage direct influence matrix

	b1	b2	b3	b4	b5	b6	b7	b8	b9	b10	b11	b12
b1	0	1.7	1.3	3	1.7	2.3	2	2.7	1	0.7	1.7	2.7
b2	2.67	0	2.7	2	2.3	2.7	2.3	3	3.3	3	1.7	4
b3	1.33	2.7	0	1	1	2	2.3	2	2.7	2.3	3.3	3.7
b4	3.33	3.7	2	0	2.3	3	2	3	2.7	3	3	3
b5	2.33	1.3	1	1.7	0	0.7	1.7	2.3	1.3	1.3	0.3	1.3
b6	1.67	2.7	1.7	2	2	0	1.7	3	2	2.3	2	1
b7	2.33	1.3	2	2.3	1.3	2.3	0	2.7	1.3	1.3	2	2.7
b8	2	2	3.3	3	3.7	3.3	3.3	0	3	2.3	3.7	3.3
b9	0.67	2.7	3	1	0.3	2	1	2	0	0.7	2	1.3
b10	1.67	1	1	2.3	1.3	1.7	1	3	0.7	0	1.7	1.3
b11	1.33	3.7	2	2.3	2.3	3	2	2	1.7	2.7	0	2
b12	0.67	3	2.3	1.7	1	1	1	0	3	2.7	2	0

Step 3: The average influence matrix was normalized by finding and dividing highest score total row from every cell in the matrix. Using formula (2), the normalized initial direct-influence matrix (D) = [dij] is measured and obtained. Each barrier in the pairwise matrix (D) had a cell value ranging from [0, 1].

$$D = \frac{B}{L} \dots\dots\dots \tag{2}$$

$$L = \max_{1<=i<=n} \sum_{j=1}^{n} bij \dots\dots \tag{3}$$

All elements in matrix (D) valued between 0 and 1. The normalized initial direct-influence matrix (D) is displayed in Table 2.

Table 3. Direct-Influence matrix

	b1	b2	b3	b4	b5	b6	b7	b8	b9	b10	b11	b12
b1	0	0.1	0	0.1	0.1	0.1	0.1	0.1	0	0	0.1	0.1
b2	0.1	0	0.1	0.1	0.1	0.1	0.1	0.1	0.1	0.1	0.1	0.1
b3	0	0.1	0	0	0	0.1	0.1	0.1	0.1	0.1	0.1	0.1
b4	0.1	0.1	0.1	0	0.1	0.1	0.1	0.1	0.1	0.1	0.1	0.1
b5	0.1	0	0	0.1	0	0	0.1	0.1	0	0	0	0
b6	0.1	0.1	0.1	0.1	0.1	0	0.1	0.1	0.1	0.1	0.1	0
b7	0.1	0	0.1	0.1	0	0.1	0	0.1	0	0	0.1	0.1
b8	0.1	0.1	0.1	0.1	0.1	0.1	0.1	0	0.1	0.1	0.1	0.1
b9	0	0.1	0.1	0	0	0.1	0	0.1	0	0	0.1	0
b10	0.1	0	0	0.1	0	0.1	0	0.1	0	0	0.1	0
b11	0	0.1	0.1	0.1	0.1	0.1	0.1	0.1	0.1	0.1	0	0.1
b12	0	0.1	0.1	0.1	0	0	0	0	0.1	0.1	0.1	0

Step 4: The total-influence matrix (T) is evaluated using the formula (4), in which I am 12*12 identity matrix. The elements t_{ij} in the total influence matrix mentions the indirect influence that barrier i has upon barrier j. The overall influence between each pair of barriers as seen in Table 3 which shows the total-influence matrix.

$$T = D(I - D)^{-1} \ \ldots\ldots.. \tag{4}$$

Table 4. Total-Influence matrix

	b1	b2	b3	b4	b5	b6	b7	b8	b9	b10	b11	b12
b1	0.11	0.2	0.2	0.2	0.2	0.2	0.2	0.2	0.2	0.1	0.2	0.2
b2	0.22	0.2	0.2	0.2	0.2	0.3	0.2	0.3	0.3	0.3	0.2	0.3
b3	0.16	0.2	0.1	0.2	0.2	0.2	0.2	0.2	0.2	0.2	0.2	0.3
b4	0.25	0.3	0.2	0.2	0.2	0.3	0.2	0.3	0.3	0.3	0.3	0.3
b5	0.15	0.1	0.1	0.1	0.1	0.1	0.1	0.2	0.1	0.1	0.1	0.1
b6	0.17	0.2	0.2	0.2	0.2	0.1	0.2	0.2	0.2	0.2	0.2	0.2
b7	0.18	0.2	0.2	0.2	0.2	0.2	0.1	0.2	0.2	0.2	0.2	0.2
b8	0.22	0.3	0.3	0.3	0.3	0.3	0.3	0.2	0.3	0.3	0.3	0.3
b9	0.11	0.2	0.2	0.1	0.1	0.2	0.1	0.2	0.1	0.1	0.2	0.2
b10	0.14	0.1	0.1	0.2	0.1	0.2	0.1	0.2	0.1	0.1	0.2	0.2
b11	0.17	0.3	0.2	0.2	0.2	0.2	0.2	0.2	0.2	0.2	0.2	0.2
b12	0.11	0.2	0.2	0.2	0.1	0.1	0.1	0.1	0.2	0.2	0.2	0.1

Step 5: The sum total of the total-influence matrix (T) rows and columns were measured one by one. Ri be the sum of ith row and Cj be the sum of jth colomn which is obtained from the total-influence matrix (T). The evaluation of Ri, Cj, (Ri + Cj) and (Ri - Cj) identifies the interdependencies among the barriers. The Ri value represents the total of the cells in the matrix given indirectly as well as the direct impact. The Cj value represents the total of the cells in the matrix given indirectly as well as the direct impact. When j = i, the obtained result of (Ri + Cj) displays the overall impact of both barriers given and received by barrier i (see table 4) .

Table 5. Sum total of the total-influence matrix

t_{ij}	b1	b2	b3	b4	b5	b6	b7	b8	b9	b10	b11	b12	Total
b1	0.11	0.2	0.2	0.2	0.2	0.2	0.2	0.2	0.2	0.1	0.2	0.2	**2.143282**
b2	0.22	0.2	0.2	0.2	0.2	0.3	0.2	0.3	0.3	0.3	0.2	0.3	**2.881103**
b3	0.16	0.2	0.1	0.2	0.2	0.2	0.2	0.2	0.2	0.2	0.2	0.3	**2.408858**
b4	0.25	0.3	0.2	0.2	0.2	0.3	0.2	0.3	0.3	0.3	0.3	0.3	**3.061695**
b5	0.15	0.1	0.1	0.1	0.1	0.1	0.1	0.2	0.1	0.1	0.1	0.1	**1.585659**
b6	0.17	0.2	0.2	0.2	0.2	0.1	0.2	0.2	0.2	0.2	0.2	0.2	**2.253334**
b7	0.18	0.2	0.2	0.2	0.2	0.2	0.1	0.2	0.2	0.2	0.2	0.2	**2.211647**
b8	0.22	0.3	0.3	0.3	0.3	0.3	0.3	0.2	0.3	0.3	0.3	0.3	**3.202395**
b9	0.11	0.2	0.2	0.1	0.1	0.2	0.1	0.2	0.1	0.1	0.2	0.2	**1.768322**
b10	0.14	0.1	0.1	0.2	0.1	0.2	0.1	0.2	0.1	0.1	0.2	0.2	**1.762526**
b11	0.17	0.3	0.2	0.2	0.2	0.2	0.2	0.2	0.2	0.2	0.2	0.2	**2.51418**
b12	0.11	0.2	0.2	0.2	0.1	0.1	0.1	0.1	0.2	0.2	0.2	0.1	**1.824637**
Total	**2**	**2.6**	**2.3**	**2.2**	**2**	**2.4**	**2.1**	**2.5**	**2.3**	**2.3**	**2.4**	**2.6**	

The value (Ri + Cj) identifies the degree of significance of barriers as shown in Figure 2, that is obtained by barrier i in the entire implementation system. The total contribution from digital technology implementation barrier I on the system is represented by (Ri - Cj). When Ri - Cj has a positive number, barrier bi has a net cause on the system and the value is negative, barrier b_i is a net effect relationship on the system. Table 8.4 analyse the degree of total influence of digital transformation technology barriers.

Step 6: The threshold value (α) is the mean of the cell elements in the total-influence matrix (T). The threshold value in the matrix T specify how one barrier influence other barriers. Threshold value obtained helps to provide and identify differences between significant and non-significant outcomes.

Figure 2. Significance of barriers

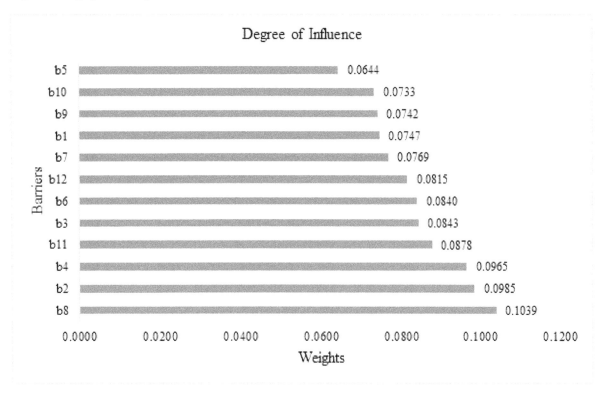

The importance and priority levels of barriers are shown in Figure 2. Lack of digital operations & Strategy (b8) has been identified as the most significant barriers. In contrast, Legal & contractual uncertainty has ranked with least score. The rankings based on priority or importance are Lack of digital operations & Strategy (5.7), Availability of training/ trainers (5.5), Huge Investment and finance (5.3), Lack of technological partnership (4.9), Organizational culture & mindset (4.7), Lack of reference and standards (4.7), Skill gap (4.5), Security & privacy (4.3), IT infrastructure & facilities (4.1), Coordination and integration (4.1), Uncertain economic benefit (4), Legal & contractual uncertainty (3.6).

Table 6. Ranking of barriers

Barrier	R	C	R+C	R-C	Rank	Cause/Effect
b1	2.1	2	4.1	0.1	9	Cause
b2	2.9	2.6	5.5	0.3	2	Cause
b3	2.4	2.3	4.7	0.1	5	Cause
b4	3.1	2.2	5.3	0.8	3	Cause
b5	1.6	2	3.6	-0.4	12	Effect
b6	2.3	2.4	4.7	-0.2	6	Effect
b7	2.2	2.1	4.3	0.2	8	Cause
b8	3.2	2.5	5.7	0.7	1	Cause
b9	1.8	2.3	4.1	-0.5	10	Effect
b10	1.8	2.3	4	-0.5	11	Effect
b11	2.5	2.4	4.9	0.2	4	Cause
b12	1.8	2.6	4.5	-0.8	7	Effect

Step 7: The cause and effect of each barrier is analysed and associations are made with the help of diagram (Table 6, figure 3). The diagram helps to identify the connections and how one barrier affects the other. It also determines the main barriers which impede the implementation of digital transformation technologies. The cause-and-effect diagram is obtained by plotting the coordinates (Ri + Cj) and (Ri - Cj). The directed graph helps to obtain inter-relationships between the barriers and influence of one barrier over other barriers. The cell elements in the total-influence matrix which is equal or greater than the threshold value which signifies high influenced power for the respective barrier. The directed graph is made by identifying impressing power of the total influence matrix.

Results

The research study aims to find the implementation barriers and challenges for adopting digital technologies as well as to obtain interdependencies and relationship between barriers in small and medium firms in India. Also, the study aims to find priority and impact levels of barriers in digital transformation technologies.

Figure 8.3 displays the cause-and-effect diagram for barriers. The cause-effect diagram of barriers is obtained by setting the coordinates $(R_i + C_j)$ and $(R_i - C_j)$. Figure 4 displays the relationship of one barrier on another. The barriers are encountered by mutual relations as well as direct single-sided relations. Both the barriers are affected one on another in mutual relation, and single-sided relation has anyone barrier affected on the other one. A black line without a pointing arrow represents mutual relations and an orange line with a pointing arrow denotes single-sided relations.

Figure 3. Cause–Effect plot

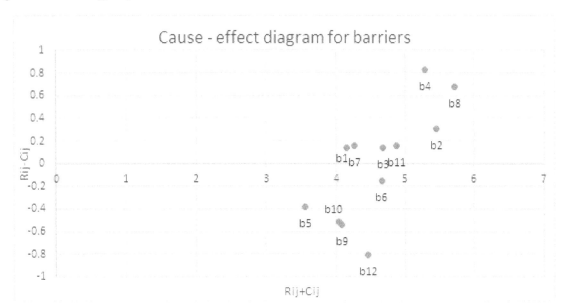

The presence of mutual and single-sided relations allows the managers to successfully handle and mitigate barriers while implementing digital transformation technologies in the firms. To understand it better, let us consider the 'IT infrastructure & facilities (b1)' and 'Huge Investment and finance (b4)' that has black line which implies these challenges have mutual relationship. Similarly, 'Lack of digital operation, and strategy (b8)' and 'Uncertain economic benefit' has mutual relationship in which one affect the other. The single sided relation where the barrier 'Skill gap (b12)' is affected by the barrier 'Lack of digital strategy (b8)'. Awareness of interactions can help decision-makers helps adopt and implement the digital transformation technologies faster and effectively in the organization.

The cause classified barriers for digital technology implementation with the help of $(R_i - C_j)$ score include Lack of digital operations & Strategy (0.7), Availability of training/ trainers (0.3), Huge Investment and finance (0.8), Lack of technological partnership (0.2), IT infrastructure & facilities (0.2), Organizational culture & mind-set (0.1), and Security & privacy (0.2). The firm needs to take proper control measures to mitigate these cause barriers. There are five effect category barriers in digital technology implementation from the study. The effect barriers are Legal & contractual uncertainty (-0.4), Lack of reference and standards (-0.2), Coordination and integration (-0.5), Uncertain economic benefit (-0.5) and Skill gap (-0.2).

Implication

The integration of digital transformation technologies can profoundly influence the growth and sustainability of Small and Medium Enterprises (SMEs) in developing nations:

a.   Enhanced Competitiveness: Embracing digitalization empowers SMEs to enhance their competitiveness by offering innovative products and services, enriching customer experiences, and streamlining operational efficiency.

b. Business Resilience: SMEs that undergo digital transformation are better positioned to navigate shifting market dynamics and external disruptions, such as the COVID-19 pandemic, by leveraging remote work, online sales channels, and digital communication tools.

c. Job Creation: Digital transformation has the potential to foster job creation within SMEs by driving demand for digital skills and fostering the emergence of new business opportunities in the digital economy.

d. Sustainable Development: Digital transformation contributes to sustainable development goals and environmental preservation by curbing resource consumption, boosting energy efficiency, and advocating for eco-friendly practices.

Therefore, the potential of digital transformation in fostering growth and sustainability within Small and Medium Enterprises (SMEs), especially in developing nations such as India, is substantial. By surmounting obstacles and adopting digital technologies, SMEs can bolster their competitive edge, broaden their market presence, and secure enduring prosperity in the digital age. Essential factors for advancing the digital transformation process of SMEs and realizing their capacity as drivers of economic growth and innovation include government backing, industry cooperation, and investment in digital infrastructure and education.

CONCLUSION

The paper aims to identify the barriers that acts as hindrances in implementing digital transformation technologies in small and medium firms. The technique of DEMATEL has been used to analyse the data and find the cause-and-effect relationship between the barriers. Implementation of digital transformation technologies must overcome multiple challenges, and it is not possible to have the solution for all challenges at the same time. Even with proper planning of implementation, DTT adoption may not provide expected beneficial. The findings are based on the expert respondents, and there are chances of bias based on the industry or institution of experts. Mitigating, handling, and controlling challenges will increase the success in the implementation of digital transformation technologies in small and medium enterprises. Identification of influence by each barrier and importance of knowledge on each barrier is incorporated in the research study, and cause-effect relationship with the help of DEMATEL method will help and assist the implementation of digital technologies in the industry. The studies and references on the implementation of digital transformation technologies in small or medium firms are limited. The removal of the gap in the transformation of small and medium firms will optimize the process of manufacturing, organisational process and help in better integration of humans and machines.

REFERENCES

Agrawal, P., Narain, R., & Ullah, I. (2019). Analysis of barriers in implementation of digital transformation of supply chain using interpretive structural modelling approach. *Journal of Modelling in Management*, *15*(1), 297–317. doi:10.1108/JM2-03-2019-0066

Cichosz, M., Wallenburg, C. M., & Knemeyer, A. M. (2020). Digital transformation at logistics service providers: Barriers, success factors and leading practices. *International Journal of Logistics Management*, *31*(2), 209–238. doi:10.1108/IJLM-08-2019-0229

Coad, A., & Tamvada, J. P. (2012). Firm growth and barriers to growth among small firms in India. *Small Business Economics*, *39*(2), 383–400. doi:10.1007/s11187-011-9318-7

Glass, R., Meissner, A., Gebauer, C., Stürmer, S., & Metternich, J. (2018). Identifying the barriers to Industrie 4.0. *Procedia CIRP*, *72*, 985–988. doi:10.1016/j.procir.2018.03.187

Hartl, E., & Hess, T. (2017). The role of cultural values for digital transformation: Insights from a delphi study. *AMCIS 2017 - America's Conference on Information Systems: A Tradition of Innovation, 2017-Augus*. AMCIS.

Hasan, A., Murni, Junita, & Rahmi, I. (2021). Ranking of Drivers and Barriers for the Green Management Implementation at MSME in Banda Aceh City, Indonesia. *Proceedings of the 2nd Borobudur International Symposium on Science and Technology (BIS-STE 2020)*, (pp. 52–61). IEEE. 10.2991/aer.k.210810.010

Huang, C. J., Chicoma, E. D. T., & Huang, Y. H. (2019). Evaluating the factors that are affecting the implementation of industry 4.0 technologies in manufacturing MSMEs, the case of Peru. *Processes (Basel, Switzerland)*, *7*(3), 161. doi:10.3390/pr7030161

Kiel, D., Arnold, C., & Müller, J. M. (2017). *Sustainable Industrial Value Creation: Benefits and Challenges of Industry 4. 0. The XXVIII ISPIM Innovation Conference – Composing the Innovation Symphony*. Research Gate.

Legner, C., Eymann, T., Hess, T., Matt, C., Böhmann, T., Drews, P., Mädche, A., Urbach, N., & Ahlemann, F. (2017). Digitalization: Opportunity and Challenge for the Business and Information Systems Engineering Community. *Business & Information Systems Engineering*, *59*(4), 301–308. doi:10.1007/s12599-017-0484-2

Machado, C. G., Winroth, M., Carlsson, D., Almström, P., Centerholt, V., & Hallin, M. (2019). Industry 4.0 readiness in manufacturing companies: Challenges and enablers towards increased digitalization. *Procedia CIRP*, *81*, 1113–1118. doi:10.1016/j.procir.2019.03.262

Medic, N., Anisic, Z., Tasic, N., Zivlak, N., & Lalic, B. (2020). Technology Adoption in the Industry 4.0 Era: Empirical Evidence from Manufacturing Companies. *IFIP Advances in Information and Communication Technology, 591 IFIP*, 115–122.

Minto-Coy, I. D., Cowell, N. M., & McLeod, M. (2016). Introduction: Breaking the barriers: Entrepreneurship, enterprise, competitiveness and growth in the Caribbean. *Social and Economic Studies*, *65*(2–3), 1–13.

Nimawat, D., & Gidwani, B. D. (2021). Identification of cause-and-effect relationships among barriers of Industry 4.0 using decision-making trial and evaluation laboratory method. *Benchmarking*, *28*(8), 2407–2431. doi:10.1108/BIJ-08-2020-0429

Norman, F. (2020). Key Factors to Promote Industry 4.0 Readiness at Indonesian Textile and Clothing Firm. *Engineering, MAthematics and Computer Science (EMACS). Journal*, *2*(2), 73–83.

Parschau, C., & Hauge, J. (2020). Is automation stealing manufacturing jobs? Evidence from South Africa's apparel industry. *Geoforum, 115*(July), 120–131. doi:10.1016/j.geoforum.2020.07.002

Rahmatullah, I., & Sahade, N., Azis, F., & Bahri. (2020). Utilization of digital technology for management effectiveness micro small and medium enterprises. *International Journal of Scientific and Technology Research, 9*(4), 1357–1362.

Raj, A., Dwivedi, G., Sharma, A., Lopes de Sousa Jabbour, A. B., & Rajak, S. (2020). Barriers to the adoption of industry 4.0 technologies in the manufacturing sector: An inter-country comparative perspective. *International Journal of Production Economics, 224*, 107546. doi:10.1016/j.ijpe.2019.107546

Ras, E., Wild, F., Stahl, C., & Baudet, A. (2017). Bridging the skills gap of workers in industry 4.0 by human performance augmentation tools - Challenges and roadmap. *ACM International Conference Proceeding Series, Part F128530*, (pp. 428–432). ACM.

Rawat, P., & Purohit, J. (2019). A Review of Challenges in Implementation of Industry 4.0 in Indian Manufacturing Industry. *International Conference on Recent Trends and Innovation in Engineering, Science & Technology*, (pp. 289–297). ACM.

Schroeder, C. (2016). The Challenges of Industry 4.0 for Small and Medium-sized Enterprises. *Friedrich Ebert Foundation*, (August), 1–28.

Shin, S. J., Woo, J., & Rachuri, S. (2014). Predictive analytics model for power consumption in manufacturing. *Procedia CIRP, 15*(December), 153–158. doi:10.1016/j.procir.2014.06.036

Türkeş, M. C., Oncioiu, I., Aslam, H. D., Marin-Pantelescu, A., Topor, D. I., & Căpuşneanu, S. (2019). Drivers and barriers in using industry 4.0: A perspective of SMEs in Romania. *Processes (Basel, Switzerland), 7*(3), 153. doi:10.3390/pr7030153

Ulas, D. (2019). Digital Transformation Process and SMEs. *Procedia Computer Science, 158*, 662–671. doi:10.1016/j.procs.2019.09.101

Vaidya, S., Ambad, P., & Bhosle, S. (2018). Industry 4.0 - A Glimpse. *Procedia Manufacturing, 20*(January), 233–238. doi:10.1016/j.promfg.2018.02.034

Wayman, O. (2019). The digitalisation of small and medium enterprise in Ireland Models for Financing Digital Projects. European Commission, 1–20.

Wiliandri, R. (2020). A Conceptual Approach to Identify Factors Affecting the Digital Transformation of Micro, Small and Medium-sized Enterprises (MSMEs) during Covid-19 Pandemic in Indonesia. *Ekonomi Bisnis, 25*(2), 66. doi:10.17977/um042v25i2p66-85

Zaoui, F., & Souissi, N. (2020). Roadmap for digital transformation: A literature review. *Procedia Computer Science, 175*, 621–628. doi:10.1016/j.procs.2020.07.090

Chapter 9
IoT and Smart Environment Solutions for SMEs

Nitsa J. Herzog
Northumbria University, UK

David J Herzog
QA Higher Education, UK

ABSTRACT

The fast development of information technologies fostered the recent flourishing of intelligent systems. While on the personal or household stratum, the usage of smart devices is quite limited in scope if not in function, on the industrial and geographical levels, various networks allow the creation of a new paradigm: Cyber-Physical space, enabled by the internet of things and smart environments. The phenomenon is truly global, encompassing all walks of life. Small and medium enterprises certainly benefit from the explosive spread of IoT and smart technologies. Industry 4.0 develops manufacturing, smart logistics and smart servitization, which are supported by just-in-time supply-chain operations. The current review of the present-day IoT, IIoT, and smart environments describes operational capabilities for innovative SMEs to expand operations and ride the wave of revolutionary change for profit and society benefits as a whole. A comprehensive assessment of potential drawbacks with technology acceptance by SMEs is done, with prospective solutions in every sphere of activities.

INTRODUCTION

Internet of Things (IoT) and smart environment technologies have significant potential to transform the way our society functions. It is especially important for most active parts of it, such as small and medium enterprises (SMEs). European Commission defines small enterprises as bodies with up to 50 workers and a turnover of up to 10 mln euros, while medium enterprises have up to 250 workers and a turnover of up to 50 mln euros (Hansen and Bøgh, 2021). Small and medium enterprises constitute as much as 90% of all companies and are accountable for at least 50% of employment worldwide. From 40% to 60% of GDP is formed by SMEs, depending on the country. IoT and smart environments are ca-

DOI: 10.4018/979-8-3693-0111-1.ch009

pable of significantly enhancing the efficiency and productivity of any business enterprise. Industry 4.0 elements are usually associated with large manufacturing, logistics and energy supply firms. However, smart environments build a basis for SMEs' growth and innovation. Every area of business activity can benefit from it, but there are some important domains where SMEs can develop unique capabilities with the help of IoT and smart environments.

THE FOURTH INDUSTRIAL REVOLUTION

The Fourth Industrial Revolution, also known as Industry 4.0, was born out of the contemporary trend of overall automation and big data flow in the manufacturing sector and other industries. It is a result of evolution in the industrial sector, characterized by the integration of modern technologies: IoT, AI, robotics, 3D printing, blockchain, digital twinning, 5G, cloud computing, edge computing, Intelligent Decision Systems (IDS) and some others (Hansen and Bøgh, 2021). The concept of Industry 4.0 is built around the creation of "smart factories," where machines, devices, and personnel are all interconnected and communicate in one Cyber-Physical Space (CPS) in real-time. It helps entrepreneurs to streamline operations, optimize Product-Service Systems (PSS) (Le-Dain et al., 2023) and create new timesaving, labour-efficient, cost-effective, customer-focused, flexible business models.

Internet of Things

IoT refers to the network of devices, vehicles, home appliances, and other objects seamlessly embedded with various sensors and actuators. It is a concept that refers to the interconnection of objects and devices to the internet, enabling them to collect, process and exchange data (Ding et al., 2023). Today ML and AI are widely used for data processing. The architecture of IoT is usually divided into layers (See Figure 1), each of them responsible for specific functions. Below are described the commonly recognized five layers of IoT and their important elements.

Layers

Figure 1. Five layers of IoT

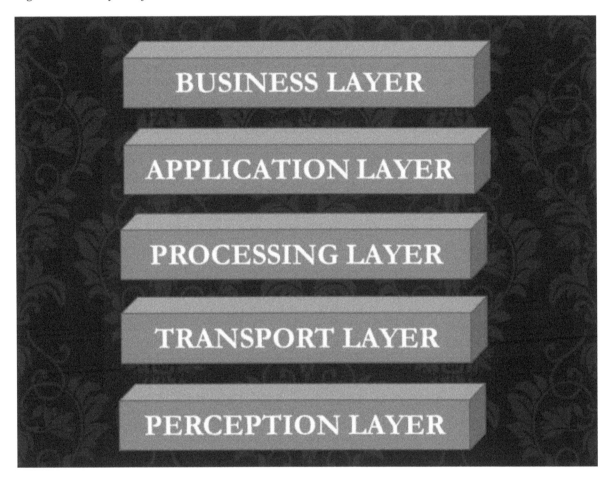

Perception Layer: The main elements are sensors, microcontrollers, actuators and smart devices (Poslad, 2011). Sensors collect physical environment data and transform it into a digitalised one. Embedded microcontrollers are actually computers on a chip or Systems-on-a-Chip (SoC) that have the ability to serve sensors for fog or edge computing. Actuators transform digital information into physical or mechanical actions. Smart devices perform more complex tasks of ubiquitous computing. Perception layer devices provide row data for analytical applications. Collected big data is processed and analysed and can be used for the modelling and prognosis. Artificial Intelligence is a powerful tool for SME business applications. Robust dataflow helps with effective methods like blockchain and digital twinning.

Sensors are doorways for inputting information into devices (McEwen and Cassimally, 2013). They can be classified by the basic principle of work. Electromagnetic ones gather data passively or actively in the electromagnetic spectrum: radio, microwave, infrared, visible light, UV, X-ray and gamma-ray detectors. Another type of electromagnetic sensor is Radio Frequency Identification (RFID) reader (Mrabet et al., 2020), inductive or capacitive. Specific magnetic sensors detect magnetic field or its distortion in the proximity. Piezoelectric sensors are built on the effect of anisotropic crystals to generate electric current under mechanical stress and, conversely, to produce mechanical stress inside of the anisotropic crystal, when an electric current flows through it. They are actively used for mechanical and audio data collection. Chemical sensors detect certain chemicals or their concentrations through the physicochemical qualities or chemical interaction (Zhu et al., 2019).

Sensors are subdivided into groups by the type of data (Verma et al., 2019). There are positioning sensors, pressure sensors, proximity sensors; level, acceleration/deceleration and gyroscope 3D space sensors; force and vibration sensors, temperature sensors, humidity and fluid property sensors, gas sensors and some others. Sensors of similar or different types can be used in batches and ensembles for the same type of data or aggregated data. Sensors can be stationary, mobile or wearable, passive or active, simple and combined with other devices.

Actuators are output devices, which convert digital data into physical force or mechanical motion (McEwen and Cassimally, 2013). Light Emitting Diodes (LED) or their analogues are the simplest known actuators. The next most widespread type is part of Micro-Electromechanical Systems (MEMS) or Nano-Electromechanical Systems (NEMS). MEMS usually combine sensors, processing parts and micro electromotive actuators (Zhu et al., 2019). They are widespread in the modern technological environment, from solenoid-based doorbells and electronic appliances to biomedical devices and automotive vehicles (Garcia et al., 2017). These actuators are programmable, clean and accurate, but delicate, depend on the environmental conditions and are relatively expensive. Hydraulic actuators are used in industry, transport and infrastructure. They are relatively swift and powerful, with a significant magnitude of force, but noisy and potentially leaky. Pneumatic actuators are low-cost and durable, with rapid reaction and calibrated power. They use gas or vacuum for mechanical action. Pneumatic actuators are widespread, with applications in industry, automotive vehicles, and robotics. Other types of actuators are thermal/mechanical, which utilize Shape Memory Alloys (SMAs) or Magnetic Shape-Memory Alloys (MSMAs), soft actuators, which are used in haptic devices or as artificial muscles, Shape Memory Polymers (SMPs) or Light-Activated Polymers (LAP) (Zhu et al., 2019).

Microcontrollers are types of self-contained Single-Board Computers (SBC) hosted on a microchip (Sugiura et al., 2023). They are usually part of a bigger system, embedded into smart devices, environment objects or networks. SBCs usually consist of a one-board microcontroller with 700-1.5 MHz processor, DDR3 512-2 GB Random Access Memory (RAM), Read-Only Memory (ROM), I/O with USB and LAN ports and Ethernet, and sometimes micro-USB (McEwen and Cassimally, 2013). Some SBCs have GPU, memory card slots, onboard flash memory, input keypad, touch panel, video and audio input devices. They run on various OS, ranging from embedded original systems to different types of Linux, BSD, Windows 10 and Android OS. Microcontrollers are low-cost computing devices but have some limitations. They can be used for limited operations simultaneously, often require a battery as a source of energy and have the drawback of restriction for direct contact with high computer power devices because of the significantly slower clock speed in CPU.

Smart devices range from smartphones and smart home appliances to industrial tools and infrastructural IoT smart objects. Their usage is widespread. Applications on a personal level include telecommunication, wearable gadgets, smart home environment, smart production lines, smart grids (Gaggero et al., 2021) and smart cities. Smart devices usually incorporate variable sensors, actuators, embedded System-on-a-Chip, microcomputers or more powerful computing units and networking I/O parts (Garcia et al., 2017). They are supplied with a human-computer interface, embedded OS, classical OS and often higher-level software. Smart devices are important for Edge and Fog computing. Smart devices, sensors, and gateways often form Fog computing level – the most extreme in Edge computing. The further extension is Mist Computing. Between Fog and Cloud computing is the level of personal computing devices – Dew computing (See Table 1)

Table 1. Types of computing by level

Computing	Level	Devices	Level above	Level below	Interactions	Environment
Mist	Extreme edge	Sensors, actuators	Fog	—	S2S, S2D/D2S	External, smart sensors and actuators network
Fog	Edge	Nodes, gateways, smart devices	Dew, Cloud	Mist	S2D/D2S, D2D, M2M, H2D/D2H,D2C	Networking devices
Dew	Local	Computing devices	Cloud	Mist, Fog	S2D/D2S, H2D/D2H, D2D, D2C	Network of devices
Cloud	Upper	Servers	—	Fog, Dew	T2C/C2T	Internet

Note. Border areas between levels are somehow blurred by the contemporary abilities of smart computing.

Network/Data Transport Layer: This layer is responsible for data communication. It plays a basic role in enabling connectivity, managing network traffic, and guaranteeing efficient data transmission (Kumar et al., 2020). In IoT, the transport layer enables and safeguards the communication of the data as it travels between layers. Physically it is represented by wired or wireless hardware networking devices, such as bridges, hubs, switches, routers, gates, repeaters, access points and other network nodes. Some microcontrollers and smart devices can double as network nodes or gateways. Protocols of this layer are presented in Table 2.

The network topology depends on the network task, network complexity, redundancy requirements and the type of protocol used (Parmar and Desai, 2016). Point-to-point and linear topologies are the simplest variants. Ring topology is one of the linear variants. Bus topology connects all devices to the common transmitting bus in a simple branching form. More complex types are star topology when devices are connected to a central switch or hub, and mesh topology, where all devices are interconnected. Tree topology is used in more complex networks, and combines hierarchical structure with nodes, branching from the common "root nodes.

By distance, networks are routinely divided into several levels, from closest to widest. It starts with Near Area Network (NAN), Personal Area Network (PAN) in the personal space, and Body Area Network (BAN) for wearable devices. It is possible to use NAN in cloud-based applications, which allow a permanent dialogue between local smart appliances. Constrained Node Networks (CNN) are built from small smart devices, such as sensors, actuators or microcomputing units. It can be part of PAN, BAN or NAN as an extension or form an independent network. Local Area Network (LAN) or Wireless Local Area Network (WLAN) covers a building or group of buildings (Verma et al., 2019). Metropolitan Area Network (MAN) is extended over a city or metropolitan area. Field Area Networks (FAN) with mobile drone-based Long Range Wide Area Network (LoRaWAN) gateways are proposed for rural areas (Gaggero et al., 2021). Wide Area Network (WAN) unites LANs and MANs, expanding over much larger geographical areas, such as countries or regions. Global Area Network (GAN) is a truly global network of networks.

Protocols. Proximity communication techniques and protocols include Bluetooth, Radio-Frequency Identification (RFID) tag technology, Near-Field Communication (NFC), and infrared (IR), Z-wave, subject to distance and compatibility (Mrabet et al., 2020). Larger coverage networks exploit other wireless technologies: Wi-Fi, Zigbee, LoRaWAN, Worldwide Interoperability for Microwave Access (WiMAX) (Verma et al., 1019), 5G, Ultra-Wideband (UWB), Sigfox and some others. TCP/IP protocol is used to connect devices to the internet. Transmission Control Protocol (TCP) is the dominant protocol for a majority of internet connectivity. Many IoT protocols utilize IPv4, while more recent ones use IPv6 (See Table 2). The last one is an update to Internet Protocol (IP), which routes traffic across the Internet and identifies and locates devices on the network. User Datagram Protocol (UDP) is a communications protocol that enables process-to-process communication and runs on top of IP (Kumar et al., 2020). While IP is a so-called logical address, a Media Access Control (MAC) address is called a physical address and is assigned to every physical device in IoT with a potential for connectivity. IP and MAC addresses are unique, but while any MAC address is globally unique, the IP address is only publicly unique, with addresses in private networks without public uniqueness. Some protocols of this layer are presented in Table 2.

Processing/Middleware layer: The name "platform" is often used interchangeably with the terms "framework" and "middleware". The platform usually represents wider scope, which includes all necessary operational systems, protocols, frameworks, databases, applications, and even hardware, when all levels of architecture are included. Middleware is an intermediate software that helps the OS interact with databases and applications. It controls data flow, synchronization and transformation, provides synchronous and asynchronous messaging and communication between different components, and enables security services, including authentication, authorization, and encryption (Kumar et al., 2020). Middleware includes an I/O handler and manages data gateways, filtering information for APIs (Application Programming Interfaces). Web servers are part of middleware. There are several types of middleware architecture: Service-Oriented Architecture (SOA), Message-Oriented Middleware (MOM), Object-Oriented Middleware (OOM), transactional and procedural. Developed, extensive middleware is appropriately called a platform when it covers numerous functions on different levels of architecture. A number of protocols of this layer are presented in Table 2.

Application layer: it is built upon previous layers. The application layer of IoT interacts with underlying layers: the network and transport layer for data transmission and connectivity, reliable data transport and physical devices communication. It effectively enables end-to-end communication, data management, and application functionality within the IoT ecosystem. This layer handles IoT applications, device management and control, user interfaces and interaction, data processing and analytics.

This level has several messaging protocols (Kumar et al., 2020). Message Queue Telemetry Transport (MQTT) and more developed Advanced Message Queuing Protocol (AMQP) are based on TCP and serve for Machine-to-Machine (M2M) communication (Mrabet et al., 2020). More universal in the industrial IoT is Data Distribution Service (DDS), a decentralised Peer-to-Peer (P2P) real-time protocol on top of UDP. Less used is Hypertext Transfer Protocol (HTTP). It has been the origin of data communication for the World Wide Web (WWW), so consequently, it is being used in the IoT. However, it is not optimised for IoT because of the time and energy-consuming issues. HTTP is still utilized in 3D printing due to the large amounts of data it can transfer. Protocols of this layer are presented in Table 2.

Business/Representation layer: It is a task-oriented layer, which principally follows the logic of external tasks, so-called "business logic", not the internal or coding protocol. The business layer usually classifies front-end software tools operations that consume data from the closely underlying application layer. It can produce data analytics for the user from data, flowing through the system and provide graphs and other visualization solutions. Human-to-Machine (H2M) communication is the principal at this level. The business layer includes operations performed by system administrators to assess, control and maintain the overall functionality of the platform/framework. Artificial Intelligence (AI) tools, designed for data analytics, presented to a user, are mainly functional on this level. It is based on the data from other levels, which combine external inflow, basic internal analytics, and ML results. It provides human-readable data. Deep Learning (DL) applications for extensive IoT systems usually utilize cloud-based computing devices. The integrative approach is embodied in the concept of smart spaces and can be united as a generalised vision of a smart environment.

Table 2. Examples of data transfer protocols distributed between three main layers

Layer	Technology type	Protocol/Standard	On top of/ with help of	Function/ Application
Perception	RFID Bluetooth NFC Ethernet Wi-Fi w-network	EPC C1G2 IEEE 802.15 NFCIP IEEE 802.3 IEEE 802.11 5G NR	RFID tag Bluetooth chip NFC tag, card TCP/UDP ports SSID NB-IoT, eMTC	RFID networking Bluetooth PAN/BAN S2D, D2D LAN, WAN WLAN MMC M2M
Transport	IP IP WWW	TCP UDP HTTP	IPv4/ IPv6 IPv4/ IPv6 TCP	P2P, M2M, D2D & Internet connectivity
Application	IoT IoT DTLS DCPS, DLRL	MQTT AMQP CoAP DDS	TCP TCP UDP UDP	P2P, M2M P2P, M2M M2M D2D, D2C/C2D

Note. The three-layer model provides a comprehensive guide for basic IoT protocol stack.

Smart Environment

A significant part of IoT is pervasive ubiquitous computing, which enables the creation of smart environments, from smart homes to smart cities and regions (See Table 3). Software applications and connectivity enable massive and effective data collection, analysis and exchange (Le-Dain et al., 2023). In a smart environment, IoT devices can control energy usage, monitor resource consumption and provide real-time data for optimization decisions (Ding et al., 2023). Smart environments often incorporate machine learning and artificial intelligence to analyse Big Data and raise the effectiveness and robustness of any response (Serrano, 2018). The smart environment can be comprehended as the integration of the system of systems where smart objects serve the basic smart components. The consequent horizontal compartmentalization and vertical stratification allow the identification of smart homes, smart cities, and smart areas.

Smart Objects

Smart object is, in effect, any object or device with sufficient computer power, means of communication with other devices or networks, analytical and executive software and, optionally, User Interface (UI), including Graphical User Interface (GUI). A smart object can be a stand-alone device or part of the network, in our case IoT (Garcia et al., 2017). Smart devices can be provided for strictly personal handling, such as smartphones, and smart glasses; broad personal usage, such as Virtual reality (VR), Augmented Reality (AR) or Mixed Reality (MR) sets; smart home appliances and so on. They can be elements of personal transport, such as smart cars, or part of the public transport system. Industrial smart devices include smart machine tools, and smart logistics network elements, such as smart trucks or other means of smart-enabled transportation. Industrial robots were the main part of classical IoT and Industry 4.0 schemes, but today IoT expanded into logistics, with smart robotic drones or logistic robotic units, often employed in groups and ensembles. Infrastructure smart objects include smart meters, smart traffic lights, smart elements of environmental control devices, smart light poles and so on (Garcia et al., 2017). They are extensively used in smart home environments.

Smart Home

The classical smart environment unit of the first degree is a smart home. It routinely has easily controlled indoor climate and ventilation systems, smart house security and alarm system, light control, smart appliances, smart utility meters, and other systems (See Figure 2). The building is supplied with necessary seamless sensors, connected by LAN or WLAN with smart devices and ubiquitous computing units (Verma et al., 2019). The central computing unit can be smartphone-based, iPad-based, a special smart home hub, on a dedicated server or in the cloud. Interaction of the user with a system is enabled through the GUI or Voice UI (VUI).

Figure 2. Smart Home (Pixabay. License: CC BY-ND 2.0 – allows to share - copy and redistribute the material in any medium or format for any purpose, even commercially)

There are specific environments created on the basis of smart home. One of the most important is the Ambient Assisted Living (AAL) system, which is suitable for elderly or home-based patients with chronic conditions. In this case, AAL includes home assistance tools, self-organization software, context-aware emergency health condition reporting tools, communication channels with healthcare services, automatic Electronic Health Records (HER) updates, and other additions. Smart homes, buildings and quarters are integral to smart cities.

Smart City

Smart city is a popular contemporary ecosystemic concept, a step forward from classical smart manufacturing IoT system (Carro-Suárez et al., 2023). A smart city is an urban environment that includes IT technologies, connectivity and Big Data analysis (see Figure 3). The main goal of smart city is to improve the quality of life of its population. The foremost elements of the objectives are efficiency, sustainability and highly functional governance. An integration of infrastructure with contemporary technological resources encompass transportation (Cirillo et al., 2020), energy, healthcare, waste management, public services and public safety. While in standard public presentation, the smart city concept is dominated by the quality of life of its inhabitants, in technological terms, it is an extensive exercise in IoT capabilities, from typical tasks to full-scale cyber-physical environments, from smart streets to smart urban areas (Lynn and Wood, 2023).

The principal backbone is an infrastructure, able to host all necessary IoT modules as a supra-structure on the city level. Intrinsic parts of it include several components. High saturation level by various sensors, collecting real-time data about transport, environment,

Figure 3. Elements of smart metropolitan area IoT

(Pixabay. License: CC BY-ND 2.0 – allows to share - copy and redistribute the material in any medium or format for any purpose, even commercially.)

grid, energy and utilities` consumption, waste management, infrastructure condition, emergencies and so on. Robust connectivity, which includes broadband, 5G, Wi-Fi coverage (Serrano, 2018). 5G enables in IoT the Massive Machine Communication (MMC). Smart devices and ubiquitous computing units, that equip the processing part of smart city IoT with capabilities of cloud computing, supported by edge and fog computing, able to process Big Data 24/7. The expansion of smart cities' capabilities to suburbia and beyond is a natural process of evolutionary growth of smart areas and regions.

Smart Territory

A smart territory idea can be approached from different directions. It might be seen as an extension of a smart metropolitan city area into the surrounding country. Another approach comes from governmental and corporation vectors. Digitalized governance, environment monitoring, resources management, the smart grid (Gaggero et al., 2021) control, smart transport and infrastructure monitoring, logistical goods movement control, just-in-time manufacturing systems, global supply chain systems, global platform services – all of them expand on a truly global level. An additional way to approach the smart territory principle comes from the digital twin conception. Total digitalization of the environment with constant bi-directional data flow is highly broadened twinning, full-scale cyber-physical space of the highest possible magnitude (Gabrys, 2020).

There are some specific elements that are instrumental for the smart territory functionality. Wide-spread usage of stationary and mobile sensing systems has to allow adequate data collection from primary sources (Serrano, 2018). There are communication means for regional and global data sharing, such as broadband, 5G, and satellite communication systems. Another critical component is the existence of powerful data centers, which provide hosting for extensive databases, global cloud applications and vigorous data processing resources. Land-based Local Positioning Systems (LPSs) and satellite space-group-based Global Positioning Systems (GPSs) are actively used for tracking and navigation (see table 3).

Table 3. Smart environment by levels

Level	Network type	Network technology	Distance	Devices
Personal	PAN BAN LAN WLAN	RFID Bluetooth NFC Wi-Fi	From less than meter to hundreds of meters	Sensors, actuators, Smart devices, Smartphones
Smart production area	LAN WLAN	RFID Bluetooth Ethernet Wi-Fi 5G	From meters to hundreds of meters	Sensors, actuators, Smart devices, Industrial robots, Smart warehouse
Smart building	LAN WLAN	Ethernet Wi-Fi 5G	From meters to hundreds of meters	Sensors, actuators, Smart devices
Smart city	MAN	Ethernet Wi-Fi 5G LPS	From meters to thousands of kilometres	Sensors, actuators, Smart devices, Smart objects, Vehicles
Smart territory	GAN	Ethernet Wi-Fi 5G GPS	From meters to thousands of kilometres	Sensors, actuators, Smart devices, Smart objects, Vehicles, Satellites

Note. There is an overlapping of some network types.

Enhanced Manufacturing Productivity

Several contributions can be named as a way to enhance productivity as part of manufacturing, service or general improvement and cost-effectiveness (Le-Dain et al., 2023). IoT is able to automate various processes, from technical ones to administrative and merchandising practices. The Industrial Internet of Things (IIoT) streamlines all production steps (see Figure 4) and within specific phases of Product Lifecycle Management (PLM) (Ding et al., 2023). Marketing information today is widely available on the internet for all magnitudes of business activities with data mining algorithms and programs (Barrenechea and Jenkins, 2018). After identifying a suitable niche product, an idea is nurtured into the conceptualization and quickly passes to the design and engineering phase.

Victualic tools, that help with materials procurement are often part of these programs. IIoT tools help with material preparation, putting it into needed shape, taking part in the assembly, enabling testing and quality control, packaging it and helping with automated storage. IoT sensors can supervise production equipment and machinery, enabling predictive maintenance and reducing downtime (Bunte et al., 2021). Small, fully automatic production lines can be made more efficient by Augmented Reality (AR) devices, additive and hybrid manufacturing and synchronized Digital Twin models, which allow in-time improvements and algorithmic control (Wuest et al., 2022). R&D, hence, can be more affordable for SMEs with IoT and smart devices. Adjustments, modifications, customizations and optimizations are also much easier on smart production lines. There are also several important principles in IioT industry 4.0 production, called X2Order: Make2Order, Build2Order, Configure2Order and Engineer2Order (Dallasega et al., 2019).

Logistics/Transportation/After-Sales Service

Figure 4. Schematic representation of interconnections between robotic operators, smart assembly line and controlling devices.

(Pixabay. License: CC BY-ND 2.0 – allows to share - copy and redistribute the material in any medium or format for any purpose, even commercially)

There are several specific IoT contributions in PLM and logistics. Augmented Reality tools and Digital Twins are extremely helpful in production and maintenance. IoT and IIoT devices can monitor and control equipment, optimize energy usage, and automate inventory management, reducing human effort and minimizing errors. In warehouses, IoT sensors and smart environment technology can be used to monitor and streamline warehouse operations, including inventory, asset tracking, and supply chain management and optimization. IoT sensors can be used to track vehicles and optimize routes. Customer support and after-sales service are also optimized by the usage of dedicated platforms and real-time product control and collaboration with customers. End-of-Life management for the product can also be semi- or fully automated.

General Cost-Effectiveness and Platforms

IoT and smart environment provide more flexible, innovative and adaptive SMEs competitive advantages. Cloud solutions and networks often use platforms for different organizational tasks. Easy collaboration for a geographically spread workforce, compliance frameworks, streamlined administrative and financial processes, and higher information security are just a few of the effective solutions. Data analytical insights are provided by analytical soft on the basis of a continuous flow of intracompany data. Micromanagement can be avoided by effective automated workers' performance control. Asset tracking, transport fleet management, predictive maintenance, remote energy and resources monitoring are often supported by a combination of IoT, smart environment and specialized cloud platforms. Continuous innovation by concurring platforms enables higher integration and compatibility for software tools. Platforms give good accessibility, quick deployment, operational scalability and optimized vertical and horizontal integration (Martikkala, A. et al., 2021). The cost is reduced on every step of the process, from the business establishment, when conceptualization, government services, and credit availability are critical, to the fully operational trade activities. There is clear evidence of the effectiveness of Digital multi-sided platforms (MSP) for B2B-SME environment (Budde et al., 2024).

Administrative and Decision-Making Process

A significant part of the time in SMEs is often taken by administrative processes. Filling out necessary forms and documentation, following compliance procedures and reporting to the authoritative bodies are greatly improved by the smart governance paradigm with the E-government approach. Operational, financial, HR, project, marketing and risk management are enhanced by time synchronized IoT information and smart environment data. While large enterprises benefit from the size and departmental specialization, SMEs are asymmetrically affected by paperwork and red line. IoT and smart environment solutions can automate and organize paperwork processes, reducing manual errors and improving productivity and refining prognostic abilities. Data-Driven Decision Making (DDDM) is enhanced by effective reporting and graphical presentation of data. Well-presented graphical data is sometimes worth a thousand words, which is critical for a highly dynamic SMEs environment.

Financial Management

Automated and algorithmic solutions are extremely important for contemporary SMEs. Digital payment solutions, such as smartphone payment apps or online payment services, simplify all steps of the process for businesses and their customers and provide the required level of security. Electronic invoicing systems, e-banking, and automatic bookkeeping help to provide healthy operational accounting, sustainable cash flow and easy reporting. Platform solutions make it easy to approach or update financial information from any geographical location and any authorized device and keep it thanks to blockchain. Financial analytical tools help establish a clear financial picture with appropriate indicators and help in financial planning. Electronic solutions for ongoing crediting, new ways of funding, easy insurance, shares and assets management create a possibility for healthy growth and future prospects. Financial education and financial advice can be made in automated and semiautomated ways, which assists SMEs in being in line with new developments or requirements. Besides that, robust security solutions, such as AI-enhanced fraud and scam detection, appropriate encryption and 24/7 assets and operations monitoring, shielding the business and shareholders, investors, entrepreneurs and employees. Berkowitz and Souchaud (2024) conducted extensive research on several French angel investment groups and platforms and demonstrated significant growth of effectivity with the application of blockchain technologies and technologically supported governance.

Sales and Marketing

IoT, smart environment and Big Data can produce necessary information for effective sales and marketing. Some customer profiles can be used to create personalized marketing campaigns for narrowly focused groups and to gather data on customer behaviour and preferences to adjust advertisements and promotions. It can help with marketing triangulation and assist with establishing future inexpensive marketing strategies for SMEs. On-the-spot, in-time, local advertisement is a possible application in smart environments. Location-based marketing is based on GPS, Wi-Fi and Bluetooth beacon technologies.

Technological sale provisions for SMEs are supported by a wide range of tools and initiatives. There are a number of technological solutions for effective sales: easy cashless techniques, including customer face recognition identification utilization RFID and Near-Field Communication (NFC) tags, QR-codes, in-store beacons, smart vending machines, and automatic sale points. Smart shopping trolleys, smart Point-Of-Sale (POS) machines, mobile POS, and interactive self-service terminals reduce customer-related time consumption. Smart shelves, equipped with weight and other sensors and integrated with a smart inventory system, guarantee product availability, quality, and expiration date control. B2B solutions are demonstrated in the case study Franze et al. (2024) in marketing, customer services, sales and after-sales.

Areas of Application by Industries: Practical Examples

IoT frameworks and smart platforms are actively used by SMEs in different areas of practical business activity: manufacturing, agriculture (Hundal et al., 2023), transport, energy and utility management, retail, healthcare, entertainment enterprises and many others. Service industries can utilize technologies for asset tracking, machinery (Ding et al., 2023) and infrastructure predictive management, security, waste management and immediate environment monitoring. Below are listed the most prominent solutions and examples in these and some other spheres.

Energy and Utility Management

SMEs often have specific energy and utility consumption patterns, such as business hours and working days, or 24/7 supply in some cases. There are multiple theoretical and empirical research papers on the importance of smart meters, smart environment/IoT, and capabilities for small and medium enterprises, working in B2B and B2C models (Franki et al., 2023). Morelli et al. (2022) demonstrated the practical importance of policies with the installation of smart meters as part of Industry 4.0 and IoT efforts for the rising effectiveness of small and medium enterprises in European countries. Mourtzis et al. (2022) proposed a Digital Twin-based Smart Grid platform for SMEs with Product-Service System (PSS) framework. SMEs have a specific role of in the internationalization of activities in clean-tech and renewables, as shown in a Finnish study (Asemokha et al., 2019). However, some earlier practical reports show a mixed picture of the appropriation of new saving technologies (Bird, 2015). There is also a tendency for smart energy SMEs to be acquired by bigger corporations through mergers and acquisitions (Giordano et al., 2011). Smart utility systems often work at the junction of several knowledge areas. There is a significant demand for high-level data and expertise support. In this case study (Happonen et al., 2020), smart monitoring of municipal and industrial water distribution systems SMEs is shown to work in collaboration with local university researchers.

Manufacturing

Smart manufacturing is usually the domain of large corporations with the capability to invest into robotic production lines and fully automated factories. However, there is significant space for SMEs, using production IoT. If smart manufacturing is comprehended as Cyber-Physical Production System (CPPS), it can be subject to Value Stream Mapping (VSM) (Martin et al., 2020), which is suitable for small and medium enterprise methods. Lean Management (LM) theory lays at the basis of Industry 4.0 production, while automation for repetitive tasks in technological inputs and reverse engineering are fundamental solutions, important for SMEs (Rauch et al., 2020). One of the cost-effective methods of implementation of IIoT for SMEs is retrofitting (Muller and Voigt, 2018). Other methods are the wide sharing of data and analytics (Baars et al., 2021) and smart Production Planning Control (PPC) (Dallasega, 2019). Chen (2019) shows IoT technologies in the textile SMEs industry with value-creation outcomes through the integration of industrial supply chains into global supply chains. Meierhofer et al. (2022) proposed an advanced method of service-oriented data valuation in manufacturing for SMEs. A case study of designing a workplace in the conditions of a digital factory is one of the examples of the successful implementation of virtual micro-logistics (Zuzik et al., 2024).

Transportation/Logistics

Modern smart transport and logistics systems are grounded in several important postulates: X2Order manufacturing, Just-In-Time (JIT) delivery (Dallasega et al., 2019), real-time tracking control, self-organization (Rauch et al., 2020) and robust analytics. Shared Vendor Managed Inventory (VMI) allows all supply chain members to participate in a collaborative Pooled Warehouse Management framework effectively (Makaci et al., 2017). Warehouse Management Systems (WMSs) employ Economic Order Quantities (EOQ) system to minimize unnecessary resources spending. Intracompany logistics, or intra-logistics, is a separate branch of Logistics 4.0 (Krowas and Riedel, 2019). Automated material transport includes machine-controlled loading-unloading operations, driverless in-warehouse and external transportation, RFID, QR-code or other digitalized follow-ups of items. Smart transport systems require today not only global position systems, telemetry or data processing but also digitalized contractual parts. There are proposed smart contracts blockchain systems for collaboration in maritime transportation (Philipp et al., 2019). Blockchain and smart sensors are employed in perishable goods transport – Cold Chain Logistics (CCL), which is critically important for SMEs involved in the production, processing, transportation, warehousing and selling to the final customer (Ramirez et al., 2022).

Agriculture

The market value of agriculture 4.0 is valued at $27 billion in the U.S. only, with a precision and smart farming share of $2.42 billion (Khan, 2020). In agriculture smart technologies are employed on all levels, from biotech R&D to global positioning for aerial or ground-based drone networks. There are smart irrigation and input delivery systems (Hundal et al., 2023), agriculture drones or Unmanned Aerial Vehicles (UAVs) for monitoring and treatment, soil and plant monitoring systems, Yield Monitoring Systems (YMSs), Farm Management Systems (FMSs), precision livestock systems with smart sensors` tagging, smart greenhouses and smart hydroponic production systems, to name just a few (Annosi et al., 2019). Smart forestry can be expanded into agroforestry (Gabrys, 2020). Precision and smart agriculture will be valued to be $43.4 billion by 2025 (Khan, 2020). It includes farm mapping, GPS-assisted soil sampling, precision pesticides, herbicides, and fertilizer applications (Mizik, 2023). Smart crop collections, automatic packaging and early processing are parts of the product delivery chain. Climate Smart Agricultural (CSA) technologies (Groot et al., 2019) are acquired slowly, but show promising potential for profitability, as demonstrated by Land Laser Leveller, which is open to contract with SMEs for levelling irrigated fields in the North of India. Spanish agricultural SMEs blockchain is successfully employed for the agricultural production supply chain (Dominigues and Roseiro, 2020). The research by Striani et al. (2024) shows clear benefits and better sustainability in aquaponics digitalization as part of the ISEPA project supported by public-private partnership (PPP).

Healthcare

The healthcare sphere is routinely highly regulated by government bodies and more often available for national medicine and social care operators. Different forms of Public-Private-Partnership (PPP) are often acceptable in this case but are usually open for "big players", such as technical, biomedical or pharmaceutical giants or large insurance companies. At the same time, there are many successful inroads of SMEs into the biomedical or social care areas. Some of them concentrate on R&D in biotech, medtech and healthcare software; others propose services for patients and their relatives. According to Horgan et al. (2019), only the European healthcare innovation market has a size of 250 bln euros, but SMEs experience serious competition pressure from multinational companies. There is clear evidence from some regions and countries, in this case, Germany, that biotech R&D is dominated by SMEs (Shkolnykova and Kudic, 2022). They also lead in radical innovations, which is reflected by a number of important patents. One of the ways to exploit this direction is to create partnerships between healthcare providers and SMEs consortiums (Doorn, 2014). Holland et al. (2024) discussed the practical implications of AI-enhanced bio-medical engineering on the basis of several case studies. While there is clear evidence of the effective application of machine-based intelligence in bioengineering and its commercialization, concerns about sustainability and social and ethical issues are raised.

Retail

Retail practices in SMEs are one of the advancing sectors, which actively adapts IoT and smart environment technologies. The most prominent development is seen in e-commerce. Platforms and online payment systems are important integral parts of it (Rivera, 2021). Blockchain inventory and supply-chain automated systems are often supplied by Decision Support Systems (DSSs). Payment and stock and asset registration systems are often integrated into accounting and bookkeeping management frameworks, stand-alone or platform based (Pantano and Dennis, 2019). PandaDoc application service and its analogues allow easy electronic document follow-up, automatic invoice, and data sharing with eSign option for contractual documents. These services are specially designed for SMEs sector, with an extensive scope of options for retail.

In-store smart technologies include partially fully automated smart shelves, combined with supply-chain electronic systems (Rivera, 2021). Smart tag systems make product item follow-up and payment easier and quickerCustomer service comprises of return customer recognition systems, including face recognition with the option of payment, customer-tailored sales and promotions, easy electronic payment systems, and automatic payment terminals (Pantano and Dennis, 2019). There is a movement towards fully automated wending kiosks or shops. In-store augmented reality application usage with the help of smartphone applications instantly provides customers with all necessary product or brand information (Nikhashemi et al., 2021).

Financial SMEs

Smart financial services and banking for SMEs are important to the contemporary business environment (Kotios et al., 2012). Assets management, blockchain applications, e-bookkeeping and other software, smartphone-enabled and platform-based solutions are mentioned above. The niche for B2B financial and banking services focused on SMEs, are occupied by many small start-ups and medium unicorns. Individual financial solutions also attract many SMEs. Over-the-border currency transactions are often cheaper from smaller, technology-oriented providers. Fintech is as a popular direction of SMEs interests as technological or biotech start-ups. Supply chain finance, blockchain finance, pear-to-pear lending, and equity crowdfunding are domains, vigorously explored by small and medium enterprises (Feyen et al., 2023. Another significant area of activity is microfinance, including emergency loans, small business and personal financial risk management, and financial consultations (Sharma et al., 2023). A case study of the implementation of digitalized micro-financial loans to the extensive network of small and medium fisheries and aquaculture enterprises by the New Hope Liuhe Group in China demonstrates significant improvement in the financial management network (Du et al., 2024). An extremely active sphere for SMEs is associated with e-tokens, e-coins and cryptocurrencies. The financial reasoning or judgment of these operations is outside this paper's scope. However, it is important to mention that the cryptocurrency market's capitalisation today is exceeding $1 trln.

Services` Enterprises

Services may include significant scope of activities. Pre-sales and post-sale solutions, construction and repairs, transportation and logistics as services, technological and expert aid, food and beverages production and distribution, beauty therapy and wellbeing, events` organization, information, communication and IT implementation support, consulting in all spheres and many others are important in post-industrial societies (Meierhofer et al., 2022). Regions with active manufacturing development also consume all services, coming along with production, supply chain, marketing and capital management. Small and medium enterprises are especially active in all service areas, often forming the backbone of whole service industries.

Tourism and Hospitality

Contemporary tourist and hospitality industries use a wide range of technological solutions. Smart city adaptation to tourism unites accommodation, transportation, cuisine, touristic attractions and accessory services in one manageable supersystem (Lee et al., 2020). Smart spots are supplied by information resources and visual presentation tools, such as touch-screens, holograms, automatic translation services or on-site games. Smart applications are used in the case of seasonal or event-driven over-tourism (Pappas et al., 2021). Internet platforms and smartphone applications-enabled services allow registration for touristic attractions, excursions, self-check-in and self-check-out in hotels, B&B and hotel-like flats. The hospitality industry is investing into smart locks, working through Bluetooth (Mercan et al., 2021). 24/7 chatbot assistants create the possibility for effective indoor service. Minibars are controlled by bar-code reading or RFID to be refilled. Smart service systems are often part of the experience in tourist trains, buses, boats or airplanes. Smart environments and IoT give more potential safety to customers and staff.

Limitations and Challenges

The Internet of Things and smart environments can provide numerous benefits for SMEs. However, there are several barriers for these enterprises to overcome. No clear solution exists for all the complex, but some difficulties can be alleviated with sufficient effort, resource allocation, proper organizational collaboration and government support.

Technical Expertise

Many SMEs do not possess enough technical expertise or technical resources to implement and operate IoT or manage smart environment solutions (Bunte et al., 2021). The heavily technical topic demands additional training for personnel, consulting specialists or the use of external services. Every effective solution is quite expensive. In the case of a business environment, there are several stakeholders, and one of the sides is associated with theoretical and practical research. It is shown that universities` clusters are instrumental in creating and supporting technological SMEs (Ardito et al., 2019). There is high importance of stakeholders' collaboration in every case of R&D. Here we can see the necessity for constant connection for every SMEs, operating in a smart environment. Another possibility is widely available expert information for any activity, linked with technological solutions (Dallasega et al., 2019). Fundamentally, the technical expertise of entrepreneurs depends on the average level of education.

Infrastructure Availability

Small and medium enterprises are sensitive to the environment in which they operate. It applies to all aspects of business activities but is very important with technical infrastructure. SMEs operate not only in metropolitan areas but often locate their activities in rural or less developed regions (Baars et al., 2021. There is sometimes no approach to broadband, sensor-rich areas, extensive infrastructural IoT networks, Big Data flow or sources of marketing information. There are advocates for widespread broadband access and recommendations to make social and governmental data widely available or free. Okkonen et al. (2020) demonstrated that open IoT platforms for SMEs allow small-scale research-driven pilot projects before massive investment or long-term projects. This approach significantly lower potential risks for small and medium enterprises.

Interoperability

Multiple standards of hardware, operational and connectivity protocols and software incompatibility make IoT and smart environments less accessible for all users (Bunte et al., 2021). Proprietary limitations also can be restrictive. Devices may not be compatible with existing infrastructure systems or smart environments, making integrating them into existing workflows and processes difficult. To overcome it general standards are applied. Middleware is developed with options to create interoperability with different platforms and APIs. There is a movement for affordable and low-cost blocks of IoT, especially

Commercial-Off-The-Shelf (COTS) IoT devices and systems. Platform interoperability for IoT in smart cities is crucial (Okkonen et al., 2020).

Security Risks

IoT devices and networks are vulnerable to cyber-attacks, compromising sensitive data and posing a risk to business operations. SMEs may not have the resources to implement robust security measures, making them more vulnerable to these risks. Security threats for IoT networks include false node Sybil attacks, two or more nodes Wormhole attacks or Distributed Denial of Service (DDoS) attacks (Empl and Pernul, 2021). Data protection is often critical, taking contractual base or customer data. One of the solutions is platform-based security arrangements. Blockchain technology gives a certain level of protection from losing sensitive and valuable data. In some types of SMEs activities, such as healthcare, financial, legal or personal services security procedures require additional investment and staff training. Collaborative solutions can be instrumental in these cases.

Data Management

IoT devices generate large amounts of data, which can be difficult to manage and analyse without the appropriate tools and expertise (Bunte et al., 2021). SMEs may not have enough resources to effectively collect, store, and analyze this data (Bettoni et al., 2021). There are several levels of data operations, which can cause concerns: collection, where many sensors have to be operational; edge computing – data from smart sensors, actuators, gates and smart devices; transfer, which sometimes requires a protected and robust medium for by-directional transmission; storing, when often extensive volumes of raw and partially-processed data are deposited; processing, which can require powerful ML and DL AI solutions; effective presentation to other programming environments and end-users. Data, metadata and processing capacities sharing can be a good solution (Baars et al., 2021). Contemporary cloud data preservation and management platforms are also beneficial for SMEs and provide practical answers to these problems.

Regulatory Compliance

IoT and smart environment solutions are often subject to regulatory requirements and standards. It can be problematic for SMEs to navigate and comply with it without appropriate digitalized governance, effective regulatory bodies` support and transparency of legislation. The smart city environment is supposed to be beneficial for enterprises` activities (Cirillo et al., 2020). However, there are necessary solutions on the level of regional, country or global compliance. Initiatives are directed at the standardization of e-governance, legal digitalization, formalization of documentary practices, easy automated taxes and duties collection and other aspects of smart government. Regulatory and government bodies have to be more resilient and tech-oriented for successful Government-to-Business (G2B) solutions on all levels, from local to international (Barrenechea and Jenkins, 2014). Some limitations can arise from rapid, successful digital innovations that make some regulations obsolete, as shown by Berkowitz and Souchaud (2024).

Financial

IoT and smart environment solutions often require a significant initial investment and costly maintenance as long as these requirements are applied on the first, critical stage (Feyen et al., 2023). SMEs prefer to avoid primary risks and choose more affordable models of business. Industrial robots are quite expensive, as well as smart warehouse solutions or highly technological smart farming. There is a necessity for SMEs to pool financial resources, and share technical assets and elements of infrastructure. The availability of specific credit lines with government guarantees can be helpful for the support of SMEs. In these cases, entrepreneurial micro-crediting, P2P finance, crowdfunding solutions, targeted e-banking assistance, and focused loans are helpful. Platforming, lease of equipment, NGO initiatives and collaboration with other stakeholders can lower expenses for SMEs.

Sociology-Psychological Barriers

A separate big area of concern is comprised of sociology-psychological barriers. Long-term merchant traditions may lead to resistance to radical change (Bunte et al., 2021). Entrepreneurs and employees alike can be accustomed to traditional ways of work routines for various reasons. Lack of awareness often comes from deficient information. Insufficiency of technical skills and domain education can result in a lack of understanding of the benefits of technologies or difficulties in implementing them. Concerns about job security are often well-based, especially for less-qualified employees (Ding et al., 2023). SMEs entrepreneurs and employees can have privacy and security concerns: IoT and smart environment technologies may involve collecting and analysing large volumes of sensitive data. Some SMEs may not have enough resources to implement robust security measures. All these issues should be addressed through education, informative guidance and problem-oriented solutions.

CONCLUSION

IoT systems are able to enhance business productivity by effective optimisation of operations. Smart devices, by operating in real-time, can monitor the hardware equipment and significantly enhance the system's maintenance. AI data-driven solutions help to identify the market trends and improve the customer experience. Furthermore, smart environmental technologies, such as waste management solutions and electricity-efficiency systems, not only improve the quality of the environment but also increase the sustainability of SMEs. IoT and smart environment technologies empower emerging markets of SMEs on a global scale and facilitate long-term sustainability.

Industry 4.0 creates an enormous shift in all entrepreneur practices. While IoT was conceived as a solution for large manufacturing enterprises and a smart environment for infrastructure management, it certainly went far beyond its primary functions. Small and medium centrepieces can fully take advantage of all elements of IoT and the smart environment alike. Certain specific areas are more prominent for SMEs than for classical initiators of Industry 4.0. Sophisticated solutions and platform-based frameworks revolutionize SMEs and help to develop a modern, flexible, sustainable, and robust opportunity-reach business environment. The cost-effective mechanism leads to the exponential growth of incomes for SMEs, creating dynamic conditions for future economic growth and sustainability in Emerging Markets.

REFERENCES

Annosi, M. C., Brunetta, F., Monti, A., & Nati, F. (2019). Is the trend your friend? An analysis of technology 4.0 investment decisions in agricultural SMEs. *Computers in Industry, 109*, 59–71. doi:10.1016/j.compind.2019.04.003

Ardito, L., Ferraris, A., Petruzzelli, A. M., Bresciani, S., & Del Giudice, M. (2019). The role of universities in the knowledge management of smart city projects. *Technological Forecasting and Social Change, 142*, 312–321. doi:10.1016/j.techfore.2018.07.030

Asemokha, A., Ahi, A., Torkkeli, L., & Saarenketo, S. (2020). Renewable energy market SMEs: Antecedents of internationalization. *Critical Perspectives on International Business, 16*(4), 407–447. doi:10.1108/cpoib-05-2018-0043

Baars, H., Tank, A., Weber, P., Kemper, H. G., Lasi, H., & Pedell, B. (2021). Cooperative approaches to data sharing and analysis for industrial internet of things ecosystems. *Applied Sciences (Basel, Switzerland), 11*(16), 7547. doi:10.3390/app11167547

Barrenechea, M. J., & Jenkins, T. (2014). e-Government or Out of Government. Open Text Corporation.

Barrenechea, M. J., & Jenkins, T. (2018). *Digital Manufacturing.* Open Text Corporation.

Berkowitz, H., & Souchaud, A. (2024). Filling successive technologically-induced governance gaps: Meta-organizations as regulatory innovation intermediaries. *Technovation, 129*, 102890. doi:10.1016/j.technovation.2023.102890

Bettoni, A., Matteri, D., Montini, E., Gładysz, B., & Carpanzano, E. (2021). An AI adoption model for SMEs: A conceptual framework. *IFAC-PapersOnLine, 54*(1), 702–708. doi:10.1016/j.ifacol.2021.08.082

Bird, J. (2015). *Developing the smarter grid: the role of domestic and small and medium enterprise customers.* Customer-Led Network Revolution.

Budde, L., Haenggi, R., Laglia, L., & Friedli, T. (2024). Leading the transition to multi-sided platforms (MSPs) in a B2B context–The case of a recycling SME. *Industrial Marketing Management, 116*, 106–119. doi:10.1016/j.indmarman.2023.12.002

Bunte, A., Richter, F., & Diovisalvi, R. (2021, February). Why It is Hard to Find AI in SMEs: A Survey from the Practice and How to Promote It. In ICAART (2) (pp. 614-620). doi:10.5220/0010204106140620

Carro-Suárez, J., Sarmiento-Paredes, S., & Nava, D. (2023). Smart and Sustainable Cities: A New Urban Transformation. In Sustainable Regional Planning. IntechOpen. doi:10.5772/intechopen.110234

Chen, C. L. (2019). Value creation by SMEs participating in global value chains under industry 4.0 trend: Case study of textile industry in Taiwan. *Journal of Global Information Technology Management, 22*(2), 120–145. doi:10.1080/1097198X.2019.1603512

Cirillo, F., Gómez, D., Diez, L., Maestro, I. E., Gilbert, T. B. J., & Akhavan, R. (2020). Smart city IoT services creation through large-scale collaboration. *IEEE Internet of Things Journal, 7*(6), 5267–5275. doi:10.1109/JIOT.2020.2978770

Dallasega, P., Woschank, M., Ramingwong, S., Tippayawong, K. Y., & Chonsawat, N. (2019, March). Field study to identify requirements for smart logistics of European, US and Asian SMEs. *In Proceedings of the International Conference on Industrial Engineering and Operations Management* (Vol. 1, No. 1, pp. 844-854). IEEE. 10.5281/zenodo.4245343

Ding, S., Tukker, A., & Ward, H. (2023). Opportunities and risks of internet of things (IoT) technologies for circular business models: A literature review. *Journal of Environmental Management, 336*, 117662. doi:10.1016/j.jenvman.2023.117662 PMID:36913854

Domínguez, J. P., & Roseiro, P. (2020). Blockchain: A brief review of agri-food supply chain solutions and opportunities. *ADCAIJ: Advances in Distributed Computing and Artificial Intelligence Journal, 9*(4), 95–106. doi:10.14201/ADCAIJ20209495106

Doorn, N. (2014). Assessing the future impact of medical devices: Between technology and application. In *Responsible Innovation 1: Innovative Solutions for Global Issues* (pp. 301–314). Springer Netherlands. doi:10.1007/978-94-017-8956-1_17

Du, Y., Xu, H., & Chen, Y. (2024). Digital empowerment and innovation in risk control strategies for fishery supply chain finance—A case study of Puhui agriculture and animal husbandry financing guarantee company limited. *Marine Development, 2*(1), 1–20. doi:10.1007/s44312-023-00013-y

Empl, P., & Pernul, G. (2021, April). A flexible security analytics service for the industrial IoT. *In Proceedings of the 2021 ACM Workshop on Secure and Trustworthy Cyber-Physical Systems* (pp. 23-32). ACM. 10.1145/3445969.3450427

Feyen, E., Natarajan, H., & Saal, M. (2023). *Fintech and the Future of Finance*. World Bank. . doi:10.1596/978-1-4648-1914-8

Franki, V., Majnarić, D., & Višković, A. (2023). A Comprehensive Review of Artificial Intelligence (AI) Companies in the Power Sector. *Energies, 16*(3), 1077. doi:10.3390/en16031077

Franzè, C., Paolucci, E., & Pessot, E. (2024). Sustained value creation driven by digital connectivity: A multiple case study in the mechanical components industry. *Technovation, 129*, 102918. doi:10.1016/j.technovation.2023.102918

Gabrys, J. (2020). Smart forests and data practices: From the Internet of Trees to planetary governance. *Big data & society, 7*(1), 2053951720904871. 0 . doi:10.1177/2053951720904871

Gaggero, G. B., Marchese, M., Moheddine, A., & Patrone, F. (2021). A possible smart metering system evolution for rural and remote areas employing unmanned aerial vehicles and internet of things in smart grids. *Sensors (Basel), 21*(5), 1627. doi:10.3390/s21051627 PMID:33652571

García, C. G., Meana-Llorián, D., & Lovelle, J. M. C. (2017). A review about Smart Objects, Sensors, and Actuators. *International Journal of Interactive Multimedia & Artificial Intelligence, 4*(3), 7. doi:10.9781/ijimai.2017.431

Giordano, V., Gangale, F., Fulli, G., Jiménez, M. S., Onyeji, I., Colta, A., Papaioannou, I., Mengolini, A., Alecu, C., Ojala, T., & Maschio, I. (2011). Smart grid projects in Europe. *JRC Ref Rep Sy, 8*. doi:10.2790/32946

Groot, A. E., Bolt, J. S., Jat, H. S., Jat, M. L., Kumar, M., Agarwal, T., & Blok, V. (2019). Business models of SMEs as a mechanism for scaling climate smart technologies: The case of Punjab, India. *Journal of Cleaner Production*, *210*, 1109–1119. doi:10.1016/j.jclepro.2018.11.054

Hansen, E. B., & Bøgh, S. (2021). Artificial intelligence and internet of things in small and medium-sized enterprises: A survey. *Journal of Manufacturing Systems*, *58*, 362–372. doi:10.1016/j.jmsy.2020.08.009

Happonen, A., Santti, U., Auvinen, H., Räsänen, T., & Eskelinen, T. (2020). Sustainable business model innovation for digital remote monitoring: a follow up study on a water Iot service. In *BIOS Forum* (pp. 98-106). IEEE. 10.5281/zenodo.4290135

Holland, C., McCarthy, A., Ferri, P., & Shapira, P. (2024). Innovation intermediaries at the convergence of digital technologies, sustainability, and governance: A case study of AI-enabled engineering biology. *Technovation*, *129*, 102875. doi:10.1016/j.technovation.2023.102875

Horgan, D., van Kranen, H. J., & Morré, S. A. (2019). Optimising SME potential in modern healthcare systems: Challenges, opportunities and policy recommendations. *Public Health Genomics*, *21*(1-2), 1–17. doi:10.1159/000492809 PMID:30145589

Hundal, G. S., Laux, C. M., Buckmaster, D., Sutton, M. J., & Langemeier, M. (2023). Exploring Barriers to the Adoption of Internet of Things-Based Precision Agriculture Practices. *Agriculture*, *13*(1), 163. doi:10.3390/agriculture13010163

Khan, T. (2020). Internet of Things: The Potentialities for Sustainable Agriculture. *International Business, Trade and Institutional Sustainability*. . doi:10.1007/978-3-030-26759-9_17

Kotios, D., Makridis, G., Walser, S., Kyriazis, D., & Monferrino, V. (2022). Personalized finance management for smes. *Big Data and Artificial Intelligence in Digital Finance*. Springer. . doi:10.1007/978-3-030-94590-9_12

Krowas, K., & Riedel, R. (2019). Planning guideline and maturity model for intra-logistics 4.0 in SME. In *Advances in Production Management Systems. Towards Smart Production Management Systems: IFIP WG 5.7 International Conference,* (pp. 331-338). Springer International Publishing. 10.1007/978-3-030-29996-5_38

Kumar, P. R., Wan, A. T., & Suhaili, W. S. H. (2020). Exploring data security and privacy issues in internet of things based on five-layer architecture. *International Journal of Communication Networks and Information Security*, *12*(1), 108–121. doi:10.17762/ijcnis.v12i1.4345

Le-Dain, M. A., Benhayoun, L., Matthews, J., & Liard, M. (2023). Barriers and opportunities of digital servitization for SMEs: The effect of smart Product-Service System business models. *Service Business*, *17*(1), 359–393. doi:10.1007/s11628-023-00520-4

Lee, P., Hunter, W. C., & Chung, N. (2020). Smart tourism city: Developments and transformations. *Sustainability (Basel)*, *12*(10), 3958. doi:10.3390/su12103958

Lynn, T., & Wood, C. (2023). Smart Streets as a Cyber-Physical Social Platform: A Conceptual Framework. *Sensors (Basel)*, *23*(3), 1399. doi:10.3390/s23031399 PMID:36772437

Makaci, M., Reaidy, P., Evrard-Samuel, K., Botta-Genoulaz, V., & Monteiro, T. (2017). Pooled warehouse management: An empirical study. *Computers & Industrial Engineering, 112*, 526–536. doi:10.1016/j.cie.2017.03.005

Martikkala, A., David, J., Lobov, A., Lanz, M., & Ituarte, I. F. (2021). Trends for low-cost and open-source iot solutions development for Industry 4.0. *Procedia Manufacturing, 55*, 298–305. doi:10.1016/j.promfg.2021.10.042

Martin, N. L., Dér, A., Herrmann, C., & Thiede, S. (2020). Assessment of smart manufacturing solutions based on extended value stream mapping. *Procedia CIRP, 93*, 371-376.. doi:10.1016/j.procir.2020.04.019

Meierhofer, J., Benedech, R. A., Schweiger, L., Barbieri, C., & Rapaccini, M. (2022, February). Quantitative modelling of the value of data for manufacturing SMEs in smart service provision. *In 12th International Conference on Exploring Service Science*, (p. 04001). EDP Sciences. 10.1051/itmconf/20224104001

Mercan, S., Cain, L., Akkaya, K., Cebe, M., Uluagac, S., Alonso, M., & Cobanoglu, C. (2021). Improving the service industry with hyper-connectivity: IoT in hospitality. *International Journal of Contemporary Hospitality Management, 33*(1), 243–262. doi:10.1108/IJCHM-06-2020-0621

Mizik, T. (2023). How can precision farming work on a small scale? A systematic literature review. *Precision Agriculture, 24*(1), 384–406. doi:10.1007/s11119-022-09934-y

Morelli, G., Magazzino, C., Gurrieri, A. R., Pozzi, C., & Mele, M. (2022). Designing Smart Energy Systems in an Industry 4.0 Paradigm towards Sustainable Environment. *Sustainability (Basel), 14*(6), 3315. doi:10.3390/su14063315

Mourtzis, D., Angelopoulos, J., & Panopoulos, N. (2022). Development of a PSS for smart grid energy distribution optimization based on digital twin. *Procedia CIRP, 107*, 1138–1143. doi:10.1016/j.procir.2022.05.121

Mrabet, H., Belguith, S., Alhomoud, A., & Jemai, A. (2020). A survey of IoT security based on a layered architecture of sensing and data analysis. *Sensors (Basel), 20*(13), 3625. doi:10.3390/s20133625 PMID:32605178

Müller, J. M., & Voigt, K. I. (2018). Sustainable industrial value creation in SMEs: A comparison between industry 4.0 and made in China 2025. *International Journal of Precision Engineering and Manufacturing-Green Technology, 5*(5), 659–670. doi:10.1007/s40684-018-0056-z

Nikhashemi, S. R., Knight, H. H., Nusair, K., & Liat, C. B. (2021). Augmented reality in smart retailing: A (n)(A) Symmetric Approach to continuous intention to use retail brands' mobile AR apps. *Journal of Retailing and Consumer Services, 60*, 102464. doi:10.1016/j.jretconser.2021.102464

Okkonen, P., Hyysalo, J., & Peltonen, E. (2020, April). Public and Open Internet of Things for Smart Cities: The SME Perspective. *In 2020 IEEE 36th International Conference on Data Engineering Workshops (ICDEW)* (pp. 48-55). IEEE. 10.1109/ICDEW49219.2020.000-8

Pantano, E., & Dennis, C. (2019). *Smart retailing*. Springer International Publishing., doi:10.1007/978-3-030-12608-7

Pappas, N., Caputo, A., Pellegrini, M. M., Marzi, G., & Michopoulou, E. (2021). The complexity of decision-making processes and IoT adoption in accommodation SMEs. *Journal of Business Research, 131*, 573–583. doi:10.1016/j.jbusres.2021.01.010

Parmar, J. K., & Desai, A. (2016). IoT: Networking technologies and research challenges. *International Journal of Computer Applications, 154*(7), 1–6. doi:10.5120/ijca2016912181

Philipp, R., Prause, G., & Gerlitz, L. (2019). Blockchain and smart contracts for entrepreneurial collaboration in maritime supply chains. *Transport and Telecommunication Journal, 20*(4), 365-378. doi:10.2478/ttj-2019-0030

Ramírez, C., Rojas, A. E., & García, A. (2022). A cold chain logistics with IoT and Blockchain scalable project for SMEs: First phase. *IFAC-PapersOnLine, 55*(10), 2336–2341. doi:10.1016/j.ifacol.2022.10.057

Rauch, E., Vickery, A. R., Brown, C. A., & Matt, D. T. (2020). SME requirements and guidelines for the design of smart and highly adaptable manufacturing systems. *Industry 4.0 for SMEs: Challenges, Opportunities and Requirements*, 39-72. doi:10.1007/978-3-030-25425-4_2

Rivera, R., Amorim, M., & Reis, J. (2021, June). Technological evolution in grocery retail: A systematic literature review. In *2021 16th Iberian Conference on Information Systems and Technologies (CISTI)* (pp. 1-8). IEEE. 10.23919/CISTI52073.2021.9476598

Serrano, W. (2018). Digital systems in smart city and infrastructure: Digital as a service. *Smart cities, 1*(1), 134-154. doi:10.3390/smartcities1010008

Sharma, S. K., Ilavarasan, P. V., & Karanasios, S. (2023). Small businesses and FinTech: A systematic review and future directions. *Electronic Commerce Research*, 1–41. doi:10.1007/s10660-023-09705-5

Shkolnykova, M., & Kudic, M. (2022). Who benefits from SMEs' radical innovations?—Empirical evidence from German biotechnology. *Small Business Economics, 58*(2), 1157–1185. doi:10.1007/s11187-021-00464-x

Sigismondi, P. (2011). *The digital glocalization of entertainment: New paradigms in the 21st century global mediascape* (Vol. 3). Springer Science & Business Media.

Stark, E., Haffner, O., & Kučera, E. (2022). Low-Cost Method for 3D Body Measurement Based on Photogrammetry Using Smartphone. *Electronics (Basel), 11*(7), 1048. doi:10.3390/electronics11071048

Sugiura, T., Yamamura, K., Watanabe, Y., Yamakiri, S., & Nakano, N. (2023). Circuits and devices for standalone large-scale integration (LSI) chips and Internet of Things (IoT) applications: A Review. *Chip (Würzburg), 100048*(3), 100048. Advance online publication. doi:10.1016/j.chip.2023.100048

Verma, A., Prakash, S., Srivastava, V., Kumar, A., & Mukhopadhyay, S. C. (2019). Sensing, controlling, and IoT infrastructure in smart building: A review. *IEEE Sensors Journal, 19*(20), 9036–9046. doi:10.1109/JSEN.2019.2922409

Wolf, M. J., & Perron, B. (Eds.). (2023). *The Routledge companion to video game studies*. Taylor & Francis., doi:10.4324/9781003214977

Wuest, T., Romero, D., Khan, M. A., & Mittal, S. (2022). *The triple bottom line of smart manufacturing technologies: an economic, environmental, and social perspective. Handbook of Smart Technologies: An Economic and Social Perspective.* Routledge., https://www.taylorfrancis.com/chapters/edit/10.4324/9780429 351921-20

Zhu, J., Liu, X., Shi, Q., He, T., Sun, Z., Guo, X., Liu, W., Sulaiman, O. B., Dong, B., & Lee, C. (2019). Development trends and perspectives of future sensors and MEMS/NEMS. *Micromachines*, *11*(1), 7. doi:10.3390/mi11010007 PMID:31861476

Zuzik, J., Furmannova, B., Dulina, L. & Kukla, S. (2024). *Digital Transformation of Material Flow and Workplace Design: A Comprehensive Case Study Analysis*. IEEE.

Chapter 10
Unlocking the Potential:
Exploring the Synergy Between Tourism and SMEs for Sustainable Economic Growth

Bindu Aggarwal
Chandigarh University, India

Ranjeet Verma
Chandigarh University, India

Pawan Kumar
https://orcid.org/0000-0001-7501-3066
Lovely Professional University, India

ABSTRACT

The dynamic interaction between tourism and small and medium enterprises (SMEs) as generators of long-term economic growth is explored in this chapter. The chapter investigates methods to unlock the potential synergy between tourism and SMEs, resulting in a paradigm of sustainable and inclusive growth, by looking at case studies, best practices, and emerging trends.

INTRODUCTION

Tourism and small and medium-sized firms (SMEs) have emerged as essential drivers of long-term economic growth in today's quickly changing global scene. Their interaction creates a dynamic and mutually beneficial connection with enormous potential for capitalizing on economic opportunities while also promoting environmental and social sustainability. We are embarking on a journey to uncover the transformative power of these industries and comprehend their joint role in crafting a successful and sustainable future as we investigate this synergy between tourism and SMEs. Tourism, as a rapidly increasing business, has proven to be a significant economic development engine in many locations throughout the world. Its potential to draw visitors, create jobs, and boost local economies is widely proven. The actual promise of tourism, however, is found not only in its ability to create cash, but also in its ability

DOI: 10.4018/979-8-3693-0111-1.ch010

to empower and uplift communities through inclusive growth. This is where SMEs, also known as the "backbone of economies," come into action (Lopes & Farinha, 2020). Small and medium-sized enterprises (SMEs) have the flexibility, ingenuity, and entrepreneurship to adapt to the particular demands and preferences of tourists. They benefit the tourism industry by providing authentic and immersive experiences that highlight local culture, heritage, and products (Mohammed, 2022). Tourists gain access to a varied range of goods and services through interacting with SMEs, allowing them to form meaningful ties with the area and its people. In turn, the symbiotic relationship between tourism and SMEs promotes SMEs' growth and development. Tourists provide a larger client base for SMEs, prompting them to extend their services, enhance product quality, and innovate to satisfy changing demands (Martucci et al., 2020). This enhanced exposure and market access enables SMEs to expand their operations, hire more people, and develop community entrepreneurship. As a result, tourism serves as a catalyst for SME expansion, transforming them into critical contributors to long-term economic development.

However, in order to fully realize the potential of the tourism-SMEs synergy, many difficulties and opportunities must be addressed. To create an enabling climate that supports SMEs in the tourism sector, governments, industry players, and local communities must work together. Access to funding, capacity-building programmes, and marketing assistance customized to the specific needs of SMEs can help them succeed and compete (Mokoena&Liambo,2023). Furthermore, pursuing sustainable practices is critical to the long-term success of tourism-SME relationships. It is critical to implement policies to reduce the harmful effects of tourism on the environment, culture, and local communities. SMEs can promote themselves as sustainability champions by embracing responsible tourism concepts, attracting aware travelers looking for authentic and eco-friendly experiences (Kadaba et al., 2023).

In this chapter, we conduct a thorough examination of the synergy between tourism and SMEs for long-term sustainable economic growth. We look at successful case studies, best practices, and innovative tactics that have unlocked the partnership's potential in various places. We hope that by conducting this investigation, policymakers, industry leaders, and academics will be inspired to work together to uncover the transformative power of tourism-SME synergy and design a route towards sustainable and inclusive economic growth. Let us begin on a journey of discovery together, uncovering the vast opportunities that exist within the synergy between tourism and SMEs. We can set the road for a future in which economic growth coexists peacefully with environmental stewardship and social well-being by doing so.

The Dynamics of Tourism and SMEs

Understanding the complex workings of the tourism business requires an understanding of the interplay between tourism and small and medium-sized enterprises (SMEs). SMEs play an important role in the global economy, contributing to job creation, economic growth, and innovation. They are essential components of the tourist industry, creating jobs in a variety of enterprises such as hotels, guesthouses, restaurants, tour operators, and souvenir stores (UNWTO, 2021).

Indeed, the World tourist Organization (UNWTO) states that SMEs employ more than 80% of the worldwide tourist workforce. These companies not only create jobs, but they also boost local economies by providing cash and tax revenue. Tourism-related SMEs generate economic links and contribute to the diversification of economic activity by sourcing goods and services from local suppliers (UNCTAD, 2021).

Furthermore, SMEs in the tourism industry are frequently incubators of innovation and entrepreneurship. Because of their versatility and flexibility, they can develop new products and services that correspond to evolving tourist preferences (Dlamini et al., 2023). They embrace specialized markets, one-of-a-kind experiences, and sustainable practices, so improving the tourist sector's overall competitiveness and sustainability (OECD, 2020). SMEs, on the other hand, suffer a number of obstacles, including limited access to capital, a shortage of skilled labour, seasonality, rivalry from larger firms, and inadequate infrastructure. Governments, business groups, and development organizations must provide supportive policies, access to money, training, and networking opportunities to solve these concerns (ILO, 2020).

Tourism and SME dynamics are critical to the growth and viability of the tourism industry. SMEs make substantial contributions to job creation, economic growth, and innovation. The tourist sector can utilize the potential of these small enterprises to create sustainable development and maximize the advantages of tourism for local communities and economies by identifying and addressing the issues faced by SMEs, as well as providing them with the necessary support.

Understanding Tourism: Catalyst for Economic Growth

Tourism is a potent economic growth driver, positively impacting many elements of the economy and society. To begin with, tourism has a big economic influence. It generates revenue from visitor spending, supports employment growth in several sectors, and creates foreign exchange earnings. Tourism activities such as lodging, food, transportation, and attractions produce cash that directly supports local companies and communities. The World Travel and Tourism Council (WTTC) estimate that the global tourism industry contributed 10.4% of global GDP in 2019 and supported over 330 million jobs (WTTC, 2020). Tourism also serves as a catalyst for infrastructural development and community empowerment. The necessity to accommodate and cater to the needs of tourists drives the development of transportation networks, lodging facilities, and recreational activities. This infrastructure development benefits not only tourists but also local inhabitants by improving transport alternatives, upgrading utilities, and upgrading public areas. Furthermore, tourism may empower local communities by fostering entrepreneurship and offering chances for the development of local businesses and industries (UNWTO, 2019).

The evolution of tourism trends has far-reaching ramifications for small and medium-sized businesses (SMEs). SMEs may reach a bigger audience and attract consumers from all over the world thanks to the rise of digitalization and online booking platforms. However, they must also deal with the difficulty of responding to changing customer preferences and needs. Sustainable tourism, experiential travel, and personalized experiences are examples of trends that allow SMEs to differentiate themselves and offer unique products and services. SMEs can improve their competitiveness and contribute to the overall growth and sustainability of the tourist industry by embracing these trends (Euromonitor International, 2021).

Tourism stimulates economic growth by creating revenue, job opportunities, and foreign exchange earnings. It promotes infrastructural development, which benefits both tourists and local populations. Furthermore, the evolution of tourist trends poses both problems and possibilities for SMEs, requiring them to adapt to shifting client expectations while also capitalizing on emergent trends (Faeni et al., 2023). Understanding the economic impact of tourism, its role in infrastructure development, and the consequences of shifting tourism trends is critical for capitalizing on tourism's potential as a driver for economic growth and long-term development.

Some Capelets

Dubai, United Arab Emirates has developed from a tiny commercial centre to a major international travel and business hub. The construction of famous buildings like the Burj Khalifa and creative tourism projects have made a substantial contribution to economic expansion, diversification, and employment generation (Jamal& Getz, 1999). Barcelona, Spain has seen a significant rise in foreign visitors as a result of its emphasis on cultural tourism, which includes its architectural gems and cultural events. Due to its ability to create jobs and strengthen the local economy, tourism has emerged as a key factor in economic growth (Prayag et al., 2013). Thailand's tourist sector has been essential to the country's economic growth. Due to its stunning beaches, rich cultural heritage, and kind welcome, the nation has become a popular travel destination worldwide, bringing in large sums of money and creating plenty of job possibilities (Song & Li, 2008).

These instances show the various ways that tourism can stimulate economic expansion, promoting growth, generating jobs, and enhancing the general well-being of an area. It goes without saying that upgrading the tourism value chain entails increasing a number of different elements to make the sector more productive and competitive.

SMALL AND MEDIUM-SIZED ENTERPRISES (SMES): PILLARS OF ECONOMIC RESILIENCE

Small and medium-sized enterprises (SMEs) are critical economic resilience pillars in global economies. SMEs are described as enterprises with a small number of employees and small assets that operate in a variety of industries such as manufacturing, services, and technology. They play an important role in economic growth, job creation, innovation, and local economic development (Molina et al., 2021).

SME agility and adaptability are important characteristics. Small and medium-sized enterprises (SMEs) have the ability to respond swiftly to market changes, emerging trends, and client requests. They are frequently more agile in modifying corporate strategy, exploring new markets, and using breakthrough technologies. This adaptability enables SMEs to better grab opportunities and handle economic problems (OECD, 2019).

Furthermore, SMEs are noted for their entrepreneurial spirit and innovative mentality. They are frequently driven by aspirant entrepreneurs and individuals prepared to take chances and seek novel ideas. SMEs act as creative incubators, stimulating innovation in products, services, and business strategies. They bring new perspectives, encourage competition, and contribute to the progress of the sector. Their ability to innovate contributes to overall economic development and competitiveness (Naidoo, 2021).

Another important contribution made by SMEs is the establishment of job possibilities. SMEs are significant job generators, particularly in emerging economies and local communities. They employ a sizable proportion of the workforce, so contributing to poverty reduction, social inclusion, and human development. Furthermore, SMEs are frequently better connected to their local communities and are more inclined to invest in and support the development of the local workforce (ILO, 2019). SMEs improve the social fabric and contribute to the economic well-being of communities by creating jobs.

SMEs are also important drivers of local economic development. They are critical to the revitalization and sustainability of local economies, particularly in rural areas or places with limited economic prospects. SMEs help local industries flourish by stimulating demand for goods and services from local suppliers. This dependency improves supply chains, promotes economic links, and helps local businesses grow. Furthermore, SMEs frequently participate in community activities, donate to local charities, and contribute to the general vibrancy and resilience of the local economy (World Bank Group, 2020).

SMEs are definitely economic resilience pillars. Their nimbleness, inventiveness, and entrepreneurial spirit, as well as their commitment to employment and local economic development, make them vital in global economies. Recognizing the importance of SMEs and enacting policies that encourage their growth and development are critical for establishing resilient economies that can endure crises, promote sustainable growth, and ensure inclusive economic opportunities for all.

REVIEW OF LITERATURE

Exploring the Synergies Between Tourism and SMEs

The research has focused on the possible benefits, obstacles, and methods for collaboration between tourism and small and medium-sized enterprises (SMEs). This review will look at the existing corpus of research and scholarly works on this topic, using a variety of scholarly articles, reports, and publications.

The research emphasizes the possible synergistic interaction between tourism and SMEs, emphasizing how SMEs help to improve the overall tourism experience. SMEs are frequently distinguished by their agility and flexibility, allowing them to respond rapidly to changing market demands and rising tourism trends. SMEs contribute value to the tourism sector by providing personalized and distinctive products and services that cater to the different preferences and needs of tourists (UNWTO, 2021). Furthermore, SMEs play a critical role in boosting tourism industry innovation and entrepreneurship by bringing new products, services, and business models that boost competitiveness and differentiation (OECD, 2020).

Tourism and SME synergies provide a variety of benefits. Job generation is an important result, especially in rural and distant places where tourism can act as a catalyst for economic progress (Hassanli et al., 2023). SMEs contribute to economic diversification by procuring goods and services from local suppliers, strengthening local supply chains and promoting local company growth (UNCTAD, 2019). Localization of economic activity encourages sustainability and inclusive development in the tourism industry. Furthermore, by providing authentic experiences and highlighting local culture and traditions, SMEs contribute to the overall vibrancy and distinctiveness of tourism destinations.

Collaboration between tourism and SMEs, on the other hand, is fraught with difficulties. Small and medium-sized enterprises (SMEs) frequently encounter challenges such as limited access to capital, a lack of marketing resources, and difficulties achieving quality standards and legal requirements. These difficulties may impede their growth and competitiveness in the tourism sector (ILO, 2020). To overcome these obstacles, the literature proposes a number of ways for encouraging collaboration and assisting SMEs. These measures include the creation of supportive policies that target the specific needs of SMEs, the provision of financial resources and business development programmes, and the promotion of capacity-building efforts to improve their skills and competencies (UNCTAD, 2019). Establishing networks and collaborations among SMEs, tourism associations, and government agencies can also allow knowledge sharing, resource pooling, and collaborative projects, leading to mutually beneficial outcomes.

SMEs play a critical role in improving the tourism experience, encouraging innovation, and contributing to the tourism industry's long-term economic success. Challenges such as limited resources and regulatory constraints, on the other hand, must be addressed by supporting policies and joint efforts. Understanding and developing synergies between tourism and SMEs is critical for policymakers, industry stakeholders, and researchers looking to maximise their combined potential for long-term economic growth.

The Role of SMEs in Tourism Value Chains

Small and medium-sized enterprises (SMEs) play an important part in tourist value chains, adding to the industry's overall success and competitiveness. This section looks at how SMEs play an important role in providing tourists with authentic and immersive experiences, how they contribute to destination branding and competitiveness, and how their involvement improves visitor happiness (see **Figure 1**).

Figure 1. Role of SMEs in tourism value chains
Source: Self-created illustration

SMEs are well-known for their capacity to provide travelers with unique and authentic experiences. SMEs, as opposed to larger corporations, have the flexibility and local knowledge to deliver personalized services and goods that reflect a destination's particular culture, customs, and heritage. These unique experiences not only enhance the travel experience of visitors, but also help to preserve and promote local cultures and traditions (Ruhanen&Weiler, 2010). Tourists can interact with local populations, sample local cuisine, participate in traditional activities, and obtain a better understanding of the destination they are visiting by working with SMEs.

Aside from providing authentic experiences, SMEs are critical to destination branding and competitiveness. SMEs frequently function as advocates for their locations, promoting the distinctive qualities and attractions that set them apart from others. SMEs contribute to developing the destination's identity and brand image through their local knowledge and tight links to the community (Sánchez, Pelegrn, & Montoro-Sánchez, 2017). Their active involvement in destination branding activities like as displaying local products and services, organising cultural events, and partnering with other local stakeholders contributes to the creation of a distinct and memorable destination experience.

Furthermore, SME participation is beneficial in increasing visitor satisfaction. Small enterprises frequently provide personalized and attentive services, providing travelers with a more intimate and memorable experience. Small and medium-sized enterprises (SMEs) have the ability to customize their products to fit the specific needs and preferences of individual travelers, hence increasing their overall satisfaction (Hall, Williams, & Lew, 2010). Furthermore, SMEs are frequently more approachable and accessible, allowing for direct contacts between tourists and business owners or workers, generating a sense of hospitality and connection that leads to visitor satisfaction and favorable word-of-mouth referrals experience.

Small and medium-sized enterprises (SMEs) play an important part in tourist value chains by providing authentic and immersive experiences, contributing to destination branding and competitiveness, and improving visitor satisfaction. Their capacity to provide personalised services, reflect local cultures, and create one-of-a-kind experiences sets them apart in the tourism sector. Engaging with SMEs benefits tourists not only by delivering enjoyable experiences, but it also supports local economies, protects local cultures, and contributes to the long-term growth of destinations.

By strengthening a number of factors throughout the tourism value chain will make the sector more productive and competitive. Travelers now plan and book their journeys in a completely new way thanks to online travel agents. For instance, Expedia and Booking.com offer platforms that make reservations easier while providing a large selection of lodging choices and travel-related services (Xiang et al., 2017). Destination Management Organizationsare essential to destination management and marketing. Visit Scotland has demonstrated efficacy in utilizing digital marketing and social media platforms to effectively captivate travelers and augment their overall travel experience (Leask et al., 2013). Pokémon GO served as an example of how augmented reality may improve traveler experiences. The game encouraged users to explore new destinations by fusing the virtual and physical worlds, demonstrating the potential of technology in the travel industry (Shin, 2018). Airbnb has caused a disruption in the conventional lodging industry by enabling people to rent out their homes to tourists. This has increased the number of lodging options and made the tourism value chain more adaptable and diverse (Guttentag, 2015).

Tourism as a Catalyst for SME Growth and Development

Tourism has shown to be a growth and development catalyst for small and medium-sized enterprises (SMEs) by extending market opportunities, encouraging innovation and product diversification, and facilitating capacity building and skill development within the tourism sector. This paragraph examines tourism's key role in supporting SME growth and development, emphasizing the benefits obtained from tourism demand, potential for innovation and quality improvement, and the necessity of capacity building for SMEs (see **Figure 2**) (Hu& Kee, 2022).

Figure 2. The cyclic framework tourism as a catalyst for SMEs growth
Source: Created by the Author

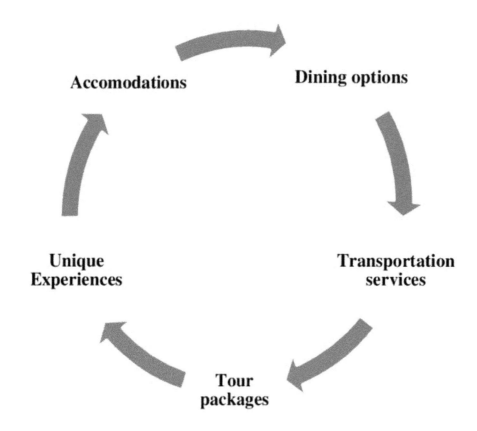

One of the keyways that tourism stimulates SME growth is by extending market prospects. The influx of tourists creates an increasing demand for diverse products and services, opening up new market niches for SMEs (UNWTO, 2021). Tourism-related SMEs have the chance to adapt to the special requirements and preferences of tourists by providing a diverse range of services such as hotels, dining alternatives, transportation services, tour packages, and unique experiences (Hall & Mitchell, 2008). This increased market demand enables SMEs to extend their customer base, improve revenue, and achieve long-term business success.

Tourism also allows SMEs to promote innovation, product variety, and quality enhancement. The tourist industry's dynamic nature, characterized by shifting client preferences and market trends, motivates SMEs to constantly innovate and differentiate themselves from competitors (Ruhanen & Weiler, 2010). Small and medium-sized enterprises (SMEs) have the agility and flexibility to create new products, services, and experiences that meet the ever-changing needs of tourists. SMEs can attract a bigger client base and increase their competitiveness by providing distinctive and creative solutions (UNWTO, 2019). Furthermore, tourism necessitates high-quality standards in order to match tourist expectations, which pushes SMEs to constantly enhance their products and services in order to preserve consumer happiness and loyalty.

Building capacity and developing skills are critical for SME growth and development in the tourism sector. Tourism-related training and support programmes equip SMEs with the information, skills, and tools they need to operate and manage their enterprises efficiently (ILO, 2020). Customer service, marketing and promotion, financial management, sustainable practices, and digital literacy are among the topics covered in these programmes. SMEs can increase their competitiveness, operational efficiency, and respond to changing tourist sector demands by investing in capacity building projects (UNCTAD, 2019). Furthermore, chances for collaboration and networking with other industry stakeholders, such as tourism groups, government agencies, and larger corporations, can provide SMEs with important resources, information exchange, and access to new markets.

Tourism promotes SME growth and development by extending market opportunities, encouraging innovation and product diversification, and facilitating capacity building and skill development within the tourism sector. Tourism SMEs gain from increased demand for products and services, which gives up new opportunities for expansion and revenue generation (Priatmoko et al., 2023). Because tourism is a dynamic industry, SMEs are encouraged to innovate and differentiate themselves, while quality improvement maintains customer happiness. Furthermore, capacity building activities provide SMEs with the skills and expertise they need to survive in the competitive tourism business. SMEs can achieve sustained growth and contribute to the overall development of the tourism sector by capitalizing on the opportunities given by tourism (Rahmawati et al., 2023).

Tourism can serve as a catalyst for Small and Medium-sized Enterprises (SMEs) growth and development by creating opportunities for entrepreneurship, job creation, and local economic stimulation. Here are examples and cases that illustrate how tourism can support SME growth:

Through fostering entrepreneurship, job creation, and local economic stimulation, tourism can act as a catalyst for the growth and development of small and medium-sized enterprises (SMEs).

Bali Indonesia's tourism sector has given local crafts people and companies a platform to flourish. Small businesses that make traditional Balinese crafts like textiles and woodcarvings profit from tourists' desire for genuine mementos (Chon& Maier,2009). Small farms in Tuscany, Italy have been able to expand their revenue streams by providing experiences like farm stays, wine tastings, and cooking workshops thanks to the agritourism sector. This has improved guests' overall travel experiences in addition to helping the farms (International Labour Organization, 2015). The adventure tourism hub of Queenstown, New Zealand has witnessed a surge in the number of small enterprises providing services like as jet boating, skiing, and bungee jumping. These businesses give visitors unique experiences while boosting the local economy (Hall & Page, 2014).

Overcoming Challenges and Seizing Opportunities

Unlocking the potential synergy between tourism and SMEs is a revolutionary endeavour that has the ability to pave the path for long-term economic growth, but it is not without its hurdles. The journey towards harnessing the combined potential of these two sectors necessitates a thorough grasp of the challenges they face, as well as the resolve to confront them head on.

Establishing effective collaboration between the tourism industry and small and medium-sized firms is one of the key problems in this respect (Dutta, 2019; Powell & Baker, 2014).

SMEs, despite being an important part of the local economy, frequently struggle to enter the tourism sector due to inadequate resources, a lack of visibility, and a limited awareness of the ever-changing global traveler's wants and preferences. The tourism sector, on the other hand, may miss the value that local

SMEs may bring to the table (Brynjolfsson & McAfee, 2014; Westerman, Bonnet, & McAfee, 2014). They frequently choose giant organizations and multinational franchises over the authentic experiences and one-of-a-kind products that local SMEs can provide.

However, the potential benefits of unleashing this synergy should not be overlooked. SMEs can provide tourists with personalized, culturally rich, and immersive experiences, thereby contributing to the variety and enrichment of the destination's tourism offerings. Tourists might be introduced to local companies and handmade products by promoting them. Unlocking the potential synergy between tourism and SMEs is a revolutionary endeavor that has the ability to pave the path for long-term economic growth, but it is not without its hurdles. The journey towards harnessing the combined potential of these two sectors necessitates a thorough grasp of the challenges they face, as well as a commitment to confront them head-on (Dweck, 2006; Duckworth, 2016).

Establishing effective collaboration between the tourism industry and small and medium-sized enterprises (SMEs) is one of the key problems in this respect. SMEs, despite being an important part of the local economy, frequently struggle to enter the tourism sector due to inadequate resources, a lack of visibility, and a limited awareness of the ever-changing global traveler's wants and preferences. However, the tourism industry may ignore the value that local SMEs may bring to the table. They frequently choose giant organizations and multinational franchises over the authentic experiences and one-of-a-kind products that local SMEs can provide.2016; Duckworth).

However, the potential benefits of unleashing this synergy should not be overlooked. SMEs may provide travelers with personalized, culturally rich, and engaging experiences, helping to diversify and expand the destination's tourism offers. Tourists can be introduced to the actual character of a place through supporting local businesses and handcrafted items, building a stronger connection and appreciation for the region. Furthermore, assisting SMEs in the tourism value chain can contribute to a more inclusive economy by creating chances for entrepreneurship and job development in local areas (Sachs, 2015; Elkington, 2018).

Adoption of sustainable practices is another critical part of this relationship. As tourism and SMEs expand together, it becomes increasingly important to guarantee that their expansion is environmentally and socially appropriate. Encouragement of responsible tourism practices among enterprises and tourists will protect natural resources, conserve cultural heritage, and reduce the negative influence on local populations. Small and medium-sized enterprises (SMEs) are well-positioned to undertake eco-friendly projects, and their active participation can pave the way for the entire tourism sector to embrace sustainability.

To summarize, realizing the potential synergy between tourism and SMEs is a process that involves perseverance, collaboration, and strategic preparation. We can unleash the actual potential of these industries, creating sustainable economic growth and fostering a brighter future for all stakeholders involved, by encouraging SMEs to participate actively in the tourism value chain and supporting responsible practices. The benefits are not only financial; they also include social, cultural, and environmental benefits that will have a long-term good impact on destinations around the world.

Developing alliances and cooperative methods that are advantageous to both the tourism industry and Small and Medium-sized Enterprises (SMEs) is necessary to fully realize the potential synergy between these two sectors. In Morocco, the tourism sector has actively collaborated with local handicraft SMEs. Tour operators include visits to artisan workshops, providing tourists with authentic experiences while supporting the economic development of local craftspeople (Boukhobza & Boumba, 2017). Travelers looking for trekking and climbing adventures can get specialized services from small and medium-sized enterprises (SMEs) in Nepal's outdoor gear and adventure tourism sectors. This collaborative effort benefits local companies and improves the travel experience overall (S. K & Chiputwa, 2019). Local service SMEs and digital tourism platforms have demonstrated cooperation in South Korea. Enhanced visitor experiences are achieved by mobile applications that link tourists with local businesses, including restaurants and transport services (Beldona et al., 2017).

These illustrations show the various ways that SMEs and tourism can work together to produce win-win results. To build a more dynamic and long-lasting tourism ecosystem, the secret is to recognize and take advantage of the complimentary qualities of both industries.

Creating an Enabling Environment for SMEs in Tourism

It is critical for the growth and success of small and medium-sized enterprises (SMEs) in the tourist sector to provide an enabling environment. This section looks at major variables that contribute to a favorable environment for SMEs, such as supporting policies, access to funding and investment, and the strengthening of SME networks and collaborations.

Supportive laws, legislation, and governance structures are critical in fostering an enabling environment for tourist SMEs. Governments and policymakers play an important role in creating a favorable business environment by promoting entrepreneurship, innovation, and SME development (Rodrguez et al., 2020). These policies may include decreasing administrative costs, simplifying bureaucratic processes, and giving incentives for SMEs to enter and succeed in the tourism business (UNWTO, 2019). Furthermore, well-defined and transparent legislation and governance frameworks assist SMEs create trust and confidence, allowing them to participate and expand in the tourist sector (UNCTAD, 2019).

Access to finance and investment is another critical component of creating an enabling environment for tourist SMEs. Small and medium-sized enterprises (SMEs) sometimes experience difficulties in acquiring appropriate capital to establish or develop their company. As a result, measures that improve SMEs' access to financing, such as targeted loan programmes, grants, and venture capital funds specifically created for the tourist sector, are critical (ILO, 2020). Furthermore, strengthening collaborations among financial institutions, government agencies, and SMEs can facilitate the provision of financial resources and improve the creditworthiness of SMEs (OECD, 2020).

It is also critical to strengthen SME networks and cooperation in order to create an enabling environment in the tourism sector. Encouragement of SMEs to interact and develop networks allows them to capitalize on collective knowledge, resources, and market opportunities. These alliances can take the shape of combined marketing campaigns, shared distribution channels, or cooperative purchasing agreements. SMEs can improve their competitiveness, get access to larger markets, and profit from economies of scale by collaborating (Hall, Williams, & Lew, 2010). Furthermore, connecting SMEs, larger firms, tourism groups, and industry platforms encourages knowledge exchange, mentorship, and innovation.

Creating an enabling environment for tourism SMEs necessitates a multifaceted approach. Supportive policies, rules, and governance frameworks provide a climate in which SMEs can operate and grow. Access to banking and investment options guarantees that SMEs have the money they need to start and grow their enterprises. SME network and collaboration strengthening facilitates cooperation, knowledge sharing, and innovation among SMEs in the tourism sector. Governments, policymakers, and industry stakeholders may establish an environment that promotes SMEs, stimulates their growth, and contributes to the overall development and sustainability of the tourist industry by concentrating on these elements (Srinamphon et al., 2022).

Establishing regulations, infrastructure, and resources that are supportive of small and medium-sized enterprises (SMEs) in the tourism industry is necessary to create an enabling environment for them. Thailand has put in place a thorough plan to assist SMEs in the travel and tourism industry. This includes working with industry groups, providing financial support, and offering training programmes to increase the competitiveness of small enterprises, particularly those in the hotel and service industries (Suntikul & Jachna,2016). The Home stay Programme in Malaysia promotes the provision of lodging and experiences to visitors by local communities. To encourage rural SMEs to engage in tourism and offer genuine experiences to tourists, the government offers infrastructure development, marketing assistance, and training (Gursoy et al., 2013). The Douro Valley in Portugal launched a cluster strategy wherein SMEs cooperate and pool resources and knowledge. This cooperative strategy has increased each company's ability to compete, encouraged innovation, and boosted the region's tourism offering as a whole (Carvalho & Costa, 2013).

These examples highlight several strategies for establishing a supportive atmosphere for small and medium-sized enterprises (SMEs) in the tourism industry, highlighting the significance of cooperation, community involvement, and government support in promoting the expansion and sustainability of these enterprises.

Sustainable Practices in Tourism-SME Collaborations

Sustainable practices are critical in the collaboration between the tourism industry and small and medium-sized enterprises (SMEs), contributing to businesses' long-term profitability, the protection of natural and cultural resources, and the overall sustainability of the tourism sector. This section examines the existing literature on sustainable practices in tourism-SME interactions, based on scholarly articles, reports, and publications.

The research emphasizes the significance of incorporating sustainable practises into tourism-SME interactions in order to reduce negative environmental impacts, promote social inclusion, and boost local economic development. Resource conservation, waste reduction, energy efficiency, biodiversity preservation, cultural heritage protection, and community participation are all examples of sustainable practices (UNWTO, 2015; UNCTAD, 2019). SMEs can help to conserve natural ecosystems, combat climate change, and preserve cultural authenticity by applying these practices.

Aside from environmental concerns, sustainable practices in tourism-SME interactions emphasize social inclusion and economic rewards. Collaboration with local communities, indigenous groups, and marginalized people is essential for establishing social equality and encouraging varied stakeholders to participate in tourist development (Hall et al., 2010). Supporting fair employment practices, offering opportunities for training and capacity-building, and procuring goods and services locally are all important components of sustainable practices that contribute to the social and economic well-being of host communities (ILO, 2020).

In tourism-SME interactions, effective collaboration and partnerships are critical for the successful adoption of sustainable practices. Engaging with tourism organizations, government agencies, non-profit organizations, and local communities to identify shared goals, exchange expertise, and build monitoring and certification procedures (UNWTO, 2019) is one way to do so. Collaborative programmes provide SMEs with the resources, skills, and finance they need to implement sustainable practices. They also promote a sustainable culture by encouraging SMEs to incorporate sustainable practices into their business plans and operations.

Sustainable practices are essential to tourism-SME interactions, assuring the tourism sector's long-term viability. SMEs may reduce their environmental impact, promote social inclusion, and contribute to local economic development by implementing sustainable practices. Effective collaboration, knowledge sharing, and capacity-building activities are required for the successful implementation of sustainable practices (Turekulova et al., 2022). SMEs may maximize the beneficial impacts of their operations and contribute to a more sustainable and responsible tourist business by collaborating with tourism organizations, government agencies, and local communities.

Sustainable tourism-SME collaboration practices are critical for long-term company viability, the protection of natural and cultural resources, and attracting aware travelers. This paragraph examines the literature on sustainable practices in tourism-SME collaborations, drawing insights from scholarly articles, reports, and publications with a focus on environmental stewardship, cultural heritage preservation, community support, and responsible tourism practices.

Environmental stewardship is a critical component of sustainable tourism-SME relationships. Small and medium-sized enterprises (SMEs) can reduce their carbon footprint by implementing energy-efficient measures, using renewable energy sources, and lowering waste and water use (UNWTO, 2019). Sustainable resource management, which includes responsible resource use, biodiversity conservation, and the protection of vulnerable ecosystems, is also critical for guaranteeing the long-term viability of tourism destinations. SMEs contribute to the overall sustainability of the tourism sector by prioritizing environmental stewardship.

Preservation of cultural assets and support for local communities are essential components of sustainable tourism-SME relationships. By promoting authentic cultural experiences, respecting local customs and traditions, and supporting local artisans and cultural projects, SMEs can actively participate in cultural heritage preservation (UNWTO, 2015). SMEs help to preserve unique cultural identities, increase the cultural value of tourism locations, and create community pride and empowerment. Supporting local communities through job creation, capacity building, and sourcing products and services locally enhances the socioeconomic benefits of tourism-SME interactions (ILO, 2020).

Responsible tourism is critical for attracting aware travelers that value ecological and ethical considerations. SMEs can promote sustainable mobility options, educate tourists about local environmental and cultural sensitivity, and encourage responsible behavior among visitors to engage in responsible tourism practices (UNWTO, 2019). By implementing responsible practices, SMEs create authentic and meaningful experiences for travelers, who are increasingly looking for places and businesses that share their values for sustainability.

It is critical to develop collaboration and knowledge exchange among SMEs, tourism organizations, local communities, and government agencies in order to effectively adopt sustainable practices in tourism-SME collaborations. Building partnerships and networks allows for the sharing of best practices, capacity building, and cooperative sustainability activities (UNWTO, 2019). Collaboration also boosts SMEs' aggregate impact in promoting sustainable practices and creates positive change in the tourism industry.

Sustainable practices in tourism-SME relationships include environmental stewardship, cultural heritage preservation, assistance for local communities, and participation in responsible tourism practices. SMEs contribute to the sustainability of the tourism sector by reducing their carbon impact, preserving cultural authenticity, and helping local communities. Responsible behavior attracts conscious travelers who appreciate sustainability. For the successful application of sustainable practices in tourist-SME collaborations, effective collaboration among SMEs, tourism organizations, communities, and governments are critical.

CASE STUDIES AND BEST PRACTICES

Case Study One

Lapa Rios Ecolodge, Costa Rica Lapa Rios Ecolodge is an exemplary case of sustainable tourism and SME collaboration. Located in a remote rainforest in Costa Rica, this eco-lodge demonstrates a commitment to environmental stewardship, cultural preservation, and community engagement. The lodge follows sustainable practices such as water and energy conservation, waste management, and organic farming (Ditton & Duffy, 2013). Lapa Rios also actively involves the local community by employing and training residents, supporting local schools, and partnering with local artisans to promote and sell their crafts (Ivanovic, 2019). This collaboration between tourism and SMEs has resulted in a successful and sustainable business that provides unique experiences for tourists while benefiting the local economy and environment.

Case Study Two

Fair Trade Tourism, South Africa Fair Trade Tourism (FTT) is a certification program in South Africa that promotes responsible tourism and supports SMEs. FTT certifies accommodations, tour operators, and attractions that adhere to strict criteria regarding fair wages, community benefits, and environmental sustainability (Butler &Hinch, 2007). By working with SMEs, FTT provides them with access to marketing platforms, capacity building, and networking opportunities. For example, the Makuleke Community Camps in Kruger National Park have partnered with FTT to create sustainable and community-owned accommodations that offer immersive cultural experiences while benefiting the local community (Sindiga, 2012). FTT's collaboration with SMEs not only promotes responsible tourism but also supports local entrepreneurship and community development.

Best Practice One

Collaboration and Cluster Development One of the best practices in tourism-SME collaborations is the establishment of collaborative networks and cluster development. In destinations such as the Basque Country in Spain, SMEs within the tourism sector have formed clusters to promote joint marketing, product development, and knowledge sharing (González et al., 2016). This collaboration enables SMEs to enhance their competitiveness, access resources, and create a unique destination experience for tourists. The Basque Country's cluster development approach has led to increased tourist arrivals, job creation, and sustainable growth in the region.

Best Practice Two

Microfinance and Entrepreneurship Support Microfinance and entrepreneurship support programs are vital for SMEs in the tourism sector, particularly in developing countries. The Grameen Bank in Bangladesh is a notable example of providing microfinance services to small businesses, including those in the tourism industry (Yunus, 2003). By providing access to credit and financial services, SMEs can invest in their businesses, improve infrastructure, and expand their operations. Microfinance programs also offer entrepreneurship training and mentoring, empowering SMEs to develop their skills and business acumen (McVay, 2011). The success of microfinance programs in supporting SMEs in tourism has been demonstrated in various contexts globally.

Successful Tourism-SME Collaborations: Lessons Learned

Tourism-SME collaborations have proven to be beneficial in developing sustainable tourist growth, promoting local economic development, and providing travelers with unique experiences. This section addresses lessons learnt from successful tourism-SMEs collaborations, focusing on insights from scholarly articles, reports, and case studies.

Initiatives focused on a specific location that support SME development and participation have been successful in promoting sustainable tourism. For instance, the 'Green Tourism Business Scheme' in the UK promotes SMEs to adopt sustainable practices by offering counseling, training, and certification (Goodwin & Francis, 2003). By providing specialized support, encouraging networking opportunities, and including SMEs into destination marketing efforts, destination management organizations (DMOs) play a critical role in fostering SME participation (Hall & Richards, 2003). Destination-based initiatives improve the competitiveness of local enterprises and contribute to the sustainable growth of tourism destinations by fostering an environment that is supportive of SMEs.

Successful tourism-SME linkages are mostly fueled by public-private partnerships and cooperation. Partnerships between governmental organizations, businesses, and SMEs produce synergies that promote the expansion of the tourism industry sustainably (Gursoy & Chi, 2013). For instance, the "New Zealand Tourism Strategy 2015" (New Zealand Tourism Strategy Group, 2007) places a strong emphasis on cooperation between the government, business, and SMEs to spur innovation and enhance visitor experiences. Through these relationships, governments and private sector organizations can take use of the innovation and adaptability of SMEs to promote tourist development while giving SMEs access to resources, knowledge, and funding opportunities.

Successful tourism-SME interactions have also shown innovative business models and entrepreneurial success stories as important lessons. Small and medium-sized businesses (SMEs) now have options to enter the tourism sector and compete with larger businesses because to the growth of the sharing economy and digital platforms. By facilitating direct bookings and eschewing conventional distribution methods, websites like Airbnb and Trip advisor have made it possible for SMEs to advertise their products to a global audience (Xiang et al., 2015). Additionally, entrepreneurial success tales emphasize the significance of innovation, differentiation, and developing distinctive client experiences. Small and medium-sized enterprises (SMEs) have prospered and contributed to the diversification of tourism services by embracing novel business models like agri-tourism, community-based tourism, and experiential tourism (Gursoy & Rutherford, 2004).

Successful tourism-SME partnerships provide important insights for promoting long-term tourism growth. The success of SMEs in the tourist sector is influenced by destination-based programmes that encourage their participation and growth, public-private partnerships and collaboration, and the implementation of cutting-edge business models. Stakeholders can foster an atmosphere that encourages entrepreneurship, supports sustainable practices, and boosts the competitiveness of SMEs in the tourism industry by putting these principles into practice.

Leveraging Technology and Digital Platforms for SMEs in Tourism

For small and medium-sized firms (SMEs) in the tourist sector to increase their competitiveness, attract a wider audience, and streamline their operations in today's digital age, technology and digital platforms have become crucial tools. With the help of case studies, reports, and scholarly articles, this paragraph analyses how technology and digital platforms might help small and medium-sized businesses (SMEs) in the tourism industry.

The capacity of technology and digital platforms to improve the accessibility and exposure of SMEs in the tourism industry is one of their main benefits. SMEs have the chance to advertise their lodgings, excursions, and experiences to a global audience through online travel agencies (OTAs) and booking platforms like Booking.com, Expedia, and Airbnb (Gretzel& Yoo, 2008). SMEs can reach new clients by utilizing these platforms that might not have been aware of their offerings through conventional marketing routes. For SMEs, this improved visibility results in improved business prospects and revenue generating.

Additionally, SMEs may streamline their operations, increase productivity, and improve the customer experience thanks to technology and digital platforms. SMEs can automate processes like inventory management, bookings, and payments thanks to cloud-based property management systems (PMS) and reservation systems, for instance (Sigala et al., 2012). Tourists may now access information, book reservations, and get real-time updates on their cellphones via mobile applications and websites, making it convenient and giving them immediate access to SMEs' services (Xiang et al., 2015). Adopting such technology not only helps SMEs save time and money, but also improves the general experience and happiness of their customers.

Technology helps SMEs in the tourist industry make data-driven decisions. SMEs can learn important information about consumer preferences, booking patterns, and market trends by using analytics tools and customer relationship management (CRM) systems (Gretzel& Yoo, 2008). SMEs can use this information to guide their pricing, product development, and marketing strategies, allowing them to customize their offers to fit market demands and maintain their competitiveness.

It is crucial to remember that adopting technology and digital platforms necessitates SMEs making investments in digital infrastructure and capabilities. Training initiatives and capacity-building projects can help SMEs build the digital skills they need to use technology successfully (UNWTO, 2020). The adoption of technology and digital solutions among SMEs can also be facilitated by cooperation with technology providers, industry associations, and governments.

For SMEs in the tourism sector, technology and digital platforms have become potent instruments for increasing their exposure, streamlining their operations, and enhancing the consumer experience. SMEs may boost their efficiency, attract a wider audience, and make data-driven decisions by utilizing these tools. To effectively utilize the potential of technology and digital platforms in the tourist sector, SMEs must invest in digital skills and work with pertinent stakeholders.

For SMEs in the travel and tourist industry to increase their market share and spur growth, e-commerce and digital marketing methods have become crucial. SMEs now have the chance to market and sell their goods and services to a worldwide clientele thanks to the growth of online marketplaces like Amazon and eBay (Sigala et al., 2012). By using e-commerce platforms, SMEs can skip conventional distribution channels and reach customers directly, cutting down on transaction expenses. Additionally, SMEs can target particular client segments, improve brand awareness, and generate leads by using digital marketing methods including search engine optimization (SEO), pay-per-click (PPC) advertising, and content marketing (Buhalis&Foerste, 2015). SMEs may boost their competitiveness and draw in more clients by utilizing e-commerce and digital marketing tactics.

Another critical component of utilizing technology for SMEs in the tourism industry is harnessing the power of social media and internet platforms. SMEs have the chance to interact with clients, create interesting material, and foster brand loyalty on social media platforms like Facebook, Instagram, and Twitter (Gretzel& Yoo, 2008). SMEs may advertise their products, build genuine relationships with their target market, and obtain immediate feedback using social media. Online review sites like Trip advisor and Yelp also significantly impact consumer opinions and encourage travel bookings (Xiang et al., 2015). SMEs may improve their reputation, acquire client trust, and increase bookings by actively managing their online presence and interacting with customers on social media and review platforms.

Additionally, a variety of tools and technology boost the competitiveness of SMEs in the digital era. Systems for managing customer relationships (CRM) give SMEs the ability to track client preferences, manage customer contacts, and customize their offers (Sigala et al., 2012). The efficiency and customer experience are improved by cloud-based property management systems (PMS) and booking engines, which also ease operational chores like reservations, inventory management, and payments. Furthermore, data analytics solutions give useful information about consumer behavior, industry trends, and performance metrics, assisting SMEs in making business decisions that are well-informed (Buhalis& Foerste, 2015). SMEs can optimize their operations, provide outstanding customer service, and maintain competitiveness in the digital environment by utilizing these tools and technology.

It is crucial to remember that embracing technology and digital platforms necessitates new skill adaptations and infrastructure investments on the part of SMEs. In order to develop their digital capabilities and keep up with technical changes, SMEs can benefit from training programmes, workshops, and partnership with industry groups (UNWTO, 2020). The competitiveness of SMEs in the digital era can also be increased by collaboration with technology providers, digital marketing agencies, and industry peers.

SMEs in the tourism industry have a variety of chances to increase their reach, communicate with clients, and become more competitive thanks to technology and digital platforms. SMEs may promote business growth and thrive in the digital age by implementing e-commerce and digital marketing strategies, utilising social media and online platforms, and utilising tools and technologies. However, it is essential for SMEs to make investments in digital infrastructure and skills, work with pertinent stakeholders, and update themselves for the rapidly evolving technology environment.

CONCLUSION

In conclusion, the study of the interactions between small and medium-sized businesses (SMEs) and tourism demonstrates the enormous potential for long-term economic growth. By producing income, opening up job opportunities, and encouraging foreign exchange revenues, tourism serves as a catalyst for SME development. SME agility, inventiveness, and entrepreneurial spirit in turn contribute to the tourism industry. They contribute to the growth of destination branding and competitiveness by acting as suppliers of genuine and immersive experiences. Additionally, SMEs are vital for advancing local economic development by serving as growth-oriented forces in their neighborhoods.

It is crucial to resolve issues and embrace opportunities if tourism-SME synergy is to achieve its full potential for sustainable economic growth. This entails increasing market prospects through tourism demand, facilitating SME innovation, product diversity, and quality improvement, as well as funding capacity-building and skill-development initiatives for SMEs in the tourism industry. The facilitation of access to finance and investment, the development of SME networks and partnerships, and the strengthening of SME collaborations are all components of building an enabling environment for SMEs (Yamak et al., 2023).

Destinations may accomplish equitable development, job creation, and sustained economic growth by utilizing the potential of tourism-SME collaboration. To create an ecosystem that supports SMEs, fosters innovation, and promotes ethical travel practices, governments, tourist organizations, and stakeholders must collaborate. With the correct assistance, SMEs may fully take advantage of the opportunities offered by the tourist sector, enhancing both the long-term viability of travel destinations and the welfare of nearby communities.

Overall, the investigation of the relationship between SMEs and tourism highlights the significance of acknowledging SMEs as key pillars of economic resilience. They are important contributors to sustainable economic growth due to their integration into the tourism value chain, capacity to generate employment, and involvement in local economic development. We can develop a robust and resilient tourist sector that benefits SMEs as well as the larger economy by maximizing their potential and encouraging collaboration.

REFERENCES

Beldona, S., Cobanoglu, C., & Perdue, R. R. (2017). Hotel guests' preferences for social media as service recovery platforms. *International Journal of Hospitality Management*, *67*, 71–80.

Boukhobza, J., & Boumba, S. (2017). Micro-enterprises and sustainable tourism development: A case study of artisan enterprises in Morocco. *Tourism Management*, *62*, 239–247.

Brynjolfsson, E., & McAfee, A. (2014). *The Second Machine Age: Work, Progress, and Prosperity in a Time of Brilliant Technologies*. W. W. Norton & Company.

Buhalis, D., & Foerste, M. (2015). SoCoMo Marketing for Travel and Tourism: Empowering Co-Creation of Value. *Journal of Destination Marketing & Management*, *4*(3), 151–161. doi:10.1016/j.jdmm.2015.04.001

Carvalho, L., & Costa, C. (2013). Promoting competitiveness in tourism: A case study of the Douro Valley. *Tourism Management Perspectives*, *6*, 15–23.

Chon, K., & Maier, T. (2009). *Welcome to Hospitality: An Introduction*. Delmar Cengage Learning.

Dlamini, T. M., Iwu, C. G., & Ogunlela, G. O. (2023). Support Strategies of Government-Owned Business Incubators for SMEs' Sustainability. In *Leadership and Governance for Sustainability* (pp. 222–241). IGI Global. doi:10.4018/978-1-6684-9711-1.ch012

Duckworth, A. L. (2016). *Grit: The Power of Passion and Perseverance*. Scribner.

Dutta, S. (2019). *The Global Innovation Index 2019: Creating Healthy Lives - The Future of Medical Innovation. World Intellectual Property Organization*. WIPO.

Dweck, C. S. (2006). *Mindset: The New Psychology of Success*. Ballantine Books.

Elkington, J. (2018). *The Triple Bottom Line: How Today's Best-Run Companies Are Achieving Economic, Social, and Environmental Success—and How You Can Too*. Routledge.

Euromonitor International (2021). *Travel and Tourism Industry Overview: Global Outlook Report*. Euromonitor International.

Faeni, D. P., Puspitaningtyas Faeni, R., Alden Riyadh, H., & Yuliansyah, Y. (2023). The COVID-19 pandemic impact on the global tourism industry SMEs: A human capital development perspective. *Review of International Business and Strategy*, *33*(2), 317–327. doi:10.1108/RIBS-08-2021-0116

Goodwin, H., & Francis, J. (2003). The Green Tourism Business Scheme and the Small Business Enterprise: An Exploratory Study of Relationships and Impacts. *Journal of Sustainable Tourism*, *11*(4), 325–347.

Gretzel, U., & Yoo, K. H. (2008). Use and Impact of Online Travel Reviews. *Information and Communication Technologies in Tourism*, *2008*, 35–46. doi:10.1007/978-3-211-77280-5_4

Gursoy, D., & Chi, C. G. Q. (2013). Understanding Chinese Outbound Tourists' Satisfaction, Destination Image, and Future Behavioral Intention: A Structural Model Approach. *Journal of Travel Research*, *52*(6), 731–742.

Gursoy, D., Chi, C. G. Q., & Lu, L. (2013). Antecedents and outcomes of travelers' information search behavior: A comparative study of pre-travel and during travel search. *Tourism Management*, *36*, 120–130.

Gursoy, D., & Rutherford, D. G. (2004). Host Attitudes toward Tourism: An Improved Structural Model. *Annals of Tourism Research*, *31*(3), 495–516. doi:10.1016/j.annals.2003.08.008

Guttentag, D. (2015). Airbnb: Disruptive innovation and the rise of an informal tourism accommodation sector. *Current Issues in Tourism*, *18*(12), 1192–1217. doi:10.1080/13683500.2013.827159

Hall, C. M., & Mitchell, R. (2008). Wine tourism in New Zealand: The visitors' perspective. *International Journal of Wine Business Research*, *20*(3), 276–293.

Hall, C. M., & Page, S. J. (2014). *The Geography of Tourism and Recreation: Environment, Place and Space*. Routledge. doi:10.4324/9780203796092

Hall, C. M., & Richards, G. (2003). *Tourism and Sustainable Community Development*. Routledge.

Hall, C. M., Williams, A. M., & Lew, A. A. (2010). *Tourism: Concepts, Impacts and Issues*. Routledge.

Hassanli, N., & Williamson, J. (2023). Minimizing the sustainability knowledge-practice gap through creating shared value: The case of small accommodation firms. *Journal of Sustainable Tourism*, 1–20. doi:10.1080/09669582.2023.2186828

Hu, M. K., & Kee, D. M. H. (2022). SMEs and business sustainability: Achieving sustainable business growth in the new normal. In *Research anthology on business continuity and navigating times of crisis* (pp. 1036–1056). IGI Global. doi:10.4018/978-1-6684-4503-7.ch052

ILO (2019). *SMEs and Decent and Productive Employment Creation*. ILO.

ILO (2020). *Tourism and COVID-19: Assessing the Economic and Social Impacts*. ILO.

International Labour Organization. (2015). *Micro-, Small and Medium-sized Enterprises*. ILO. https://www.ilo.org/global/topics/micro-and-small enterprises/WCMS_437530/lang--en/index.htm

Jamal, T., & Getz, D. (1999). Community roundtables for tourism-related conflicts: The dialectics of consensus and process structures. *Journal of Sustainable Tourism*, 7(3-4), 290–313. doi:10.1080/09669589908667341

Kadaba, D. M. K., & Aithal, P. S., & KRS, S. (2023). Government Initiatives and Digital Innovation for AtmaNirbhar MSMEs/SMEs: To Achieve Sustainable and Inclusive Economic Growth. [IJMTS]. *International Journal of Management, Technology, and Social Sciences*, 8(1), 68–82.

Leask, A., Fyall, A., & Barron, P. (2013). Generation Y: Opportunity or challenge - strategies to engage Generation Y in the destination. *Tourism Management*, 35, 190–200.

Lopes, J., & Farinha, L. (2020). Knowledge and Technology Transfer in Tourism SMEs. In *Multilevel Approach to Competitiveness in the Global Tourism Industry* (pp. 198–210). IGI Global. doi:10.4018/978-1-7998-0365-2.ch012

Martucci, O., Acampora, A., Arcese, G., & Poponi, S. (2020). The Development of Smart Tourism Destinations Through the Integration of ICT Innovations in SMEs of the Commercial Sector: Practical Experience from Central Italy. In *Handbook of Research on Smart Territories and Entrepreneurial Ecosystems for Social Innovation and Sustainable Growth* (pp. 124–151). IGI Global. doi:10.4018/978-1-7998-2097-0.ch008

Mohammed, A. H. A. (2022). SMEs' sustainable development challenges post-COVID-19: The tourism sector. *World Journal of Entrepreneurship, Management and Sustainable Development*, 18(3), 407–424.

Mokoena, S. L., &Liambo, T. F. (2023). The sustainability of township tourism SMMEs. *International Journal of Research in Business and Social Science (2147-4478)*, 12(1), 341-349.

Molina, M. Y. S., Espinoza, L. C. G., & Tarabó, A. E. M. (2021). Small businesses like a sign of innovation and sustainable development in the community tourism centers in Santa Elena. In *Innovation and Entrepreneurial Opportunities in Community Tourism* (pp. 15–36). IGI Global.

Naidoo, V. (2021). SME sustainability in South Africa post-COVID-19. In *Handbook of Research on Sustaining SMEs and Entrepreneurial Innovation in the Post-COVID-19 Era* (pp. 419–437). IGI Global. doi:10.4018/978-1-7998-6632-9.ch020

New Zealand Tourism Strategy Group. (2007). *New Zealand Tourism Strategy 2015*. Ministry of Tourism.

OECD. (2019). *Small, Medium, Strong*. Trends in SME Performance and Business Conditions.

OECD. (2020). *Tourism Policy Responses to the Coronavirus (COVID-19)*. Pandemic.

Powell, T. C., & Baker, T. (2014). Learning from Crises: How Governance and Relationships Affect Innovation During Industry Downturns. *Strategic Management Journal*, 35(7), 1054–1073.

Prayag, G., Hosany, S., & Odeh, K. (2013). The role of tourists' emotional experiences and satisfaction in understanding behavioral intentions. *Journal of Destination Marketing & Management*, 2(2), 118–127. doi:10.1016/j.jdmm.2013.05.001

Priatmoko, S., Kabil, M., Akaak, A., Lakner, Z., Gyuricza, C., & Dávid, L. D. (2023). Understanding the Complexity of Rural Tourism Business: Scholarly Perspective. *Sustainability (Basel)*, *2023*(15), 1193. doi:10.3390/su15021193

Rahmawati, R., Handayani, S. R., Suprapti, A. R., Airawaty, D., & Latifah, L. (2023). Green Entrepreneurship Based on Local Characteristics and Culture to Support Sustainable Eco-Tourism: A Case Study. *Journal of Intercultural Communication*, *23*(1), 66–75. doi:10.36923/jicc.v23i1.71

Rodríguez, A. J. G., Barón, N. J., & Martínez, J. M. G. (2020). Validity of dynamic capabilities in the operation based on new sustainability narratives on nature tourism SMEs and clusters. *Sustainability (Basel)*, *12*(3), 1004. doi:10.3390/su12031004

Ruhanen, L., & Weiler, B. (2010). Authenticity and Small Tourism Business Development in Rural Areas. *Journal of Sustainable Tourism*, *18*(3), 367–381.

S. K. & Chiputwa, B. (2019). Adventure tourism in Nepal: Challenges and opportunities. *Tourism Management Perspectives*, *32*, 100569.

Sachs, J. D. (2015). *The Age of Sustainable Development*. Columbia University Press. doi:10.7312/sach17314

Sánchez, J., Pelegrín, A., & Montoro-Sánchez, Á. (2017). Stakeholder Collaboration and Destination Branding. *Annals of Tourism Research*, *67*, 125–134.

Shin, D. H. (2018). Augmented reality: A new digital marketing tool in tourism. *Journal of Destination Marketing & Management*, *8*, 1–5.

Sigala, M., Christou, E., & Gretzel, U. (2012). *Social Media in Travel, Tourism and Hospitality: Theory, Practice and Cases*. Ashgate Publishing.

Song, H., & Li, G. (2008). Tourism demand modelling and forecasting—A review of recent research. *Tourism Management*, *29*(2), 203–220. doi:10.1016/j.tourman.2007.07.016

Srinamphon, P., Chernbumroong, S., & Tippayawong, K. Y. (2022). The Effect of Small Particulate Matter on Tourism and Related SMEs in Chiang Mai, Thailand. *Sustainability (Basel)*, *14*(13), 8147. doi:10.3390/su14138147

Suntikul, W., & Jachna, T. (2016). SME competitiveness in tourism: The role of financial and non-financial support institutions. *Current Issues in Tourism*, *19*(2), 144–161.

Turekulova, D., Beisengaliyev, B., Valiyeva, S., Kurmankulova, N., & Saimagambetova, G. (2022). Analysis of sustainable development of SMEs and factors influencing to the ecotourism industry. *Journal of Environmental Management & Tourism*, *13*(1), 211–222. doi:10.14505/jemt.v13.1(57).19

UNCTAD. (2019). *Policy Guide on Entrepreneurship for Development*. UNCTAD.

UNCTAD. (2021). *Tourism for Development: Volume II - Good Practices in Tourism*. UNCTAD.

UNWTO (2019). *Tourism for Sustainable Development: Toolkit for Business*. UNWTO.

UNWTO. (2020). *Harnessing Innovation in Tourism: Case Studies*. World Tourism Organization.

UNWTO. (2021). *Global Report on Small and Medium-sized Enterprises in Tourism*. UN.

Westerman, G., Bonnet, D., & McAfee, A. (2014). *Leading Digital: Turning Technology into Business Transformation*. Harvard Business Review Press.

World Bank Group (2020). *Supporting SMEs During the COVID-19 Crisis: A Policy Handbook for Developing Countries*. World Bank Group.

WTTC. (2020). *Travel and Tourism: Economic Impact 2020*. WTTC.

Xiang, Z., Du, Q., Ma, Y., & Fan, W. (2015). An Empirical Investigation of the Impacts of Social Media Interactions on Destination Image. *Tourism Management*, 46.

Xiang, Z., Du, Q., Ma, Y., & Fan, W. (2017). A comparative analysis of major online review platforms: Implications for social media analytics in hospitality and tourism. *Tourism Management*, *58*, 51–65. doi:10.1016/j.tourman.2016.10.001

Yamak, S., Karatas-Ozkan, M., Godwin, E. S., Mahmood, S., & Rahimi, R. (2023). Transformation or Retaining the Status Quo: Multinational Hospitality Companies and SME Collaboration on Sustainability in Emerging Countries. In Handbook of Research on Sustainable Tourism and Hotel Operations in Global Hypercompetition (pp. 490-516). IGI Global.

Chapter 11
Women's Empowerment Through Entrepreneurship in Emerging Economies:
Analyzing the Dimensions and Policy Implications

Manpreet Arora
https://orcid.org/0000-0002-4939-1992

School of Commerce and Management Studies, Central University of Himachal Pradesh, Dharamshala, India

Swati Singh

Maharaja Agresen University, Baddi, India

ABSTRACT

The concept of women entrepreneurship has the ability to transform the whole society, it gains more relevance in emerging economies. Through women's entrepreneurship, not only the economic freedom of women can be ensured but it also fosters creativity innovation, and productivity in emerging nations. One of the best ways to make women empower along with education is "women entrepreneurship." In the process of women entrepreneurship, women not only earn self-respect, but they also understand the peculiarities of economic and social dimensions of life. The abilities of women are many-fold, which can be harnessed easily by adopting the path of women entrepreneurship. The tool of women entrepreneurship can act as a facilitator, motivator as well as moderator of fostering women empowerment. If access to finance through microfinance and other interventions, is provided to women they become empowered in many aspects. This chapter highlights the role of women entrepreneurship for women empowerment in emerging economies. This piece of research highlights various policy implications also in order to nurture women entrepreneurship.

DOI: 10.4018/979-8-3693-0111-1.ch011

INTRODUCTION

In emerging nations, women entrepreneurship is surfacing as a new engine for the growth and development of the economy (Vossenberg, 2013). It has the ability to bring prosperity as well as welfare. The concept of women entrepreneurship has the ability to transform the whole society. It not only has the capacity to promote skill development, employment, and eradication of poverty and hunger but also has the ability to pave the way for education of the weaker sections of society. Through women's entrepreneurship, not only the economic freedom of women ensured but it also foster creativity innovation, and productivity (Setini et al., 2020). Instances are available where cultural and social impacts of women entrepreneurship can also be seen. Further, there is a great possibility of upliftment of the whole family and ultimately the society through economic and social freedom of women. Women are considered to be the pillar of every society; therefore, the whole society gets empowered. Though women are considered vulnerable and weaker sections of society, they are regarded as instrumental in the transformation of society in various parts of the world (Mandal, 2013). The authors believe that women can play an important role in achieving the sustainable development goals of the entire world. But for that policy interventions are required at the grassroots level for developing the entrepreneurial ecosystem for nurturing, and budding women across the globe (Singh et al. 2021).

When women are empowered and have equal access to education, resources, and opportunities, they become empowered and can actively participate in the workforce. Increased female labor force participation has been linked to higher economic growth rates in many countries (Gaddis & Klasen, 2014). By utilizing the full potential of women, economies can benefit from a larger talent pool and increased productivity. Women bring diverse perspectives, experiences, and skills when they are at leadership roles (Lu & Herremans, 2019). When we empower women it encourages their participation in decision-making processes, entrepreneurship, and leadership roles. This diversity promotes innovation and creativity, leading to the development of new products, services, and solutions that can drive economic progress (Bassett-Jones, 2005).

Empowering women economically has a substantial impact on poverty reduction (Wei et.al.,2021). Women constitute a noteworthy portion of the world's poor, and when they are empowered, they can improve their own economic situations and those of their families. Women have a general tendency to invest a higher percentage of their income in education, health, and nutrition for their children, leading to better overall living standards and breaking the vicious circle of poverty. Further various social goals can be achieved through women entrepreneurship (Chhabra, et.al., (2020)). Empowering women contributes to social stability and development. When women are economically empowered, they gain greater control over their lives, which can lead to improved health, reduced gender-based violence, and increased political participation. These factors contribute to more inclusive and stable societies, which are essential for sustainable economic growth. In order to gain the holistic objectives of the nations, it is very important to invest in women's education, skills training, and healthcare. It not only benefits individual women but also enhances human capital development. When women are educated and healthy, they can contribute more effectively to the workforce, resulting in a more skilled and productive labor force. When we use the term women empowerment, it simply conveys the idea that they need steps for efforts to be empowered. There is therefore absence of gender equality, or they are not treated equal as other men. In every economy it should be ensured that women participate in economic and social lives in a very wider sense in order to derive the benefits of equality. Women are the most vulnerable if we talk about the developing nations. The implications of women empowerment are manifold. It signifies the control of women on resources, assets, income and much largely their own lives. When women are empowered, they gain the ability as well as power to manage various types of risks associated in their personal or professional lives. Various societal barriers, cultural norms, customs and religions across the world demarcate women from other genders in one form or another. But largely a concept of inferiority towards woman could be seen in various communities. The social status of the women is not at par with men. Women are still lagging behind in attaining same social status as men in many communities across the world. Less percentage of women are involved in economic activities. In rural areas, the women are less educated. The level of confidence and other entrepreneurial skills are very low. To build stronger economies, sustainable societies and a better planet it is necessary to provide equal opportunity to everyone. In the pursuit of achieving sustainable goals of the nations and creating equal opportunity for all, it is necessary to create a supportive environment for the women as well as women entrepreneurs. Further during and after pandemic entrepreneurship has been regarded as an effective resilience strategy (Arora & Sharma, 2021a, Arora & Sharma, 2021b).

Women entrepreneurship plays an important role in empowering women. It assists in making women economically independent. By women entrepreneurship women own their businesses, have control over finances and create possibilities of earning not only for themselves but for many others. It boosts their confidence, help to improve their decision-making abilities and increases their overall empowerment. When women act as entrepreneurs, they enter into leadership roles which allows them to shape the direction of their enterprises. By this they not only contribute towards the economic development of the country but help in achieving various sustainable development goals like removing of poverty and creating access to decent lives. They also learn various managerial skills like negotiation skills, conflict resolution and conflict management, problem-solving, and critical thinking, which can be applied not only in business but also in other aspects of their lives. Women as entrepreneurs create possibilities of challenging traditional gender roles as well as societal norms and rituals when they enter into male dominated industries. They set an example for young minds by encouraging them to pursue unlimited possibilities of entrepreneurial aspirations and break free from stereotypes. Women-led businesses have the potential to create job opportunities not only for themselves but also for others in their communities, thereby fostering the process of community development. By employing both women and men, women entrepreneurs contribute to economic growth, poverty reduction, and community development. Undoubtedly, women entrepreneurs often face several constraints, and their entrepreneurial journey can be quite challenging. Their social networks are limited as compared to men in business, they also face constraints in having access to financial resources. Therefore, various initiatives, policy interventions, organizational policies, and support systems are required to address these barriers and provide women with the necessary resources, funding, training, and networking opportunities. By facilitating access to these resources, through various policy interventions, women entrepreneurship can help in overcoming the existing gender gaps and can accelerate the process of promotion of women's economic empowerment.

The social impacts of women entrepreneurship are plenty which have long lasting and deeper impacts. Successful women entrepreneurs serve as role models and sources of inspiration for other women and girls around them promoting a sense of positivity and encouragement for the vulnerable sections of the society. Their achievements validate that women can overcome obstacles, prosper in business, and contribute to the economy in a meaningful manner. This inspiration fosters a sense of possibility and encourages other women to pursue entrepreneurship and strive for their own empowerment. Women entrepreneurs often prioritize community development by creating a social impact and contribute to community development in the most sustainable fashion. They may create businesses that address societal challenges, promote sustainable practices, or support marginalized communities. Through their entrepreneurial endeavors, women can drive positive change and make a difference in their communities.

Need of the Study

Women entrepreneurship is an important area in many dimensions. Not only it contributes towards the growth and development of an emerging economy, but it is equally important for creating ample opportunities for women in order to create gender equality. Various SDGs also reflect towards issues pertaining to women like gender, equality, decent work and economic growth, reducing inequalities, good health and well-being, which can be achieved through women entrepreneurship. So, it becomes important to understand various challenges to women entrepreneurship and its perception by people. How people perceive the concept of women entrepreneurship is equally important as it effects, its growth, accessibility, and opportunities. Therefore, understanding their sentiments can give us directions in this area.

Research Questions

The following research questions will be achieved conceptually:

1. What is the concept of women entrepreneurship? How challenging / critical is entrepreneurship for women?
2. What are public sentiments about entrepreneurship and innovation in general and women entrepreneurship in particular on Twitter?
3. Policy recommendations for nurturing women entrepreneurship ecosystem

Methodology

The conceptual background of the chapter is literature based. To understand the concept of women empowerment the literature from SCOPUS is extracted and a key word analysis is performed on 857 documents, in order to highlight the thrust areas contributing towards women empowerment. Visual analysis has been performed by Vosviewer Software.

The study is also based upon analyzing the public sentiments, which has been extracted from social media platform, i.e., Twitter. Qualitative software named NVivo has been used for content analysis as well as sentiment analysis. The present chapter is basically a knowledge-contributing perspective. The literature available on women entrepreneurship has served as the conceptual foundation of the chapter. The chapter is qualitative in approach. Further, an attempt has been made to put forward the policy recommendations for nurturing women's entrepreneurship in this chapter. Through content analysis, the challenges and opportunities of this ecosystem have been explored and policy recommendations have been framed accordingly.

Discussion

What is the concept of women entrepreneurship? How challenging / critical is entrepreneurship for women?

Women's lives are transformed as a result of economic or social empowerment. This process begins with the mobilization of credit especially lent to women and then when they work together, particularly, in group lending programmes; it creates positive change in their lives (Porter, 2013, Arora & Singh, 2018). For example, in India, a pilot programme called as the SHG Bank Linkage Programme has remained one of the most effective programmes for empowering women. According to the reports of a leading bank of India, NABARD, 87% of SHGs are women SHGs. SHG's have provided the opportunity to the women to have direct access to the financial resources. They can use the borrowed capital either for personal consumption or for any income generating activities. This essentially helps to improve their economic situation by giving them the opportunity to invest in micro-level businesses, thereby directly and indirectly supporting family businesses. When women are financially independent and have control over their income and savings, they gain confidence and feel empowered (Bansal & Singh, 2020). They also gain confidence and feel empowered if they have free access to employment. Self-help group programmes or group lending systems have shown positive impact on the lives of women and vulnerable in many developing nations. Still, there are number of challenges faced by the women while setting up enterprises.

The state of women still is in bad shape in many aspects. Women account for roughly half of the world's population, but till now many women have less control over their lives and make fewer decisions than men (Sarfaraz, Faghih & Majd, 2014). According to Bansal & Singh (2020) women lack in awareness, have high family responsibility, and they lack in support from family members. There are also gender inequality issues. Gender inequalities in any national economies are associated to factors like as the types of work undertaken by men and women, the places and areas in which they typically work, or the distribution of paid and unpaid work within households (Ruth, Summers, & Carter, 2013). However, a greater proportion of women worked as self-employed or as casual informal labourers which is also major issue of concern (Samantroy, & Tomar, 2018).

In order to understand the literature on women and empowerment, especially in the field of business and management, a Scopus search was made. Articles which were published in the Scopus database in English only on "women empowerment" were attempted to be analyzed. The database gave result of 896 documents. The keyword analysis revealed certain important aspects of the literature on women empowerment. There were many clusters where the subject of women empowerment was researched upon in which majority of the clusters talked about the challenges of women empowerment, women in tourism, and about the constraints women are facing in empowerment. Then there were certain areas which were based upon the social empowerment of women and were talking about the role of women in agriculture, especially in the developing nations. The literature also suggested that the tourism market is also providing opportunities to empower women, especially in the developing nations. A good chunk of literature highlighted the concept of glass ceiling also (Chhabra & Karmarkar, 2016). Another thrust area of research was how the rural population is coming up for women empowerment by the help of NGOs and community-based programs relating with self-help groups as well as tourism. Figure 1 and figure 2 highlights the various clusters which show the research areas pertaining to this concept.

Figure 1. Keyword analysis A
Source: Authors creation using SCOPUS database

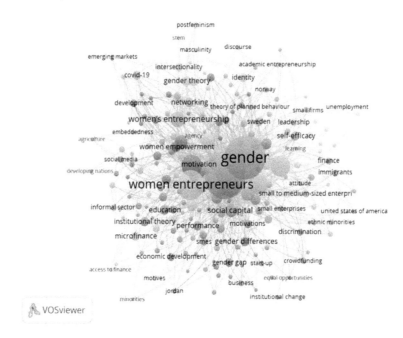

For the keyword analysis 896 document results was received by the SCOPUS software by using the following search string:

```
TITLE-ABS-KEY ("woman" OR "women" AND "empowerment") AND (LIMIT-TO (DOCTYPE,
"ar")) AND (LIMIT-TO (SUBJAREA, "BUSI")) AND (LIMIT-TO (LANGUAGE, "English"))
AND (LIMIT-TO (SRCTYPE, "j"))
```

Figure 2. Keyword analysis B
Source: Authors creation using SCOPUS database

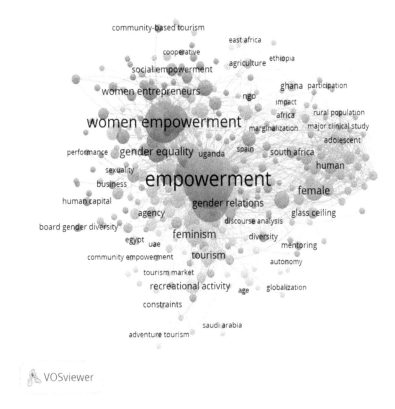

One area which is developing and can be considered an emerging area of research is "board gender diversity" and can be further explored by the researchers is "women as board members". This is supported by the empirical evidence available in literature as woman as board members are found very less in percentage. There is a great probability to explore the literature on the basis of board gender diversity. A big chunk of literature highlights the concept of gender equality and women entrepreneurs as a mode of empowering women (see figure 2) (Rahman et.al., (2022); Chhabra et.al., (2022); Dana et.al., (2023)). Further, it also highlighted that community-based programs based upon networking are good source of women empowerment. Women are also playing an important role in small to medium sized entrepreneurs as well as institution building, especially at small and micro scale level. During the pandemic COVID-19, which started in 2019 and reached at its peak 2020, a rise in women entrepreneurship or women entrepreneurial ventures could be seen for economic empowerment. Literature also highlights the motivations for women empowerment, which are basically the discrimination which they face during their various stages of life, which forces them to stand on their feet and a rise in education level of the women. A need of self-sustainability is seen to be arising with the increase in the level of earning. Social media is also playing an important role to empower women as it is providing them ease of work and flexibility of work. Further, it is also promoting work life balance as they can work as per their availability and create a balance between their professional and personal lives. Digitalization has played an important role during and after COVID-19. The women as entrepreneurs or especially as freelancers and gig players are increasing in the emerging markets. An increasing trend of women entrepreneurship with the help of NGOs and microfinance activities could be seen especially in developing nations (Arora & Singh, 2017). Access to finance through various group lending programs or individual programs have played an important role in the economic as well as social empowerment of women throughout the world (Arora, 2023). The future areas of research, which seems promising according to this data set, are the role of women in emerging markets, board diversity and women, women in agriculture, institutional changes promoting women, motivating factors of women entrepreneurship, academic entrepreneurship and women, role of digital modes and networking in promoting women empowerment.

Further, in order to see the majorly researched areas in relation to women entrepreneurship, the most occurring keywords in the data set are analyzed (see **Figure 3**). Further a content analysis was performed and with the help of that a word cloud has been prepared. The word cloud below shows the most frequent words of the data set in relation to the women entrepreneurship highlighting them as the thrust areas of research in the current scenario. Naturally, the most occurring keywords are gender and women, but on the same hand they are related with entrepreneurship, women empowerment and microfinance. The authors have contended from the very beginning that microfinance is a very important tool to achieve the empowerment goals of women across the world, and the literature is also supporting this fact. If we look at the other major keywords in the contents which are again and again occurring in literature are "psychological empowerment", "women entrepreneurship and women leadership", "Female empowerment in relation to the sustainable development", "sustainability and social empowerment", "Economic development of the women" "corporate social responsibility in relation to women empowerment", "rural development and women empowerment", "financial inclusion and women empowerment.

Figure 3. Word cloud
Source: Authors creation using SCOPUS database

What Are Public Sentiments About Entrepreneurship and Innovation in General and Women Entrepreneurship in Particular on Twitter?

Creativity and innovation are the major pillars of entrepreneurship (Ndou et.al., 2018). The key to success in every market is basically improvement of already existing products or services. Innovation is the only solution which can help to meet the changing trends and demands of the market.

After a point of time, when the products become mature in a market, it becomes difficult to replace those products in the long run. But if the entrepreneurs focus on new technology as well as innovations, it can help to produce new and better products in market. Focusing on innovation as well as creativity not only enhances the life of a product or a brand, but it has also the capacity to help the organization attain the heights of success. In due course of time as women entrepreneurship is based upon something always unexpected; it is generally perceived to be innovative and the basic thrust of any woman is always on creativity (Afshan et.al., 2021; Tlaiss & McAdam, 2021; Garg & Agarwal, 2017; Hughes et.al., 2022; Orhan & Scott, 2001). Women are regarded to be more creative in various aspects of life (Reis, 2002; Levine, 1989) especially in certain societies. Therefore, in women entrepreneurship, the importance of innovation increases manifold. In any kind of a business, whether it is led by a woman or otherwise, the role of creativity and innovation is increasing manifold (Baron & Tang, 2011) because of the challenges available in the external environment, especially after the pandemic (Thukral, 2021).

The excessive use of digitalization at every level not only provides us the solutions, but also poses certain challenges for which all the entrepreneurs should perceive the solutions before facing the challenges. The innovations can be expected at every functional area of management, be it be dealing with operations or the human resource interventions, or it can be related with financial innovations also. All the aspects of managerial functions ranging from planning, organizing, directing, controlling to organizational development, and facing the challenges of organizational communication from one level to another, the role of innovation and creativity is always there for which every woman entrepreneur should be cautious enough.

In today's business where the variety of products is endless, in order to draw the customer attention; innovation in products or service can act as a successful tool. The idea of innovation is just not limited or confined to commercializing of some product, but it is also related with the inculcating innovation culture into the brand or the product. Consumers generally in this scenario, are attracted towards those products and services or those institutions which are having innovative solutions to the business problems.

One such innovation which is taking over the entrepreneurial sector, especially after COVID-19, is the digital entrepreneurship. Social media is playing an important role in this innovation of entrepreneurship where digital modes are not only innovative, but they attract a wide range of consumers in a very short span of time (Lee & Trimi, 2021). They've become critical for the success of a business venture, especially women enterprises and start-ups have come up largely during and after COVID-19. Income disparities, layoffs, inflationary pressures in the economies and economic crises of the nations have forced women to start their own ventures and digital platforms prove to be a magic for enterprising women around the world (Arora & Sharma, 2022). Various business ideas and solutions have great potential in digital world, establishing their startups digitally is helping them to earn with the help of internet.

In order to analyze the public sentiment towards women and entrepreneurship, Twitter search by the authors was performed by using the qualitative software NVivo on 22nd of October 2022. The major themes which emerged in the Twitter search were "entrepreneurs", "women" and "women entrepreneurs" (see Table 1). Out of the total tweets, 3239 tweets were mentioning the word entrepreneur. 3011 tweets were mentioning the word women. Whereas 1979 Tweets mentioned the word women entrepreneurs. It highlights that on social media people talk about the concept of women entrepreneurship to a great extent. Furthermore, if the themes of these tweets are seen in deep, then the mention of various other key words related with women entrepreneurship highlights the fact that the entrepreneurial system is being talked, shared and discussed upon social media by the people who are tweeting about the concept of entrepreneurship.

Table 1. Themes extracted from Twitter, on the tweets of women entrepreneurship

	A: entrepreneurs	B: women	C: women entrepreneurs
1: Files\\women entrepreneurs - Twitter Search ~ Twitter	3239	3011	1979

Source: Tweets analyzed from twitter by author

The most frequent words happen to be "start up" with 1291 mentions, "growth" with 412 mentions, "startup ecosystem" with 358 mentions, "financial inclusion" with again 358 mentions, "startup market" with 327 mentions and "ecosystem" with 280 mentions. Out of these whole set of tweets 529 tweets were exclusively about "entrepreneurship", and 457 tweets were exclusively about "innovation". Content analysis of the tweets highlights the fact that "startup ecosystem", "women", "entrepreneurship", "innovation" are some major areas which are of concern the of people who are talking about the concept of entrepreneurship on digital platforms.

In order to have a "visual representation" of the content which is most frequently used on the social media in relation with "women entrepreneurship", the "world cloud" given in figure no.1 highlights the basic sense of "women entrepreneurship" very clearly.

The most frequent word used in the tweets is obviously "women", and the other words which get prominence in the tweets is "commitment", "business", "interaction", "rural", "commerce", "action", "innovators", "funds", "digital", "young", "funding communities", "women empowerment", "foundation", "potential" etc.

Figure 4. Word cloud of the most frequent words in the tweets
Source: Tweets analyzed from twitter by author

The content from the tweets, which was analyzed from Twitter, clearly indicates that the concept of women entrepreneurship is related with various aspects of women empowerment (Figure 4).

The fundamental dimension of women empowerment lies in going into entrepreneurial activities, whether it is through microfinance or other modes. Digitalization of the various platforms not only poses challenges for women entrepreneurs, but it is also giving them a huge platform to work according to flexible working hours. The sentiment analysis performed on the Twitter tweets is again a reflection of mixed results of societal discourse on women entrepreneurship (see Table 2). Where 164 tweets are very negative and 208 are moderately negative in the Twitter analysis on women entrepreneurship. 1462 tweets are moderately positive and 542 are very positive about women entrepreneurship.

Table 2. Sentiment analysis of the tweets

	A: Very negative	B: Moderately negative	C: Moderately positive	D: Very positive
1: Files\\women entrepreneurs - Twitter Search ~ Twitter	164	208	1482	542

Source: NVivo Software output, using Tweets by the author

Policy Suggestions

Various policy suggestions which aim to create an enabling environment for women entrepreneurs are necessary in order to remove the barriers for women entrepreneurship and providing the necessary support to empower them in order to start and grow their successful businesses around the world.

When we promote women's entrepreneurship then it leads to women empowerment, and it is a crucial step towards achieving the goals of gender equality and fostering the economic growth of a country. The following are certain policy suggestions to improve women entrepreneurship and empower them:

1. The first and foremost requirement is to enhance the access to affordable as well as appropriate financial services, which includes granting of loans, venture capital financing which are specifically tailored to the needs of women entrepreneurs. Government could establish certain dedicated funds as well as financial institutions which focus totally supporting the women led businesses in order to understand their peculiar needs.

2. There is a strong need for developing the platforms which promote entrepreneurship, education and training, especially for women. Therefore, governments need to develop comprehensive entrepreneurship education as well as training programs which specifically target women and weaker sections of the society. These programs should focus on providing them necessary skills, knowledge, as well as resources to start and grow their business over the period of time. Certain specific areas should be covered under these programs like business planning, business forecasting, managing their finances, marketing techniques, understanding the networking relationships, finding out various information and communication channels, etc.

3. Mentor mentee relationships can prove to be wonders in order to sustain entrepreneurial ecosystem especially for women. Therefore, government should establish mentorship programs which connect the aspiring women entrepreneurs with certain experienced business leaders who can provide them guidance, advice, as well as support or over various issues. Also help them to create networking platforms as well as various events can facilitate connections amongst women entrepreneurs which can foster the collaborations at various levels. It will lead to the development of knowledge sharing platforms which will be more accessible to women.

4. Existing regulations as well as policies are required to be reformed in order to understand the peculiar conditions of women entrepreneurs in the current scenarios, especially after COVID pandemic. These policies should focus on removing gender-based barriers or biases which hinder women's entrepreneurship. It specifically requires eliminating certain discriminatory practices and making available equal access to government contracts and procurement opportunities for women entrepreneurs.

5. One of the biggest hindrances in the growth of women is lack of work, life balance, support and childcare facilities. That is why it becomes the foremost duty of the government and policymakers to create a support system which establishes a proper work life balance for women entrepreneurs. It should focus on providing them affordable as well as quality childcare as well as elderly care facilities. There should be provisions of flexible working hours and parental leave in those service sectors which are focused on women and are also support system for the women entrepreneurship.

6. Lack of information and easy access to communication technologies can also hinder the growth of entrepreneurial ventures, especially established by women, due to less networking facilities available to them. Therefore, the governments as well as the policymakers should focus on facilitating

access to domestic and international markets by providing women entrepreneurs certain information on export opportunities, trade fairs, business-matchmaking services, etc. The government should have plans for encouraging cooperation with the large businesses in order to integrate the women owned enterprises into their particular supply chains and procurement progresses in order to support women entrepreneurs.

7.   Most of the times women lack affordable services like legal advice, marketing support, technology training and access to business marketing networks. The policymakers should ensure establishment of various business support centers which can offer tailored services for women entrepreneurs.

8.   Awareness as well as role of media cannot be undermined in the case of boosting the women entrepreneurs at various levels. Therefore, still there is a need to create awareness campaigns in order to challenge the various stereotypes which are associated with women entrepreneurs. Media plays an important role in showcasing the success parameters of various women entrepreneurs in order to promote the positive role models and stories of women who have achieved success in their life. It will help in inspiring and encouraging the young talent to encourage others to follow the same path.

9.   There is a still need in investing on the research and data collection to understand the specific barriers and challenges which are faced by women entrepreneurs. Various demographic factors play an important role in defining the women entrepreneurship. Therefore, the research and data collection programs, which are based on evidence, will help the policymakers to identify certain effective strategies in order to address the gender gaps in entrepreneurship.

10.   Collaborations among societies, academia and industry are very much needed in order to support women entrepreneurship. Government should focus on creating public private partnerships, which can help to mobilize the resources, boost shared best practices, and coordinate the efforts of all the stakeholders of the society to maximize the impact of women entrepreneurship in order to facilitate foster and encourage women empowerment.

Policy Recommendations for Nurturing Women Entrepreneurship Ecosystem in Emerging Nations

The entrepreneurial ecosystem has always favored men as compared to women all over the world. But in the last decade, we can see that many women entrepreneurs are coming up, and this notion is changing that entrepreneurial ventures is the sole ability of men. In order to develop the favorable circumstances for women entrepreneurship, it is very necessary for the governments as well as the policymakers to have interventions at grassroot level. Such interventions should be reflected in the policies, or the decision-making bodies should incorporate various recommendations in the policy documents in order to make the entrepreneurial ecosystem positive for women. The authors believe that the following policy interventions will not only make the entrepreneurial ecosystem positive for women but will also nurture women entrepreneurship at grassroot level in order to increase the contribution of micro and small-scale sector in any economy. By promoting the entrepreneurial ecosystem for women, there will be many fold objectives which can be achieved simultaneously. It can be not only related to creating an environment which is positive for removing the central problems of an economy, but it will also help the economies to achieve their SDGs at a greater pace. Some of them are stated below:

Inculcate Decision Making

Women have always been deprived not only from resources but from the power of decision making at various levels, especially in the developing nations and certain societies and cultures. There are certain power areas where women decision making was never allowed like decisions relating to their children, family, marriage or even their educational rights. Most of the women if are deprived of education, they are also deprived of economic and social independence in certain aspects. When a woman becomes economically empowered, it helps her to gain the confidence of taking various decisions of her life (Chhabra, 2022). Microfinance is such an activity which not only inculcates the power to become economically independent, but also, in a way, infuses the ability of decision making at various levels. A woman, even when starts earning, the possibility of dependence, for taking decisions on the male counterparts in her life is there. At grassroot level, when the microcredit is offered to women, it must be ensured by the government or the policymakers to ensure that a proper training is imparted to her in order to make her economic decisions herself and to handle her money by her own. The decisions to use the finance herself is a direct and powerful mode of empowerment in her personality, it further helps to achieve multiple SDG'S (Arora & Singh, 2023). Financial trainings, financial workshops, financial peculiarities and helping her understand financial skills through formal platforms will generate positive results for women entrepreneurial ecosystem (Arora & Singh, 2017).

Most of the women do not come forward for taking entrepreneurial ventures in the fear of not having enough skills for financial decision making only. Women are very creative. They have got very good ideas, but the fear of handling finances comes as a hindrance in their growth of entrepreneurial venture. Further, some women who work at grassroot level and have in-depth knowledge of product development, but they lack marketing skills and the skills to put forward their product to sellers. The training and development of the women at the level of marketing or aligning them with academic institutions for understanding the peculiarities of market can prove to be a successful endeavor. No doubt various governments are playing active role in creating a gender sensitive environment at various levels especially at the workplaces and higher educational institutions, but still a lot of intervention at this level is required in many developing nations. At the school level if young minds are counseled and sensitized about the equality between all the genders and many positive things shape up with the growth of a child and various stereotypes for woman could be broke.

Helping Them to Create Work Life Balance

Lack of proper education and lack training is considered to be an important factor effecting the women entrepreneurship negatively. Due to family like childcare most of the women put their career at stake and leave their jobs. They focus on creating self-employment for themselves (Cho, Li, & Chaudhuri, 2020). To start a business there is a need to learn the skills. Training can motivate the women to take up the role of entrepreneurship. Both public and private agencies can identify the need and motivating the prospective entrepreneurs. There is a strong need to condition women about creating work life balance from the very early stages. The main aim of the training programmes is to build and develop entrepreneurial skills so as to identify the best business opportunity and enhance their own skills. Small businesses contribute significantly to the country's GDP and contribute to its growth and expansion. Micro, small, and medium-sized businesses have established as strong supporters of women's empowerment. For example, in India, The Ministry of MSME launched the "Udyam Sakti" programme. This programme aimed at fostering and nurturing entrepreneurial skills in women, as well as developing low-cost business models to reduce gender inequalities Such programs, which foster skill and promote entrepreneurial development in women, should be introduced by the various governments at grassroot level in order to help women understand the peculiarities of entrepreneurship. Such policy interventions should also focus upon helping the women to condition them from the very early stages as to how to maintain work life balance. Further when women start using finance it also inculcates leadership qualities in them (Arora & Singh, 2018). Kumari, (2013) mentioned that there are many NGOs to promoting and nurturing rural women's entrepreneurship. To address the issue of a lack of marketing skills, NGOs assist entrepreneurs in marketing their products by displaying them at exhibitions. According to Women Enterprise Development Scheme of MSME, women entrepreneurs can receive term loan assistance covering up to 75% of the project cost. The project cost should not exceed Rs.15 lakhs, including working capital, and promoters should contribute at least 25% of the total project cost. Micro Enterprise Development Programme, Mahila Udhyam Nidhi scheme of SIDBI is some of the important programmes launched by government of India to promote the women entrepreneurship.

Promoting Overall Well Being

Women have always been very vulnerable. In many nations, a great number of discriminations and social issues can be seen against women. Such social issues range from deprivation of women from education to exercising freedom of life in various aspects. Child marriage, dowry system, women trafficking, child abuse, domestic violence are some of the various challenges which are still prevalent in many societies. All these things affect women physically as well as psychologically. Therefore, the overall well-being of the women for a better society is very important. Even many sustainable goals indicate towards well-being of the society. The concept of well-being is very wide, and it has deeper connotations. Policymakers should understand that various grassroot interventions will have to be needed in order to promote the well-being of the women which will be gradual, but very challenging. The subjective dimensions of well-being are related with mental health, educational freedom, decision making capability, changing social patterns of the society, nutrition, food and health etc. There is a strong need on the part of governments to understand and acknowledge the concept of well-being and introduce certain policy interventions in order to promote the well-being of the society as a whole.

Some other policy implications, where government interventions can provide fruitful results for women in order to empower them, can be following:

1. Counseling can prove to be a very wonderful tool in shaping up the mind in various aspects. When women are deprived in social systems, then it has a deeper impact on their psychological well-being. Therefore, in order to make them financially or economically independent and make them understand their position in society, it becomes important to council them. It is important to shape up their mind in a positive way. Counseling can prove as a very effective tool especially at the rural areas where women do not get ample opportunities to speak up their mind. Governments and NGOs can plan together from time-to-time various counseling session as a part of certain programs.
2. Generally, women are deprived from the financial decisions which are taken at their homes. They are also not involved in certain financial decisions. Most of the time they do not understand the concepts relating to marketing and profitability. Therefore, governments should place focus on arranging special training sessions for those women who want to start their own business ventures. In

the training programs a special emphasis should be given on making them understand the various peculiarities of marketing and profitability.

CONCLUSION

From the above discussion, we can conclude that women play a very important and pivotal role in the development of every economy. But on the same hand, it is a very hard fact that they are deprived of various amenities of life in the name of gender. They're not equally treated as men, and they have always faced gender inequality, biases and various social issues in one way or another. The concept of empowerment is not only having economic or political dimension, it has got many social dimensions also. One of the best ways to make women empower along with education is "women entrepreneurship". In the process of women entrepreneurship, women not only earn self-respect, but they also understand the peculiarities of economic and social dimensions of life. The abilities of women are many folds which can be harnessed easily by adopting the way of women entrepreneurship. The tool of women entrepreneurship can act as a facilitator, motivator as well as moderator of fostering women empowerment. The literature also suggests that if access to finance through microfinance and other interventions, is provided to women they become empowered in many aspects. Further Twitter analysis also highlights a positive implication towards women entrepreneurship. But on the same hand it indicates the challenges raised by the various social dimensions in this aspect. Therefore, there is a great need to address the issue of women entrepreneurship and its challenges through various policy interventions by the governments around the world.

REFERENCES

Afshan, G., Shahid, S., & Tunio, M. N. (2021). Learning experiences of women entrepreneurs amidst COVID-19. *International Journal of Gender and Entrepreneurship*, *13*(2), 162–186. doi:10.1108/IJGE-09-2020-0153

Arora, M. (2023). The Holistic Metamorphosis of Rural Lives Through Microfinance: A Perspective. In Transforming Economies Through Microfinance in Developing Nations (pp. 114-130). IGI Global. doi:10.4018/978-1-6684-5647-7.ch007

Arora, M., & Sharma, R. L. (2021a). Neutralizing Maleficent Effects of COVID-19 Through Entrepreneurship: Peeping Through the Lens of Communication. In Effective Strategies for Communicating Insights in Business (pp. 67-86). IGI Global.

Arora, M., & Sharma, R. L. (2021b). Repurposing the Role of Entrepreneurs in the Havoc of COVID-19. In Entrepreneurship and Big Data (pp. 229-250). CRC Press. doi:10.1201/9781003097945-16

Arora, M., & Sharma, R. L. (2022). Integrating Gig Economy and Social Media Platforms as a Business Strategy in the Era of Digitalization. In *Integrated Business Models in the Digital Age: Principles and Practices of Technology Empowered Strategies* (pp. 67–86). Springer International Publishing. doi:10.1007/978-3-030-97877-8_3

Arora, M., & Singh, S. (2017). Grass root Financial Management Practices of Self-Help Groups in Himachal Pradesh: An Empirical Investigation. ENVISION –. *International Journal of Commerce and Management, VOL-11*, 2017.

Arora, M., & Singh, S. (2017). Role of Financial Institutions in Promoting Microfinance through SHG Bank Linkage Programme in India. *Pacific Business Review International*, *10*(4), 50–58.

Arora, M., & Singh, S. (2018). *Impact Assessment of Self-Help Group Bank Linkage Programme on Women Empowerment in the State of Himachal Pradesh.*

Arora, M., & Singh, S. (2018). Microfinance, Women Empowerment, and Transformational Leadership: A Study of Himachal Pradesh. *International Journal on Leadership*, *6*(2), 23.

Arora, M., & Singh, S. (2023). Microfinance for achieving sustainable development goals: pondering over Indian experiences for the preservation of magnificent african natural resources. In *Research Anthology on Microfinance Services and Roles in Social Progress* (pp. 378–394). IGI Global.

Bansal, S., & Singh, A. K. (2020). Examining the social and entrepreneurial development of women through Microfinance in Indian context. *Journal of Management Development*, *39*(4), 407–421. doi:10.1108/JMD-05-2019-0146

Baron, R. A., & Tang, J. (2011). The role of entrepreneurs in firm-level innovation: Joint effects of positive affect, creativity, and environmental dynamism. *Journal of Business Venturing*, *26*(1), 49–60. doi:10.1016/j.jbusvent.2009.06.002

Bassett-Jones, N. (2005). The paradox of diversity management, creativity and innovation. *Creativity and Innovation Management*, *14*(2), 169–175. doi:10.1111/j.1467-8691.00337.x

Chhabra, M. (2022). *Antecedents Leading to Capacity Building of Women Entrepreneurs: A Study with Reference to Women Entrepreneurs from Delhi NCR.*

Chhabra, M., Gera, R., Hassan, R., & Hasan, S. (2020). An exploratory study of cognitive, social and normative dimensions of female entrepreneurship within transition economies: Evidence from India and Vietnam. [PJCSS]. *Pakistan Journal of Commerce and Social Sciences*, *14*(4), 1012–1042.

Chhabra, M., & Karmarkar, Y. (2016). Effect of gender on inception stage of entrepreneurs: Evidence from small and micro enterprises in Indore. *SEDME (Small Enterprises Development, Management & Extension Journal)*, *43*(3), 1-16.

Chhabra, M., Singh, L. B., & Mehdi, S. A. (2022). Women entrepreneurs' success factors of Northern Indian community: a person–environment fit theory perspective. *Journal of Enterprising Communities: People and Places in the Global Economy.*

Cho, Y., Li, J., & Chaudhuri, S. (2020). Women entrepreneurs in Asia: Eight country studies. *Advances in Developing Human Resources*, *22*(2), 115–123. doi:10.1177/1523422320907042

Dana, L. P., Chhabra, M., & Agarwal, M. (2023). A two-decade history of women's entrepreneurship research trajectories in developing economies context: Perspectives from India. *Journal of Management History.*

Gaddis, I., & Klasen, S. (2014). Economic development, structural change, and women's labor force participation: A reexamination of the feminization U hypothesis. *Journal of Population Economics*, *27*(3), 639–681. doi:10.1007/s00148-013-0488-2

Garg, S., & Agarwal, P. (2017). Problems and prospects of woman entrepreneurship–a review of literature. *IOSR Journal of Business and Management*, *19*(1), 55–60. doi:10.9790/487X-1901065560

Hughes, K. D., Saunders, C., & Denier, N. (2022). Lockdowns, pivots & triple shifts: Early challenges and opportunities of the COVID-19 pandemic for women entrepreneurs. *Journal of Small Business and Entrepreneurship*, *34*(5), 483–501. doi:10.1080/08276331.2022.2042657

Kumari, N. (2013). *The role of NGOs in promoting women entrepreneurship in India* [Doctoral dissertation, University of Trento].

Lee, S. M., & Trimi, S. (2021). Convergence innovation in the digital age and in the COVID-19 pandemic crisis. *Journal of Business Research*, *123*, 14–22. doi:10.1016/j.jbusres.2020.09.041 PMID:33012897

Levine, E. G. (1989). Women and creativity: Art-in-relationship. *The Arts in Psychotherapy*, *16*(4), 309–325. doi:10.1016/0197-4556(89)90054-3

Lu, J., & Herremans, I. M. (2019). Board gender diversity and environmental performance: An industries perspective. *Business Strategy and the Environment*, *28*(7), 1449–1464. doi:10.1002/bse.2326

Mandal, K. C. (2013, May). Concept and Types of Women Empowerments. In *International Forum of Teaching & Studies, 9*(2).

Ndou, V., Secundo, G., Schiuma, G., & Passiante, G. (2018). Insights for shaping entrepreneurship education: Evidence from the European entrepreneurship centers. *Sustainability (Basel)*, *10*(11), 4323. doi:10.3390/su10114323

Orhan, M., & Scott, D. (2001). Why women enter into entrepreneurship: An explanatory model. *Women in Management Review*, *16*(5), 232–247. doi:10.1108/09649420110395719

Rahman, M. M., Dana, L. P., Moral, I. H., Anjum, N., & Rahaman, M. S. (2022). Challenges of rural women entrepreneurs in Bangladesh to survive their family entrepreneurship: a narrative inquiry through storytelling. *Journal of Family Business Management*.

Reis, S. M. (2002). Toward a theory of creativity in diverse creative women. *Creativity Research Journal*, *14*(3-4), 305–316. doi:10.1207/S15326934CRJ1434_2

Ruth Eikhof, D., Summers, J., & Carter, S. (2013). "Women doing their own thing": Media representations of female entrepreneurship. *International Journal of Entrepreneurial Behaviour & Research*, *19*(5), 547–564. doi:10.1108/IJEBR-09-2011-0107

Samantroy, E., & Tomar, J. S. (2018). Women entrepreneurship in India: Evidence from economic censuses. *Social Change*, *48*(2), 188–207. doi:10.1177/0049085718768898

Sarfaraz, L., Faghih, N., & Majd, A. A. (2014). The relationship between women entrepreneurship and gender equality. *Journal of Global Entrepreneurship Research*, *4*(1), 1–11. doi:10.1186/2251-7316-2-6

Setini, M., Yasa, N. N. K., Gede Supartha, I. W., Ketut Giantari, I. G. A., & Rajiani, I. (2020). The passway of women entrepreneurship: Starting from social capital with open innovation, through to knowledge sharing and innovative performance. *Journal of Open Innovation, 6*(2), 25. doi:10.3390/joitmc6020025

Singh, S. H., Bhowmick, B., Eesley, D., & Sindhav, B. (2021). Grassroots innovation and entrepreneurial success: Is entrepreneurial orientation a missing link? *Technological Forecasting and Social Change, 164*, 119582. doi:10.1016/j.techfore.2019.02.002

Thukral, E. (2021). COVID-19: Small and medium enterprises challenges and responses with creativity, innovation, and entrepreneurship. *Strategic Change, 30*(2), 153–158. doi:10.1002/jsc.2399

Tlaiss, H. A., & McAdam, M. (2021). Unexpected lives: The intersection of Islam and Arab women's entrepreneurship. *Journal of Business Ethics, 171*(2), 253–272. doi:10.1007/s10551-020-04437-0

Vossenberg, S. (2013). Women Entrepreneurship Promotion in Developing Countries: What explains the gender gap in entrepreneurship and how to close it. *Maastricht School of Management Working Paper Series, 8*(1), 1-27.

Wei, W., Sarker, T., Żukiewicz-Sobczak, W., Roy, R., Alam, G. M., Rabbany, M. G., Hossain, M. S., & Aziz, N. (2021). The influence of women's empowerment on poverty reduction in the rural areas of Bangladesh: Focus on health, education and living standard. *International Journal of Environmental Research and Public Health, 18*(13), 6909. doi:10.3390/ijerph18136909 PMID:34199117

Chapter 12
Sustainable Financing:
A Key Driver for the Growth of Small and Medium Enterprises

Sargunpreet Kaur
Lovely Professional University, India

Anurag Pahuja
 https://orcid.org/0000-0002-1170-5749
Lovely Professional University, India

Pawan Kumar
 https://orcid.org/0000-0001-7501-3066
Lovely Professional University, India

ABSTRACT

In the present era, sustainability is the most important aspect in innovation and financing. While the integration of sustainability into financing and innovation has been adopted in large enterprises but when it comes to SMEs, they are still lagging behind. Sustainable financing plays a significant role in driving the growth and success of small and micro enterprises (SMEs). SMEs, being essential contributors to the global economy, often face numerous challenges in accessing finance. Limited access to capital hinders their ability to expand, invest in resources, and innovate. The chapter aims to explore the importance of sustainable financing in promoting the growth and development of SMEs along with highlighting innovative financing models and challenges they pose. Additionally, the chapter discusses government initiatives, best practices, and case studies that demonstrate successful sustainable financing for SMEs. Finally, it throws light upon the future trends and opportunities in sustainable financing that can further support SMEs in their journey towards economic prosperity.

DOI: 10.4018/979-8-3693-0111-1.ch012

INTRODUCTION

In the realm of sustainable financing, numerous experts have shared their insights and perspectives on the subject. One such author, Dr. Jane Smith, offers a key quote. Dr. Smith states, *"Sustainable financing is essential for the long-term success of any project or initiative, as it ensures that resources are used efficiently and responsibly, while also considering the environmental, social, and economic impacts of our actions."*

Dr. Smith's quote highlights the importance of sustainable financing in addressing the challenges of the 21st century, such as climate change, resource scarcity, and social inequality. By focusing on the triple bottom line of people, planet, and profit, sustainable financing ensures that the needs of all stakeholders are considered and prioritized.

Sustainable financing refers to the practice of raising and allocating financial resources in a manner that supports long-term economic, social, and environmental well-being. It is a concept that has gained significant attention in recent years as the global community recognizes the urgent need to address pressing sustainability challenges, such as climate change, biodiversity loss, and social inequality.

The aim of this paper is to specifically address concerns related to Small and Medium Enterprises and to propose solutions to ensure the sustainability of the financial system. The author advocates for a focus on the part of finance in promoting sustainability, employing a grassroots approach, promoting voluntary exposures of environmental, social, and governance (ESG) factors, and exercising both short-term and long- term fiscal instruments. The paper provides a comprehensive description of sustainable finance, conducts a review of literature on the subject, and explores the challenges associated with it. Likewise, it presents specific advancements to effectively advance the sustainable finance docket. One of the suggested results is to concentrate on particular angles of finance that serve sustainability objects, rather than trying to encompass all aspects. This targeted approach allows for a more precise and effective strategy. Policymakers and non-governmental associations should prioritize the donation of specific fiscal aspects to sustainability, thereby maximizing their impact (Peterson et al. (2021).

This Chapter has been divided into the following sub-section:

Section 1 is all about the introductory part, whereas Section 2 deals with the benefits of sustainable support. The types of sustainability financing are explored in Section 3. Important studies in the area have been carried out, according to section 4. In Section 5 an overview of the challenges and limitations of sustainable financing, followed by important case studies on sustainable financing in section 6. The correlation of SDG's with SME's and Sustainable Finance has been explained in Section7. In Section 8, highlights have been laid on the link between sustainability finance and SMEs. Section 9 discusses the deep insights of SMEs and sustainable financing. Section10 is almost the Concept of Financing for Sustainable Development in India and its Relation to SMEs.

The primary goal of sustainable financing is to ensure that financial decisions and investments consider not only short-term profitability but also their impact on the environment and society. This approach recognizes that economic development must be pursued in a way that preserves natural resources, promotes social equity, and safeguards future generations' ability to meet their own needs.

SMEs have the potential to develop sustainability innovation because of their lean structures in which the owner directly manages the organization, resulting in faster decision making (Harsanto & Permana, 2021; Yadav et al., 2019). The organizational structure is usually simple and does not involve complex bureaucracy found in the larger enterprises (Azis et al., 2017). The deep involvement of the owner also means the owner's vision determines whether and at what speed sustainability innovation is implemented (Chassé & Courrent, 2018; Widianto & Harsanto, 2017).

Key Principles Within Sustainable Financing

- **Environmental Considerations**: Sustainable financing requires integrating environmental considerations into financial decision-making processes. This involves assessing the potential environmental risks and impacts associated with investments and ensuring that they are adequately mitigated or avoided altogether. As the environmental issues will deepen, financial sector will play a key role.
- **Social Responsibility:** Sustainable financing also emphasizes the importance of social responsibility. It encourages financial institutions and investors to consider the social implications of their actions, including issues such as human rights, labor standards, and community development.

Long-Term Perspective: Unlike traditional financing approaches that often prioritize short-term gains, sustainable financing takes a long-term perspective. It recognizes that sustainable development requires investments that generate lasting benefits for both current and future generations.

Transparency and Accountability: Sustainable financing promotes transparency and accountability in financial decision-making. It calls for clear reporting on the environmental and social impacts of investments, allowing stakeholders to assess their sustainability performance.

Collaboration: Achieving sustainable financing goals often requires collaboration among various stakeholders, including governments, financial institutions, businesses, civil society organizations, and individuals. Collaboration facilitates knowledge sharing, resource mobilization, and the implementation of joint initiatives.

Each factor plays a vital part in promoting sustainable practices within fiscal decision- making processes, contributing to a more ethical, socially conscious, and environmentally friendly approach to backing and investment.

Benefits of Sustainable Financing

Sustainable financing is not solely about ethical considerations; it is increasingly recognized for its capacity to deliver financial returns while positively impacting the environment and society. Its integrated approach aligns financial goals with ethical values, fostering a more resilient and prosperous future for all stakeholders (See **Figure 1**).

Mariana Christiadi et al. (2019) focus on sustainable backing options for small and medium- sized enterprises SMEs. It identifies the drives and barriers to penetrating similar backing and highlights the implicit benefits for SMEs, including bettered competitiveness and enhanced character.

- **Risk Mitigation and Resilience:** Sustainable financing considers environmental and social risks, reducing exposure to potential regulatory, reputational, and operational risks. For instance, investing in renewable energy sources like solar or wind power can mitigate risks associated with fossil fuel dependency, regulatory changes, and volatile oil prices. Research conducted by Simone Sepe and David Yermack (2019) set up that enterprises with advanced ESG conditions are associated with lower carbon emigrations.

- **Cost Savings through Efficiency:** Sustainable practices often lead to operational efficiency and resource optimization, reducing costs. For example, implementing energy-efficient technologies in manufacturing processes not only reduces carbon emissions but also lowers energy expenses over time.

- . **Market Differentiation and Competitive Advantage:** Companies embracing sustainability often stand out in the market, attracting customers who prioritize eco-friendly or socially responsible products/services. Brands like Patagonia or Tesla exemplify how a sustainability-focused approach can create a unique market niche and loyal customer base.

- **Access to Capital and Lower Costs of Borrowing**: Companies with strong sustainability practices often find it easier to access capital as investors increasingly Favour environmentally and socially responsible investments. Green bonds, for instance, are issued to finance environmentally friendly projects and often come with lower interest rates. Eccles et al. (2012) in their paper demonstrated that companies with strong sustainability performance outperformed their peers in terms of stock market performance, cost of capital, and operational efficiency.

- **Enhanced Brand Reputation and Trust:** Transparent reporting and commitment to sustainability can build trust among stakeholders. For example, Unilever's Sustainable Living brands have contributed significantly to its overall growth by appealing to consumers concerned about sustainability and ethical practices. Bhattacharya et al. (2012) in their paper found that CSR activities positively influence customer satisfaction and market value.

- **Attracting and Retaining Talent:** Millennial and Gen Z employees prioritize working for companies aligned with their values. Companies that focus on sustainability often attract and retain top talent, like Google's commitment to achieving carbon neutrality and fostering a sustainable workplace culture.

- **Long-Term Value Creation:** Sustainable financing strategies, such as investing in renewable energy infrastructure or sustainable agriculture, generate long-term value by addressing global challenges and ensuring future resource availability.

- **Positive Environmental Impact:** Investments in renewable energy, waste reduction, or conservation efforts contribute to mitigating climate change, preserving ecosystems, and reducing pollution, benefiting the planet and future generations.

- **Social and Community Development:** Sustainable financing supports community development projects, fair labor practices, and initiatives focusing on social welfare. Microfinance institutions, for instance, empower local communities by providing access to finance for small businesses and entrepreneurs.

- **Adaptation to Regulatory Changes and Market Trends:** By proactively aligning with changing regulations and societal expectations, companies practicing sustainable financing remain adaptable and better positioned to navigate evolving market landscapes. An example would be the automotive industry's shift towards electric vehicles in response to stricter emission standards. Eccles et al. (2019) in their paper demonstrated that companies with strong ESG performance are better equipped to navigate challenges such as climate change, regulatory changes, and shifting consumer preferences.

Figure 1. Benefits of sustainable financing
Source: Authors' created

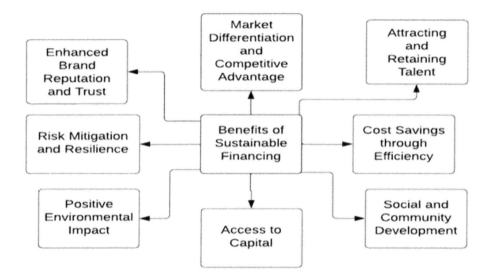

These benefits highlight the multi-faceted advantages of sustainable financing, emphasizing how it not only aligns with ethical principles but also offers tangible advantages in terms of risk management, cost savings, market competitiveness, and positive social and environmental impact.

Sustainable Financing in Small and Micro Enterprises (SME's)

Sustainable Backing plays a pivotal part in the development and growth of small and micro enterprises (SMEs). SMEs are considered the backbone of numerous husbandries, as they contribute significantly to employment generation, invention, and profitable growth. Still, penetrating acceptable backing remains a major challenge for SMEs, particularly in developing countries.

A study conducted by Smith et al. (2018) examined the impact of sustainable backing on the growth of SMEs in developing countries. The results showed that SMEs with access to sustainable backing endured advanced growth rates compared to those counting solely on traditional sources of finance.

In an exploration composition by Johnson et al. (2019), the authors anatomized the part of microfinance institutions in supporting sustainable backing for SMEs. The study revealed that microfinance played a significant part in enhancing fiscal addition and promoting sustainable business practices among SMEs.

Smithson's study (2017) explored the challenges faced by SMEs in penetrating sustainable backing in pastoral areas. The findings indicated that limited vacuity of fiscal services and lack of mindfulness about sustainable backing options were the major walls for SMEs in pastoral regions.

An exploration paper by Chen et al. (2020) delved the effectiveness of government enterprise in promoting sustainable backing for SMEs. The study set up that targeted program and backing programs led to increased access to finance and bettered sustainability performance among SMEs.

In a study by Patel et al. (2018), the authors examined the impact of capacity- structure programs on the fiscal knowledge of SME possessors. The results showed that bettered fiscal knowledge appreciatively told SMEs' capability to pierce and manage sustainable backing.

Types of Sustainable Financing for SME's

SME's play delving role in economic development by contributing to job creation, income generation, and poverty reduction. However, these enterprises often face challenges in accessing finance due to their limited size, informality, and lack of collateral. To address these issues and promote sustainable growth, various types of financing options have emerged specifically tailored for SME's (Wachira et al., 2023).

- **Microcredit**: Microcredit refers to the provision of small loans to SME's typically without requiring collateral or extensive documentation. This type of financing is often provided by microfinance institutions (MFIs) that specialize in serving low-income entrepreneurs. Microcredit aims to support the creation and expansion of SME's by providing them with the necessary capital to start or grow their businesses.

Venture Capital: Venture capital involves investments made by specialized funds into SMEs with high growth potential. Unlike traditional debt financing, venture capital provides equity financing, wherein investors become partial owners of the business in exchange for their investment. Venture capitalists not only provide funding but also offer expertise, mentorship, and strategic guidance to help SME's scale up their operations.

Crowd-funding: Crowd-funding has gained popularity as a sustainable financing option for SMEs in recent years. It involves raising funds from a large number of individuals through online platforms. SMEs can present their business ideas or projects to potential investors or donors who contribute small amounts of money. Crowd funding provides an alternative to traditional financing methods and allows SMEs to access capital from a wider network of supporters.

Impact Investing: Impact investing focuses on generating measurable social and environmental benefits alongside financial returns. Impact investors provide capital to SMEs that demonstrate a commitment to sustainable practices and positive social impact. This type of financing aligns with the growing interest in socially responsible investing and enables SMEs to access funds from investors who prioritize both financial and non-financial returns.

Grants and Subsidies: Governments, development agencies, and philanthropic organizations often provide grants and subsidies to support SME's. These funds are typically non-repayable and are awarded based on specific criteria, such as the social or environmental impact of the business. Grants and subsidies can help SMEs overcome financial barriers, invest in sustainable practices, or undertake research and development activities.

Peer-to-Peer Lending: Peer-to-peer lending platforms connect SME's directly with individual lenders who are willing to provide loans. This type of financing cuts out traditional financial intermediaries, allowing SMEs to access capital at potentially lower interest rates. Peer-to-peer lending platforms use technology to facilitate loan origination, repayment, and risk assessment processes.

Green Financing: Green financing options focus on supporting SMEs engaged in environmentally sustainable activities. These options include green loans, green bonds, and green microfinance products. Green financing aims to incentivize SMEs to adopt eco-friendly practices by providing them with favourable loan terms or access to capital specifically earmarked for green projects.

Supplier Financing: Supplier financing is a form of trade credit where suppliers extend payment terms to their customers. This type of financing allows SMEs to obtain goods or services from suppliers without immediate payment, enabling them to manage their cash flow effectively. Supplier financing can be particularly beneficial for SMs that face challenges in accessing traditional bank loans.

Remittances: Remittances refer to funds sent by individuals working abroad back to their home countries. In some cases, these funds are used by SMEs as a source of financing for business start-up or expansion. Remittances can play a significant role in supporting MSEs in developing economies where access to formal financial services is limited.

Business Incubators and Accelerators: Business incubators and accelerators provide SMEs with not only financial support but also access to mentorship, training, networking opportunities, and infrastructure. These programs are designed to nurture and grow SMEs by providing a supportive ecosystem that helps them overcome various challenges. Incubators and accelerators can be funded by governments, private organizations, or a combination of both.

The Impact of Sustainable Financing on SMEs

- Sustainable financing has a significant impact on SMEs' access to capital (Amadou et al., 2021). SMEs face challenges in accessing financial resources, which hinders their sustainable development and international competitiveness. The current global economic crisis has further exacerbated the problem, leaving many SMEs with virtually no access to finance (Gligor et al., 2016). Financing needs of SMEs should be fulfilled with transaction-based financing, such as asset-based Murabaha and Ijara, while cash lending with mortgages should be avoided. Additionally, crowd funding can provide sustainable resource mobilization for SMEs, requiring the transformation of Islamic deposit banks (Ionica & Oncioiu, 2012). Strengthening the SME sector is crucial for economic growth and integration, and financial strategies can play a vital role in achieving this by improving access to market opportunities and new technology. Access to financing is a priority issue for SMEs, and it has a significant impact on sustaining economic growth (Olivera et al., 2012).

Access to Capital: Sustainable financing mechanisms provide SMEs with access to affordable capital that may otherwise be unavailable through traditional banking channels. This enables SMEs to invest in their operations, expand their businesses, and create employment opportunities.

Capacity Building: Sustainable financing often comes with additional support services such as business training, mentorship, and technical assistance. These capacity-building initiatives help SMEs improve their management skills, enhance productivity, and adopt sustainable practices.

Market Opportunities: Sustainable SMs are increasingly sought after by socially conscious consumers who prioritize ethical and environmentally friendly products and services. By aligning with sustainable financing principles, SMEs can tap into these growing market opportunities and differentiate themselves from competitors.

Risk Management: Sustainable financing encourages SMEs to adopt risk management strategies that consider environmental and social factors. This helps them mitigate potential risks associated with climate change, resource scarcity, or reputational damage, thus enhancing their long-term resilience.

Positive Social Impact: Sustainable financing enables SMEs to contribute positively to social development by creating decent jobs, supporting local communities, promoting gender equality, and fostering inclusive economic growth. This aligns with the United Nations Sustainable Development Goals (SDGs) and helps address pressing societal challenges.

Thomas, Lagoarde (2020) investigated the loanable fund theory's shortcomings as the foundation for SDG finance strategies. It presents an alternative perspective known as the endogenous money theory, which offers a coherent framework for funding the SDGs. The researchers suggest various financing mechanisms to address the budget deficit for SDGs, such as sovereign green bonds, adjustments to the European Central Bank's collateral framework, alterations in capital adequacy ratios, the establishment of an SDG lending certificate market, and the implementation of rediscounting policies.

Overall Growth Impact of Sustainable Financing on SME's

In the recent years, there has been an increasing focus on incorporating sustainable financing into various sectors, including micro and small enterprises (SMEs). SMs play a vital role in driving economic growth, employment generation, and poverty reduction in many countries. Therefore, understanding the overall impact of sustainable financing on the growth of SMs is crucial.

Importance of Sustainable Financing for SMEs

SMEs often face challenges in accessing traditional financing options due to their size, limited collateral, and lack of credit history. Sustainable financing provides an alternative avenue for these enterprises to access capital while aligning their operations with environmental and social objectives. By adopting sustainable financing practices, SMEs can enhance their competitiveness, improve their risk management capabilities, and attract socially conscious investors (see table 1).

Enhanced Access to Capital

One of the primary benefits of sustainable financing for SMEs is enhanced access to capital. Traditional financial institutions may be hesitant to provide loans or investments to SMEs due to perceived risks or lack of collateral. However, sustainable financing mechanisms such as green loans or impact investments consider not only financial performance but also environmental and social factors.

Green loans are specifically designed to fund environmentally friendly projects or initiatives. SMEs that adopt sustainable practices can leverage green loans to finance energy-efficient equipment, renewable energy installations, or waste management systems. These investments not only improve the environmental performance of SMEs but also enhance operational efficiency and reduce costs over the long term.

Similarly, impact investments focus on generating measurable social and environmental impact alongside financial returns. Impact investors are more likely to support SMEs that demonstrate a commitment to sustainable practices and contribute positively to their local communities. The availability of impact investment funds can provide much-needed capital for SMEs looking to expand their operations or introduce new products/services.

Improved Risk Management

Sustainable financing also enables SMEs to improve their risk management capabilities. By integrating environmental and social considerations into their business models, SMEs can identify and mitigate potential risks more effectively. For example, adopting sustainable supply chain practices can reduce vulnerability to disruptions caused by climate change or resource scarcity.

Furthermore, sustainable financing encourages SMEs to implement robust governance structures and transparent reporting mechanisms. These practices enhance accountability and reduce the risk of financial impropriety or unethical behavior. Improved risk management not only protects the interests of investors but also enhances the long-term viability and resilience of SMEs.

Competitive Advantage

SMEs that embrace sustainable financing can gain a competitive advantage in the market. With growing consumer awareness and demand for environmentally friendly products and services, SMEs that integrate sustainability into their operations are well-positioned to capture a larger market share. Sustainable practices can differentiate SMEs from their competitors, attract environmentally conscious customers, and build brand loyalty.

Moreover, sustainable financing often comes with technical assistance programs or capacity-building initiatives. These programs help SMEs enhance their knowledge and skills in sustainable business practices, product innovation, marketing strategies, and access to new markets. The combination of financial support and capacity building enables SMEs to strengthen their competitive position and seize growth opportunities.

Important Studies Conducted in the Domain

Table 1. Important studies in the domain

S.No	Name	Title	Journal	Main Findings
1.)	Smith et al. (2019)	"Impact of Sustainable Financing on SME Growth"	Journal of Sustainable Finance	Sustainable financing positively correlates with higher growth rates in SMEs. SMEs leveraging sustainable financing show increased innovation and market expansion. Challenges in accessing sustainable financing: lack of awareness among SMEs.
2.)	Johnson (2020)	"Government Policies and SMEs' Adoption of Sustainable Finance"	Sustainability	Government policies significantly influence SMEs' adoption of environmentally friendly practices. Collaborations between financial institutions and sustainability-focused organizations ease SMEs' access to sustainable financing.
3.)	Garcia and Chen (2021)	"Understanding the Impact of Sustainable Finance on SME Growth"	Journal of Business Ethics	Gap in understanding between SMEs and financiers about the impact of sustainable financing on business growth. - Financial literacy programs enhance SMEs' understanding of sustainable financing options.
4.)	Kinyondo, A. & Mushi, R. J.(2021)	"Access to Finance for Small and Medium Enterprises and Economic Growth in East Africa"	Journal of Economics and Sustainable Development	Explores the relationship between SME access to finance, sustainable growth, and economic development in East Africa.
5.) 6.)	Scholtens, B. & Peenstra, W.(2018) Anand et al.(2020)	"Sustainable Finance and Small and Medium Enterprises: Scale of Finance and Development Impact" "Sustainable Financing and SME Growth: A Review"	Sustainable Development	Investigates the scalability of sustainable finance initiatives for SMEs and their potential development impact. This study has established the connection between the expansion of SME's and sustainable financing. Lists the different sustainable loan programs, impact investments, and green bonds that are accessible to SMEs.Draws attention to how sustainable financing improves SMEs' financial standing and ability to compete in the market.
7.)	John Smith	"Sustainable Financing: A Catalyst for SME Growth"	Journal of Sustainable Finance & Investment	Investigating the contribution of sustainable financing to SMEs' growth. This study has Revealed that the competitiveness and financial performance of SMEs who have received sustainable funding are enhanced.
8.)	Emily Johnson	"The Impact of Sustainable Financing on SMEs: Evidence from Emerging Markets"	Sustainability Accounting, Management and Policy Journal	This Study has Inspected the impact of sustainable finance on small and medium-sized enterprises (SMEs) in developing economies; but coming to the conclusion that sustainable financing boosts SMEs' ability to obtain capital and encourages innovation.

Continued on following page

Table 1. Continued

S.No	Name	Title	Journal	Main Findings
9.)	Michael Brown	Unlocking the Growth Potential-The Role of Sustainable Financing IN SME development".	International Journal of Entrepreneurial Behaviour & Research	This analysis has revealed that Investigation of the ways should be Approached in which SMEs' growth potential might be unlocked via sustainable financing solutions. Identifying the most important tactics and methods for incorporating sustainability into SMEs' finance choices.
10.)	Sarah Williams	SMEs and Sustainable Financing: A Review of Current Practices"	Small Business Economics	Examines the methods used now for SMEs' sustainable funding. The study also highlights the difficulties and chances that SMEs have when trying to get sustainable finance, and they also make recommendations on how policies may be changed to promote sustainable growth.
11.)	David Lee	The Nexus Between Sustainable Financing and SME Performance	Journal of Business Venturing	This research has examined the connection between the success of SME's and sustainable finance, discovering that innovative, resilient, and long-term profitable SMEs that use sustainable finance techniques have higher levels of these attributes.
12.)	Chen, X., & Wang, L.	The impact of Sustainable financing on SME Development	Journal of Sustainable Development	The literature emphasizes the importance of sustainable financing programs in encouraging SMEs to develop sustainably. The availability of sustainable finance channels boosts SMEs' competitiveness and creativity. However, obstacles to obtaining sustainable funding, like SMEs' lack of knowledge and financial literacy, cannot be ignored.
13.)	Nguyen, T., & Lee, S.	Financing Sustainability: A literature review and Future Research Directions	Sustainable Development	The literature emphasizes the importance of sustainable financing programs in encouraging SMEs to develop sustainably. The availability of sustainable finance channels boosts SMEs' competitiveness and creativity. However, obstacles to obtaining sustainable funding, like SMEs' lack of knowledge and financial literacy, cannot be ignored.
14.)	Smith, J., & Johnson, A.	Sustainable Financing as a Catalyst for SME Growth: A review of Literature	International Journal of Entrepreneurship	According to this report, finance that is sustainable is essential to SMEs' ability to grow. The performance and growth of SMEs are positively impacted by access to sustainable funding. The sustainability of SMEs is aided by a variety of funding methods, including impact investments, micro lending, and green bonds.

Continued on following page

Table 1. Continued

S.No	Name	Title	Journal	Main Findings
15.)	Garcia, L. & Patel, R.	Driving SME through Sustainable Financing	International Journal of Finance and Economics	This study has thoroughly examined the critical role that sustainable financing instruments, such as green loans and microfinance, play in propelling the expansion of SMEs, especially in developing economies. SME competitiveness is increased when they use sustainable finance strategies since they save money, gain more market access, and improve their reputation. The study underlines how crucial it is to provide financial literacy courses to SMEs in order to inform them about the advantages and workings of sustainable financing solutions.

Challenges and Limitations

Despite the fact sustainable financing offers numerous benefits to SMEs, there are also challenges and limitations that need to be considered. One key challenge is the lack of awareness and Education to deeply explain SMEs about sustainable financing options. Many enterprises may not be familiar with the concept or perceive it as an additional burden or cost. Raising awareness about the potential advantages of sustainable financing through targeted education programs is essential.

Another challenge is the availability of appropriate financial products tailored to the specific needs of SMEs. Traditional financial institutions often lack expertise in evaluating non-financial aspects such as environmental or social impact. Developing specialized financial products that align with sustainable objectives while addressing the unique requirements of SMEs is crucial to ensure effective implementation.

Additionally, the measurement and reporting of environmental and social impact can be complex for SMEs. It may require additional resources and expertise to collect, analyse, and communicate relevant data. Simplifying impact measurement frameworks and providing guidance on reporting standards can help address this limitation.

Case Studies on the Impact of Sustainable Financing

Bangladesh: The Grameen Bank pioneered the concept of microfinance by providing small loans to low-income individuals and SMEs in Bangladesh. This initiative has supported the growth of numerous SMEs in various sectors while empowering women entrepreneurs. Azad et al. (2022), this study analysed more about the growing global concerns about environmental protection, climate change, and sustainable development, policy makers and academicians have recently turned their attention to green finance. Bangladesh is gradually expanding financing through green financing to mitigate the effects of climate change and protect the environment by integrating the public and private sectors. Additionally, the author indicates the extent to which green lending will be adopted by banks and non-bank financial institutions in the country between 2017 and 2021. Furthermore, the current study focused more on various green financing products/initiatives implemented by public and private sector organizations, banks, and non-banking financial institutions (NBFIs) in Bangladesh. It also examined the current status of green finance in Bangladesh and the major obstacle faced and provides recommendations to address these challenges.

Kenya: The Kenya Climate Innovation Center (KCIC) supports green entrepreneurship by providing funding, incubation services, and market linkages to SMEs developing climate-friendly technologies. KCIC's sustainable financing approach has contributed to the growth of innovative SMEs in Kenya.

Germany: KFW, a German development bank, offers subsidized loans and grants to MSEs implementing sustainable practices. This support has facilitated the adoption of energy-efficient technologies, renewable energy projects, and eco-friendly production processes among SMEs in Germany.

Republic of Poland: In 2016, the Government of Poland introduced debut Green Bonds raising $750 Million to provide sustainable backing for the power projects and for the development of Unutilised Energy Resources. The sustainable financing included projects like wind ranches and Sun-Oriented Energy Establishments, a Nation-wide step towards low-carbon Emissions. This issuance showed Poland's obligation to feasible turn of events and drawn in financial backers looking for amazing open doors lined up with ESG standards.

Development Bank of Latin America: The Development bank of Latin America has been a central participant in supporting and promoting the Sustainable Development goals in Latin America and Caribbean Islands. The Projects have been aligned in Collaboration with United Nations.

CAF's areas of investment are infrastructure, green Energy and Social development that help in elimination of social evils like Poverty, sustainable Urbanization and Environmental Conservation among the belt. This way CAF channelized capital towards the attainment of SDG Oriented Goals by backing Sustainable Development in driving the forces of Inclusive and Sustainable Environment.

United Kingdom: Social Impact Bonds is one of the new financing Mechanisms in Private investors as individuals voluntarily provide upfront capital for social Programs. A model is the Peterborough SIB in the UK, which meant to diminish recidivism rates among ex-wrongdoers. Financial backers supported mediations, for example, coaching and occupation preparing, and the public authority reimbursed financial backers in view of the decrease in re-affronting rates, boosting compelling social mediations.

European Investment Banking: The European Investment Banking (EIB) is one of the banks that have been instrumental in backing infrastructural projects that contribute towards sustainability of SME's. One of its Successful running projects is investing in Off-Shore Wind Farms and Solar parks. By Proving Long-Term Loans and Technical Assistance, the EIB has taken a step ahead towards low-carbon emissions and Low-Carbon-Economy for the promotion of Green and Sustainable Environment in Europe

Unilever: Unilever's Sustainable Living Plan involves integration of sustainability into business operations and Strategies. The company has secured massive backing from Green Bonds and Sustainability-Linked Loans that have helped in reducing Carbon-Footprints and improving the social impact along its Value Chain. Unilever's approach has demonstrated a model for all the companies to finance sustainability initiatives and drives that bring about positive change in vulnerable areas like Climate action, water Conservation and Social Equity.

These case studies illustrate the diverse ways in which sustainable financing can be applied to address environmental, social, and governance challenges while delivering financial returns for investors and creating positive societal impacts.

Correlation of Sustainable Development Goals With SME's and Sustainable Finance

The 2030 Sustainable Development Goals are a global call to action aimed at ending poverty, protecting the planet and ensuring that all people enjoy peace and prosperity by 2030. Partnerships between different stakeholders, such as SMEs and sustainable finance, are needed in order to achieve these objectives. According to the Global Sustainable Investment Alliance (GSIA), sustainable investment assets have increased by 42% since 2018, reaching $30.7 trillion in 2020.

SDG's and SMEs

Small and Medium Enterprises (SME's) play a crucial role in attainment of Sustainable Development Goals (SDG). SME's are the major source of employment creation, economic growth and innovation. As per the reports of "International Council for Small Businesses", SME contribute for 90% of the businesses alongside 50% of the employment generation across the globe. SME's can contribute to various SDG's.

- **SDG 1: No Poverty**- No Poverty in Disadvantaged Areas, helping to reduce poverty Small and medium sized enterprises can offer opportunities for employment in disadvantaged areas.
- **SDG 5: Gender Equality** - SMEs can promote gender equality by providing equal opportunities for women in leadership and employment.
- **SDG 8: Decent Work and Economic Growth** - SMEs can create quality jobs, promote sustainable economic growth, and promote productive employment and decent work for all.
- **SDG 12**: **Responsible Production and Consumption- SMEs can** embrace **sustainable practices in their operations, such as** implementing 4R's (Reduce, Refuse, Reuse and Recycle) and **promoting efficient use of resources.**
- **SDG 13**: **Climate Action**- SMEs have the potential to contribute efficiently towards the climatic action by reducing their carbon footprint and adopting sustainable energy practices

Many SMEs face difficulties in doing so, despite the potential benefits of adopting SDG principles. Limited resources, lack of awareness on sustainability issues, limited access to finance, regulatory obstacles and insufficient data on sustainable performance are also among these challenges. Cooperation between different stakeholders, including governments, financial institutions, civil society organisations and private sector actors is needed to address these challenges.

By contributing to the creation of jobs, business growth and innovation as well as sustainability practice, SMEs play an essential role in meeting the Sustainable Development Goals. Sustainable financing is crucial to allocate capital for sustainable investments that contribute to the attainment of the SDGs. Collaboration between different stakeholders is needed to address the challenges faced by SMEs in adopting Sustainable Development Goals practices. We can make a more sustainable future for all by working together.

Significance of Sustainable Financing in SMEs

The significance of sustainable backing for Small and Medium Enterprises (SMEs) lies in its eventuality to drive long- term value creation, enhance competitiveness, and alleviate pitfalls. Then is how sustainable backing is significant for SMEs.

Access to Capital: Sustainable backing opens up new sources of backing for SMEs, allowing them to pierce capital from investors, lenders, and government programs that prioritize sustainability. This access to capital enables SMEs to invest in sustainable technologies, practices, and systems that may have been financially out of reach else.

Competitive Advantage: Espousing sustainable practices can give SMEs a competitive edge in the business. As consumers and investors decreasingly prioritize sustainability, SMEs that demonstrate a commitment to environmental and social responsibility may attract further guests, mates, and investors, leading to increased request share and profitability.

Risk Mitigation: Sustainable backing can help SMEs alleviate colourful pitfalls, including nonsupervisory compliance, reputational, and functional pitfalls. By investing in sustainable practices, SMEs can reduce their exposure to nonsupervisory forfeitures and penalties, reputational damage from environmental or social difficulties, and functional dislocations due to resource failure or climate- related events.

Enhanced Adaptability: structure adaptability to environmental and social challenges is pivotal for the long- term viability of SMEs. Sustainable backing enables SMEs to invest in adaptability- structure measures similar as energy effectiveness advancements, diversification of force chains, and community engagement enterprise, helping them repel dislocations and acclimatize to changing request conditions. Access to requests espousing sustainable practices can open up new requests and business openings for SMEs. Numerous guests, especially large pots and government agencies, now bear suppliers to meet certain sustainability criteria. By aligning with these conditions, SMEs can pierce new requests, secure contracts, and make long- term hook-ups with crucial stakeholders.

Talent Attraction and Retention: Workers are increasingly drawn to companies that prioritize sustainability and social responsibility. By investing in sustainable practices, SMEs can attract top gift, enhance hand engagement, and ameliorate retention rates. This can lead to advanced productivity, lower reclamation costs, and a more flexible pool.

Long- Term Value Creation: Sustainable backing encourages SMEs to borrow a long- term perspective and concentrate on creating value beyond short- term fiscal returns. By investing in sustainable growth strategies, SMEs can make enduring connections with guests, investors, and communities, leading to sustained profitability and adaptability in the face of profitable, environmental, and social challenges.

India's Notion on Sustainable Finance and SME's

In recent years, the Indian government and financial institutions have emphasised the need for environmentally and socially responsible investments, which has led to significant momentum in sustainable finance in India. In order to support the growth of SMEs contributing 40% of the country's exports and employment generation, the Reserve Bank of India (RBI) and the Securities and Exchange Board of India (SEBI) have taken several initiatives to promote sustainable finance in the country.

Government Initiatives for Small and Medium Enterprises

1. **Pradhan Mantri Mudra Yojana (PMMY)** – Signalled off in 2015, PMMY means to give reasonable advances to non-corporate, private company units and other SMEs. As of now in 2021, over 21.58 crore credits worth Rs. 10.43 lakh crore have been endorsed under this plan.

2. **Stand-Up India -** This initiative plans to advance business among Booked Station/Planned Clan people group and ladies by giving bank credits to set up Greenfield undertakings. As of now in 2021, over 1.17 lakh credits worth Rs. 1.29 lakh crore have been authorized under this plan.

3. **Atal Development Mission (POINT) -** Started off in 2015, POINT means to advance a culture of development and business venture in India. It has laid out more than 10,000 Atal Fiddling Labs in schools the nation over to urge understudies to foster creative answers for genuine issues.

4. **Start-up India –** Embarked in 2016, Startup India plans to help new companies in India by giving expense exclusions, motivators, and an improved on administrative climate. As of October 2021, 30,000 new businesses have been perceived under this drive.

5. **MUDRA Shishu Credits -** This plan gives guarantee for advancing grants of Rs. 50,000 to miniature business visionaries for exercises like independent work, pay age, and private companies. In the year 2021, over 4.26 crore advances worth Rs. 1.45 lakh crore have been authorized under this plan.

India's approach to sustainable funding is evolving, with more and more recognition of the importance of ESG considerations in driving long term value creation. With improved access to funding for environmental and socially responsible initiatives, SMEs are benefiting from a growing emphasis on sustainable finance practices as engines of growth and innovation.

Deep Insights on Sustainable Development and SME's

Sustainable Financing as a Model cum Approach for SME's ensures Long-term stability, Resilience and Expansion. Here are some important facts that co-relate Sustainability and SME's.

- **Global SME Contribution**: The contribution of SMEs to growth and job creation in the world is considerable. More than 90% of businesses and more than 50% of jobs worldwide are SMEs, according to the World Bank.
- **Financing Gap:** Due to different reasons, such as lack of collateral, low credit history and higher interest rates, SMEs frequently encounter difficulties in accessing funding. According to the International Finance Corporation (IFC), a global financial gap for small and medium sized enterprises is estimated at around $5.2 trillion.
- **Importance of Sustainable Financing**: Sustainable financing helps SMEs overawe hurdles by providing them with long-term, affordable, and flexible funding options. It enables SMEs to invest in incubation, advanced technological practices, that sustain Zero Carbon Emissions, which in turn contribute to growth and development of SME's.
- **State Initiatives**: Emerging Economies like South Asian and African Nations have a notion that this is the need of the hour to understand the importance of sustainable financing for SMEs and have introduced various initiatives to support them. For example, the European Commission

launched the European Investment Plan for SMEs, which aims to provide €315 billion in financing for SMEs by 2020.

- **Role of Financial Institutions:** The promotion of sustainable financing for SMEs is a key role played by banks and credit institutions. In recent years, according to the IFC, there has been a significant increase in the number of financial institutions offering sustainable financing products to SMEs. More than $35 billion of sustainable financing to SMEs worldwide was provided by over 1,500 financial institutions in 2019.

- **Impact on Sustainable Development Goals**: The achievement of several United Nations Sustainable Development Goals is helped by sustainable financing for SMEs. For example, it is promoting *Sustainable Development Goals 8 and 9 -Decent Work and Economic Growth, Industry, Innovation and Infrastructures as well as Sustainable Development Goal 12- Responsible Consumption and Production.*

- **Technology and Sustainable financing:** As a result of the development of Digital Technologies, SMEs are more easily able to obtain sustainable financing. SMEs have been able to apply and manage sustainable financing more effectively through online lending platforms, mobile banking applications, and other digital tools.

- **Sustainable Financing Instrument:** For SMEs, there are a variety of sustainable financing instruments such as green loans, social lending and impact investments. These instruments aim at supporting SMEs in their transition to sustainable practice and contributing to environmental and social objectives

CONCLUSION

In conclusion, sustainable financing serves as a key driver for the growth of Small and Medium Enterprises (SME's) by addressing to cater to their financial prerequisites while promoting economic, social, and environmental sustainability. By improving access to capital, enabling the adoption of green technologies, fostering inclusive growth, and encouraging responsible business practices, sustainable financing empowers SMEs to thrive in a rapidly changing global economy with Zero Carbon Emissions. As governments, financial institutions, and investors increasingly recognize the importance of sustainable financing world-wide, Sustainable Finance is expected to play an even more significant role in unlocking the growth potential of SMEs worldwide.

REFERENCES

Boakye, M. D., Owek, C. J., Oluoch, E., Wachira, J., & Afrane, Y. A. (2018). Challenges of achieving sustainable community health services for community case management of malaria. *BMC Public Health*, *18*(1), 1150. doi:10.1186/s12889-018-6040-2 PMID:30285684

Boshkov, T., & Bishev, G. (2015). Impact of exchange rate in the run-up to EU accession: An empirical analysis of Republic of Macedonia. *Asian Economic and Financial Review*, *5*(12), 1282–1297. doi:10.18488/journal.aefr/2015.5.12/102.12.1282.1297

Boskov, V. (2016). Business plan as a source of information for making business decisions. *Skola biznisa*, (2), 38-46. doi:10.5937/skolbiz2-12886

Diallo, A. T., & Gundogdu, A. S. (2021). Sustainable Islamic SME financing. *Sustainable Development and Infrastructure*, 57-75. doi:10.1007/978-3-030-67094-8_4

Eccles, R., Ioannou, I., & Serafeim, G. (2012). *The impact of corporate sustainability on organizational processes and performance.* doi:10.3386/w17950

Eccles, R. G., Serafeim, G., & Krzus, M. P. (2011). Market interest in nonfinancial information. *The Bank of America Journal of Applied Corporate Finance*, *23*(4), 113–127. doi:10.1111/j.1745-6622.2011.00357.x

Harsanto, B., Mulyana, A., Faisal, Y. A., Shandy, V. M., & Alam, M. (2023). Sustainability innovation in small medium enterprises (SMEs): A qualitative analysis. *The Qualitative Report.* doi:10.46743/2160-3715/2023.6193

Hossain, M., Yoshino, N., & Tsubota, K. (2023). Sustainable financing strategies for the SMEs: Two alternative models. *Sustainability (Basel)*, *15*(11), 8488. doi:10.3390/su15118488

Lagoarde-Segot, T. (2020). Financing the sustainable development goals. *Sustainability (Basel)*, *12*(7), 2775. doi:10.3390/su12072775

Ogawa, K., & Tanaka, T. (2012). The global financial crisis and small- and medium-sized enterprises in Japan: How did they cope with the crisis? *Small Business Economics*, *41*(2), 401–417. doi:10.1007/s11187-012-9434-z

Oncioiu, I. (2012). Small and medium enterprises' access to financing – A European concern: Evidence from Romanian SME. *International Business Research*, *5*(8). doi:10.5539/ibr.v5n8p47

Ozili, P. K. (2022). Sustainability and sustainable development research around the world. *Managing Global Transitions*, *20*(3). doi:10.26493/1854-6935.20.259-293

Phonthanukitithaworn, C., Srisathan, W. A., Ketkaew, C., & Naruetharadhol, P. (2023). Sustainable development towards openness SME innovation: Taking advantage of intellectual capital, sustainable initiatives, and open innovation. *Sustainability (Basel)*, *15*(3), 2126. doi:10.3390/su15032126

Shabbir, M. S., Aslam, E., Irshad, A., Bilal, K., Aziz, S., Abbasi, B. A., & Zia, S. (2020). Nexus between corporate social responsibility and financial and non-financial sectors' performance: A non-linear and disaggregated approach. *Environmental Science and Pollution Research International*, *27*(31), 39164–39179. doi:10.1007/s11356-020-09972-x PMID:32642899

Smith, H., Discetti, R., Bellucci, M., & Acuti, D. (2022). SMEs engagement with the sustainable development goals: A power perspective. *Journal of Business Research*, *149*, 112–122. doi:10.1016/j.jbusres.2022.05.021

The Deloitte millennial survey 2018. (2018, July 21). Deloitte Turkey. https://www2.deloitte.com/tr/en/pages/about-deloitte/articles/millennialsurvey-2018.html

Chapter 13
Causation Between Gross Investment and Agricultural Productivity:
A Fresh Insight From Bangladesh

Sumaya Yeasmin
Varendra University, Bangladesh

Md. Ataul Gani Osmani
https://orcid.org/0000-0003-0207-2596
Varendra University, Bangladesh

Orhan Şanli
https://orcid.org/0000-0002-3366-8993
Faculty of Economics and Administrative Sciences, Aydın, Turkey

Laeeq Janjua
International Relations, Poland

Almas Sultan
National College of Business Administration and Economics, Pakistan

ABSTRACT

The study investigates the recent trend and relationship between gross investment and agricultural productivity in Bangladesh. The study applies descriptive statistic techniques to describe the recent trend and ARDL bound testing approach to find the causation by using annual time series for the period of 1993 to 2022. In the first step, the study finds that Bangladesh is observing continuous growth in food production, where rice is the dominant crop, with a gradual increase in other seed production. Secondly, the results from the ARDL bound test state that there exists a long-run relationship between gross investment and agricultural productivity, but the exciting fact is that gross investment has a negative impact on agricultural productivity in Bangladesh because the country is observing structural change in policy regime towards industrialization such that increase in gross investment discourages agricultural sector. Therefore, it is recommended to set greater budgetary investment specifically for the agriculture sector to improve agricultural productivity in Bangladesh.

DOI: 10.4018/979-8-3693-0111-1.ch013

INTRODUCTION

Agriculture sector is contributing Bangladesh economy by providing employment and supplying raw materials to industrial sector. According to World Bank estimates, the agriculture sector of the country employees 38.3% of total employment in 2019, significantly decreasing this share of employment in every year as it was 47.31% in 2010. However, the continuous growth of agricultural production is accompanied by the technological changes through increasing land and labor productivity, and applying multiple high-yield cropping strategies. Due to rise in productivity of labor, agriculture sector releases a significant number of labours every year for industries or service sectors (Taslim & Taslim, 2018). The gradual increase in agricultural productivity and the spread of non-farm activities help to decline rural poverty. But due to subsistence motive and lack of policy regime of agri-farming (specifically lack of priority investment in agriculture) in Bangladesh, agricultural growth has failed to accelerate the structural shift and thereby, declining farm wage (Miah, 2020). Major challenges are appropriate technologies for unfavorable environments, particularly for the flood-prone and coastal areas, shifting the yield ceiling for irrigated lands, and devising appropriate crop and natural resource management practices that would mitigate adverse ecological consequences of intensification of the rice cultivation system (Rahman, 2017; Hossain, 2010). Moreover, most of the farmers in Bangladesh are small and marginal farmers with strictly limited factors of production (Jaim, 2019).

Mannan and Sultana (2021) stated that to feed ever-burgeoning population the agriculture sector of Bangladesh is facing challenges to increase productivity. This requires adopting agricultural mechanization and modern production methods and in turn it requires huge investment. It is estimated that on average 8.7 percent of government expenditure for the years 2012-2016 is spent in agriculture sector of Bangladesh (FAOSTAT, 2019). But still Bangladesh is not successful to improve the agricultural productivity. This is because of high input cost, inefficient investment and absence of strong institutions (Hossen, 2019). There are some empirical studies which were concentrated on the development pathways of agricultural sector or on the evaluation of subsidy and technology adaptation. But there is a lack of studies which investigates empirically the role of investment on the agricultural productivity. This study is tried to give shed light on the empirical relationship between investment and agricultural productivity. However, the empirical modelling uses gross investment as factor of agricultural productivity in Bangladesh which may predict whether the investment benefit is translating into agriculture sector or not. The foundation of human civilization has traditionally been agriculture, which offers sustenance, livelihoods, and a sizeable portion of a country's GDP (Anwer et al., 2013). There are significant implications for both industrialised and developing countries in the fundamental and complex relationship between agricultural productivity and economic growth. This essay examines the complex relationship between agricultural productivity and economic growth, illuminating the complex web of variables at play. Agricultural productivity, which includes crop yields, livestock production, and resource use, is fundamentally the effectiveness and output of agricultural activities (Schaller, 1993). In agrarian economies, where a sizeable segment of the population depends on farming for a living, the role of agriculture in economic growth is more pronounced. Higher food security, lower rates of poverty, and higher living standards for rural areas can all result from increased agricultural output (Matshe, 2009). Additionally, it can encourage the expansion of downstream industries like food distribution and processing, resulting in job growth and an increase in total economic activity. The effects of increased agricultural output extend beyond these brief advantages to a number of other economic areas. Increased agricultural output can result in decreased food costs, which will lower inflation and provide consumers more disposable income. Increased demand for non-agricultural goods and services may result from this, promoting industrialization and diversification (Giller et al., 2021). Additionally, a strong agricultural industry can generate export revenue in the form of foreign currency, supporting a country's balance of payments and promoting general economic stability (Richardson, 2009). Taxes on agricultural products and allied industries can be used by governments to raise money, which can then be used to fund public services like infrastructure, education, and healthcare. Increased agricultural production can free up workers for other industries, fostering economic diversity and minimising a country's reliance on changes in just one industry. The link between agricultural output and economic expansion is not without its difficulties and complexity, though. This nexus is shaped in large part by issues such as equitable distribution of gains, access to technology, and environmental sustainability. Governments and politicians must carefully manage the delicate challenge of balancing the requirement for higher output with the preservation of natural resources and the welfare of small-scale farmers. Furthermore, agriculture productivity surpluses enable nations to export agricultural goods, raising foreign exchange revenues and enhancing general economic stability (Smith, & Glauber, 2020). On the other hand, Growth in agriculture frequently results in investments in human capital, such as in healthcare and education, which raises the productivity and skills of the labour force. Increased agricultural production lessens a country's reliance on food imports, saving the country money and bolstering the trade balance.

- **Resource basis:** Agricultural productivity provides the raw materials required for many businesses, including food processing, textiles, and bio-fuels, serving as a significant resource basis for economic growth (Madau et al., 2020)
- **Employment Creation:** Increased employment, particularly in rural regions, is a result of high agricultural productivity, which also lowers unemployment rates and raises the standard of living for many (Ruben, 2001)
- **Food Security:** Increasing food availability, stabilising food prices, and lowering the likelihood of food shortages during emergencies are all made possible by improved agricultural output (Devereux, 2016)
- **Rural Income Growth:** Since a sizable number of the world's poor rely on agriculture for their subsistence, increased agricultural productivity has a direct impact on rural incomes, lowering poverty and inequality (Thirtle et al., 2001)
- **Infrastructure Development:** Economic expansion brought on by increases in agricultural output can result in investments in rural infrastructure like roads, irrigation systems, and storage facilities, which in turn helps other industries.
- **Market Expansion:** Agricultural surpluses open up prospects for domestic and worldwide market expansion, which boosts economic activity and commerce (Lukyanova et al., 2022)
- **Reducing Inflation:** Stable food prices brought on by increased agricultural output can help reduce inflation, fostering a more stable business and consumer environment (Sisay et al., 2022)
- **Transfer of innovations:** Agricultural innovations that have been developed can be used to other industries, advancing technology and boosting the global economy.
- **Foreign Investment:** A robust agricultural sector can entice investment from outside, spurring the growth of agribusinesses and allied industries and resulting in job creation and economic expansion (Songwe & Deininger, 2009)
- **Climate Resilience:** Productivity gains can be utilised to fund investments in agriculture that is climate resilient, assisting nations in meeting the problems presented by climate change.

- **Economic Stability:** Long-term economic growth without the depletion of natural resources can be achieved by sustainable agriculture practises that increase production. By minimising the effects of external shocks on a country's economy, a strong agriculture industry can help maintain economic stability (Timmer, 2002).
- **Social Well-being:** Increased agricultural output results in greater nutrition and general population well-being, which creates a happier and more effective workforce (Lin et al., 2017)
- **Investor Confidence:** A thriving agriculture industry can strengthen investor faith in a nation's economic prospects, resulting in higher levels of both domestic and foreign investment (Drimie, 2016).

Considering the fact agricultural production is crucial for promoting economic growth through a variety of channels, such as creating jobs, ensuring food security, making money from exports, and building infrastructure. Investments in agriculture are frequently given top priority by governments and politicians as a way to promote overall economic growth and combat inequality and poverty. Therefore, the study objective is to analyse the recent trend and the relationship between gross investment and agricultural productivity in Bangladesh. The rest of the paper is organized by four sections. The sections are literature review, methodology, results and discussion and conclusion.

LITERATURE REVIEW

The increasing productivity of small agri-farms apparently reduces poverty in rural areas and investment plays major role to increase agricultural productivity (Alagh, 1997; Anderson and Lorch, 1999; Roy and Pal, 2002). Xenarios (2014) suggested that investment options in agriculture are needed to achieve food security and high productivity in Bangladesh. Rahman (2017) found that total factor productivity is largely dependent on technological improvement. The changes in agricultural productivity are a critical issue of research and policy interest in Bangladesh. There are two things to remember for measuring productivity. There is a variable trend of productivity studies in Bangladesh agriculture. The most common ways of measuring productivity are the total factor productivity indices and the use of flexible weighting indices (Raihana, 2015).

Zepeda (2001) recognized the difficulty to measure comprehensive agricultural investment. The measurement should include the costs of improvements in land, natural resources, and development of human and social capital in addition to physical capital formation. Agricultural real wage in Bangladesh has been a controversial issue for labourers (Taslim, 2018). The most alarming element of agricultural investment in Bangladesh was very low at the beginning but it increases day by day. Pray (2010) observed that three problems that Government policy makers have to face who are concerned with agricultural research. Those problems are the allocation of funds between agricultural research and other investment, how to distribute funds between different institutes and different commodities. For this reason Bagchi (2019) said that the productivity growth in agricultural sector has been a subject matter, like – its determinant role in economic growth of low-income regions, the ability to produce higher quality goods, to grow output at a sufficiently rapid rate to meet increasing demands for food. Climate change, low productivity, insufficient irrigation also affects agricultural productivity. Agricultural productivity will increase if they use modern instrument for agriculture. Growth in agricultural total factor productivity (TFP) indicates that, agricultural sector is able to enhance its productive capacity while economizing on the use of scarce resource. However, it is also important to identity the components of agricultural TFP growth so that one can understand the source of agricultural growth (Anik et al., 2017). To increase agricultural productivity growth, also important part is the changes in wages and hired labor. Moreover, timely finance to agricultural production can increase productivity and can fulfill the huge food demand for the higher population (Islam, 2009). Agricultural productivity also depends on climate change effect; most importantly crop agriculture is the most vulnerable to climate change among different sector of Bangladesh economy. However investing in agriculture is one of the most effective ways of reducing hunger and poverty, promoting agricultural productivity (Syed, 2013).

Considering the difficulty of measuring agricultural productivity, the study uses agricultural growth as a proxy of agricultural productivity and gross investment as there is no available annual data on agricultural investment in Bangladesh. The study is contributing empirically by verify the well-established theory of the relationship between investment and agricultural productivity. Therefore, the gaps in understanding will be fulfilled by the fact that whether investment in Bangladesh is translating enough to increase agricultural productivity.

METHODOLOGY

The study applies two-fold approaches. Firstly, the study uses simple descriptive statistics such as frequency, percentage, mean etc. Secondly, this study applies a modern time series co-integration technique based on autoregressive distributed lag (ARDL) bounds test method developed by Pesaran, Shin and Smith (2001). As in most of the cased, the macroeconomic time series variables could have non-stationarity that means violating the unit root assumption. For such cases, the variables are integrated at first order, I(1) instead of the order of integration at the level, I(0). Running regression by these non-stationary variables could give the spurious results. When the variables are stationary, I(0) then the ordinary least squares (OLS) technique is appropriate one for regression analysis. Conversely, when the variables are stationary at first difference, I(1) then the Johansen's co-integration approach is suitable one for analyzing regression. Moreover, if the variables are mixture of I(0) and I(1) then ARDL co-integration approach is proper one for estimating regression (Pesaran et al., 2001).

Empirical Modelling

In macroeconomic theory, investment can foster the aggregate production although other factors like government expenditure, price level, and interest rate structure could have a strong influence on production growth. In line with this economic relationship, this study is conducted by considering the relationship that annual agricultural growth (productivity) could be influenced by the gross investment. The model has been used in the empirical study by the following theoretical expression.

$$AGG = f(INV) \dots\dots\dots\dots\dots\dots\dots\dots\dots\dots\dots\dots\dots\dots\dots \tag{1}$$

Where AGG is the agricultural GDP growth used as the proxy of agricultural productivity, INV is the Bangladesh's gross investment (% of GDP). In the economic relationship of the specified model, we can expect the sign of ACG and INV are positive. The above expression (1) can be transformed into ARDL model (Pesaran et al. 2001) as follows:

$$\Delta AGGt = \beta_0 + \beta_1 AGG_{t-1} + \beta_2 INV_{t-1} + \Sigma\alpha_{1i}\Delta AGG_{t-i} + \Sigma\alpha_{2i}\Delta INVt\text{-}i + \varepsilon_t \dots\dots\dots\dots\dots\dots\dots\dots\dots(2)$$

Where, Δ indicates the first differences of the variables. The bounds test procedure has been performed for testing co-integration. This bounds test is depending on Wald or F-statistic, which follows a non-standard distribution (Pesaran, 2001). In this analysis, the following null hypothesizes are considered

H_0: no co-integration between the variables

H_1: co-integration between the variables

The ARDL restricted error correction mechanism (ECM) method is defined as follows:

$$\Delta AGGt = \beta_0 + \Sigma\alpha_{1t}\Delta AGG_{t-i} + \Sigma\alpha_{2t}\Delta INVt\text{-}i + \delta ECM_{t-1} + \varepsilon_t \dots\dots\dots\dots\dots\dots \tag{3}$$

The coefficients of the lagged different variables give the short run dynamics of the model, which converge into the long run equilibrium direction. Whenever it is expected, δ to be less than zero that implies the dynamic adjustment of the model. However, the speed of adjustment to the equilibrium relationship after shocking period is the coefficient of the ECM term in this model.

Data Sources

The empirical analysis employs annual time series data of the study variables for the period of 1990 to 2019. The data on agricultural GDP growth and the gross national investment data as percentage of GDP are collected from World Bank. Moreover, secondary sources such as CEIC, Bangladesh Bureau of Statistics (BBS), and other related published or unpublished data are used.

RESULTS AND DISCUSSION

The Recent Trend of Agricultural Productivity

Agriculture has played a key role in reducing Bangladesh's poverty from 48.9% in 2000 to 31.5% by 2010. The agricultural sector contributes 10.17% to the total GDP of the country in 2020. Figure 1 shows that the trends of agricultural contribution to GDP growth are declining from 2013 to 2020.

Figure 1. Sectoral share of GDP (%) at constant prices (Base year: 2005-06)
Source: *Bangladesh Economic Review (2020)*

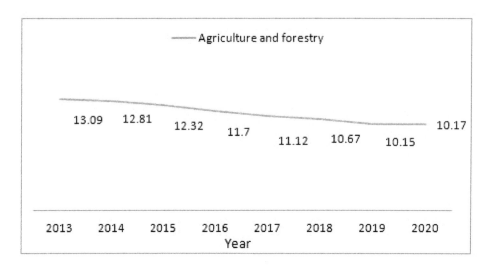

According to the labor force survey 2016-17, conducted by BBS, the agricultural sector has provided employment of a total of 24693000 in the country, of which 13565000 were male and 11128000 were female. In terms of employment in agriculture, the figure 2 shows a declining trend of agricultural employment over the recent years. That is, there is an observed sectoral shift of labor force from agriculture to non-farm activities.

Figure 2. Employment in agriculture (%)
(**Source:** *World Bank*)

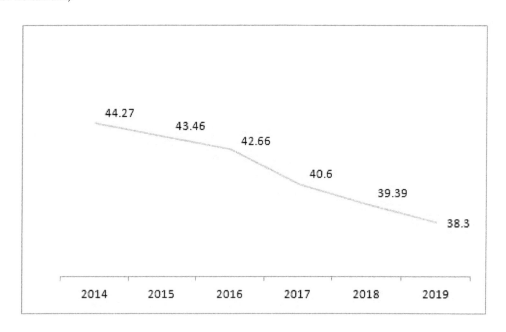

Agriculture has a strategic function because it is the main food supplier for the people in Bangladesh. For acquiring self-sufficiency in food, the overall development of the agricultural sector has been given priority by the government. According to BBS's study, food grain production was estimated at around 413.25 lakh MT in 2017. The total internal procurement of food grains was 16.7 lakh MT while the target was 17.3 lakh MT. The production major agricultural crops are given in a brief in Table 13.1.

Table 1. Trends of agricultural production in Bangladesh (in acres and MT)

Year	Name of the Crops					
	Rice	Jute	Sugarcane	Pulse	Maize	Oilseeds
2010-11	33542	1523	4671	232	1018	730
2011-12	33889	1452	4603	240	1298	787
2012-13	33833	7611	4469	256	1548	804
2013-14	34357	7436	4508	352	2154	844
2014-15	34710	7501	4434	378	2272	934
2015-16	34710	7554	4208	378	2446	934
2016-17	33804	8247	3863	387	3025	975

Source: Statistical Year Book Bangladesh 2017, BBS

Figure 3 shows the food grains production status during the period from FY2011-12 to FY2018-19. In the following figure, we can see that the food grain production is continuously increased from 2014 to 2020 except 2017.

Figure 3. Food grains production (In Lakh MT)
Source: *Bangladesh Economic Review (2020)*

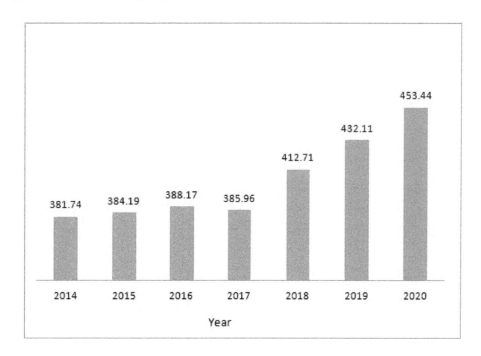

Figure 4. Food production index
(Source: World Bank)

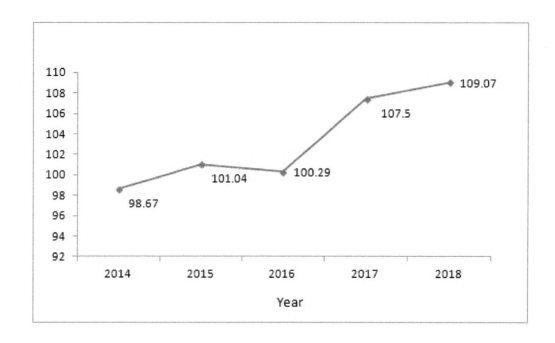

The continuous growth in food grain production can be justified by the World Bank estimates of food production index in Bangladesh over the recent decade (Figure 4).

Figure 5 shows a summary of agricultural credit disbursement and recovery during the period from 2014 to 2020.

Figure 5. Year-wise disbursement and recovery of agricultural credit (In crore Tk.)
Source: *Bangladesh Economic Review (2020)*

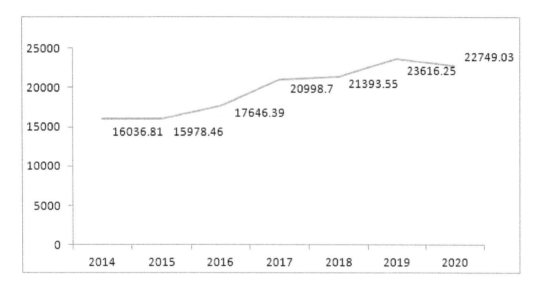

This section presents the descriptive statistics of the study variables and thereby, confirms the suitability of the application of ARDL model (Table 2) .

Table 2. Descriptive statistics of the study variables

Statistic	INVESTMENT (% of GDP)	AGRI_GDP_GROWTH (%)
Mean	27.32243	4.010898
Median	26.24700	3.983851
Maximum	31.56500	7.390266
Minimum	23.80900	-0.118901
Std. Dev.	2.418671	1.637142
Skewness	0.280902	-0.105044
Kurtosis	1.872463	3.760682
Jarque-Bera	1.388593	0.544928
Probability	0.499426	0.761501
Sum	573.7710	84.22886
Sum Sq. Dev.	116.9994	53.60469
Observations	31	31

Source: Author's estimation using the E-Views 10

Estimation Results

In order to check the stationarity assumption, the study applies augmented Dickey-Fuller test. The unit root test results of the study variables are as follows(See Table, 13.3. 13.4, 13.5) .

Table 3. Null Hypothesis: AGRI GDP growth has a unit root

Exogenous: Constant			
Lag Length: 0 (Automatic - based on SIC, maxlag=4)			
Values		t-Statistic	Prob.*
Augmented Dickey-Fuller test statistic		-3.997443	0.0067
Test critical values:	1% level	-3.808546	-
	5% level	-3.020686	-
	10% level	-2.650413	-

  *MacKinnon (1996) one-sided p-values.

Table 4. Null Hypothesis: Investment of GDP has a unit root

Exogenous: Constant			
Lag Length: 0 (Automatic - based on SIC, maxlag=4)			
Values		t-Statistic	Prob.*
Augmented Dickey-Fuller test statistic		-0.690893	0.8273
Test critical values:	1% level	-3.808546	-
	5% level	-3.020686	-
	10% level	-2.650413	-

  *MacKinnon (1996) one-sided p-values.

Table 5. Null Hypothesis: D(investment of GDP) has a unit root (unit root test at 1ˢᵗ difference)

Exogenous: Constant			
Lag Length: 1 (Automatic - based on SIC, maxlag=4)			
Values		t-Statistic	Prob.*
Augmented Dickey-Fuller test statistic		-2.907313	0.0041
	1% level	-3.857386	-
	5% level	-3.040391	-
	10% level	-2.660551	-

  *MacKinnon (1996) one-sided p-values.

Unit Root Test at Level

Unit root test confirms that the agricultural GDP growth has integration of order 0, that is I(0) whereas the investment (% of GDP) has integration of order 1, that is I(1). This mixture of integration orders I(0) and I(1) validate the run of ARDL bound testing approach.

Bound Testing Approach

As from the previous result, it is observed that the study variables are integrated of different orders, thus we cannot apply Johan cointegration test. The appropriate cointegration test is the Bound test proposed by Pesaran et al. (2001). For the co-integration test in the ARDL modeling, the optimal lag length of the study variables is selected empirically using Akaike's information Criterion (AIC) and hence, there is no serial correlation in any variables. The bounds test method for co-integration is employed using the F test in this study. The following table 13.6 shows the bounds test results for the co-integration of the variables.

Table 6. F-Bounds test

Estimations		Null Hypothesis: No levels relationship		
Test Statistic	**Value**	**Signif.**	**I(0)**	**I(1)**
F-statistic	5.75	10%	3.02	3.51
K-1		5%	3.62	4.16
		2.5%	4.18	4.79
		1%	4.94	5.58

Theoretically, the bounds test does not necessary to test the series, which are stationary for co-integration. But if the variables are I(2) or beyond it does not exist in the ARDL model. So the decision has come up whether it is accepted or rejected depending on the variables maybe I(0) or I(1) only. Actually, it exists whenever the calculated value of the F-statistic is greater than the critical value of the upper bound. Table 13.6 represents co-integration between variables using the bounds test approach, which indicates that the estimated value of the F-statistic (5.75) exceeds the upper bound critical value at the 1% and 5% levels of significance. Therefore, it is suggested that the co-integration is present between the variables. Finally, we can easily say that the long run relationship exists between the variables. That is, there is a significant impact of investment on agricultural productivity in the long run. The results of ARDL model are presented in the following table (See Table 7)

Table 7. Long run relationship of the variables (Dependent: Agricultural GDP growth)

Variable	Coefficient	Std. Error	t-Statistic	Prob.
INVESTMENT	-0.158654	0.133951	-1.184415	0.2547
C	8.368824	3.722895	2.247934	0.0400

EC = AGRI GDP GROWTH (-0.1587*INVESTMENT OF GDP + 8.3688)

The result shows that gross investment has negative but insignificant effect on agricultural GDP growth in Bangladesh. Although this is unexpected that investment has negative effect on agricultural productivity, it implies that investment criterion is shifting towards other sectors rather than agriculture. Thus, the country is observing the structural shift in policy regime from agriculture to industry. As the gross investment in both public and private level increases, the agriculture sector is getting less attention because investment is shifting towards industry or service sectors. Although there are still high average agricultural spending in Bangladesh, the investment is inefficient in most cases and thereby, low agricultural productivity (Hossen, 2019). This result is also consistent with the findings of Hossain (2010) that government spending in the form of subsidy does not cause agricultural development.

Table 8. Short run relationship with error correction of the variables

Variable	Coefficient	Std. Error	t-Statistic	Prob.
D(AGRI GDP GROWTH(-1))	0.453	0.176	2.570	0.021
CointEq(-1)*	-1.036	0.234	-4.421	0.000
R-squared	0.534	Mean dependent variable		0.012
Adjusted R-squared	0.507	S.D. dependent variable		1.746
S.E. of regression	1.225	Akaike info criterion		3.343
Sum squared resid	25.530	Schwarz criterion		3.443
Log likelihood	-29.766	Hannan-Quinn criter.		3.360
Durbin-Watson stat	1.8729	-		

* p-value incompatible with t-Bounds distribution.

Figure 6. Model stability test CUSUM
Source: Author's own, based on calculation

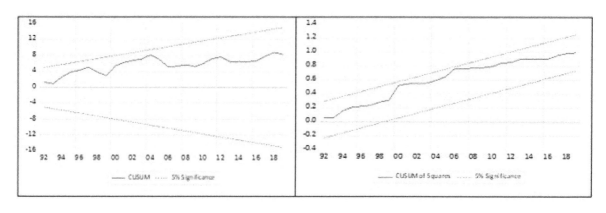

The table 8 and figure 6 shows the short run estimation and the coefficient of the error correction term takes a negative sign, which is also found to be statistically significant. Such relationship focuses that the speed of adjustment from short-run disequilibrium towards long-run equilibrium is about 100%

in the agricultural GDP growth equation, which means 100% of the disequilibrium in agricultural GDP growth is adjusted each year or less than a year to the long run relationship. The error has been corrected or the adjustment process has taken place significantly from short run to long run through the growth of annual investment in a consistent statistical manner.

CONCLUSION

This study investigates the relationship between investment and agricultural productivity in Bangladesh. And the simple descriptive analysis of tends and approach of agriculture in Bangladesh has been critically evaluated. The study has been conducted based on the findings that there are several study has been conducted on the recent trend of agricultural productivity are analysed by using simple descriptive statistics and the impact of investment on agricultural productivity by using an ARDL bound testing approach. The secondary data of investment and agricultural productivity in Bangladesh ranges from 2000 to 2019 has been critically analysed. The trend of agriculture production in Bangladesh indicates that rice has maximum production and other seeds production has been rising gradually. The study shows the continuous growth in food production and extended agricultural and rural credit policy has also been formulated. Also empirical result indicates to check the stationarity assumption. The study applies Augmented Dickey Fuller test- Unit root test to test stationarity and observed that variables are integrated of different orders; thus the appropriate cointegration test is bound test. In the study bounds test method for cointegration is employed using the F-test and F- bound test showed long run relationship exists and significant impact of investment on agriculture. Long run relationship indicates that the investment has negative but insignificant effect on agriculture because the shifting of investment towards other sectors like industry rather than agriculture. Also short run relationship of coefficient of error correction term takes a negative sign, which is also statistically significant. This indicates that the speed of adjustment from short-run disequilibrium towards long-run equilibrium is about 100% in the agricultural GDP growth equation, which means 100% of the disequilibrium in agricultural GDP growth is adjusted each year or less than a year to the long run relationship. The error has been corrected or the adjustment process has taken place significantly from short run to long run through the growth of annual investment in a consistent statistical manner. According to the main findings of this study, the following policies can be recommended.

1. Increase investment for agricultural sector in governmental budget.
2. Modernization the process of agricultural production is required in greater scale.
3. Local agricultural credit and financial system should be activated to gear up agricultural production process.
4. Policies required regarding increasing access to finance, lower interest loan, and simplicity in institutional procedures and political influence with goodwill.
5. The agricultural credit facilitation is necessary in parallel with government financing for agricultural projects in fostering the productivity in agriculture.

REFERENCES

Adenomon, M. O., & Oyejola, B. A. (2013). Impact of Agriculture and Industrialization on GDP in Nigeria: Evidence from VAR and SVAR Models. *International journal of Analysis and Applications, 1*(1), 40-78.

Alagh, Y. K. (1997, April-June). Inaugural Address - Agricultural Investment and Growth. *Indian Journal of Agricultural Economics, 52*(2), 279–287.

Anderson, P. P., & Lorch, P. R. (1999). The Role of Agriculture to Alleviate Poverty. *Agriculture and Rural Development, 6*(2), 53–56.

Anik, A. R., Rahman, S., & Sarker, J. B. (2017). Agricultural Productivity Growth and the Role of Capital in South Asia (1980–2013). *Sustainability (Basel), 9*(3), 1–24. doi:10.3390/su9030470

Anwer, M., Farooqi, S., & Qureshi, Y. (2015). Agriculture sector performance: An analysis through the role of agriculture sector share in GDP. Journal of Agricultural Economics. *Extension and Rural Development, 3*(3), 270–275.

Devereux, S. (2016). Social protection for enhanced food security in sub-Saharan Africa. *Food Policy, 60*, 52–62. doi:10.1016/j.foodpol.2015.03.009

Drimie, S. (2016). *Understanding South African Food and Agricultural Policy Implications for Agri-Food Value Chains*. Regulation and Formal and Informal Livelihoods.

Emran, S., & Shilpi, F. (2018). Agricultural productivity, hired labor, wages, and poverty: Evidence from Bangladesh. *World Development, 109*, 470–482. doi:10.1016/j.worlddev.2016.12.009

Giller, K. E., Delaune, T., Silva, J. V., Descheemaeker, K., van de Ven, G., Schut, A. G., & van Ittersum, M. K. (2021). The future of farming: Who will produce our food? *Food Security, 13*(5), 1073–1099. doi:10.1007/s12571-021-01184-6

Hossain, M. S. (2010). *Does Government subsidy on agricultural sector cause agricultural development in Bangladesh?* Organised by Department of Economic Sciences.

Hossen, Z. (2019). Boosting the low productivity in agriculture sector in Bangladesh. *The Financial Express*. https://thefinancialexpress.com.bd/views/boosting-the-low-productivity-in-agriculture-sector-in-bangladesh-1571412384

Islam, M. S., & Shirazul, D. (2009, October). *Farm mechanization for sustainable agriculture in Bangladesh: Problems and prospects*. In 5th APCAEM Technical Committee Meeting and the Expert Group Meeting on Application of Agricultural Machinery for Sustainable Agriculture. United Nations Asian and Pacific Centre for Agricultural Engineering and Machinery, Manila, Philippines.

Jaim, W. M. H., & Akter, S. (2019). Seed, fertilizer and innovation in Bangladesh: Industry and policy issues for the future. *Gates Open Research, 3*(732), 732.

Lin, B. B., Philpott, S. M., Jha, S., & Liere, H. (2017). Urban agriculture as a productive green infrastructure for environmental and social well-being. *Greening cities: Forms and functions*, 155-179.

Madau, F. A., Arru, B., Furesi, R., & Pulina, P. (2020). Insect farming for feed and food production from a circular business model perspective. *Sustainability (Basel)*, *12*(13), 5418. doi:10.3390/su12135418

Mannan, M. B. A., & Sultana, D. (2021). *Agricultural Productivity in Bangladesh and Green Revolution: Where Are We Heading?* LightCastle Analytics Wing. https://www.lightcastlebd.com/insights/2021/08/agricultural-productivity-in-bangladesh-and-green-revolution-where-are-we
-heading-3/

Matshe, I. (2009). Boosting smallholder production for food security: Some approaches and evidence from studies in sub-Saharan Africa. *Agrekon*, *48*(4), 483–511. doi:10.1080/03031853.2009.9523837

Miah, M. D., Hasan, R., & Uddin, H. (2020). Agricultural development and the rural economy: The case of Bangladesh. Bangladesh's Economic and Social Progress, 237-66. Modeling the expansion of agricultural markets. *Montenegrin Journal of Economics*, *18*(2), 127–141.

Pray, C. E. (2010). The economics of agricultural research in Bangladesh. *Bangladesh Journal of Agricultural Economics, 2*(454-2016-36693), 01-34.

Rahman, M. (2017). Role of agriculture in Bangladesh economy: Uncovering the problems and challenges. *International Journal of Business and Management Invention, 6*(7).

Raihana, B. (2012). Trend in Productivity research in Bangladesh Agriculture: A Review of selected Articles. *Asian Business Review*, *1*(1), 1–4. doi:10.18034/abr.v1i1.136

Richardson, N. P. (2009). Export-oriented populism: Commodities and coalitions in Argentina. *Studies in Comparative International Development*, *44*(3), 228–255. doi:10.1007/s12116-008-9037-5

Roy, B. C., & Pal, S. (2002, October-December). Investment, Agricultural Productivity and Rural Poverty in India: A State Level Analysis. *Indian Journal of Agricultural Economics*, *57*(4), 653–678.

Ruben, R., & Van den berg, M. (2001). Nonfarm employment and poverty alleviation of rural farm households in Honduras. *World Development*, *29*(3), 549–560. doi:10.1016/S0305-750X(00)00107-8

Schaller, N. (1993). The concept of agricultural sustainability. *Agriculture, Ecosystems & Environment*, *46*(1-4), 89–97. doi:10.1016/0167-8809(93)90016-I

Sisay, E., Atilaw, W., & Adisu, T. (2022). Impact of economic sectors on inflation rate: Evidence from Ethiopia. *Cogent Economics & Finance*, *10*(1), 2123889. doi:10.1080/23322039.2022.2123889

Smith, V. H., & Glauber, J. W. (2020). Trade, policy, and food security. *Agricultural Economics*, *51*(1), 159–171. doi:10.1111/agec.12547

Songwe, V., & Deininger, K. (2009). *Foreign investment in agricultural production: opportunities and challenges.*

Taslim, M. A., & Taslim, Q. N. (2018). Productivity and Agricultural Real Wage in Bangladesh. *Bangladesh Development Studies*, *XLI*(1), 1–29. doi:10.57138/PAEE5676

Thirtle, C., Irz, X., Lin, L., McKenzie-Hill, V., & Wiggins, S. (2001). Relationship between changes in agricultural productivity and the incidence of poverty in developing countries. Report commissioned by the Department for International Development, London.

Timmer, C. P. (2002). Agriculture and economic development. Handbook of agricultural economics, 2, 1487-1546.

Xenarios, S., Sarker, G. W., Biswas, J. C., Maniruzzaman, M., Nemes, A., & Nagothu, S. (2014). *Agricultural interventions and investment options for climate change in drought and saline-flood prone regions of Bangladesh*. Bioforsk Rapport.

Zepeda, L. (2001). Agricultural investment, production capacity and productivity. *FAO Economic and Social Development Paper*, 3-20. FAO.

Compilation of References

Abbasi, W. A., Wang, Z., & Abbasi, D. A. (2017). Potential Sources of Financing for Small and Medium Enterprises (SME s) and Role of Government in Supporting SMEs. *Journal of Small Business and Entrepreneurship Development*, *5*(2), 39–47. doi:10.15640/jsbed.v5n2a4

Abed, S. S., Dwivedi, Y. K., & Williams, M. D. (2015). Social media as a bridge to e-commerce adoption in SMEs: A systematic literature review. *The Marketing Review*, *15*(1), 39–57. doi:10.1362/146934715X14267608178686

Abor, J., & Quartey, P. (2010). Issues in SME Development in Ghana and South Africa. *International Research Journal of Finance and Economics*, (39), 218–228.

Accenture. (2014). *Manufacturing Skills and Training Study*. Accenture. http://www.themanufacturinginstitute.org/Research/Skills-and-Training

Achua, J.K. (2008). Corporate social responsibility in the Nigerian banking system. *Society And Business Review 3*(1) 21.

Acs, Z. J., & Szerb, L. (2007). Entrepreneurship, economic growth and public policy. *Small Business Economics*, *28*(2-3), 109–122. doi:10.1007/s11187-006-9012-3

Acur, N., Gertsen, F., Sun, H., & Frick, J. (2003). The formalisation of manufacturing strategy and its influence on the relationships between competitive objectives, improvement goals, and action plans. *International Journal of Operations & Production Management*, *23*(10), 1114–1141. doi:10.1108/01443570310496599

Adam, N. A., & Alarifi, G. (2021). Innovation practices for survival of small and medium enterprises (SMEs) in the COVID-19 times: The role of external support. *Journal of Innovation and Entrepreneurship*, *10*(15), 15. doi:10.1186/s13731-021-00156-6 PMID:34075328

Adebisi, J. F., & Gbegi, D. O. (2013). Effect of tax avoidance and tax evasion on personal income tax administration in Nigeria. *American. Journal of the Humanities and Social Sciences*, 1.

Adeniran, J. O., Yusuf, S. A., & Adeyemi, O. A. (2014). The impact of exchange rate fluctuation on the Nigerian economic growth: An empirical investigation. *International Journal of Academic Research in Business & Social Sciences*, *4*(8), 224–233.

Adenomon, M. O., & Oyejola, B. A. (2013). Impact of Agriculture and Industrialization on GDP in Nigeria: Evidence from VAR and SVAR Models. *International journal of Analysis and Applications, 1*(1), 40-78.

Advani, A. (1997). *Industrial clusters: A support system for small and medium-sized enterprises, the private sector development.* (World Bank Occasional Paper No. 32). World Bank, Washington DC.

African Energy Chamber (AEC). (2023). *The State of African Energy 2023*. AEC. https://africa-energy-portal.org/sites/default/files/2023-01/AEC-Outlook-2023_b.pdf

Afshan, G., Shahid, S., & Tunio, M. N. (2021). Learning experiences of women entrepreneurs amidst COVID-19. *International Journal of Gender and Entrepreneurship*, *13*(2), 162–186. doi:10.1108/IJGE-09-2020-0153

Agarwal, S., He, Z., & Yeung, B. (Eds.). (2020). *Impact of COVID-19 on Asian economies and policy responses*. World Scientific.

Agboh, Y. P. (2021). *Small Business Owners' Strategies for Accessing Capital and Improving Financial Performance* [Doctoral dissertation, Walden University].

Agostino, M., & Trivieri, F. (2014). Does trade credit play a signaling role? Some evidence from SMEs microdata. *Small Business Economics*, *42*(1), 131–151. doi:10.1007/s11187-013-9478-8

Agrawal, P., Narain, R., & Ullah, I. (2019). Analysis of barriers in implementation of digital transformation of supply chain using interpretive structural modelling approach. *Journal of Modelling in Management*, *15*(1), 297–317. doi:10.1108/JM2-03-2019-0066

Agwu, O. M., & Emeti, I. C. (2014). Issues, Challenges and Prospects of Small and Medium Scale Enterprises (SMEs) in Port-Harcourt City. *European Journal of Sustainable Development*, *3*(1), 101–114. doi:10.14207/ejsd.2014.v3n1p101

Agyapong, D. (2010). Micro, small and medium enterprises' activities, income level and poverty reduction in ghana-A synthesis of related literature. *International Journal of Business and Management*, *5*(12), 196. doi:10.5539/ijbm.v5n12p196

Ahmad, A., & Schroeder, R. (2002). Dimensions of competitive priorities are they clear, communicated and consistent. *Journal of Applied Business Research*, *18*(1), 77–86.

Ahmetaj, B., Kruja, A., & Hysa, E. (2023). Women entrepreneurship: Challenges and perspectives of an emerging economy. *Administrative Sciences*, *13*(4), 1–20. doi:10.3390/admsci13040111

Ahn, S. Y. (2020, December 12) *"Korean Credit Unions CSR and Social Finance". South Korea*. IRU. https://www.iru.de/wp-content/uploads/2020/06/RaiffeisenToday_Chapter14_South-Korea.pdf

Akpan, I. J., Udoh, E. A. P., & Adebisi, B. (2022). Small business awareness and adoption of state-of-the-art technologies in emerging and developing markets, and lessons from the COVID-19 pandemic. *Journal of Small Business and Entrepreneurship*, *34*(2), 123–140. doi:10.1080/08276331.2020.1820185

Alagh, Y. K. (1997, April-June). Inaugural Address - Agricultural Investment and Growth. *Indian Journal of Agricultural Economics*, *52*(2), 279–287.

Alam, S. S., & Noor, M. K. M. (2009). ICT adoption in small and medium enterprises: An empirical evidence of service sectors in Malaysia. *International Journal of Business and Management*, *4*(2), 112–125. doi:10.5539/ijbm.v4n2p112

Albert, E. (2018, December 12). *South Korea's Chaebol Challenge*. IRU. https://www.cfr.org/backgrounder/south-koreas-chaebol-challenge

Aliyu, S. U. R. (2011). *Real exchange rate misalignment: An application of behavioural equilibrium exchange rate (BEER) to Nigeria*. Munich Personal RePEc Archive.

Almeshqaba, F., & Ustunb, T. S. (2019). Lessons learned from rural electrification initiatives in developing countries: Insights for technical, social, financial and public policy aspects. *Renewable & Sustainable Energy Reviews*, *102*, 35–53. doi:10.1016/j.rser.2018.11.035

Alvarez-Salazar, J. (2020). The fuzzy boundaries in start-up firms industries. a social network analysis. *Journal of Technology Management & Innovation*, *15*(4), 30–42. doi:10.4067/S0718-27242020000400030

Alvi, M. H. (2016). *A Manual for Selecting Sampling Techniques in Research [Internet].* MPRA. https://mpra.ub.uni-muenchen.de/70218/

Amoako-Gyampah, K., & Acquaah, M. (2008). Manufacturing strategy, competitive strategy and firm performance: An empirical study in a developing economy environment. *International Journal of Production Economics, 111*(2), 575–592. doi:10.1016/j.ijpe.2007.02.030

Anand, J., McDermott, G., Mudambi, R., & Narula, R. (2021). Innovation in and from emerging economies: New insights and lessons for international business research. *Journal of International Business Studies, 52*(4), 545–559. doi:10.1057/s41267-021-00426-1

Anderson, P. P., & Lorch, P. R. (1999). The Role of Agriculture to Alleviate Poverty. *Agriculture and Rural Development, 6*(2), 53–56.

Andulkar, M., Le, D. T., & Berger, U. (2018): A multi-case study on Industry 4.0 for SMEs in Brandenburg, Germany. In: *Proceedings of the Annual Hawaii International Conference on System Sciences.* IEEE. 10.24251/HICSS.2018.574

Angela, R. & Diana, R. (2022). DIGITAL TECHNOLOGIES AND THE PERFORMANCE OF SMALL AND MEDIUM ENTERPRISES. *Studies in Business and Economics, 17*(3).

Anigbogu, T. U., Onwuteaka, C. I., Edoko, T. D., & Okoli, M. I. (2014). Roles of small and medium scale enterprises in community development: Evidence from Anambra south senatorial zone, Anambra State. *International Journal of Academic Research in Business & Social Sciences, 4*(8), 302. doi:10.6007/IJARBSS/v4-i8/1099

Anik, A. R., Rahman, S., & Sarker, J. B. (2017). Agricultural Productivity Growth and the Role of Capital in South Asia (1980–2013). *Sustainability (Basel), 9*(3), 1–24. doi:10.3390/su9030470

Annosi, M. C., Brunetta, F., Monti, A., & Nati, F. (2019). Is the trend your friend? An analysis of technology 4.0 investment decisions in agricultural SMEs. *Computers in Industry, 109*, 59–71. doi:10.1016/j.compind.2019.04.003

Anwer, M., Farooqi, S., & Qureshi, Y. (2015). Agriculture sector performance: An analysis through the role of agriculture sector share in GDP. Journal of Agricultural Economics. *Extension and Rural Development, 3*(3), 270–275.

Apulu, I., & Ige, E. O. (2011). Are Nigeria SMEs effectively utilizing ICT. *Internatiom Journal Business Management, 6*(6), 207–214.

Ardito, L., Ferraris, A., Petruzzelli, A. M., Bresciani, S., & Del Giudice, M. (2019). The role of universities in the knowledge management of smart city projects. *Technological Forecasting and Social Change, 142*, 312–321. doi:10.1016/j.techfore.2018.07.030

Aremu, M. A., & Adeyemi, S. L. (2011). Small and Medium Scale Enterprises as: A Survival Strategy for Employment Generation in Nigeria. *Journal of Sustainable Development, 4*(1), 200–206.

Arghode, V. (2012). Qualitative and Quantitative Research: Paradigmatic Differences. *Global Education Journal, 4*, 1–12.

Arofatkhan, K. (2023). The Impact of Small Business on Economic Growth in Developing Countries. *EPRA International Journal of Economics* [EBMS]. *Business and Management Studies, 10*(8), 12–14.

Arora, M. (2023). The Holistic Metamorphosis of Rural Lives Through Microfinance: A Perspective. In Transforming Economies Through Microfinance in Developing Nations (pp. 114-130). IGI Global. doi:10.4018/978-1-6684-5647-7.ch007

Arora, M., & Sharma, R. L. (2021a). Neutralizing Maleficent Effects of COVID-19 Through Entrepreneurship: Peeping Through the Lens of Communication. In Effective Strategies for Communicating Insights in Business (pp. 67-86). IGI Global.

Arora, M., & Sharma, R. L. (2021b). Repurposing the Role of Entrepreneurs in the Havoc of COVID-19. In Entrepreneurship and Big Data (pp. 229-250). CRC Press. doi:10.1201/9781003097945-16

Arora, M., & Sharma, R. L. (2022). Integrating Gig Economy and Social Media Platforms as a Business Strategy in the Era of Digitalization. In *Integrated Business Models in the Digital Age: Principles and Practices of Technology Empowered Strategies* (pp. 67–86). Springer International Publishing. doi:10.1007/978-3-030-97877-8_3

Arora, M., & Singh, S. (2017). Grass root Financial Management Practices of Self-Help Groups in Himachal Pradesh: An Empirical Investigation. ENVISION –. *International Journal of Commerce and Management, VOL-11*, 2017.

Arora, M., & Singh, S. (2017). Role of Financial Institutions in Promoting Microfinance through SHG Bank Linkage Programme in India. *Pacific Business Review International, 10*(4), 50–58.

Arora, M., & Singh, S. (2018). *Impact Assessment of Self-Help Group Bank Linkage Programme on Women Empowerment in the State of Himachal Pradesh.*

Arora, M., & Singh, S. (2018). Microfinance, Women Empowerment, and Transformational Leadership: A Study of Himachal Pradesh. *International Journal on Leadership, 6*(2), 23.

Arora, M., & Singh, S. (2023). Microfinance for achieving sustainable development goals: pondering over Indian experiences for the preservation of magnificent african natural resources. In *Research Anthology on Microfinance Services and Roles in Social Progress* (pp. 378–394). IGI Global.

Aruwa, S., & Gugong, B. (2007) An assessment of Small and Medium Industries Equity Investment Scheme (SMIEIS) Implementation Guidelines. Journal of Humanities, Kaduna State University.

Asemokha, A., Ahi, A., Torkkeli, L., & Saarenketo, S. (2020). Renewable energy market SMEs: Antecedents of internationalization. *Critical Perspectives on International Business, 16*(4), 407–447. doi:10.1108/cpoib-05-2018-0043

Aswani, F. (2007). *Barriers and facilitators to transitioning of small businesses (SMMEs) from the second to the first economy in South Africa* [Unpublished Masters thesis, Pretoria: University of Pretoria].

Aterido, R., Hallward-Driemeier, M., & Pages, C. (2009). *Big constraints to small firms' growth? business environment and employment growth across firms.* (Policy Research Working Paper Series 5032) The World Bank.

Ates, A. (2008). Strategy process in manufacturing SMEs. [PhD dissertation, University of Strathclyde, Glasgow].

Ates, A., & Acur, N. (2022). Making obsolescence obsolete: Execution of digital transformation in a high-tech manufacturing SME. *Journal of Business Research, 152*, 336–348. doi:10.1016/j.jbusres.2022.07.052

Audretsch, D. B., & Keilbach, M. (2004). Does entrepreneurship capital matter? *Entrepreneurship Theory and Practice, 28*(5), 419–430. doi:10.1111/j.1540-6520.2004.00055.x

Autio, E., Nambisan, S., Thomas, L. D. W., & Wright, M. (2018). Digital affordances, spatial affordances, and the genesis of entrepreneurial ecosystems. *Strategic Entrepreneurship Journal, 12*(1), 72–95. doi:10.1002/sej.1266

Ayanda, A. M., & Laraba, A. S. (2011). Small and Medium Scale Enterprises as a survival strategy for employment generation in Nigeria. *Journal of Sustainable Development, 4*(1), 200–206.

Ayanruoh, F. (2013). Why privatising Nigeria 's Refineries. ' *The Guardian* (Nigeria), www.ngrguardiannews.com

Ayuba, B. (2014). Assessment of Factors Influencing Consumer Satisfaction: A Survey of Customers of Nigerian Manufacturing Companies. *World Review of Business Research, 3*(4), 148–161.

Ayyagari, M., Demirgüç-Kunt, A., & Maksimovic, V. (2011). Small vs. young firms across the world: contribution to employment, job creation, and growth. *World Bank Policy Research Working Paper*, (5631).

Baars, H., Tank, A., Weber, P., Kemper, H. G., Lasi, H., & Pedell, B. (2021). Cooperative approaches to data sharing and analysis for industrial internet of things ecosystems. *Applied Sciences (Basel, Switzerland)*, *11*(16), 7547. doi:10.3390/app11167547

Bagheri, M., Mitchelmore, S., Bamiatzi, V., & Nikolopoulos, K. (2019). Internationalization orientation in SMEs: The mediating role of technological innovation. *Journal of International Management*, *25*(1), 121–139. doi:10.1016/j.intman.2018.08.002

Baimukhamedova, A., & Baimukhamedov, M. (2023). Digital Transformation of Small and Medium Businesses. In *Advancing SMEs Toward E-Commerce Policies for Sustainability* (pp. 19–43). IGI Global.

Bala, M., & Verma, D. (2018). A critical review of digital marketing. International Journal of Management. *IT & Engineering*, *8*(10), 321–339.

Bansal, S., & Singh, A. K. (2020). Examining the social and entrepreneurial development of women through Microfinance in Indian context. *Journal of Management Development*, *39*(4), 407–421. doi:10.1108/JMD-05-2019-0146

Banwo, A. O., Du, J., & Onokala, U. (2017). The determinants of location specific choice: Small and medium-sized enterprises in developing countries. *Journal of Global Entrepreneurship Research*, *7*(1), 1–17. doi:10.1186/s40497-017-0074-2

Barad, M., & Gien, D. (2001). Linking improvement models to manufacturing strategies – a methodology for SMEs and other enterprises. *International Journal of Production Research*, *39*(12), 2675–2695. doi:10.1080/00207540110051824

Barnes, D. (2002a). The complexities of the manufacturing strategy formation process in practice. *International Journal of Operations & Production Management*, *22*(10), 1090–1111. doi:10.1108/01443570210446324

Barnes, D. (2002b). The manufacturing strategy formation process in small and medium-sized enterprises. *Journal of Small Business and Enterprise Development*, *9*(2), 130–149. doi:10.1108/14626000210427384

Baron, R. A., & Tang, J. (2011). The role of entrepreneurs in firm-level innovation: Joint effects of positive affect, creativity, and environmental dynamism. *Journal of Business Venturing*, *26*(1), 49–60. doi:10.1016/j.jbusvent.2009.06.002

Barrenechea, M. J., & Jenkins, T. (2014). e-Government or Out of Government. Open Text Corporation.

Barrenechea, M. J., & Jenkins, T. (2018). *Digital Manufacturing*. Open Text Corporation.

Bartlett, C. (1983). MNCs: Get off the reorganizational merry-go-round. *Harvard Business Review*, (March-April), 138–145.

Bassett-Jones, N. (2005). The paradox of diversity management, creativity and innovation. *Creativity and Innovation Management*, *14*(2), 169–175. doi:10.1111/j.1467-8691.00337.x

Beaver, G., & Prince, C. (2004). Management, strategy, and policy in the UK small business sector: A critical review. *Journal of Small Business and Enterprise Development*, *11*(1), 34–49. doi:10.1108/14626000410519083

Becker, W., & Schmid, O. (2020). The right digital strategy for your business: An empirical analysis of the design and implementation of digital strategies in SMEs and LSEs. *Business Research*, *13*(3), 985–1005. doi:10.1007/s40685-020-00124-y

Beck, T., Demirguc-Kunt, A., & Levine, R. (2005). SMEs, growth, and poverty: Cross-country evidence. *Journal of Economic Growth*, *10*(3), 199–229. doi:10.1007/s10887-005-3533-5

Beldona, S., Cobanoglu, C., & Perdue, R. R. (2017). Hotel guests' preferences for social media as service recovery platforms. *International Journal of Hospitality Management, 67*, 71–80.

Bellamy, L. C. (2009). Strategy formulation in SMEs: Indications from a longitudinal study. *International Journal of Entrepreneurship and Small Business, 8*(4), 534–549. doi:10.1504/IJESB.2009.025697

Bell, E., Bryman, A., & Harley, B. (2022). *Business research methods.* Oxford University Press. doi:10.1093/hebz/9780198869443.001.0001

Berkowitz, H., & Souchaud, A. (2024). Filling successive technologically-induced governance gaps: Meta-organizations as regulatory innovation intermediaries. *Technovation, 129*, 102890. doi:10.1016/j.technovation.2023.102890

Berman, S. J. (2012). Digital transformation: Opportunities to create new business models. *Strategy and Leadership, 40*(2), 16–24. doi:10.1108/10878571211209314

Berniak-Woźny, J., Kwasek, A., Gąsiński, H., Maciaszczyk, M., & Kocot, M. (2023). Business Case for Corporate Social Responsibility in Small and Medium Enterprises—Employees' Perspective. *Sustainability (Basel), 15*(2), 1660. doi:10.3390/su15021660

BERR. (2009). *Manufacturing: New Challenges.* New Opportunities. September.

Bettoni, A., Matteri, D., Montini, E., Gładysz, B., & Carpanzano, E. (2021). An AI adoption model for SMEs: A conceptual framework. *IFAC-PapersOnLine, 54*(1), 702–708. doi:10.1016/j.ifacol.2021.08.082

Bharati, P., Zhang, W., & Chaudhury, A. (2015). Better knowledge with social media? Exploring the roles of social capital and organizational knowledge management. *Journal of Knowledge Management, 19*(3), 456–475. doi:10.1108/JKM-11-2014-0467

Bhorat, H., Asmal, Z., & Lilenstein, K. & Van der zee K. (2018). *SMMEs in South Africa: Understanding the constraints on growth and performance.* (Development Policy Research Unit (DPRU) Working Paper 201802).University of Cape Town

Biahmou, A., Emmer, C., Pfouga, A., & Stjepandić, J. (2016). Digital master as an enabler for industry 4.0. *Advances in Transdisciplinary Engineering, 4*, 672–681.

Billen, A. (2023). *News and Events.* Maastrichit School of Management. https://www.msm.nl/news-events-and-blogs/blog/the-crucial-role-of-smes-in-emerging-markets

Bird, J. (2015). *Developing the smarter grid: the role of domestic and small and medium enterprise customers.* Customer-Led Network Revolution.

Błach, J. (2020). Barriers to financial innovation: Corporate finance perspective. *Journal of Risk and Financial Management, 13*(11), 1–23. doi:10.3390/jrfm13110273

Boakye, M. D., Owek, C. J., Oluoch, E., Wachira, J., & Afrane, Y. A. (2018). Challenges of achieving sustainable community health services for community case management of malaria. *BMC Public Health, 18*(1), 1150. doi:10.1186/s12889-018-6040-2 PMID:30285684

Boddu, R. S. K., Santoki, A. A., Khurana, S., Koli, P. V., Rai, R., & Agrawal, A. (2022). An analysis to understand the role of machine learning, robotics and artificial intelligence in digital marketing. *Materials Today: Proceedings, 56*, 2288–2292. doi:10.1016/j.matpr.2021.11.637

Boshkov, T., & Bishev, G. (2015). Impact of exchange rate in the run-up to EU accession: An empirical analysis of Republic of Macedonia. *Asian Economic and Financial Review, 5*(12), 1282–1297. doi:10.18488/journal.aefr/2015.5.12/102.12.1282.1297

Boskov, V. (2016). Business plan as a source of information for making business decisions. *Skola biznisa*, (2), 38-46. doi:10.5937/skolbiz2-12886

Boukhobza, J., & Boumba, S. (2017). Micro-enterprises and sustainable tourism development: A case study of artisan enterprises in Morocco. *Tourism Management*, *62*, 239–247.

Bouri, A., Breij, M., Diop, M., Kempner, R., Klinger, B., & Stevenson, R. (2011). *Report on support to SMEs in developing countries through financial intermediaries*. Dalberg Global Development Advisors.

Bouwmana, H., Nikoub, S., & Reuver, M. D. (2019). Digitalization, business models, and SMEs: How do business model innovation practices improve performance of digitalizing SMEs? *Telecommunications Policy*, *43*(9), 101828. doi:10.1016/j.telpol.2019.101828

Brem, A., & Wolfram, P. (2014). Research and development from the bottom up-introduction of terminologies for new product development in emerging markets. *Journal of Innovation and Entrepreneurship*, *3*(1), 1–22. doi:10.1186/2192-5372-3-9

Brodny, J., & Tutak, M. (2022). Digitalization of Small and Medium-Sized Enterprises and Economic Growth: Evidence for the EU-27 Countries. *Journal of Open Innovation*, *8*(2), 67. doi:10.3390/joitmc8020067

Brooks, J. (2014). Young people with diabetes and their peers - an exploratory study of peer attitudes, beliefs, responses and influences. Project report to Diabetes UK, University of Huddersfield.

Bruwer, J. (2020). Fortifying South African small medium and micro-enterprise sustainability through a proposed internal control framework: The sustenance framework. *Expert Journal of Business and Management*, *8*(2), 147–158.

Bryman, A. (2012). *Social Research Methods* (4th ed.). Oxford University Press.

Brynjolfsson, E., & McAfee, A. (2014). *The Second Machine Age: Work, Progress, and Prosperity in a Time of Brilliant Technologies*. W. W. Norton & Company.

Budde, L., Haenggi, R., Laglia, L., & Friedli, T. (2024). Leading the transition to multi-sided platforms (MSPs) in a B2B context–The case of a recycling SME. *Industrial Marketing Management*, *116*, 106–119. doi:10.1016/j.indmarman.2023.12.002

Buer, S. V., Fragapane, G. I., & Strandhagen, J. O. (2018). The data driven process improvement cycle: Using digitalization for continuous improvement. *IFAC-PapersOnLine*, *51*(11), 1035–1040. doi:10.1016/j.ifacol.2018.08.471

Buhalis, D., & Foerste, M. (2015). SoCoMo Marketing for Travel and Tourism: Empowering Co-Creation of Value. *Journal of Destination Marketing & Management*, *4*(3), 151–161. doi:10.1016/j.jdmm.2015.04.001

Buldyrev, S., Parshani, R., Paul, G., Stanley, H., & Havlin, S. (2010). Catastrophic cascade of failures in interdependent networks. *Nature*, *464*(7291), 1025–1028. doi:10.1038/nature08932 PMID:20393559

Bunte, A., Richter, F., & Diovisalvi, R. (2021, February). Why It is Hard to Find AI in SMEs: A Survey from the Practice and How to Promote It. In ICAART (2) (pp. 614-620). doi:10.5220/0010204106140620

Cagliano, R., & Spina, G. (2002). A comparison of practice-performance models between small manufacturers and subcontractors. *International Journal of Operations & Production Management*, *22*(12), 1367–1388. doi:10.1108/01443570210452057

Capozza, C., & Divella, M. (2019). Human capital and firms' innovation: Evidence from emerging economies. *Economics of Innovation and New Technology*, *28*(7), 741–757. doi:10.1080/10438599.2018.1557426

Carey, G., Braunack-Mayer, A., & Barraket, J. (2009). Spaces of care in the third sector: Understanding the effects of professionalization. *Health*, *13*(6), 629–646. doi:10.1177/1363459308341866 PMID:19841023

Carey, G., Buick, F., & Malbon, E. (2018). The unintended consequences of structural change: When formal and informal institutions collide in efforts to address wicked problems. *International Journal of Public Administration*, *41*(14), 1169–1180. doi:10.1080/01900692.2017.1350708

Carro-Suárez, J., Sarmiento-Paredes, S., & Nava, D. (2023). Smart and Sustainable Cities: A New Urban Transformation. In Sustainable Regional Planning. IntechOpen. doi:10.5772/intechopen.110234

Carvalho, L., & Costa, C. (2013). Promoting competitiveness in tourism: A case study of the Douro Valley. *Tourism Management Perspectives*, *6*, 15–23.

Central Bank of Nigeria. (2013). *Statistical Bulletin* (Vol. 23). CBN.

Chatha, K. A., & Butt, I. (2015). Themes of study in manufacturing strategy literature. *International Journal of Operations & Production Management*, *35*(4), 604–698. doi:10.1108/IJOPM-07-2013-0328

Chea, A. C. (2023). Global Marketing: Emerging Market Economies' Challenges, Opportunities and Effective Marketing Strategy for Success. *Business and Economic Review*, *13*(4), 103–122. doi:10.5296/ber.v13i4.21482

Chen, C. L. (2019). Value creation by SMEs participating in global value chains under industry 4.0 trend: Case study of textile industry in Taiwan. *Journal of Global Information Technology Management*, *22*(2), 120–145. doi:10.1080/1097198X.2019.1603512

Chhabra, M. (2022). *Antecedents Leading to Capacity Building of Women Entrepreneurs: A Study with Reference to Women Entrepreneurs from Delhi NCR*.

Chhabra, M., & Karmarkar, Y. (2016). Effect of gender on inception stage of entrepreneurs: Evidence from small and micro enterprises in Indore. *SEDME (Small Enterprises Development, Management & Extension Journal)*, *43*(3), 1-16.

Chhabra, M., Singh, L. B., & Mehdi, S. A. (2022). Women entrepreneurs' success factors of Northern Indian community: a person–environment fit theory perspective. *Journal of Enterprising Communities: People and Places in the Global Economy*.

Chhabra, M., Gera, R., Hassan, R., & Hasan, S. (2020). An exploratory study of cognitive, social and normative dimensions of female entrepreneurship within transition economies: Evidence from India and Vietnam. [PJCSS]. *Pakistan Journal of Commerce and Social Sciences*, *14*(4), 1012–1042.

Chittithaworn, C., Islam, A., & Yusuf, D. H. M. (2011). Factors affecting Business Success of Small and Medium Enterprises in Thailand. *Asian Social Science*, *7*(5), 180–190. doi:10.5539/ass.v7n5p180

Chon, K., & Maier, T. (2009). *Welcome to Hospitality: An Introduction*. Delmar Cengage Learning.

Cho, Y., Li, J., & Chaudhuri, S. (2020). Women entrepreneurs in Asia: Eight country studies. *Advances in Developing Human Resources*, *22*(2), 115–123. doi:10.1177/1523422320907042

Cichosz, M., Wallenburg, C. M., & Knemeyer, A. M. (2020). Digital transformation at logistics service providers: Barriers, success factors and leading practices. *International Journal of Logistics Management*, *31*(2), 209–238. doi:10.1108/IJLM-08-2019-0229

Cirillo, F., Gómez, D., Diez, L., Maestro, I. E., Gilbert, T. B. J., & Akhavan, R. (2020). Smart city IoT services creation through large-scale collaboration. *IEEE Internet of Things Journal*, *7*(6), 5267–5275. doi:10.1109/JIOT.2020.2978770

Coad, A., & Tamvada, J. P. (2012). Firm growth and barriers to growth among small firms in India. *Small Business Economics*, *39*(2), 383–400. doi:10.1007/s11187-011-9318-7

Cole, M. A., Elliot, R. J. R., Occhiali, G., & Strobl, E. (2018, September). Power outages and firm performance in Sub-Saharan Africa, ‖. *Journal of Development Economics*, *134*, 150–159. Advance online publication. doi:10.1016/j.jdeveco.2018.05.003

Crabtree, B. F., & Miller, W. L. (1999) Doing qualitative research, 2nd edn. Thousand Oaks, Calif: London: Sage.

Creswell, J. W. (2009). *Research Design: qualitative, quantitative and mixed approaches* (3rd ed.). Sage.

D'Erasmo, P. N., Hernan, J. N., Boedo, M. H., & Şenkal, A. (2014). Misallocation, Informality, and Human Capital: Understanding the Role of Institutions. *Journal of Economic Dynamics & Control*, *42*(3), 122–142. doi:10.1016/j.jedc.2014.03.009

da Costa, L. S., Munhoz, I. P., Pereira, L., & Akkari, A. C. S. (2022). Assessing the digital maturity of micro and small enterprises: A focus on an emerging market. *Procedia Computer Science*, *200*, 175–184. doi:10.1016/j.procs.2022.01.216

Dallasega, P., Woschank, M., Ramingwong, S., Tippayawong, K. Y., & Chonsawat, N. (2019, March). Field study to identify requirements for smart logistics of European, US and Asian SMEs. *In Proceedings of the International Conference on Industrial Engineering and Operations Management* (Vol. 1, No. 1, pp. 844-854). IEEE. 10.5281/zenodo.4245343

Danaan, V. V. (2018). Analysing poverty in Nigeria through theoretical lenses. *Journal of Sustainable Development*, *11*(1), 20. doi:10.5539/jsd.v11n1p20

Dana, L. P., Chhabra, M., & Agarwal, M. (2023). A two-decade history of women's entrepreneurship research trajectories in developing economies context: Perspectives from India. *Journal of Management History*.

Daniel, K., Per, C., & Tomas, N. (2022). Challenges for growing SMEs: A managerial perspective, Journal of Small Business Management, Demir, R., Wennberg, K., and McKelvie, A. (2017). The strategic management of high-growth firms: A review and theoretical conceptualization. *Long Range Planning*, *50*(4), 431–456.

de Soto, H. (1989). *The Other Path: The Invisible Revolution in the Third World*. I.B. Tauris.

Deloof, M., & La Rocca, M. (2015). Local financial development and the trade credit policy of Italian SMEs. *Small Business Economics*, *44*(4), 905–924. doi:10.1007/s11187-014-9617-x

Denicolai, S., Zucchella, A., & Magnani, G. (2021). Internationalization, digitalization, and sustainability: Are SMEs ready? A survey on synergies and substituting effects among growth paths. *Technological Forecasting and Social Change*, *166*, 120650. doi:10.1016/j.techfore.2021.120650

Denzin, N. K., & Lincoln, Y. S. (2011) The Sage Handbook of Qualitative Research 4th edn. Thousand Oaks, Sage. California

Department of Minerals and Energy. (2008). *National Response to South Africa's Electricity Shortage*. DME. http://www.dme.gov.za/energy/efficiency_sectors.stm

Desta, C. G. (2018). The urban informal economy in Ethiopia: Theory and empirical evidence. *Eastern Africa Social Science Research Review*, *34*(1), 37–64. doi:10.1353/eas.2018.0001

Devereux, S. (2016). Social protection for enhanced food security in sub-Saharan Africa. *Food Policy*, *60*, 52–62. doi:10.1016/j.foodpol.2015.03.009

Diallo, A. T., & Gundogdu, A. S. (2021). Sustainable Islamic SME financing. *Sustainable Development and Infrastructure*, 57-75. doi:10.1007/978-3-030-67094-8_4

Ding, S., Tukker, A., & Ward, H. (2023). Opportunities and risks of internet of things (IoT) technologies for circular business models: A literature review. *Journal of Environmental Management, 336*, 117662. doi:10.1016/j.jenvman.2023.117662 PMID:36913854

Dixit, S. (2023, June 20). India's digital transformation could be a game-changer for economic development. *World Bank Blogs*. World Bank. https://blogs.worldbank.org/developmenttalk/indias-digital-transformation-could-be-game-changer-economic-development

Dlamini, T. M., Iwu, C. G., & Ogunlela, G. O. (2023). Support Strategies of Government-Owned Business Incubators for SMEs' Sustainability. In *Leadership and Governance for Sustainability* (pp. 222–241). IGI Global. doi:10.4018/978-1-6684-9711-1.ch012

Dodd, N., van der Merwe, J., Bond, P., & Dodd, N. (2019). *BRICS'trade with Africa: Long live the new king, just like the old king. BRICS and Resistance in Africa: Contention, Assimilation and Co-optation*. Zed Books.

Domínguez, J. P., & Roseiro, P. (2020). Blockchain: A brief review of agri-food supply chain solutions and opportunities. *ADCAIJ: Advances in Distributed Computing and Artificial Intelligence Journal, 9*(4), 95–106. doi:10.14201/ADCAIJ20209495106

Doorn, N. (2014). Assessing the future impact of medical devices: Between technology and application. In *Responsible Innovation 1: Innovative Solutions for Global Issues* (pp. 301–314). Springer Netherlands. doi:10.1007/978-94-017-8956-1_17

Dourado Freire, C., Sacomano Neto, M., Moralles, H. F., & Rodrigues Antunes, L. G. (2023). Technology-based business incubators: The impacts on resources of startups in Brazil. *International Journal of Emerging Markets, 18*(12), 5778–5797. doi:10.1108/IJOEM-08-2020-0900

Drimie, S. (2016). *Understanding South African Food and Agricultural Policy Implications for Agri-Food Value Chains. Regulation and Formal and Informal Livelihoods.*

Dube, C., & Erinah, C. (2016). Response of the Manufacturing Sector to the Zimbabwe Economic Crisis. In K. George & O. O. Raphael (Eds.), *Economic Management in a Hyperinflationary Environment: The Political Economy of Zimbabwe, 1980–2008*. Academic. doi:10.1093/acprof:oso/9780198747505.003.0003

Duckworth, A. L. (2016). *Grit: The Power of Passion and Perseverance*. Scribner.

Duncombe, R., Heeks, R., Kintu, R., Nakangu, B., & Abraham, S. (2006). Ecommerce for small enterprise development. *A Handbook for entrepreneurs in developing countries*, 7-22.

Duttagupta, R. & Pazarbasioglu, C. (2017). *Miles to Go: The Future of Emerging Markets – IMF F&D*. Finance and Development World Bank blog.

Dutta, S. (2019). *The Global Innovation Index 2019: Creating Healthy Lives - The Future of Medical Innovation. World Intellectual Property Organization*. WIPO.

Du, Y., Xu, H., & Chen, Y. (2024). Digital empowerment and innovation in risk control strategies for fishery supply chain finance—A case study of Puhui agriculture and animal husbandry financing guarantee company limited. *Marine Development, 2*(1), 1–20. doi:10.1007/s44312-023-00013-y

Dweck, C. S. (2006). *Mindset: The New Psychology of Success*. Ballantine Books.

Dzansi, D. Y., & Tasssin-Njike, R. (2014). Understanding the transition from informal to formal business: A conceptual framework. *Mediterranean Journal of Social Sciences, 5*(20), 664–664. doi:10.5901/mjss.2014.v5n20p664

Easterby-Smith, M., Thorpe, R., & Jackson, P. (2012). *Management Research* (4th ed.). Sage.

Eccles, R., Ioannou, I., & Serafeim, G. (2012). *The impact of corporate sustainability on organizational processes and performance*. doi:10.3386/w17950

Eccles, R. G., Serafeim, G., & Krzus, M. P. (2011). Market interest in nonfinancial information. *The Bank of America Journal of Applied Corporate Finance*, *23*(4), 113–127. doi:10.1111/j.1745-6622.2011.00357.x

Economy, E., & Levi, M. (2014). *By all means necessary: How China's resource quest is changing the world*. Oxford University Press.

Edmiston, K. D. (2007). The role of small and large businesses in economic development. *Economic Review*, 73-97

Ehie, I., & Muogboh, O. (2016). Analysis of manufacturing strategy in developing countries. *Journal of Manufacturing Technology Management*, *27*(2), 234–260. doi:10.1108/JMTM-07-2014-0094

Elkington, J. (2018). *The Triple Bottom Line: How Today's Best-Run Companies Are Achieving Economic, Social, and Environmental Success—and How You Can Too*. Routledge.

Eller, R., Alford, P., Kallmünzer, A., & Peters, M. (2020). Antecedents, consequences, and challenges of small and medium-sized enterprise digitalization. *Journal of Business Research*, *112*, 119–127. doi:10.1016/j.jbusres.2020.03.004

ElNaggar, R. A., & ElSayed, M. F. (2023). Drivers of business model innovation in micro and small enterprises: Evidence from Egypt as an emerging economy. *Future Business Journal*, *9*(1), 4. doi:10.1186/s43093-022-00180-2

Empl, P., & Pernul, G. (2021, April). A flexible security analytics service for the industrial IoT. *In Proceedings of the 2021 ACM Workshop on Secure and Trustworthy Cyber-Physical Systems* (pp. 23-32). ACM. 10.1145/3445969.3450427

Emran, S., & Shilpi, F. (2018). Agricultural productivity, hired labor, wages, and poverty: Evidence from Bangladesh. *World Development*, *109*, 470–482. doi:10.1016/j.worlddev.2016.12.009

Eniola, A. A. (2014). The Role of SME Firm Performance in Nigeria. *Arabian Journal of Business and Management Review*, *3*(12), 33–47. doi:10.12816/0016552

Eniola, A. A., & Entebang, H. (2015). Government policy and performance of small and medium business management. *International Journal of Academic Research in Business & Social Sciences*, *5*(2), 237–248. doi:10.6007/IJARBSS/v5-i2/1481

Erixon, F. (2009). SMEs in Europe: Taking stock and looking forward. *Centre for European Studies*, *8*(8), 293–300. doi:10.1007/s12290-009-0093-7

Escribano, A., Guasch, J. L., & Pena, J. (2009). *Assessing the Impact of Infrastructure Constraints on Firm Productivity in Africa*. (Working Paper 9). Africa Infrastructure Sector Diagnostic, World Bank. Washington D.C.

Esteve-Pérez, S., Pieri, F., & Rodriguez, D. (2022). One swallow does not make a summer: Episodes and persistence in high growth. *Small Business Economics*, *58*(3), 1517–1544. doi:10.1007/s11187-020-00443-8

Euromonitor International (2021). *Travel and Tourism Industry Overview: Global Outlook Report*. Euromonitor International.

European Commision. (2013). *SMEs*. European Commission. https://ec.europa.eu/.../en/opportunities/fp7/calls/fp7-sme-2013.html

European Commission (2003). *Recommendation 2003/361/EC regarding the SME definition*. EC.

Faeni, D. P., Puspitaningtyas Faeni, R., Alden Riyadh, H., & Yuliansyah, Y. (2023). The COVID-19 pandemic impact on the global tourism industry SMEs: A human capital development perspective. *Review of International Business and Strategy, 33*(2), 317–327. doi:10.1108/RIBS-08-2021-0116

Falkena, H., Abedian, I., von Blottnitz, M., Coovadia, C., Davel, G., Madungandaba, J., Masilela, E., & Rees, S. (2001). *SMEs access to finance in South Africa – supply side regulatory review*. Policy Board for Financial Services and Regulation, South Africa: Pretoria. www.treasury.gov.za/documents/me/p1 24.pdf

Feyen, E., Natarajan, H., & Saal, M. (2023). *Fintech and the Future of Finance*. World Bank. . doi:10.1596/978-1-4648-1914-8

Fida, B. A. (2008). The Role of Small and Medium Enterprises (SMEs) in Economic Development. Enterprise Development, Free Online Library.

Fiseha, G. G., & Oyelana, A. A. (2015). An assessment of the roles of small and medium enterprises (SMEs) in the local economic development (LED). *The South African Journal of Economics, 6*(3), 280–290.

Foroudi, P., Gupta, S., Nazarian, A., & Duda, M. (2017). Digital technology and marketing management capability: Achieving growth in SMEs. *Qualitative Market Research, 20*(2), 230–246. doi:10.1108/QMR-01-2017-0014

Franki, V., Majnarić, D., & Višković, A. (2023). A Comprehensive Review of Artificial Intelligence (AI) Companies in the Power Sector. *Energies, 16*(3), 1077. doi:10.3390/en16031077

Franzè, C., Paolucci, E., & Pessot, E. (2024). Sustained value creation driven by digital connectivity: A multiple case study in the mechanical components industry. *Technovation, 129*, 102918. doi:10.1016/j.technovation.2023.102918

Frimpong, S., Agyapong, G., & Agyapong, D. (2022). Financial literacy, access to digital finance and performance of SMEs: Evidence From Central region of Ghana. *Cogent Economics & Finance, 10*(1), 2121356.

Gabrys, J. (2020). Smart forests and data practices: From the Internet of Trees to planetary governance. *Big data & society, 7*(1), 2053951720904871. 0 . doi:10.1177/2053951720904871

Gaddis, I., & Klasen, S. (2014). Economic development, structural change, and women's labor force participation: A reexamination of the feminization U hypothesis. *Journal of Population Economics, 27*(3), 639–681. doi:10.1007/s00148-013-0488-2

Gaggero, G. B., Marchese, M., Moheddine, A., & Patrone, F. (2021). A possible smart metering system evolution for rural and remote areas employing unmanned aerial vehicles and internet of things in smart grids. *Sensors (Basel), 21*(5), 1627. doi:10.3390/s21051627 PMID:33652571

García, C. G., Meana-Llorián, D., & Lovelle, J. M. C. (2017). A review about Smart Objects, Sensors, and Actuators. *International Journal of Interactive Multimedia & Artificial Intelligence, 4*(3), 7. doi:10.9781/ijimai.2017.431

Garg, S., & Agarwal, P. (2017). Problems and prospects of woman entrepreneurship–a review of literature. *IOSR Journal of Business and Management, 19*(1), 55–60. doi:10.9790/487X-1901065560

Garvin, D. A. (1987). Competing on the eight dimensions of quality. *Harvard Business Review, 65*(6), 101–109.

Garzoni, A., De Turi, I., Secundo, G., & Del Vecchio, P. (2020). Fostering digital transformation of SMEs: A four levels approach. *Management Decision, 58*(8), 1543–1562. doi:10.1108/MD-07-2019-0939

Gatewood, E. J., & Boko, S. (2009). Globalization: Entrepreneurial challenges and opportunities in the developing world. In Z. J. Acs, H. E. Aldrich, & D. B. Audretsch, (Eds.), *The Role of SMEs and Entrepreneurship in a Globalized Economy. Expert Report No. 34 to Sweden's Globalisation Council.* Globalisation Council.

Gavrila, S. G., & de Lucas Ancillo, A. (2021). Spanish SMEs' digitalization enablers: E-Receipt applications to the offline retail market. *Technological Forecasting and Social Change, 162*, 120381. doi:10.1016/j.techfore.2020.120381 PMID:33082601

Gazem, N., Abdul Rahman, A., & Saeed, F. (2017). Using TRIZ systematic innovation methods for redesign services in small and medium enterprises [IJISSS]. *International Journal of Information Systems in the Service Sector, 9*(3), 78–92. doi:10.4018/IJISSS.2017070105

Gereffi, G., Humphrey, J., & Sturgeon, T. (2005). The governance of global value chains. *Review of International Political Economy, 12*(1), 78–104. doi:10.1080/09692290500049805

Ghobakhloo, M. (2018). The future of manufacturing industry: A strategic roadmap toward Industry 4.0. *Journal of Manufacturing Technology Management, 29*(6), 910–936. doi:10.1108/JMTM-02-2018-0057

Gibson, W., & Brown, A. (2009). Working with Qualitative Data. London.SAGE Publications. *Qualitative Report, 8*(4), 597–607.

Giller, K. E., Delaune, T., Silva, J. V., Descheemaeker, K., van de Ven, G., Schut, A. G., & van Ittersum, M. K. (2021). The future of farming: Who will produce our food? *Food Security, 13*(5), 1073–1099. doi:10.1007/s12571-021-01184-6

Gilmore, A., & Carson, D. (2018). SME marketing: Efficiency in practice. *Small Enterprise Research, 25*(3), 213–226. doi:10.1080/13215906.2018.1521740

Giordano, V., Gangale, F., Fulli, G., Jiménez, M. S., Onyeji, I., Colta, A., Papaioannou, I., Mengolini, A., Alecu, C., Ojala, T., & Maschio, I. (2011). Smart grid projects in Europe. *JRC Ref Rep Sy, 8*. doi:10.2790/32946

Giovannetti, G., Marvasi, E., & Sanfilippo, M. (2015). Supply chains and the internationalization of small firms. *Small Business Economics, 44*(4), 845–865. doi:10.1007/s11187-014-9625-x

Giunipero, L. C., Denslow, D., & Rynarzewska, A. I. (2022). Small business survival and COVID-19-An exploratory analysis of carriers. *Research in Transportation Economics, 93*, 101087. doi:10.1016/j.retrec.2021.101087

Glass, R., Meissner, A., Gebauer, C., Stürmer, S., & Metternich, J. (2018). Identifying the barriers to Industrie 4.0. *Procedia CIRP, 72*, 985–988. doi:10.1016/j.procir.2018.03.187

Gleed, S. (2023). Opinion: How Technology has revolutionized small business. *Deseret News.* https://www.deseret.com/opinion/2023/5/20/23727697/technology-revolution-small-business

Godinho, C. (2023). The Eskom crisis update: Where we are now. *Energy for Growth.* https://energyforgrowth.org/article/the-eskom-crisis-update-where-we-are-now/

González-Benito, J., & Suárez-González, I. (2010). A study of the role played by manufacturing strategic objectives and capabilities in understanding the relationship between Porter's generic strategies and business performance. *British Journal of Management, 21*(4), 1027–1043. doi:10.1111/j.1467-8551.2008.00626.x

Goodwin, H., & Francis, J. (2003). The Green Tourism Business Scheme and the Small Business Enterprise: An Exploratory Study of Relationships and Impacts. *Journal of Sustainable Tourism, 11*(4), 325–347.

Gosa, T. (2012). *Sustainable energy and policy design on the energy transition to renewable energy systems in Stellenbosch, case study: Stellenbosch solar water heater bylaw.* https://scholar.sun.ac.za/handle/10019.1/71957

Govindan, K., Shankar, K. M., & Kannan, D. (2020). Achieving sustainable development goals through identifying and analyzing barriers to industrial sharing economy: A framework development. *International Journal of Production Economics, 227*, 107575. doi:10.1016/j.ijpe.2019.107575

Gregory, G., Harvie, C., & Lee, H. H. (2002). *Korean SMEs in the Wake of the Financial Crisis: Strategies, Constraints, and Performance in a Global Economy.* Department of Economics, University of Wollongong, 2002. https://ro.uow.edu.au/cgi/viewcontent.cgi?referer=&httpsredir=1&article=1057&context=commwkpapers

Gregory, R., Failing, L., Harstone, M., Long, G., McDaniels, T., & Ohlson, D. (2012). *Structured decision making: a practical guide to environmental management choices.* John Wiley & Sons. doi:10.1002/9781444398557

Gretzel, U., & Yoo, K. H. (2008). Use and Impact of Online Travel Reviews. *Information and Communication Technologies in Tourism, 2008,* 35–46. doi:10.1007/978-3-211-77280-5_4

Groeßler, A. (2007). A dynamic view on strategic resources and capabilities applied to an example from the manufacturing strategy literature. *Journal of Manufacturing Technology Management, 18*(3), 250–266. doi:10.1108/17410380710730594

Groot, A. E., Bolt, J. S., Jat, H. S., Jat, M. L., Kumar, M., Agarwal, T., & Blok, V. (2019). Business models of SMEs as a mechanism for scaling climate smart technologies: The case of Punjab, India. *Journal of Cleaner Production, 210,* 1109–1119. doi:10.1016/j.jclepro.2018.11.054

Größler, A., & Grübner, A. (2006). An empirical model of the relationships between manufacturing capabilities. *International Journal of Operations & Production Management, 26*(5), 458–485. doi:10.1108/01443570610659865

Guest, G., Namey, E., & Chen, M. (2020). A simple method to assess and report thematic saturation in qualitative research. *PLoS One, 15*(5), e0232076. doi:10.1371/journal.pone.0232076 PMID:32369511

Gündüz, N., Küfeoğly, S., & Lehtonen, M. (2017). Impacts of natural disasters on Swedish electric power policy: A case study. *Sustainability (Basel), 9*(2), 230. doi:10.3390/su9020230

Gunningham, N., & Sinclair, D. (2017). *Leaders and laggards: next-generation environmental regulation.* Routledge. doi:10.4324/9781351282000

Guo, H., Yang, Z., Huang, R., & Guo, A. (2020). The digitalization and public crisis responses of small and medium enterprises: Implications from a COVID-19 survey. *Frontiers of Business Research in China, 14*(1), 1–25. doi:10.1186/s11782-020-00087-1

Gursoy, D., & Chi, C. G. Q. (2013). Understanding Chinese Outbound Tourists' Satisfaction, Destination Image, and Future Behavioral Intention: A Structural Model Approach. *Journal of Travel Research, 52*(6), 731–742.

Gursoy, D., Chi, C. G. Q., & Lu, L. (2013). Antecedents and outcomes of travelers' information search behavior: A comparative study of pre-travel and during travel search. *Tourism Management, 36,* 120–130.

Gursoy, D., & Rutherford, D. G. (2004). Host Attitudes toward Tourism: An Improved Structural Model. *Annals of Tourism Research, 31*(3), 495–516. doi:10.1016/j.annals.2003.08.008

Guttentag, D. (2015). Airbnb: Disruptive innovation and the rise of an informal tourism accommodation sector. *Current Issues in Tourism, 18*(12), 1192–1217. doi:10.1080/13683500.2013.827159

Hall, C. M., & Mitchell, R. (2008). Wine tourism in New Zealand: The visitors' perspective. *International Journal of Wine Business Research, 20*(3), 276–293.

Hall, C. M., & Page, S. J. (2014). *The Geography of Tourism and Recreation: Environment, Place and Space.* Routledge. doi:10.4324/9780203796092

Hall, C. M., & Richards, G. (2003). *Tourism and Sustainable Community Development.* Routledge.

Hall, C. M., Williams, A. M., & Lew, A. A. (2010). *Tourism: Concepts, Impacts and Issues.* Routledge.

Hallgren, M., Olhager, J., & Schroeder, R. G. (2011). A hybrid model of competitive capabilities. *International Journal of Operations & Production Management*, *31*(5), 511–526. doi:10.1108/01443571111126300

Hammond, J. S., Keeney, R. L., & Raiffa, H. (2015). *Smart choices: A practical guide to making better decisions*. Harvard Business Review Press.

Hansen, E. B., & Bøgh, S. (2021). Artificial intelligence and internet of things in small and medium-sized enterprises: A survey. *Journal of Manufacturing Systems*, *58*, 362–372. doi:10.1016/j.jmsy.2020.08.009

Happonen, A., Santti, U., Auvinen, H., Räsänen, T., & Eskelinen, T. (2020). Sustainable business model innovation for digital remote monitoring: a follow up study on a water Iot service. In *BIOS Forum* (pp. 98-106). IEEE. 10.5281/zenodo.4290135

Harrigan, P., Ramsey, E., & Ibbotson, P. (2011). Critical factors underpinning the e-CRM activities of SMEs. *Journal of Marketing Management*, *27*(5-6), 503–529. doi:10.1080/0267257X.2010.495284

Harsanto, B., Mulyana, A., Faisal, Y. A., Shandy, V. M., & Alam, M. (2023). Sustainability innovation in small medium enterprises (SMEs): A qualitative analysis. *The Qualitative Report*. doi:10.46743/2160-3715/2023.6193

Hart, K. (1973). Informal income opportunities and urban employment in Ghana. *The Journal of Modern African Studies*, *2*(1), 61–89. doi:10.1017/S0022278X00008089

Hartl, E., & Hess, T. (2017). The role of cultural values for digital transformation: Insights from a delphi study. *AMCIS 2017 - America's Conference on Information Systems: A Tradition of Innovation, 2017-Augus*. AMCIS.

Hasan, A., Murni, Junita, & Rahmi, I. (2021). Ranking of Drivers and Barriers for the Green Management Implementation at MSME in Banda Aceh City, Indonesia. *Proceedings of the 2nd Borobudur International Symposium on Science and Technology (BIS-STE 2020)*, (pp. 52–61). IEEE. 10.2991/aer.k.210810.010

Hasan, I., Jackowicz, K., Kowalewski, O., & Kozłowski, Ł. (2017). Do local banking market structures matter for SME financing and performance? New evidence from an emerging economy. *Journal of Banking & Finance*, *79*, 142–158. doi:10.1016/j.jbankfin.2017.03.009

Hasan, M. M., Yajuan, L., & Mahmud, A. (2020). Regional development of China's inclusive finance through financial technology. *SAGE Open*, *10*(1), 2158244019901252. doi:10.1177/2158244019901252

Hashim, I. A., & Zarma, A. B. (1996), "The Impact of Parallel Market on the Stability of Exchange Rate: Evidence from Nigeria", NDIC Quarterly, Vol. 7 No. 2.

Hassanli, N., & Williamson, J. (2023). Minimizing the sustainability knowledge-practice gap through creating shared value: The case of small accommodation firms. *Journal of Sustainable Tourism*, 1–20. doi:10.1080/09669582.2023.2186828

Heckathorn, D. D. (1997). Respondent-driven sampling: A new approach to the study of hidden populations. *Social Problems*, *44*(2), 174–199. doi:10.2307/3096941

Hill, T. (2000). Manufacturing Strategy—Text and Cases 2nd edition. Palgrave.

Hill, A., & Hill, T. (2009). *Manufacturing Operations Strategy* (3rd ed.). Palgrave Macmillan. doi:10.1007/978-1-137-07690-8

Hillenkamp, I., Lapeyre, F., & Lemaître, A. (Eds.). (2013). *Securing livelihoods: Informal economy practices and institutions*. OUP Oxford. doi:10.1093/acprof:oso/9780199687015.001.0001

Hirasawa, K. (2019). *Globalization and small businesses* (No. 2019-06). Ordnungspolitische Diskurse.

Hitt, M. A., Ireland, R. D., & Hoskisson, R. E. (2007). *Strategic management: Competitiveness and globalization* (5th edition.). Cincinnati, OH: Southwestern College Publishing Company Houndmills, Hampshire. https://databank.world-bank.org/data/home.aspx

Ho, C. Q., Hensher, D. A., Mulley, C., & Wong, Y. Z. (2018). Potential uptake and willingness-to-pay for Mobility as a Service (MaaS): A stated choice study. *Transportation Research Part A, Policy and Practice, 117*, 302–318. doi:10.1016/j. tra.2018.08.025

Holland, C., McCarthy, A., Ferri, P., & Shapira, P. (2024). Innovation intermediaries at the convergence of digital technologies, sustainability, and governance: A case study of AI-enabled engineering biology. *Technovation, 129*, 102875. doi:10.1016/j.technovation.2023.102875

Hong, Y., Hammad, A., Sepasgozar, S., & Akbarnezhad, A. (2019). BIM adoption model for small and medium construction organisations in Australia. *Engineering, Construction, and Architectural Management, 26*(2), 154–183. doi:10.1108/ ECAM-04-2017-0064

Horgan, D., van Kranen, H. J., & Morré, S. A. (2019). Optimising SME potential in modern healthcare systems: Challenges, opportunities and policy recommendations. *Public Health Genomics, 21*(1-2), 1–17. doi:10.1159/000492809 PMID:30145589

Horn, A. (2011). Who's out there? A profile of informal traders in four South African city central business districts. *Town and Regional Planning, 59*, 1–6.

Hossain, M. S. (2010). *Does Government subsidy on agricultural sector cause agricultural development in Bangladesh?* Organised by Department of Economic Sciences.

Hossain, M., Yoshino, N., & Tsubota, K. (2023). Sustainable financing strategies for the SMEs: Two alternative models. *Sustainability (Basel), 15*(11), 8488. doi:10.3390/su15118488

Hossen, Z. (2019). Boosting the low productivity in agriculture sector in Bangladesh. *The Financial Express.* https:// thefinancialexpress.com.bd/views/boosting-the-low-productivity-in-agriculture-sector-in-bangladesh-1571412384

Ho, T. C. F., Ahmad, N. H., & Ramayah, T. (2016). Competitive Capabilities and Business Performance among Manufacturing SMEs: Evidence from an Emerging Economy, Malaysia. *Journal of Asia-Pacific Business, 17*(1), 37–58. doi :10.1080/10599231.2016.1129263

Hsieh, H.-F., & Shannon, S. E. (2005). Three Approaches to Qualitative Content Analysis. *Qualitative Health Research, 15*(9), 1277–1288. doi:10.1177/1049732305276687 PMID:16204405

Huang, C. J., Chicoma, E. D. T., & Huang, Y. H. (2019). Evaluating the factors that are affecting the implementation of industry 4.0 technologies in manufacturing MSMEs, the case of Peru. *Processes (Basel, Switzerland), 7*(3), 161. doi:10.3390/pr7030161

Hughes, K. D., Saunders, C., & Denier, N. (2022). Lockdowns, pivots & triple shifts: Early challenges and opportunities of the COVID-19 pandemic for women entrepreneurs. *Journal of Small Business and Entrepreneurship, 34*(5), 483–501. doi:10.1080/08276331.2022.2042657

Hu, M. K., & Kee, D. M. H. (2022). SMEs and business sustainability: Achieving sustainable business growth in the new normal. In *Research anthology on business continuity and navigating times of crisis* (pp. 1036–1056). IGI Global. doi:10.4018/978-1-6684-4503-7.ch052

Hundal, G. S., Laux, C. M., Buckmaster, D., Sutton, M. J., & Langemeier, M. (2023). Exploring Barriers to the Adoption of Internet of Things-Based Precision Agriculture Practices. *Agriculture, 13*(1), 163. doi:10.3390/agriculture13010163

Hussain, A., Jeddi, S., Lakmeeharan, K., & Muzaffar, H. (2019, October 10). *Unlocking private sector financing in emerging markets infrastructure.* Mckinsey & Conpany. https://www.mckinsey.com/industries/private-equity-and-principal-investors/our-insights/unlocking-private-sector-financing-in-emerging-markets-infrastructure

Ihua, U. B. (2009). SMEs Key Failure-Factors: A Comparison between the United Kingdom and Nigeria. *Journal of Social Sciences, 18*(3), 199–207. doi:10.1080/09718923.2009.11892682

ILO (2019). *SMEs and Decent and Productive Employment Creation.* ILO.

ILO (2020). *Tourism and COVID-19: Assessing the Economic and Social Impacts.* ILO.

IMF. (2019). *Enhancing the Role of SMEs in the Arab World—Some Key Considerations.* IMF. https://www.imf.org/en/Publications/Policy-Papers/Issues/2019/12/13/Enhancing-the-Role-of-SMEs-in-the-Arab-World-Some-Key-Considerations-48873

IMF. (2020). Republic of Korea: Financial System Stability Assessment and Press Release for the Republic of Korea. *IMF Country Report, 20*(120).

Indarti, N., & Langenberg, M. (2004). *Factors affecting business success among SMEs: Empirical evidence from Indonesia.* U Twente. http://www.utwente.nl/niks/achief/research/conference/esu/papers/indartilagenbe rg.pdf (Accessed 10 March 2015)

Independent Online. (2021). eThekwini Municipality to host informal traders indaba aimed at boosting local economy in wake of unrest. *Independent Online.* https://www.iol.co.za/mercury/news/ethekwini-municipality-to-host-informal-traders-indaba-aimed-at-boosting-local-economy-in-wake-of-unrest-0b7c6362-7a8a-4c69-b382-fb5354f5e2d0

Industrial Development Corporation. (2015). *Economic Overview of the Department of Research and Information: Recent developments in the global and South African economies.* IDC. www.idc.co.za/images/downloadfiles/economicoverviews/economic_overview_jun_2015.pdf

International Labour Oorganisation. (2019, September 10) *The power of small: Unlocking the potential of SME.* ILO. https://www.ilo.org/infostories/en-GB/Stories/Employment/SMEs#footer

International Labour Organisation. (2015). *Transitioning from the Informal to Formal Economy [Internet].* Geneva: International Labour Office. https://www.ilo.org/wcmsp5/groups/public/@ed_dialogue/@actrav/documents/publication/wcms_545928.pdf

International Labour Organisation. (2017). *Enterprise Formalisation.* Geneva: International Labour Office. https://www.ilo.org/wcmsp5/groups/public/---ed_emp/---emp_ent/---ifp_seed/documents/publication/wcms_544828.pdf

International Labour Organisation. (2018). *World employment social outlook.* Geneva: International Labour Office. https://www.ilo.org/wcmsp5/groups/public/---dgreports/---dcomm/---publ/documents/publication/wcms_615594.pdf

International Labour Organisation. (2020). *Brief: Impact of Lockdown Measures on the Informal Economy [Internet].* Geneva (Switzerland): International Labour Organization. http://www.ilo.org/global/topics/employment-promotion/informal-economy/publications/WCMS_743523/lang--en/index.htm

International Labour Organization. (2015). *Micro-, Small and Medium-sized Enterprises.* ILO. https://www.ilo.org/global/topics/micro-and-small enterprises/WCMS_437530/lang--en/index.htm

International Monetary Fund. (2020). *South Africa.* IMF. https://www.tralac.org/documents/news/3097-south-africa-selected-issues-paper-january-2019-imf/file.html (Accessed 21 June 2023).

International Monetary Fund. (2021, September 20). *Emerging markets must balance overcoming the pandemic, returning to more normal policies, and rebuilding their economies.* IMF. https://www.imf.org/external/pubs/ft/fandd/2021/06/pdf/the-future-of-emerging-markets-duttagupta-and-pazarbasioglu.pdf

International Monetary Fund. (2023). *World Economic Outlook: Navigating Global Divergences.* Washington, DC.

Isensee, C., Teuteberg, F., Griese, K.-M., & Topi, C. (2020). The relationship between organizational culture, sustainability, and digitalization in SMEs: A systematic review. *Journal of Cleaner Production, 275,* 122944. doi:10.1016/j.jclepro.2020.122944

Ishengoma, E., & Kappel, R. (2006) Economic Growth and Poverty: Does Formalisation of Informal Enterprises Matter. *GIGA Working Papers 20.*

Islam, M. S., & Shirazul, D. (2009, October). *Farm mechanization for sustainable agriculture in Bangladesh: Problems and prospects.* In 5th APCAEM Technical Committee Meeting and the Expert Group Meeting on Application of Agricultural Machinery for Sustainable Agriculture. United Nations Asian and Pacific Centre for Agricultural Engineering and Machinery, Manila, Philippines.

Jaim, W. M. H., & Akter, S. (2019). Seed, fertilizer and innovation in Bangladesh: Industry and policy issues for the future. *Gates Open Research, 3*(732), 732.

Jamal, T., & Getz, D. (1999). Community roundtables for tourism-related conflicts: The dialectics of consensus and process structures. *Journal of Sustainable Tourism, 7*(3-4), 290–313. doi:10.1080/09669589908667341

Jeong, S., McLean, G. N., & Park, S. (2018). Understanding informal learning in small-and medium-sized enterprises in South Korea. *Journal of Workplace Learning, 30*(2), 89–107. doi:10.1108/JWL-03-2017-0028

Julta, D., Bodorick, P., & Dhaliwal, J. (2002). Supporting the e-business readiness of small and medium sized enterprises: Approaches and metrics. *Internet Research, 12*(2), 139–164. doi:10.1108/10662240210422512

Kabonga, I., Zvokuomba, K., & Nyagadza, B. (2021). The challenges faced by young entrepreneurs in informal trading in Bindura, Zimbabwe. *Journal of Asian and African Studies, 56*(8), 1780–1794. doi:10.1177/0021909621990850

Kadaba, D. M. K., & Aithal, P. S., & KRS, S. (2023). Government Initiatives and Digital Innovation for AtmaNirbhar MSMEs/SMEs: To Achieve Sustainable and Inclusive Economic Growth. [IJMTS]. *International Journal of Management, Technology, and Social Sciences, 8*(1), 68–82.

Kang, H. S., Lee, J. Y., Choi, S., Kim, H., Park, J. H., Son, J. Y., Kim, B. H., & Do Noh, S. (2016). Smart manufacturing: Past research, present findings, and future directions. *International Journal of Precision Engineering and Manufacturing-Green Technology., 3*(1), 111–128. doi:10.1007/s40684-016-0015-5

Karadag, H. (2015). The role and challenges of small and medium-sized enterprises (SMEs) in emerging economies: An analysis from Turkey. *Business and Management Studies, 1*(2), 179–188. doi:10.11114/bms.v1i2.1049

Karlan, D., & Morduch, J. (2010). Access to finance. In *Handbook of development economics* (Vol. 5, pp. 4703–4784). Elsevier. doi:10.1016/B978-0-444-52944-2.00009-4

Kateja, A. (2012). Building infrastructure: Private participation in emerging economies. *Procedia: Social and Behavioral Sciences, 37,* 368–378. doi:10.1016/j.sbspro.2012.03.302

Kato, A. I. (2021). A Literature Review of Venture Capital Financing and Growth of SMEs in Emerging Economies and a Agenda for Future Research. *Academy of Entrepreneurship Journal, 27*(1), 1–17.

Keskġn, H., Ġentürk, C., Sungur, O., & Kġrġġ, H. M. (2010). The importance of SMEs in developing economies. In *2nd international symposium on sustainable development* (pp. 183-192). IEEE.

Kgosana, C. (2013). *Small businesses failure rate high.* Sowetanlive. https://www.sowetanlive.co.za/news/business-news/2013/05/16/small-businesses-failure-rate-high

Khaksar, S. (2011). The role of government policy and the growth of entrepreneurship in the micro, small (&) medium-sized enterprises in India: An overview. *Australian Journal of Basic and Applied Sciences, 5*(6), 1563–1571.

Khambule, I. (2022). COVID-19 and the informal economy in a small town in South Africa: Governance implications in the post-COVID era. *Cogent Social Sciences, 8*(1), 2078528. doi:10.1080/23311886.2022.2078528

Khamis, M. (2014) Formalisation of jobs and firms in emerging market economies through registration reform. *IZA World of Labour.* Bhorat, H and Köhler, T., 2020 COVID-19, social protection, and the labour market in South Africa: Are social grants being targeted at the most vulnerable? *Working Papers 202008, University of Cape Town, Development Policy Research Unit.*

Khan, T. (2020). Internet of Things: The Potentialities for Sustainable Agriculture. *International Business, Trade and Institutional Sustainability.* . doi:10.1007/978-3-030-26759-9_17

Khanna, G. (2016). *How companies can transform from product to platform ecosystem* [Doctoral dissertation, Massachusetts Institute of Technology].

Kiel, D., Arnold, C., & Müller, J. M. (2017). *Sustainable Industrial Value Creation: Benefits and Challenges of Industry 4. 0. The XXVIII ISPIM Innovation Conference – Composing the Innovation Symphony.* Research Gate.

Kim, C., & Lee, J. (2018). The Effect of Network Structure on Performance in South Korea SMEs: The Moderating Effects of Absorptive Capacity. *Sustainability (Basel), 10*(9), 3174. doi:10.3390/su10093174

King, N. (2009). Book review: Phenomenological psychology: Theory research and method. *Qualitative Research in Organizations and Management, 2*(2).

King, N., Brooks, M., Turley, S., & Emma, L. (2015). The Utility of Template Analysis in Qualitative Psychology Research. *Qualitative Research in Psychology, 12*(2), 202–222. doi:10.1080/14780887.2014.955224 PMID:27499705

Kongolo, M. (2010). Job creation versus job shedding and the role of SMEs in economic development. *African Journal of Business Management, 4*(11), 2288–2295.

Konieczny, G., Kolisnichenko, P., Górska, M., & Górski, T. (2023). The role of well-being in sustainable corporate development of companies. *Economics. Finance and Management Review,* (3), 59–67.

Korea Credit Guarantee Fund. (2022, December 11). *Annual Report.* Kodit. https://www.kodit.co.kr/synap/skin/doc.html?fn=2022%EB%85%84%EB%8F%84%20%EC%98%81%EB%AC%B8%20%EC%97%B0%EC%B0%A8%EB%B3%B4%EA%B3%A0%EC%84%9C.pdf&rs=/serverFiles/synap/20230807181004788_4392/output

Kotios, D., Makridis, G., Walser, S., Kyriazis, D., & Monferrino, V. (2022). Personalized finance management for smes. *Big Data and Artificial Intelligence in Digital Finance.* Springer. . doi:10.1007/978-3-030-94590-9_12

Kovalevska, N., Nesterenko, I., Lutsenko, O., Nesterenko, O., & Hlushach, Y. (2022). Problems of accounting digitalization in conditions of business processes digitalization. *Amazonia Investiga, 11*(56), 132–141. doi:10.34069/AI/2022.56.08.14

Kraft, C., Lindeque, J. P., & Peter, M. K. (2022). The digital transformation of Swiss small and medium-sized enterprises: Insights from digital tool adoption. *Journal of Strategy and Management, 15*(3), 468–494. doi:10.1108/JSMA-02-2021-0063

Kraus, S., Palmer, C., Kailer, N., Kallinger, F. L., & Spitzer, J. (2019). Digital entrepreneurship: A research agenda on new business models for the twenty-first century. *International Journal of Entrepreneurial Behaviour & Research, 25*(2), 353–375.

Krippendorff, K. (2018). *Content analysis: An introduction to its methodology.* Sage Publications.

Krowas, K., & Riedel, R. (2019). Planning guideline and maturity model for intra-logistics 4.0 in SME. In *Advances in Production Management Systems. Towards Smart Production Management Systems: IFIP WG 5.7 International Conference,* (pp. 331-338). Springer International Publishing. 10.1007/978-3-030-29996-5_38

Krüger, N., & Teuteberg, F. (2016). IT consultants as change agents in digital transformation initiatives. In Multikonferenz Wirtschaftsinformatik (Vol. 2, pp. 1019-1030). Universitätsverlag Ilmenau, Ilmenau, Germany, March 9-11.

Kumar, A., Pujari, P., & Gupta, N. (2021). Artificial Intelligence: Technology 4.0 as a solution for healthcare workers during COVID-19 pandemic. *Acta Universitatis Bohemiae Meridionales, 24*(1), 19–35. doi:10.32725/acta.2021.002

Kumari, N. (2013). *The role of NGOs in promoting women entrepreneurship in India* [Doctoral dissertation, University of Trento].

Kumar, P. R., Wan, A. T., & Suhaili, W. S. H. (2020). Exploring data security and privacy issues in internet of things based on five-layer architecture. *International Journal of Communication Networks and Information Security, 12*(1), 108–121. doi:10.17762/ijcnis.v12i1.4345

Kumar, V., Verma, P., Mittal, A., Tuesta Panduro, J. A., Singh, S., Paliwal, M., & Sharma, N. K. (2023). Adoption of ICTs as an emergent business strategy during and following COVID-19 crisis: Evidence from Indian MSMEs. *Benchmarking, 30*(6), 1850–1883. doi:10.1108/BIJ-11-2021-0685

Laforet, S., & Tann, J. (2006). Innovative characteristics of small manufacturing firms. *Journal of Small Business and Enterprise Development, 13*(3), 363–380. doi:10.1108/14626000610680253

Lagoarde-Segot, T. (2020). Financing the sustainable development goals. *Sustainability (Basel), 12*(7), 2775. doi:10.3390/su12072775

Langa, M. T., & Govender, K. K. (2019). The need for agile relationship lending between small business and banks, towards a more engaged relationship: A case study in Khayelitsha, South Africa. *Asian Business Research Journal, 4*(1), 29–34. doi:10.20448/journal.518.2019.41.29.34

Leach, J. C., & Melicher, R. W. (2020). *Entrepreneurial finance.* Cengage Learning.

Leask, A., Fyall, A., & Barron, P. (2013). Generation Y: Opportunity or challenge - strategies to engage Generation Y in the destination. *Tourism Management, 35*, 190–200.

Le-Dain, M. A., Benhayoun, L., Matthews, J., & Liard, M. (2023). Barriers and opportunities of digital servitization for SMEs: The effect of smart Product-Service System business models. *Service Business, 17*(1), 359–393. doi:10.1007/s11628-023-00520-4

Lee, D.-H. (2015). *Commercializing Excellent Ideas for Creative Economy: Focusing on the Six Months Challenge Platform Project. Research Report 2015–047.* Korea Institute of SandT Evaluation and Planning.

Lee, K. W. (2016, December 12). *Skills Training by Small and Medium-Sized Enterprises: Innovative Cases and the Consortium Approach in the Republic of Korea.* (ADBI Working Paper Series). ADBI. https://www.adb.org/sites/default/files/publication/188802/adbi-wp579.pdf

Lee, C. K. M., Zhang, S., & Ng, K. K. H. (2017). Development of an industrial Internet of things suite for smart factory towards re-industrialization. *Advances in Manufacturing*, *5*(4), 335–343. doi:10.1007/s40436-017-0197-2

Lee, P., Hunter, W. C., & Chung, N. (2020). Smart tourism city: Developments and transformations. *Sustainability (Basel)*, *12*(10), 3958. doi:10.3390/su12103958

Lee, S. M., & Trimi, S. (2021). Convergence innovation in the digital age and in the COVID-19 pandemic crisis. *Journal of Business Research*, *123*, 14–22. doi:10.1016/j.jbusres.2020.09.041 PMID:33012897

Legner, C., Eymann, T., Hess, T., Matt, C., Böhmann, T., Drews, P., Mädche, A., Urbach, N., & Ahlemann, F. (2017). Digitalization: Opportunity and Challenge for the Business and Information Systems Engineering Community. *Business & Information Systems Engineering*, *59*(4), 301–308. doi:10.1007/s12599-017-0484-2

Legodi, K., & Kanjere, M. (2015). The challenges faced by informal traders in greater Letaba municipality in Limpopo province, *South Africa. Africa's Public Service Delivery and Performance Review*, *3*(4), 57–75. doi:10.4102/apsdpr.v3i4.98

Leino, J. (2009). *Formal and informal Microenterprises, Enterprise Surveys. Enterprise Note No. 5, Informality*. World Bank.

Lekhanya, L. M. (2016). *Determinants of Survival and Growth of Small and Medium Enterprises in Rural KwaZulu-Natal* [Ph.D. Thesis, Cape Town: University of the Western Cape].

Leng, Y., Yu, L., & Niu, X. (2022). Dynamically aggregating individuals' social influence and interest evolution for group recommendations. *Information Sciences*, *614*, 223–239. doi:10.1016/j.ins.2022.09.058

Levine, R. (2005). *Does firm size matter for growth and poverty alleviation? Prepared for the Brookings Blum Round table: The Private Sector in the Fight against Global Poverty*. Brown University and the National Bureau of Economic Research. https://www.brookings.edu/global/200508blum_levine.pdf

Levine, E. G. (1989). Women and creativity: Art-in-relationship. *The Arts in Psychotherapy*, *16*(4), 309–325. doi:10.1016/0197-4556(89)90054-3

Levine, R. (2005). "Finance and Growth: Theory and Evidence," Handbook of Economic Growth. In P. Aghion & S. Durlauf (Eds.), *Handbook of Economic Growth*. Elsevier.

Levy, S. (2010). *Good intentions, bad outcomes: Social policy, informality, and economic growth in Mexico*. Brookings Institution Press.

Liang, L., Gao, Y., Huang, B., & Liao, C. (2017). The impact of SMEs' lending and credit guarantee on bank efficiency in South Korea. *Review of Development Finance*, *7*(2), 134–141. doi:10.1016/j.rdf.2017.04.003

Liberto, D., James, M., & Kvilhaug, S. (2023, September 10) *Small and Midsize Enterprise (SME) Defined: Types Around the World the World*. Investiopedia. https://www.investopedia.com/terms/s/smallandmidsizeenterprises.asp#citation-8

Li, L., Su, F., Zhang, W., & Mao, J.-Y. (2017). Digital transformation by SME entrepreneurs: A capability perspective (. Portico). *Information Systems Journal*, *28*(6), 1129–1157. doi:10.1111/isj.12153

Lin, B. B., Philpott, S. M., Jha, S., & Liere, H. (2017). Urban agriculture as a productive green infrastructure for environmental and social well-being. *Greening cities: Forms and functions*, 155-179.

Lin, Y., Ma, S., & Zhou, L. (2012). Manufacturing strategies for time based competitive advantages. *Industrial Management & Data Systems*, *112*(5), 729–747. doi:10.1108/02635571211232299

Liu, Y., Dilanchiev, A., Xu, K., & Hajiyeva, A. M. (2022). Financing SMEs and business development as new post Covid-19 economic recovery determinants. *Economic Analysis and Policy*, *76*, 554–567. doi:10.1016/j.eap.2022.09.006

Lockett, S. H., Hatton, J., Turner, R., Stubbins, C., Hodgekins, J., & Fowler, D. (2012). Using a semi-structured interview to explore imagery experienced during social anxiety for clients with a diagnosis of psychosis: An exploratory study conducted within an early intervention for psychosis service. *Behavioural and Cognitive Psychotherapy*, *40*(1), 55–68. doi:10.1017/S1352465811000439 PMID:21729340

Löfving, M., Säfsten, K., & Winroth, M. (2014). Manufacturing strategy frameworks suitable for SMEs. *Journal of Manufacturing Technology Management*, *25*(1), 7–26. doi:10.1108/JMTM-08-2012-0081

Long, J., Jiang, C., Dimitrov, S., & Wang, Z. (2022). Clues from networks: Quantifying relational risk for credit risk evaluation of SMEs. *Financial Innovation*, *8*(1), 1–41. doi:10.1186/s40854-022-00390-1

Lopes, J., & Farinha, L. (2020). Knowledge and Technology Transfer in Tourism SMEs. In *Multilevel Approach to Competitiveness in the Global Tourism Industry* (pp. 198–210). IGI Global. doi:10.4018/978-1-7998-0365-2.ch012

López Salazar, A., Contreras Soto, R., & Espinosa Mosqueda, R. (2012). The impact of financial decisions and strategy on small business competitiveness. *Global. Journal of Business Research*, *6*(2), 93–103.

Loucks, E. S., Martens, M. L., & Cho, C. H. (2010). Engaging small-and medium-sized businesses in sustainability. *Sustainability Accounting. Management and Policy Journal*, *1*(2), 178–200.

Lucas, H. Jr, Agarwal, R., Clemons, E. K., El Sawy, O. A., & Weber, B. (2013). Impactful Research on Transformational Information Technology: An Opportunity to Inform New Audiences. *Management Information Systems Quarterly*, *37*(2), 371–382. https://www.jstor.org/stable/43825914. doi:10.25300/MISQ/2013/37.2.03

Lu, J., & Herremans, I. M. (2019). Board gender diversity and environmental performance: An industries perspective. *Business Strategy and the Environment*, *28*(7), 1449–1464. doi:10.1002/bse.2326

Lukacs, E. (2005). The economic Role of SMEs in world economy, especially in Europe. *European Integration Studies, Miskolc*, *4*(1), 3–12.

Lukin, A., & Xuesong, F. (2019). What is BRICS for China? *Strategic Analysis*, *43*(6), 620–631. doi:10.1080/097001 61.2019.1669896

Luo, Y., Xue, Q., & Han, B. (2010). How emerging market governments promote outward FDI: Experience from China. *Journal of World Business*, *45*(1), 68–79. doi:10.1016/j.jwb.2009.04.003

Lutfi, A., Alkelani, S. N., Al-Khasawneh, M. A., Alshira'h, A. F., Alshirah, M. H., Almaiah, M. A., Alrawad, M., Al-syouf, A., Saad, M., & Ibrahim, N. (2022). Influence of Digital Accounting System Usage on SMEs Performance: The Moderating Effect of COVID-19. *Sustainability (Basel)*, *14*(22), 15048. doi:10.3390/su142215048

Lu, Z., Wu, J., Li, H., & Nguyen, D. (2022). Local Bank, Digital Financial Inclusion and SME Financing Constraints: Empirical Evidence from China. *Emerging Markets Finance & Trade*, *58*(6), 1712–1725. doi:10.1080/1540496X.2021.1923477

Lynn, T., & Wood, C. (2023). Smart Streets as a Cyber-Physical Social Platform: A Conceptual Framework. *Sensors (Basel)*, *23*(3), 1399. doi:10.3390/s23031399 PMID:36772437

Machado, C. G., Winroth, M., Carlsson, D., Almström, P., Centerholt, V., & Hallin, M. (2019). Industry 4.0 readiness in manufacturing companies: Challenges and enablers towards increased digitalization. *Procedia CIRP*, *81*, 1113–1118. doi:10.1016/j.procir.2019.03.262

Machado, H. P. V. (2016). Growth of small businesses: A literature review and perspectives of studies. *Gestão & Produção*, *23*, 419–432. doi:10.1590/0104-530x1759-14

Macht, S. A., & Weatherston, J. (2014). The benefits of online crowdfunding for fund-seeking business ventures. *Strategic Change, 23*(1-2), 1–14. doi:10.1002/jsc.1955

Madau, F. A., Arru, B., Furesi, R., & Pulina, P. (2020). Insect farming for feed and food production from a circular business model perspective. *Sustainability (Basel), 12*(13), 5418. doi:10.3390/su12135418

Maheshkar, C., & Soni, N. (2021). Problems Faced by Indian Micro, Small and Medium Enterprises (MSMEs). *SEDME (Small Enterprises Development, Management & Extension Journal), 48*(2), 142-159.

Makaci, M., Reaidy, P., Evrard-Samuel, K., Botta-Genoulaz, V., & Monteiro, T. (2017). Pooled warehouse management: An empirical study. *Computers & Industrial Engineering, 112*, 526–536. doi:10.1016/j.cie.2017.03.005

Malhotra, M. (2007). *Expanding access to finance: Good practices and policies for micro, small, and medium enterprises.* World Bank Publications. doi:10.1596/978-0-8213-7177-0

Malik, A., Teal, F., & Baptist, S. (2006). Performance of Nigerian Manufacturing Firms: Report on the Nigerian Manufacturing Enterprise Survey. United Nations Industrial Development Organization (UNIDO), Nigerian Federal Ministry of Industry and Centre for the Study of African Economies, Department of Economics, University of Oxford, United Kingdom.

Mamman, A., Bawole, J., Agbebi, M., & Alhassan, A. R. (2019). SME policy formulation and implementation in Africa: Unpacking assumptions as opportunity for research direction. *Journal of Business Research, 97*, 304–315. doi:10.1016/j.jbusres.2018.01.044

Mandal, K. C. (2013, May). Concept and Types of Women Empowerments. In *International Forum of Teaching & Studies, 9*(2).

Mannan, M. B. A., & Sultana, D. (2021). *Agricultural Productivity in Bangladesh and Green Revolution: Where Are We Heading?* LightCastle Analytics Wing. https://www.lightcastlebd.com/insights/2021/08/agricultural-productivity-in-bangladesh-and-green-revolution-where-are-we-heading-3/

Martikkala, A., David, J., Lobov, A., Lanz, M., & Ituarte, I. F. (2021). Trends for low-cost and open-source iot solutions development for Industry 4.0. *Procedia Manufacturing, 55*, 298–305. doi:10.1016/j.promfg.2021.10.042

Martin, N. L., Dér, A., Herrmann, C., & Thiede, S. (2020). Assessment of smart manufacturing solutions based on extended value stream mapping. *Procedia CIRP, 93*, 371-376. . doi:10.1016/j.procir.2020.04.019

Martucci, O., Acampora, A., Arcese, G., & Poponi, S. (2020). The Development of Smart Tourism Destinations Through the Integration of ICT Innovations in SMEs of the Commercial Sector: Practical Experience from Central Italy. In *Handbook of Research on Smart Territories and Entrepreneurial Ecosystems for Social Innovation and Sustainable Growth* (pp. 124–151). IGI Global. doi:10.4018/978-1-7998-2097-0.ch008

Marzuki, S. Z. S., Osman, C. A., Buyong, S. Z., & Zreik, M. (2021). Design Thinking Mini Project Approach Using Factor Analysis. *Environment-Behaviour Proceedings Journal, 6*(17), 93–98. doi:10.21834/ebpj.v6i17.2797

Masarira, S., & Msweli, P. (2013). The role of SMEs in national economies: the case of South Africa. *Economic and Social Development: Book of Proceedings*, 1484.

Matshe, I. (2009). Boosting smallholder production for food security: Some approaches and evidence from studies in sub-Saharan Africa. *Agrekon, 48*(4), 483–511. doi:10.1080/03031853.2009.9523837

Mauro, P. (2017, May 04). Emerging economy consumers drive infrastructure needs. *IMF Blog.* IMF. https://www.imf.org/en/Blogs/Articles/2017/05/04/emerging-economy-consumers-drive-infrastructure-needs

Mazurek, G. (2019). *Transformacja cyfrowa. Perspektywa marketing (The Digital Transformation. A Marketing Outlook)*. Warszawa PWN.

Mazzarol, T. (2015). SMEs engagement with e-commerce, e-business and e-marketing. *Small Enterprise Research*, *22*(1), 79–90. doi:10.1080/13215906.2015.1018400

McKenzie, D., & Sakho, Y. S. (2010). Does it pay firms to register for taxes? The impact of formality on firm profitability. *Journal of Development Economics*, *91*(1), 15–24. doi:10.1016/j.jdeveco.2009.02.003

McKillop, D. G., & Wilson, J. O. S. (2015). Credit Unions as Cooperative Institutions: Distinctiveness, Performance and Prospects. *Social and Environmental Accountability Journal*, *35*(2), 96–112. doi:10.1080/0969160X.2015.1022195

Mckinsey (2013). *Manufacturing the future: The next era of global growth*. McKinsey. www.mckinsey.com/.../our-insights/the-future-of-manufacturing (Accessed 12 November, 2015).

McKinsey. (2016). *Why customer analytics matter*. McKinsey Global Institute.

McPeak, J. G., Little, P. D., & Doss, C. R. (2011). *Risk and social change in an African rural economy: livelihoods in pastoralist communities*. Routledge Taylor & Francis. doi:10.4324/9780203805824

Mechman, A., Omar, S. S., Hamawandy, N. M., Abdullah, A. S., & Qader, A. N. (2022). The Effect of Digital Marketing, And E-Commence on SMEs performance of Baghdad. *Journal of Positive School Psychology*, *6*(3), 4197–4212.

Medic, N., Anisic, Z., Tasic, N., Zivlak, N., & Lalic, B. (2020). Technology Adoption in the Industry 4.0 Era: Empirical Evidence from Manufacturing Companies. *IFIP Advances in Information and Communication Technology, 591 IFIP*, 115–122.

Meierhofer, J., Benedech, R. A., Schweiger, L., Barbieri, C., & Rapaccini, M. (2022, February). Quantitative modelling of the value of data for manufacturing SMEs in smart service provision. *In 12th International Conference on Exploring Service Science*, (p. 04001). EDP Sciences. 10.1051/itmconf/20224104001

Mei, Y., Mao, D., Lu, Y., & Chu, W. (2020). Effects and mechanisms of rural E-commerce clusters on households' entrepreneurship behavior in China. *Growth and Change*, *51*(4), 1588–1610. doi:10.1111/grow.12424

Melo, S. C., Queiroz, G. A., & Junior, P. A. (2023). Sustainable digital transformation in small and medium enterprises (SMEs): A review on performance. *Heliyon*, *9*(3), e13908. doi:10.1016/j.heliyon.2023.e13908 PMID:36915489

Mercan, S., Cain, L., Akkaya, K., Cebe, M., Uluagac, S., Alonso, M., & Cobanoglu, C. (2021). Improving the service industry with hyper-connectivity: IoT in hospitality. *International Journal of Contemporary Hospitality Management*, *33*(1), 243–262. doi:10.1108/IJCHM-06-2020-0621

Miah, M. D., Hasan, R., & Uddin, H. (2020). Agricultural development and the rural economy: The case of Bangladesh. Bangladesh's Economic and Social Progress, 237-66. Modeling the expansion of agricultural markets. *Montenegrin Journal of Economics*, *18*(2), 127–141.

Migilinskas, D., Popov, V., Juocevicius, V., & Ustinovichius, L. (2013). The Benefits, Obstacles and Problems of Practical Bim Implementation. *Procedia Engineering*, *57*, 767–774. doi:10.1016/j.proeng.2013.04.097

Miller, J. L. (2010). Sustainability: Is It a Good Choice for Small Companies?. *Inquiries Journal, 2*(10).

Minto-Coy, I. D., Cowell, N. M., & McLeod, M. (2016). Introduction: Breaking the barriers: Entrepreneurship, enterprise, competitiveness and growth in the Caribbean. *Social and Economic Studies*, *65*(2–3), 1–13.

Mishra, R., & Shukla, A. (2015). Counterfeit Purchase Intentions Among College Students: An Empirical Investigation. In S. Chatterjee, N. P. Singh, D. P. Goyal, & N. Gupta (Eds.), *Managing in Recovering Markets*. Springer. doi:10.1007/978-81-322-1979-8_16

Mizik, T. (2023). How can precision farming work on a small scale? A systematic literature review. *Precision Agriculture*, *24*(1), 384–406. doi:10.1007/s11119-022-09934-y

Mkhize, S., Dube, S., & Skinner, C. (2013). Stre*et Vendors in Durban, South Africa*. South Africa: Women in informal Employment: Globalizing and Organizing (WIEGO).

Mohammed, A. H. A. (2022). SMEs' sustainable development challenges post-COVID-19: The tourism sector. *World Journal of Entrepreneurship, Management and Sustainable Development*, *18*(3), 407–424.

Mokoena, S. L., &Liambo, T. F. (2023). The sustainability of township tourism SMMEs. *International Journal of Research in Business and Social Science (2147-4478), 12*(1), 341-349.

Molina, M. Y. S., Espinoza, L. C. G., & Tarabó, A. E. M. (2021). Small businesses like a sign of innovation and sustainable development in the community tourism centers in Santa Elena. In *Innovation and Entrepreneurial Opportunities in Community Tourism* (pp. 15–36). IGI Global.

Mont, O., Curtis, S. K., & Palgan, Y. V. (2021). Organisational response strategies to COVID-19 in the sharing economy. *Sustainable Production and Consumption*, *28*, 52–70. doi:10.1016/j.spc.2021.03.025 PMID:34786447

Morelli, G., Magazzino, C., Gurrieri, A. R., Pozzi, C., & Mele, M. (2022). Designing Smart Energy Systems in an Industry 4.0 Paradigm towards Sustainable Environment. *Sustainability (Basel)*, *14*(6), 3315. doi:10.3390/su14063315

Morkovina, S. S., Malitskaya, V., Panyavina, E. A., & Sibiryatkina, I. (2018). *Export potential and measures to support small and medium-sized enterprises*. Research Gate.

Mottaeva, A., & Gritsuk, N. (2017). Development of infrastructure of support of small and medium business. In *MATEC Web of Conferences* (*Vol. 106*, p. 08083). EDP Sciences. 10.1051/matecconf/201710608083

Mourtzis, D., Angelopoulos, J., & Panopoulos, N. (2022). Development of a PSS for smart grid energy distribution optimization based on digital twin. *Procedia CIRP*, *107*, 1138–1143. doi:10.1016/j.procir.2022.05.121

Moyi, E. D. (2003). Networks, information and small enterprises: New technologies and the ambiguity of empowerment. *Information Technology for Development*, *10*(4), 221–232. doi:10.1002/itdj.1590100402

Moyo, B. (2022). Factors affecting the probability of formalizing informal sector activities in Sub-Saharan Africa: Evidence from World Bank enterprise surveys. *African Journal of Economic and Management Studies*, *13*(3), 480–507. doi:10.1108/AJEMS-06-2021-0304

Mrabet, H., Belguith, S., Alhomoud, A., & Jemai, A. (2020). A survey of IoT security based on a layered architecture of sensing and data analysis. *Sensors (Basel)*, *20*(13), 3625. doi:10.3390/s20133625 PMID:32605178

Mubarak, M. F., Shaikh, F. A., Mubarik, M., Samo, K. A., & Mastoi, S. (2019). The Impact of Digital Transformation on Business Performance. Engineering, Technology &. *Applied Scientific Research*, *9*(6), 5056–5061.

Muchichwa, N. (2017). *Decent work in the informal economy: towards formalisation of the informal economy*. Labour and Economic Development Research Institute of Zimbabwe (LEDRIZ) / Friedrich-Ebert-Stiftung (FES). https://library.fes.de/pdf-files/bueros/simbabwe/13742.pdf

Mugisha, H., Omagwa, J., & Kilika, J. (2020). Short-Term Debt and Financial Performance of Small and Medium Scale Enterprises in Buganda Region, Uganda. *International Journal of Finance & Banking Studies, 9*(4), 58–69. doi:10.20525/ijfbs.v9i4.910

Müller, J. M., & Voigt, K. I. (2018). Sustainable industrial value creation in SMEs: A comparison between industry 4.0 and made in China 2025. *International Journal of Precision Engineering and Manufacturing-Green Technology, 5*(5), 659–670. doi:10.1007/s40684-018-0056-z

Muske, G., & Woods, M. (2004). Micro businesses as an economic development tool: What they bring and what they need. *Community Development (Columbus, Ohio), 35*(1), 97–116.

Mutula, S. M., & Brakel, P. V. (2007). ICT skills readiness for the emerging global digital economy among the SMEs in developing economies: Case study of Botswana. *Library Hi Tech News*, (25), 231–245. doi:10.1108/07378830710754992

Mzini, L., & Lukamba-Muhiya, T. (2014). An assessment of electricity supply and demand at Emfuleni Local Municipality. *Journal of Energy in Southern Africa, 25*(3), 20–26. doi:10.17159/2413-3051/2014/v25i3a2654

Naidoo, V. (2021). SME sustainability in South Africa post-COVID-19. In *Handbook of Research on Sustaining SMEs and Entrepreneurial Innovation in the Post-COVID-19 Era* (pp. 419–437). IGI Global. doi:10.4018/978-1-7998-6632-9.ch020

Narula, R. (2020). Policy opportunities and challenges from the COVID-19 pandemic for economies with large informal sectors. *Journal of International Business Policy, 3*(3), 302–310. doi:10.1057/s42214-020-00059-5

Ndou, V., Secundo, G., Schiuma, G., & Passiante, G. (2018). Insights for shaping entrepreneurship education: Evidence from the European entrepreneurship centers. *Sustainability (Basel), 10*(11), 4323. doi:10.3390/su10114323

New Zealand Tourism Strategy Group. (2007). *New Zealand Tourism Strategy 2015*. Ministry of Tourism.

Newberry, D. (2006). *The Role of Small and Medium-Sized Enterprises in the Futures of Emerging Economies*. Earth Trends. http://earthtrends.wri.org/features/view

Ngida, S. (2023). *Community Engagement: How Businesses can foster Local Impact*. LinkedIn. https://www.linkedin.com/pulse/community-engagement-how-businesses-can-foster-positive-ngida/

Ng, K. K., Chen, C. H., Lee, C. K., Jiao, J. R., & Yang, Z. X. (2021). A systematic literature review on intelligent automation: Aligning concepts from theory, practice, and future perspectives. *Advanced Engineering Informatics, 47*, 101246. doi:10.1016/j.aei.2021.101246

Niazi, T., Cole, R., Lee, L., Kim, S. S., & Han, J. (2021, December 11). *Public Lending Schemes for SMEs in Asia and the Pacific: Lessons from the Republic of Korea and the United States*. ADB. https://www.adb.org/sites/default/files/publication/753586/adb-brief-201-lending-smes-asia-pacific-lessons-rok-usa.pdf

Nieto, M. J., & Santamaria, L. (2010). Technological collaboration: Bridging the innovation gap between small and large firms. *Journal of Small Business Management, 48*(1), 44–69. doi:10.1111/j.1540-627X.2009.00286.x

Nikhashemi, S. R., Knight, H. H., Nusair, K., & Liat, C. B. (2021). Augmented reality in smart retailing: A (n)(A) Symmetric Approach to continuous intention to use retail brands' mobile AR apps. *Journal of Retailing and Consumer Services, 60*, 102464. doi:10.1016/j.jretconser.2021.102464

Nimawat, D., & Gidwani, B. D. (2021). Identification of cause-and-effect relationships among barriers of Industry 4.0 using decision-making trial and evaluation laboratory method. *Benchmarking, 28*(8), 2407–2431. doi:10.1108/BIJ-08-2020-0429

NIRP. (2014). *Nigeria Industrial Revolution Plan*. NIRP. http://www.nepza.gov.ng/downloads/nirp.pdf

Noreen, A. (2022). *6 Benefits of small businesses in community development.* Read Write. https://readwrite.com/benefits-of-small-businesses-in-a-community/

Norman, F. (2020). Key Factors to Promote Industry 4.0 Readiness at Indonesian Textile and Clothing Firm. *Engineering, MAthematics and Computer Science (EMACS). Journal, 2*(2), 73–83.

North, K., Aramburu, N., & Lorenzo, O. J. (2019). Promoting digitally enabled growth in SMEs: A framework proposal. *Journal of Enterprise Information Management, 33*(1), 238–262. doi:10.1108/JEIM-04-2019-0103

Nwosa, P. I., & Oseni, I. O. (2013). The Impact of Banks Loan to SMEs on Manufacturing Output in Nigeria. *Journal of Social and Development Sciences, 4*(5), 212–217. doi:10.22610/jsds.v4i5.754

O'Connor, C., & Joffe, H. (2020). Intercoder reliability in qualitative research: Debates and practical guidelines. *International Journal of Qualitative Methods, 19*, 1–13. doi:10.1177/1609406919899220

O'Flynn, J. (2020). Confronting the big challenges of our time: Making a difference during and after. *COVID, 19.* https://www.tandfonline.com/doi/full/10.1080/14719037.2020.1820273

O'Regan, N., & Ghobadian, A. (2006). Perceptions of generic strategies of small and medium sized engineering and electronics manufacturers in the UK. *Journal of Manufacturing Technology Management, 17*(5), 603–620. doi:10.1108/17410380610668540

Ocheni, S. I., & Gemade, T. I. (2015). *Effects of Multiple Taxation on the Performance of Small and Medium Scale Business Enterprises in Benue State International Journal of Academic Research in Business and Social Sciences, 5*(3), 345–364.

Oda Abunamous, M., Boudouaia, A., Jebril, M., Diafi, S., & Zreik, M. (2022). The decay of traditional education: A case study under covid-19. *Cogent Education, 9*(1), 2082116. doi:10.1080/2331186X.2022.2082116

Odili, O. (2014). Exchange Rate and Balance of Payment: An Autoregressive Distributed Lag (Ardl). *Econometric Investigation on Nigeria Journal of Economics and Finance, 4*(6), 21–30.

Oduyoye, O. O., Adebola, S. A., & Binuyo, A. O. (2013). Empirical study of infrastructure support and small business growth in Ogun state, Nigeria. *Journal of Research and Development (Srinagar), 1*(1), 14–22.

OECD. (2017). *Enhancing the Contributions of SMEs in a Global and Digitalised Economy.* OECD. https://www.oecd.org/industry/C-MIN-2017-8-EN.pdf

OECD. (2019). *Small, Medium, Strong.* Trends in SME Performance and Business Conditions.

OECD. (2019, September 16) *"Access to Finance". SME and Entrepreneurship Outlook.* OECD. https://www.oecd-ilibrary.org/sites/8082995b-en/index.html?itemId=/content/component/8082995b

OECD. (2020). *Tourism Policy Responses to the Coronavirus (COVID-19).* Pandemic.

OECD. (2020, December 11). *Key Facts on SMEs Financing-Korea.* OECD. https://www.oecd-ilibrary.org/sites/9fd590e7-en/index.html?itemId=/content/component/9fd590e7-en

OECD. (2021a, September 20). *The SME Financing Gap:Theory and Evidence.* OECD. https://www.oecd-ilibrary.org/finance-and-investment/the-sme-financing-gap-vol-i_9789264029415-en#:~:text=The%20lack%20of%20funding%20available,countries%20and%20non%2DOECD%20economies

OECD. (2021b, September 19). *Business Insights on Emerging Markets 2021. OECD Emerging Markets Network*, OECD Development Centre, Paris. https://www.oecd.org/dev/oecdemnet.htm

OECD. (2022, December 7). *Financing SMEs and Entrepreneurs 2022: An OECD Scoreboard.* OECD.

OECD. (2023, September 20). *Financing SMEs and Entrepreneurs 2020:An OECD Scoreboard.* OECD. https://www. oecd-ilibrary.org/sites/9fd590e7-en/index.html?itemId=/content/component/9fd590e7-en#wrapper

Ogawa, K., & Tanaka, T. (2012). The global financial crisis and small- and medium-sized enterprises in Japan: How did they cope with the crisis? *Small Business Economics, 41*(2), 401–417. doi:10.1007/s11187-012-9434-z

Ogboru, P. L. (2005). *An Evaluation of Funding Arrangements for Small and Medium Scale Enterprises (SMEs) in Nigeria.* [PhD Dissertation, St Clements University].

Ojo, O. (2009) Impact of microfinance on entrepreneurial development: the case of nigeria. *The International Conference on Economics and Administration.* University of Bucharest, Romania. <http://www.itchannel.ro/faa/536_pdf-sam_ICEA_FAA_2009.pdf>

Oke, A. (2013). Linking manufacturing flexibility to innovation performance in manufacturing plants. *International Journal of Production Economics, 143*(2), 242–247. doi:10.1016/j.ijpe.2011.09.014

Okkonen, P., Hyysalo, J., & Peltonen, E. (2020, April). Public and Open Internet of Things for Smart Cities: The SME Perspective. *In 2020 IEEE 36th International Conference on Data Engineering Workshops (ICDEW)* (pp. 48-55). IEEE. 10.1109/ICDEW49219.2020.000-8

Okpara, J. O. (2011). Factors constraining the growth and survival of SMEs in Nigeria: Implications for poverty alleviation. *Management Research Review, 34*(2), 156–171. doi:10.1108/01409171111102786

Okungu, V. R., & McIntyre, D. (2019). Does the informal sector in Kenya have financial potential to sustainably prepay for health care? Implications for financing universal health coverage in low-income settings. *Health Systems and Reform, 5*(2), 145–157. doi:10.1080/23288604.2019.1583492 PMID:30924731

Olapade, M. (2015). *Microfinance and Formalization of Enterprises in the Informal Sector.* (Working Paper No, 62). ILO.

Olayinka, O., & Wynn, M. G. (2022). Digital transformation in the Nigerian small business sector. In Handbook of Research on Digital Transformation, Industry Use Cases, and the Impact of Disruptive Technologies (pp. 359-382). IGI Global. doi:10.4018/978-1-7998-7712-7.ch019

Olugbenga, T. K., Jumah, A. A., & Phillips, D. A. (2013). The Current and Future Challenges of Electricity Market in Nigeria in the face of Deregulation Process [March.]. *American Journal of Engineering Research, 1*(2), 33–39.

Omrani, N., Rejeb, N., Maalaoui, A., Dabi, M., & Kraus, S. (2022). Drivers of Digital Transformation in SMEs. *IEEE Transactions on Engineering Management.*

Oncioiu, I. (2012). Small and medium enterprises' access to financing – A European concern: Evidence from Romanian SME. *International Business Research, 5*(8). doi:10.5539/ibr.v5n8p47

Onourah, P. (2009). *The role of Small and Medium Sized Enterprises for Economic Growth: A Case Study of Matori LGA in Lagos, Nigeria.* [Master's Thesis, School of Management, Blekinge Institute of Technology].

Onugu, B. A. N. (2005). *Small and medium enterprises (SMEs) in Nigeria: Problems and Challenges.* [PhD Thesis, St. Clements's University]. https://www.stclements.edu/grad/gradonug.pdf

Opazo-Basáez, M., Vendrell-Herrero, F., & Bustinza, O. F. (2022). Digital service innovation: A paradigm shift in technological innovation. *Journal of Service Management, 33*(1), 97–120. doi:10.1108/JOSM-11-2020-0427

O'Regan N, Ghobadian A, Sims M. (2006). *Fast tracking innovation in manufacturing.* Research Gate.

Orhan, M., & Scott, D. (2001). Why women enter into entrepreneurship: An explanatory model. *Women in Management Review, 16*(5), 232–247. doi:10.1108/09649420110395719

Ortiz-de-Mandojana, N., & Bansal, P. (2016). The long-term benefits of organizational resilience through sustainable business practices. *Strategic Management Journal, 37*(8), 1615–1631. doi:10.1002/smj.2410

Osabohien, R., Worgwu, H., & al-Faryan, M. A. S. (2023). Social entrepreneurship, technology diffusion and future employment in Nigeria. *Social Enterprise Journal, 19*(1), 40–50. doi:10.1108/SEJ-03-2022-0032

Oseni, M. O. (2012). Power Outages and the Costs of Unsupplied Electricity: Evidence from Backup Generation among Firms in Africa. *Proceedings of the USAEE 2012.* Austin: Internation Association of Energy Economics. USAEE. https://www.usaee.org/usaee2012/submissions/OnlineProceedings/IEE%20PAPER%20FRST%20YEAR%20EDITED%20LAST%201%20LATEST.pdf

Osmundsen, K., Iden, J., & Bygstad, B. (2018). Digital transformation: Drivers, success factors, and implications. In *Proceedings of the MCIS 2018*, Corfu, Greece.

Owen, B. M., Sun, S., & Zheng, W. (2008). China's competition policy reforms: The anti-monopoly law and beyond. *Antitrust Law Journal, 75*(1), 231–265.

Ozili, P. K. (2022). Sustainability and sustainable development research around the world. *Managing Global Transitions, 20*(3). doi:10.26493/1854-6935.20.259-293

Pagani, M., & Pardo, C. (2017). The Impact of Digital Technology on Relationships in a Business Network. *Industrial Marketing Management, 67*(2), 185–192. doi:10.1016/j.indmarman.2017.08.009

Paiola, M. (2017). Digitalization and servitization: opportunities and challenges for Italian SMES. Sinergie italian journal of management, 36(107).

Pandya, V. M. (2012, September). Comparative analysis of development of SMEs in developed and developing countries. In *The 2012 International Conference on Business and Management* (*Vol. 6*, No. 7, pp. 1-20).

Pan, H., Kang, M., & Ha, H. (2017). Do trade area grades really affect credit ratings of small businesses? An application of big data. *Management Decision, 55*(9), 2038–2052. doi:10.1108/MD-11-2016-0834

Pansiri, J., & Temtime, Z. T. (2008). Assessing managerial skills in SMEs for capacity building. *Journal of Management Development, 27*(2), 251–260. doi:10.1108/02621710810849362

Pantano, E., & Dennis, C. (2019). *Smart retailing.* Springer International Publishing., doi:10.1007/978-3-030-12608-7

Pappas, N., Caputo, A., Pellegrini, M. M., Marzi, G., & Michopoulou, E. (2021). The complexity of decision-making processes and IoT adoption in accommodation SMEs. *Journal of Business Research, 131*, 573–583. doi:10.1016/j.jbusres.2021.01.010

Pardiman, J. (2022), Impact of financial capital, social capital, and business digitalization on business sustainability of SMEs in Indonesia. Journal Manajemen dan Pemasaran Jasa, 15(1).

Parker, G. G., Van Alstyne, M. W., & Choudary, S. P. (2016). *Platform revolution: How networked markets are transforming the economy and how to make them work for you.* WW Norton & Company.

Parmar, J. K., & Desai, A. (2016). IoT: Networking technologies and research challenges. *International Journal of Computer Applications, 154*(7), 1–6. doi:10.5120/ijca2016912181

Parrott, W. (2023, September 20) *What is an SME?* Acca Global. https://www.accaglobal.com/gb/en/student/exam-support-resources/fundamentals-exams-study-resources/f9/technical-articles/sme-finance.html Accessed 18/09/2023

Parschau, C., & Hauge, J. (2020). Is automation stealing manufacturing jobs? Evidence from South Africa's apparel industry. *Geoforum, 115*(July), 120–131. doi:10.1016/j.geoforum.2020.07.002

Pendleton, E. (2013). *The advantages of doing business in an emerging market*. Chron. https://smallbusiness.chron.com/advantages-doingbusiness-emerging-market-22717.html

Penz, E., Schlegemilch, B. B., & Stottinger, B. (2009). Voluntary Purchase of Counterfeit Products: Empirical Evidence from Four Countries. *Journal of International Consumer Marketing*, *21*(1), 67–84. doi:10.1080/08961530802125456

Perifanis, N. A., & Kitsios, F. (2023). Investigating the influence of artificial intelligence on business value in the digital era of strategy: A literature review. *Information (Basel)*, *14*(2), 85. doi:10.3390/info14020085

Perks, S., & Smith, E. E. (2008). Focused training programmes for solving growth problems of very small businesses. *Acta Commercii*, *8*(1), 145–159. doi:10.4102/ac.v8i1.77

Pham, Q. H., & Vu, K. P. (2022). Digitalization in small and medium enterprise: A parsimonious model of digitalization of accounting information for sustainable innovation ecosystem value generation. *Asia Pacific Journal of Innovation and Entrepreneurship*, *16*(1), 2–37. doi:10.1108/APJIE-02-2022-0013

Pham, T. T. T., Nguyen, T. V. H., Nguyen, S. K., & Nguyen, H. T. H. (2023). Does planned innovation promote financial access? Evidence from Vietnamese SMEs. *Eurasian Business Review*, *13*(2), 281–307. doi:10.1007/s40821-023-00238-3

Philbin, S., Viswanathan, R., & Telukdarie, A. (2022). Understanding how digital transformation can enable SMEs to achieve sustainable development: A systematic literature review. *Small Business International Review*, *6*(1), e473. doi:10.26784/sbir.v6i1.473

Philipp, R., Prause, G., & Gerlitz, L. (2019). Blockchain and smart contracts for entrepreneurial collaboration in maritime supply chains. *Transport and Telecommunication Journal*, *20*(4), 365-378. doi:10.2478/ttj-2019-0030

Phonthanukitithaworn, C., Srisathan, W. A., Ketkaew, C., & Naruetharadhol, P. (2023). Sustainable development towards openness SME innovation: Taking advantage of intellectual capital, sustainable initiatives, and open innovation. *Sustainability (Basel)*, *15*(3), 2126. doi:10.3390/su15032126

Ponmani, R. (2011). Infrastructure and SMEs development in selected Asian countries. *Asian Journal of Research in Social Sciences and Humanities*, *1*(4), 465–473.

Popović, J., Dudas, I., Milošević, D., & Luković, J. (2022). Digital Transformation as a chance for Small Business Development. *International Journal of Management Trends: Key Concepts and Research*, *1*(1), 29–38. doi:10.58898/ijmt.v1i1.29-38

Powell, T. C., & Baker, T. (2014). Learning from Crises: How Governance and Relationships Affect Innovation During Industry Downturns. *Strategic Management Journal*, *35*(7), 1054–1073.

Pradhan, P., Nigam, D., & Ck, T. (2018). Digital marketing and SMES: An identification of research gap via archives of past research. *Journal of Internet Banking and Commerce*, *23*(1), 1–14.

Pradhan, R. P., Arvin, M. B., Nair, M., & Bennett, S. E. (2020). The dynamics among entrepreneurship, innovation, and economic growth in the Eurozone countries. *Journal of Policy Modeling*, *42*(5), 1106–1122. doi:10.1016/j.jpolmod.2020.01.004

Pray, C. E. (2010). The economics of agricultural research in Bangladesh. *Bangladesh Journal of Agricultural Economics, 2*(454-2016-36693), 01-34.

Prayag, G., Hosany, S., & Odeh, K. (2013). The role of tourists' emotional experiences and satisfaction in understanding behavioral intentions. *Journal of Destination Marketing & Management*, *2*(2), 118–127. doi:10.1016/j.jdmm.2013.05.001

Priatmoko, S., Kabil, M., Akaak, A., Lakner, Z., Gyuricza, C., & Dávid, L. D. (2023). Understanding the Complexity of Rural Tourism Business: Scholarly Perspective. *Sustainability (Basel)*, *2023*(15), 1193. doi:10.3390/su15021193

Qian, Y. (2008). Impacts of Entry by Counterfeiters. *The Quarterly Journal of Economics*, 123–124.

Qiu, D., Lin, P. M., Feng, S. Y., Peng, K. L., & Fan, D. (2020). The future of Airbnb in China: Industry perspective from hospitality leaders. *Tourism Review*, *75*(4), 609–624. doi:10.1108/TR-02-2019-0064

Quatraro, F., & Vivarelli, M. (2015). Drivers of entrepreneurship and post-entry performance of newborn firms in developing countries. *The World Bank Research Observer*, *30*(2), 277–305. doi:10.1093/wbro/lku012

Quinton, S., Canhoto, A., Molinillo, S., Pera, R., & Budhathoki, T. (2017). Conceptualising a digital orientation: Antecedents of supporting SME performance in the digital economy. *Journal of Strategic Marketing*, 1–13.

Rahman, M. M., Dana, L. P., Moral, I. H., Anjum, N., & Rahaman, M. S. (2022). Challenges of rural women entrepreneurs in Bangladesh to survive their family entrepreneurship: a narrative inquiry through storytelling. *Journal of Family Business Management*.

Rahman, M. (2017). Role of agriculture in Bangladesh economy: Uncovering the problems and challenges. *International Journal of Business and Management Invention*, *6*(7).

Rahman, S. (2001). A comparative study of TQM practice and organisational performance of SMEs with and without ISO 900 certification. *International Journal of Quality & Reliability Management*, *8*(1), 35–49. doi:10.1108/02656710110364486

Rahmatullah, I., & Sahade, N., Azis, F., & Bahri. (2020). Utilization of digital technology for management effectiveness micro small and medium enterprises. *International Journal of Scientific and Technology Research*, *9*(4), 1357–1362.

Rahmawati, R., Handayani, S. R., Suprapti, A. R., Airawaty, D., & Latifah, L. (2023). Green Entrepreneurship Based on Local Characteristics and Culture to Support Sustainable Eco-Tourism: A Case Study. *Journal of Intercultural Communication*, *23*(1), 66–75. doi:10.36923/jicc.v23i1.71

Raihana, B. (2012). Trend in Productivity research in Bangladesh Agriculture: A Review of selected Articles. *Asian Business Review*, *1*(1), 1–4. doi:10.18034/abr.v1i1.136

Raj, A., Dwivedi, G., Sharma, A., Lopes de Sousa Jabbour, A. B., & Rajak, S. (2020). Barriers to the adoption of industry 4.0 technologies in the manufacturing sector: An inter-country comparative perspective. *International Journal of Production Economics*, *224*, 107546. doi:10.1016/j.ijpe.2019.107546

Ramdani, B., Raja, S., & Kryukova, M. (2021). Digital innovation in SMEs: A systematic review, synthesis and research agenda. *Information Technology for Development*.

Ramírez, C., Rojas, A. E., & García, A. (2022). A cold chain logistics with IoT and Blockchain scalable project for SMEs: First phase. *IFAC-PapersOnLine*, *55*(10), 2336–2341. doi:10.1016/j.ifacol.2022.10.057

Ranchhod, V. (2019). *Why is South Africa's unemployment rate so high?* Ground Up. https://www.groundup.org.za/article/why-south-africas-unemployment-rate-so-high/.

Rao, P., Kumar, S., Chavan, M., & Lim, W. M. (2023). A systematic literature review on SME financing: Trends and future directions. *Journal of Small Business Management*, *61*(3), 1247–1277. doi:10.1080/00472778.2021.1955123

Ras, E., Wild, F., Stahl, C., & Baudet, A. (2017). Bridging the skills gap of workers in industry 4.0 by human performance augmentation tools - Challenges and roadmap. *ACM International Conference Proceeding Series, Part F128530*, (pp. 428–432). ACM.

Rauch, E., Vickery, A. R., Brown, C. A., & Matt, D. T. (2020). SME requirements and guidelines for the design of smart and highly adaptable manufacturing systems. *Industry 4.0 for SMEs: Challenges, Opportunities and Requirements*, 39-72. doi:10.1007/978-3-030-25425-4_2

Rawat, P., & Purohit, J. (2019). A Review of Challenges in Implementation of Industry 4.0 in Indian Manufacturing Industry. *International Conference on Recent Trends and Innovation in Engineering, Science & Technology*, (pp. 289–297). ACM.

Raymond, L., & Croteau, A. M. (2006). Enabling the strategic development of SMEs through advanced manufacturing systems: A configurational perspective. *Industrial Management & Data Systems*, *106*(7), 1012–1032. doi:10.1108/02635570610688904

Raynard, P., & Forstater, M. (2002). *Corporate Social Responsibility: Implications for Small and Medium Enterprises in Developing Countries. United Nations Industrial Development Organization.* UNIDO.

Reis, S. M. (2002). Toward a theory of creativity in diverse creative women. *Creativity Research Journal*, *14*(3-4), 305–316. doi:10.1207/S15326934CRJ1434_2

Revell, A., Stokes, D., & Chen, H. (2010). Small businesses and the environment: Turning over a new leaf? *Business Strategy and the Environment*, *19*(5), 273–288. doi:10.1002/bse.628

Richardson, N. P. (2009). Export-oriented populism: Commodities and coalitions in Argentina. *Studies in Comparative International Development*, *44*(3), 228–255. doi:10.1007/s12116-008-9037-5

Ritala, P., Baiyere, A., Hughes, M., & Kraus, S. (2021). Digital strategy implementation: The role of individual entrepreneurial orientation and relational capital [Published by Elsevier Inc.]. *Technological Forecasting and Social Change*, *171*, 171. doi:10.1016/j.techfore.2021.120961

Rivera, R., Amorim, M., & Reis, J. (2021, June). Technological evolution in grocery retail: A systematic literature review. In *2021 16th Iberian Conference on Information Systems and Technologies (CISTI)* (pp. 1-8). IEEE. 10.23919/CISTI52073.2021.9476598

Roberts, H., Cowls, J., Morley, J., Taddeo, M., Wang, V., & Floridi, L. (2021). The Chinese approach to artificial intelligence: An analysis of policy, ethics, and regulation. *AI & Society*, *36*(1), 59–77. doi:10.1007/s00146-020-00992-2

Robinson, K. L., Dassie, W., & Christy, R. D. (2004). Entrepreneurship and small business development as a rural development strategy. *Journal of Rural Social Sciences*, *20*(2), 1.

Rodríguez, A. J. G., Barón, N. J., & Martínez, J. M. G. (2020). Validity of dynamic capabilities in the operation based on new sustainability narratives on nature tourism SMEs and clusters. *Sustainability (Basel)*, *12*(3), 1004. doi:10.3390/su12031004

Rogan, M. & Skinner, C. (2020). The COVID-19 crisis and the South African informal economy. *Locked out of livelihoods and employment. National Income Dynamics Study-Coronavirus Rapid Mobile Survey (NIDS-CRAM)*.

Romanovich, G. L., Romanovich, A. M., Vybornova, V. V., & Nikolayevna, R. V. (2014). Small businesses is a sphere of innovation in the age of globalization. *Journal of Applied Engineering Science*, *12*(4), 297–301. doi:10.5937/jaes12-7155

Rowinski, M. (2022). How Small Businesses Drive The American Economy. *Contribution to the Forbes Business Council*. https://www.forbes.com/sites/forbesbusinesscouncil/2022/03/25/how-small-businesses-drive-the-american-economy/?sh=460a8daa4169

Roy, B. C., & Pal, S. (2002, October-December). Investment, Agricultural Productivity and Rural Poverty in India: A State Level Analysis. *Indian Journal of Agricultural Economics*, *57*(4), 653–678.

Ruben, R., & Van den berg, M. (2001). Nonfarm employment and poverty alleviation of rural farm households in Honduras. *World Development, 29*(3), 549–560. doi:10.1016/S0305-750X(00)00107-8

Rud, J. P. (2012). Electricity Provision and Industrial development: Evidence from India. *Journal of Development Economics, 97*(2), 352–367. doi:10.1016/j.jdeveco.2011.06.010

Ruhanen, L., & Weiler, B. (2010). Authenticity and Small Tourism Business Development in Rural Areas. *Journal of Sustainable Tourism, 18*(3), 367–381.

Rusjan, B. (2006). The impact of a manufacturing focus on manufacturing and business unit performance: an empirical investigation. *Economic and business review, 8*(1), 5-18.

Rustamovna, T. H., & Anvarovich, K. A. (2016). The role of small businesses to improve the export potential. *Academy,* (12 (15)), 21–23.

Ruth Eikhof, D., Summers, J., & Carter, S. (2013). "Women doing their own thing": Media representations of female entrepreneurship. *International Journal of Entrepreneurial Behaviour & Research, 19*(5), 547–564. doi:10.1108/IJEBR-09-2011-0107

S. K. & Chiputwa, B. (2019). Adventure tourism in Nepal: Challenges and opportunities. *Tourism Management Perspectives, 32*, 100569.

Saah, P. (2021). The impact of small and medium-sized enterprises on the economic development of South Africa. *Technium Soc. Sci. J., 24*, 549.

Saban, K. A., Rau, S., & Wood, C. A. (2021). SME executives' perceptions and the information security preparedness model. *Information and Computer Security, 29*(2), 263–282. doi:10.1108/ICS-01-2020-0014

Sachs, J. D. (2015). *The Age of Sustainable Development.* Columbia University Press. doi:10.7312/sach17314

Sahut, J. M., & Peris-Ortiz, M. (2014). Small business, innovation, and entrepreneurship. *Small Business Economics, 42*(4), 663–668. doi:10.1007/s11187-013-9521-9

Saka, A., & Chan, D. (2020). Profound barriers to building information modelling (BIM) adoption in construction small and medium-sized enterprises (SMEs). *Construction Innovation, 20*(2), 261–284. doi:10.1108/CI-09-2019-0087

Saleh, A. S., & Ndubisi, N. O. (2006). An Evaluation of SME Development in Malaysia. *International Review of Business Research Papers, 2*(1), 1–14.

Samantroy, E., & Tomar, J. S. (2018). Women entrepreneurship in India: Evidence from economic censuses. *Social Change, 48*(2), 188–207. doi:10.1177/0049085718768898

Sánchez, J., Pelegrín, A., & Montoro-Sánchez, Á. (2017). Stakeholder Collaboration and Destination Branding. *Annals of Tourism Research, 67*, 125–134.

Sandada, M. (2014). Transition from informality to formality perceptions of informal traders in the Harare Metropolitan Area. *International Journal of Economics. Commerce & Management, 2*(12), 1–11.

Sanni, A (2012). Multiplicity of Taxes in Nigeria: Issues, Problems and Solutions International *Journal of Business and Social Science 17*(3).

Santos-Jaén, J. M., Gimeno-Arias, F., León-Gómez, A., & Palacios-Manzano, M. (2023, September 26). The Business Digitalization Process in SMEs from the Implementation of e-Commerce: An Empirical Analysis. *Journal of Theoretical and Applied Electronic Commerce Research, 18*(4), 1700–1720. doi:10.3390/jtaer18040086

Sarfaraz, L., Faghih, N., & Majd, A. A. (2014). The relationship between women entrepreneurship and gender equality. *Journal of Global Entrepreneurship Research*, 4(1), 1–11. doi:10.1186/2251-7316-2-6

Sarmiento, R., Byrne, M., Contreras, L. R., & Rich, N. (2008). Delivery reliability, manufacturing capabilities and new models of manufacturing efficiency. *Journal of Manufacturing Technology Management*, 18(4), 367–386. doi:10.1108/17410380710743761

Schaller, N. (1993). The concept of agricultural sustainability. *Agriculture, Ecosystems & Environment*, 46(1-4), 89–97. doi:10.1016/0167-8809(93)90016-I

Schoemaker, P. J., Heaton, S., & Teece, D. (2018). Innovation, dynamic capabilities, and leadership. *California Management Review*, 61(1), 15–42. doi:10.1177/0008125618790246

Schroeder, R. G., Flynn, B., & Flynn, E. (2006). *The high-performance manufacturing projects.* (Working Paper) University of Minnesota, Wake Forest University, USA.

Schroeder, C. (2016). The Challenges of Industry 4. 0 for Small and Medium-sized Enterprises. *Friedrich Ebert Foundation*, (August), 1–28.

Scuotto, V., Nicotra, M., Del Giudice, M., Krueger, N., & Gregori, G. L. (2021). A micro foundational perspective on SMEs' growth in the digital transformation era. *Journal of Business Research*, 129, 382–392. doi:10.1016/j.jbusres.2021.01.045

SEDA (Small Enterprise Development Agency). (2018). *Annual report 2017/2018.* Unpublished Report, RP368/2018, Pretoria.

SEDA (Small Enterprise Development Agency). (2019). *SMME Quarterly Update 3rd Quarter 2018.* SEDA. http://www.seda.org.za/Publications/Publications/SMME%20Quarterly,%202018-Q3.pdf

Segal, D. L., Coolidge, F. L., O'Riley, A., & Heinz, B. A. (2006). Structured and semistructured interviews. In M. Hersen (Ed.), *Clinician's handbook of adult behavioral assessment* (pp. 121–144). Elsevier Academic Press. doi:10.1016/B978-012343013-7/50007-0

Serrano, W. (2018). Digital systems in smart city and infrastructure: Digital as a service. *Smart cities, 1*(1), 134-154. doi:10.3390/smartcities1010008

Setia, P., Venkatesh, V., & Joglekar, S. (2013). Leveraging digital technologies: How information quality leads to localized capabilities and customer service performance. *Management Information Systems Quarterly*, 37(2), 565–590. doi:10.25300/MISQ/2013/37.2.11

Setini, M., Yasa, N. N. K., Gede Supartha, I. W., Ketut Giantari, I. G. A., & Rajiani, I. (2020). The passway of women entrepreneurship: Starting from social capital with open innovation, through to knowledge sharing and innovative performance. *Journal of Open Innovation*, 6(2), 25. doi:10.3390/joitmc6020025

Shabbir, M. S., Aslam, E., Irshad, A., Bilal, K., Aziz, S., Abbasi, B. A., & Zia, S. (2020). Nexus between corporate social responsibility and financial and non-financial sectors' performance: A non-linear and disaggregated approach. *Environmental Science and Pollution Research International*, 27(31), 39164–39179. doi:10.1007/s11356-020-09972-x PMID:32642899

Sharafat, A. L. I., Rashid, H., & Khan, M. A. (2014). The role of small and medium enterprises and poverty in Pakistan: An empirical analysis. *Theoretical and Applied Economics*, 18(4), 593.

Sharma, S. K., Ilavarasan, P. V., & Karanasios, S. (2023). Small businesses and FinTech: A systematic review and future directions. *Electronic Commerce Research*, 1–41. doi:10.1007/s10660-023-09705-5

Shields, J., & Shelleman, J. M. (2015). Integrating sustainability into SME strategy. [archive only]. *Journal of Small Business Strategy*, *25*(2), 59–78.

Shin, D. H. (2018). Augmented reality: A new digital marketing tool in tourism. *Journal of Destination Marketing & Management*, *8*, 1–5.

Shin, S. J., Woo, J., & Rachuri, S. (2014). Predictive analytics model for power consumption in manufacturing. *Procedia CIRP*, *15*(December), 153–158. doi:10.1016/j.procir.2014.06.036

Shkolnykova, M., & Kudic, M. (2022). Who benefits from SMEs' radical innovations?—Empirical evidence from German biotechnology. *Small Business Economics*, *58*(2), 1157–1185. doi:10.1007/s11187-021-00464-x

Sigala, M., Christou, E., & Gretzel, U. (2012). *Social Media in Travel, Tourism and Hospitality: Theory, Practice and Cases*. Ashgate Publishing.

Sigismondi, P. (2011). *The digital glocalization of entertainment: New paradigms in the 21st century global mediascape* (Vol. 3). Springer Science & Business Media.

Singh, S. H., Bhowmick, B., Eesley, D., & Sindhav, B. (2021). Grassroots innovation and entrepreneurial success: Is entrepreneurial orientation a missing link? *Technological Forecasting and Social Change*, *164*, 119582. doi:10.1016/j.techfore.2019.02.002

Sisay, E., Atilaw, W., & Adisu, T. (2022). Impact of economic sectors on inflation rate: Evidence from Ethiopia. *Cogent Economics & Finance*, *10*(1), 2123889. doi:10.1080/23322039.2022.2123889

Siu, W. S. (2005). An institutional analysis of marketing practices of small and medium-sized enterprises (SMEs) in China, Hong Kong and Taiwan. *Entrepreneurship and Regional Development*, *17*(1), 65–88. doi:10.1080/08985620052000330306

Śledziewska, K., Gabryelczyk, R., & Włoch, R. (2015). *Go digital! Diagnoza luki w kompetencjach cyfrowych MŚP (Go Digital! Gap Analysis in Digital Competences of SMEs)* (Working paper delab UW, 38).

SMEDAN. (2009). *Small and Medium Enterprise Development Agency of Nigeria*. Small Business in Nigeria.

SMEDAN. (2013). Small and Medium Enterprise Development Agency of Nigeria, Small Business in Nigeria, Abuja. SMEs. *Technovation*, *26*, 251–261.

Smit, W. (2017). *SMMEs contribute 36% to economy*. IOL. https://www.iol.co.za/business-report/entrepreneurs/smmes-contribute-36-to-economy-8269623

Smith, H., Discetti, R., Bellucci, M., & Acuti, D. (2022). SMEs engagement with the sustainable development goals: A power perspective. *Journal of Business Research*, *149*, 112–122. doi:10.1016/j.jbusres.2022.05.021

Smith, V. H., & Glauber, J. W. (2020). Trade, policy, and food security. *Agricultural Economics*, *51*(1), 159–171. doi:10.1111/agec.12547

Soften, K., & Winroth, M. (2002). Analysis of the congruence between manufacturing strategy and production system in SMME. *Computers in Industry*, *49*(1), 91–106. doi:10.1016/S0166-3615(02)00061-1

Song, H., & Li, G. (2008). Tourism demand modelling and forecasting—A review of recent research. *Tourism Management*, *29*(2), 203–220. doi:10.1016/j.tourman.2007.07.016

Songwe, V., & Deininger, K. (2009). *Foreign investment in agricultural production: opportunities and challenges*.

South Africa. (1996). Small Business Act, No, 102 of 1966. South Africa: Pretoria.

Srinamphon, P., Chernbumroong, S., & Tippayawong, K. Y. (2022). The Effect of Small Particulate Matter on Tourism and Related SMEs in Chiang Mai, Thailand. *Sustainability (Basel)*, *14*(13), 8147. doi:10.3390/su14138147

Srivastava, R. K., & Jena, D. (2011). *Manufacturing: A Case Based Approach Process Improvement in Precision Component Manufacturing: A Case Based Approach.* IAENG. https://www.iaeng.org/publication/IMECS2011/IMECS2011_pp1269-1274.pdf

Stark, E., Haffner, O., & Kučera, E. (2022). Low-Cost Method for 3D Body Measurement Based on Photogrammetry Using Smartphone. *Electronics (Basel)*, *11*(7), 1048. doi:10.3390/electronics11071048

Statista. (2023). *Number of small and medium-sized enterprises (SMEs) in South Korea from 2017 to 2020 (in 1,000s).* Statista. https://www.statista.com/statistics/1223066/south-korea-small-and-medium-enterprises-number/#:~:text=In%20 2020%2C%20there%20were%20around,million%20in%20the%20previous%20year

Stats S. A. (2020). *How unequal is South Africa?* StatsSA. https://www.statssa.gov.za/?p=12930 (Accessed 23 September 2022).

Stats, S. A. (2022). *Quarterly Labour Force Survey (QLFS) – Q2:2022.* StatsSA. https://www.statssa.gov.za/?p=15685#:~:text=The%20official%20unemployment%20rate%20was,QLFS)%20for%20Q2%3A%202022. (Accessed 23 January 2023).

Stats, S. A. (2023). Be*yond unemployment – Time-Related Underemployment in the SA labour market.* https://www.statssa.gov.za/?p=16312#:~:text=Quarter%2Dto%2Dquarter%20changes%20indicate,9%25%20in%20Q1%3A2023

Storey, D. J. (2016). *Understanding the small business sector.* Routledge. doi:10.4324/9781315544335

Straková, J., Talíř, M., & Váchal, J. (2022). Opportunities and threats of digital transformation of business models in SMEs. *Economics & Sociology (Ternopil)*, *15*(3), 159–171. doi:10.14254/2071-789X.2022/15-3/9

Stryszowski, P., & Kazimierczak, M. (2016). *Trade in counterfeit and pirated goods mapping the economic impact.* Office for Harmonization in the Internal Market; Organisation for Economic Co-Operation and Development; European Union. https://euipo.europa.eu/tunnel...the.../Mapping_the_Economic_Impact_en.pdf.

Stubblefield Loucks, E., Martens, M. L., & Cho, C. H. (2010). Engaging small-and medium-sized businesses in sustainability. *Sustainability Accounting. Management and Policy Journal*, *1*(2), 178–200.

Sugiura, T., Yamamura, K., Watanabe, Y., Yamakiri, S., & Nakano, N. (2023). Circuits and devices for standalone large-scale integration (LSI) chips and Internet of Things (IoT) applications: A Review. *Chip (Würzburg)*, *100048*(3), 100048. Advance online publication. doi:10.1016/j.chip.2023.100048

Suntikul, W., & Jachna, T. (2016). SME competitiveness in tourism: The role of financial and non-financial support institutions. *Current Issues in Tourism*, *19*(2), 144–161.

Suutari, T., Lähdesmäki, M., & Kurki, S. (2023). Doing well and doing good? Small rural businesses' performance and responsibility towards local communities. *Journal of Rural Studies*, *102*, 103097. doi:10.1016/j.jrurstud.2023.103097

Swamidass, P., & Newell, W. (1987). Manufacturing strategy, environmental uncertainty and performance: A path analytic model. *Management Science*, *33*(4), 509–524. doi:10.1287/mnsc.33.4.509

Swierczek, F. W., & Ha, T. T. (2003). Entrepreneurial orientation, uncertainty avoidance and firm performance: An analysis of Thai and Vietnamese SMEs. *International Journal of Entrepreneurship and Innovation*, *4*(1), 46–58. doi:10.5367/000000003101299393

Tajudeen, F. P., Jaafar, N. I., & Ainin, S. (2018). The impact of social media usage among organizations. *Information & Management*, *55*(3), 308–321. doi:10.1016/j.im.2017.08.004

Tarigan, R. (2005). An evaluation of the relationship between alignment of strategic priorities and manufacturing performance. *International Journal of Management*, *22*(4), 586–597.

Tarutėa, A., & Gatautisa, R. (2013). ICT impact on SMEs performance. Contemporary Issues in Business, Management and Education conference. *Procedia - Social and Behavioral Sciences 110* (2014) 1218 – 1225.

Tarutė, A., Duobienė, J., Klovienė, L., Vitkauskaitė, E., & Varaniūtė, V. (2018). Identifying factors affecting digital transformation of SMEs. In *Proceedings of The 18th International Conference on Electronic Business* (pp. 373- 381). ICEB.

Taslim, M. A., & Taslim, Q. N. (2018). Productivity and Agricultural Real Wage in Bangladesh. *Bangladesh Development Studies*, *XLI*(1), 1–29. doi:10.57138/PAEE5676

Telukdarie, A., Dube, T., Matjuta, P., & Philbin, S. (2023). The opportunities and challenges of digitalization for SME's. *Procedia Computer Science*, *217*, 689–698. doi:10.1016/j.procs.2022.12.265

Teng, X., Wu, Z., & Yang, F. (2022). Research on the Relationship between Digital Transformation and Performance of SMEs. *Sustainability, 14*, 6012.

Teng, X., Wu, Z., & Yang, F. (2022). Research on the Relationship between Digital Transformation and Performance of SMEs. *Sustainability (Basel)*, *14*(10), 6012. doi:10.3390/su14106012

Thaha, A. R.; Maulina, E.; Muftiadi, R. A.; & Alexandri, M. B., (2021). Digital Marketing and SMEs: A Systematic Mapping Study. *Library Philosophy and Practice (e-journal)*, 5113.

Thanetsunthorn, N., & Wuthisatian, R. (2023). Do business-friendly regulations foster corporate social performance? Evidence from 20 emerging market countries. *International Journal of Business and Globalisation*, *34*(2), 219–236. doi:10.1504/IJBG.2023.132801

The Deloitte millennial survey 2018. (2018, July 21). Deloitte Turkey. https://www2.deloitte.com/tr/en/pages/about-deloitte/articles/millennialsurvey-2018.html

The World Bank. (2023). *Small and Medium Enterprises Finance*. The World Bank. https://www.worldbank.org/en/topic/smefinance

Thirtle, C., Irz, X., Lin, L., McKenzie-Hill, V., & Wiggins, S. (2001). Relationship between changes in agricultural productivity and the incidence of poverty in developing countries. Report commissioned by the Department for International Development, London.

Thompson, A. R., Smith, J. A., & Larkin, M. (2011, June). Interpretative phenomenological analysis and clinical psychology training: Results from a survey of the group of trainers in clinical psychology. *Clinical Psychology Forum*, *1*(222), 15–19. doi:10.53841/bpscpf.2011.1.222.15

Thukral, E. (2021). COVID-19: Small and medium enterprises challenges and responses with creativity, innovation, and entrepreneurship. *Strategic Change*, *30*(2), 153–158. doi:10.1002/jsc.2399

Tien, N. H., Hiep, P. M., Dai, N. Q., Duc, N. M., & Hong, T. T. K. (2020). Green entrepreneurship understanding in Vietnam. *International Journal of Entrepreneurship*, *24*(2), 1–14.

Tierno, P. (2019, July 29). *Can Korea Move Beyond Government-Backed Small Business Lending?* FRBSF. https://www.frbsf.org/banking/asia-program/pacific-exchange-blog/beyond-small-business-lending-korea/

Timmer, C. P. (2002). Agriculture and economic development. Handbook of agricultural economics, 2, 1487-1546.

295

Tlaiss, H. A., & McAdam, M. (2021). Unexpected lives: The intersection of Islam and Arab women's entrepreneurship. *Journal of Business Ethics*, *171*(2), 253–272. doi:10.1007/s10551-020-04437-0

Treadwell, J. (2011). From the car boot to booting it up? eBay, online counterfeit crime and the transformation of the criminal marketplace. *Criminology & Criminal Justice*, *12*(2), 175–191. doi:10.1177/1748895811428173

Troise, C., Battisti, E., Christofi, M., van Vulpen, N. J., & Tarba, S. (2023). How can SMEs use crowdfunding platforms to internationalize? The role of equity and reward crowdfunding. *Management International Review*, *63*(1), 117–159. doi:10.1007/s11575-022-00493-y PMID:36465887

Tu, J. J., & Akhter, S. (2023). Exploring the role of entrepreneurial education, technology and teachers' creativity in excelling sustainable business competencies. *Ekonomska Istrazivanja*, *36*(1), 2119429. doi:10.1080/1331677X.2022.2119429

Turekulova, D., Beisengaliyev, B., Valiyeva, S., Kurmankulova, N., & Saimagambetova, G. (2022). Analysis of sustainable development of SMEs and factors influencing to the ecotourism industry. *Journal of Environmental Management & Tourism*, *13*(1), 211–222. doi:10.14505/jemt.v13.1(57).19

Türkeş, M. C., Oncioiu, I., Aslam, H. D., Marin-Pantelescu, A., Topor, D. I., & Căpuşneanu, S. (2019). Drivers and barriers in using industry 4.0: A perspective of SMEs in Romania. *Processes (Basel, Switzerland)*, *7*(3), 153. doi:10.3390/pr7030153

Tushman, M., Newman, W., & Romanelli, E. (1986). Managing the unsteady pace of organizational evolution. *California Management Review*, *29*(Fall), 29–44. doi:10.2307/41165225

U.S Small Business Administration. (2023, September 10). *"Size Standards"*. SBA. https://www.sba.gov/federal-contracting/contracting-guide/size-standards

Ulas, D. (2019). Digital Transformation Process and SMEs. *Procedia Computer Science*, *158*, 662–671. doi:10.1016/j.procs.2019.09.101

UNCTAD. (2019). *Policy Guide on Entrepreneurship for Development*. UNCTAD.

UNCTAD. (2021). *Tourism for Development: Volume II - Good Practices in Tourism*. UNCTAD.

UNIDO. (2013). *Emerging trends in global manufacturing industries*. UNDO. https://www.manufacturing-policy.eng.cam.ac.uk/policies-documents-folder/2013-emerging-trends-in-global-manufacturing-industries-unido/at_download/file(Accessed 05/01/15).

UNWTO (2019). *Tourism for Sustainable Development: Toolkit for Business*. UNWTO.

UNWTO. (2020). *Harnessing Innovation in Tourism: Case Studies*. World Tourism Organization.

UNWTO. (2021). *Global Report on Small and Medium-sized Enterprises in Tourism*. UN.

Vaidya, S., Ambad, P., & Bhosle, S. (2018). Industry 4.0 - A Glimpse. *Procedia Manufacturing*, *20*(January), 233–238. doi:10.1016/j.promfg.2018.02.034

Van Alstyne, M. W., Parker, G. G., & Choudary, S. P. (2016). Pipelines, platforms, and the new rules of strategy. *Harvard Business Review*, *94*(4), 54–62.

Van der Molen, P. (2018). Informal economies, state finances and surveyors. *Survey Review*, *50*(358), 16–25. doi:10.1080/00396265.2016.1216922 van Rhyn, L. (2023). *Challenges Faced by Small Business Corporations in South Africa*. Thrive CFO. https://thrivecfo. cloud/challenges-faced-by-small-business-corporations-in-southafrica/#Government_Support_Programs_for_Small_ Businesses.

Varga, J. (2021). Defining the economic role and benefits of micro small and medium-sized enterprises in the 21st century with a systematic review of the literature. *Acta Polytechnica Hungarica, 18*(11), 209–228. doi:10.12700/ APH.18.11.2021.11.12

Vásquez, J., Bruno, G., Settineri, L., & Aguirre, S. (2018). Conceptual Framework for Evaluating the Environmental Awareness and Ecoefficiency of SMEs. *Procedia CIRP, 78*, 347–352. doi:10.1016/j.procir.2018.09.062

Venkatesh, J., & Kumari, R. L. (2015). Performance of Mudra Bank: A Study on Financial Assistance to MSME Sector. *International Journal of Research in Economics and Social Sciences, 5*, 185–191.

Verma, A., Prakash, S., Srivastava, V., Kumar, A., & Mukhopadhyay, S. C. (2019). Sensing, controlling, and IoT infrastructure in smart building: A review. *IEEE Sensors Journal, 19*(20), 9036–9046. doi:10.1109/JSEN.2019.2922409

Vidalakis, C., Abanda, F., & Oti, A. (2020). BIM adoption and implementation: Focusing on SMEs. *Construction Innovation, 20*(1), 128–147. doi:10.1108/CI-09-2018-0076

Viljoen, J., Blaauw, D., & Schenck, C. (2019). The opportunities and value-adding activities of buy-back centres in South Africa's recycling industry: A value chain analysis. Local Economy, London South Bank University.

Von ketelhodt, A. & Wocke, A. (2008). The impact of electricity crises on the consumption behaviour of small and medium enterprises. *J. energy South Africa, 19*(1), 4-12.

Vos, A., & Willemse, I. (2011, December 12). *Leveraging Training Skills Development in SMEs:An Analysis Of East Flaunders*. OECD. https://www.oecd.org/cfe/leed/49180408.pdf

Vossenberg, S. (2013). Women Entrepreneurship Promotion in Developing Countries: What explains the gender gap in entrepreneurship and how to close it. *Maastricht School of Management Working Paper Series, 8*(1), 1-27.

Vrontis, D., Chaudhuri, R., & Chatterjee, S. (2022). Adoption of Digital Technologies by SMEs for Sustainability and Value Creation: Moderating Role of Entrepreneurial Orientation. *Sustainability (Basel), 14*(13), 7949. doi:10.3390/su14137949

Wagner, J. (2007). Exports and productivity: A survey of the evidence from firm-level data. *World Economy, 30*(1), 60–82. doi:10.1111/j.1467-9701.2007.00872.x

Wang, L., & Klugman, J. (2020). How women have fared in the labour market with China's rise as a global economic power. *Asia & the Pacific Policy Studies, 7*(1), 43–64. doi:10.1002/app5.293

Wang, X. (2020). *Blockchain chicken farm: And other stories of tech in China's countryside*. FSG Originals.

Wang, Y., Ali, Z., Mehreen, A., & Hussain, K. (2023). The trickle-down effect of big data use to predict organization innovation: The roles of business strategy alignment and information sharing. *Journal of Enterprise Information Management, 36*(1), 323–346. doi:10.1108/JEIM-10-2021-0439

Wasiuzzaman, S., Nurdin, N., Abdullah, A., & Vinayan, G. (2020). Creditworthiness and access to finance: A study of SMEs in the Malaysian manufacturing industry. *Management Research News, 43*(3), 293–310.

Wayman, O. (2019). The digitalisation of small and medium enterprise in Ireland Models for Financing Digital Projects. European Commission, 1–20.

Wei, W., Sarker, T., Żukiewicz-Sobczak, W., Roy, R., Alam, G. M., Rabbany, M. G., Hossain, M. S., & Aziz, N. (2021). The influence of women's empowerment on poverty reduction in the rural areas of Bangladesh: Focus on health, education and living standard. *International Journal of Environmental Research and Public Health*, *18*(13), 6909. doi:10.3390/ijerph18136909 PMID:34199117

Wennekers, S., Van Wennekers, A., Thurik, R., & Reynolds, P. (2005). Nascent entrepreneurship and the level of economic development. *Small Business Economics*, *24*(3), 293–309. doi:10.1007/s11187-005-1994-8

Westerman, G., Bonnet, D., & McAfee, A. (2014). *Leading Digital: Turning Technology into Business Transformation.* Harvard Business Review Press.

Wheelwright, S. (1984). Manufacturing strategy: Defining the missing link. *Strategic Management Journal*, *5*(1), 77–91. doi:10.1002/smj.4250050106

Wieland, A., & Wallenburg, C. M. (2013). The influence of relational competencies on supply chain resilience: A relational view. *International Journal of Physical Distribution & Logistics Management*, *43*(4), 300–320. doi:10.1108/IJPDLM-08-2012-0243

Wiliandri, R. (2020). A Conceptual Approach to Identify Factors Affecting the Digital Transformation of Micro, Small and Medium-sized Enterprises (MSMEs) during Covid-19 Pandemic in Indonesia. *Ekonomi Bisnis*, *25*(2), 66. doi:10.17977/um042v25i2p66-85

Woetzel, J., Orr, G., Lau, A., Yougang, C., Chang, E., Seong, J., Chui, M., & Qiu, A. (2014). *China's digital transformation: The Internet's impact on productivity and growth.* Mckinsey Global Institute.

Wolf, M. J., & Perron, B. (Eds.). (2023). *The Routledge companion to video game studies.* Taylor & Francis., doi:10.4324/9781003214977

World Bank Data (2017). *Sustainable development goals.* World Bank Data.

World Bank Group (2020). *Supporting SMEs During the COVID-19 Crisis: A Policy Handbook for Developing Countries.* World Bank Group.

World Bank. (2015). *Nigeria economic report. Nigeria economic report; no. 3.* World Bank Group.

World Bank. (2017). *What's Happening in the Missing Middle? Lessons from Financing.* World Bank. https://www.worldbank.org/en/topic/financialsector/publication/whats-happening-in-the-missing-middle-lessons-from-financing-smes

World Bank. (2023, July 29). *Small and Medium Enterprises (SMEs) Finance: Improving SMEs' access to Finance and Finding Innovative Solutions to unlock Sources of Capital.* World Bank. https://www.worldbank.org/en/topic/smefinance

Writer, S. (2022). *South Africa's horror year of load shedding – here's how it compares.* Business Tech. https://businesstech.co.za/news/energy/630667/south-africas-horror-year-of-load-shedding-heres-how-it-compares/

WTTC. (2020). *Travel and Tourism: Economic Impact 2020.* WTTC.

Wuest, T., Romero, D., Khan, M. A., & Mittal, S. (2022). *The triple bottom line of smart manufacturing technologies: an economic, environmental, and social perspective. Handbook of Smart Technologies: An Economic and Social Perspective.* Routledge., https://www. taylorfrancis.com/chapters/edit/10.4324/9780429351921-20

Xenarios, S., Sarker, G. W., Biswas, J. C., Maniruzzaman, M., Nemes, A., & Nagothu, S. (2014). *Agricultural interventions and investment options for climate change in drought and saline-flood prone regions of Bangladesh.* Bioforsk Rapport.

Xiang, Z., Du, Q., Ma, Y., & Fan, W. (2015). An Empirical Investigation of the Impacts of Social Media Interactions on Destination Image. *Tourism Management*, *46*.

Xiang, Z., Du, Q., Ma, Y., & Fan, W. (2017). A comparative analysis of major online review platforms: Implications for social media analytics in hospitality and tourism. *Tourism Management, 58*, 51–65. doi:10.1016/j.tourman.2016.10.001

Yadava, A. K., Khan, I. A., Pandey, P., Aarif, M., Khanna, G., & Garg, S. (2022). Impact of marketing communication and information sharing on the productivity of India's small and medium-sized businesses (SMEs). *International Journal of Health Sciences, 6*, 12745–12755. doi:10.53730/ijhs.v6nS2.8352

Yamak, S., Karatas-Ozkan, M., Godwin, E. S., Mahmood, S., & Rahimi, R. (2023). Transformation or Retaining the Status Quo: Multinational Hospitality Companies and SME Collaboration on Sustainability in Emerging Countries. In Handbook of Research on Sustainable Tourism and Hotel Operations in Global Hypercompetition (pp. 490-516). IGI Global.

Ye, J., & Kulathunga, K. M. M. C. B. (2019). How does financial literacy promote sustainability in SMEs? A developing country perspective. *Sustainability (Basel), 11*(10), 2990. doi:10.3390/su11102990

Yeung, G., He, C., & Zhang, P. (2017). Rural banking in China: Geographically accessible but still financially excluded. *Regional Studies, 51*(2), 297–312. doi:10.1080/00343404.2015.1100283

Yip, G. S., & McKern, B. (2016). *China's next strategic advantage: From imitation to innovation.* MIT press.

Yoon, L. (2023, September 20). *SMEs in South Korea -Statistics and Fact.* Statista. https://www.statista.com/topics/10036/smes-in-south-korea/#topicOverview

Yoshino, N., & Taghizadeh-Hesary, F. (2019). *Unlocking SME finance in Asia: Roles of credit rating and credit guarantee schemes (First ed.).* SAGE Publications

Zahoor, N., Zopiatis, A., Adomako, S., & Lamprinakos, G. (2023). The micro-foundations of digitally transforming SMEs: How digital literacy and technology interact with managerial attributes. *Journal of Business Research, 159*, 113755. doi:10.1016/j.jbusres.2023.113755

Zaoui, F., & Souissi, N. (2020). Roadmap for digital transformation: A literature review. *Procedia Computer Science, 175*, 621–628. doi:10.1016/j.procs.2020.07.090

Zepeda, L. (2001). Agricultural investment, production capacity and productivity. *FAO Economic and Social Development Paper*, 3-20. FAO.

Zha, Q., Kou, G., Zhang, H., Liang, H., Chen, X., Li, C., and Dong, Y. (2021). Opinion dynamics in finance and business: A literature review and research opportunities. *Financial Innovation (Heidelberg), 6*(1), 1-22.

Zhang, M., Lian, Y., Zhao, H., & Xia-Bauer, C. (2020). Unlocking green financing for building energy retrofit: A survey in the western China. *Energy Strategy Reviews, 30*, 100520. doi:10.1016/j.esr.2020.100520

Zhang, X., Xu, Y., & Ma, L. (2022). Research on Successful Factors and Influencing Mechanism of the Digital Transformation in SMEs. *Sustainability (Basel), 14*(5), 2549. doi:10.3390/su14052549

Zhao, W., Wang, A., & Chen, Y. (2019). How to maintain the sustainable development of a business platform: A case study of Pinduoduo social commerce platform in China. *Sustainability (Basel), 11*(22), 6337. doi:10.3390/su11226337

Zhu, J., Liu, X., Shi, Q., He, T., Sun, Z., Guo, X., Liu, W., Sulaiman, O. B., Dong, B., & Lee, C. (2019). Development trends and perspectives of future sensors and MEMS/NEMS. *Micromachines, 11*(1), 7. doi:10.3390/mi11010007 PMID:31861476

Zikmund, W. G. (2003). *Business Research Methods* (7th ed.). Thompson South-Western.

Zreik, M. (2021). The Regional Comprehensive Economic Partnership and Its Impact on the US-China Trade War. *Journal of Asia Pacific Studies, 6*(3), 339–348.

Zreik, M. (2023). From Boom to Bust: A Study of China's Economy in the Wake of COVID-19 Outbreak in H1 2020. *BRICS Journal of Economics*, *4*(1), 147–171. doi:10.3897/brics-econ.4.e101050

Zreik, M., Iqbal, B. A., & Rahman, M. N. (2022). Outward FDI: determinants and flows in emerging economies: evidence from China. *China and WTO Review*, *8*(2), 385–402. doi:10.14330/cwr.2022.8.2.07

Zuboff, S. (2022). Surveillance capitalism or democracy? The death match of institutional orders and the politics of knowledge in our information civilization. *Organization Theory*, *3*(3), 26317877221129290. doi:10.1177/26317877221129290

Zuzik, J., Furmannova, B., Dulina, L. & Kukla, S. (2024). *Digital Transformation of Material Flow and Workplace Design: A Comprehensive Case Study Analysis*. IEEE.

Zwane, S. (2023). *Poultry sector suffering as loadshedding persists*. Zimoja. https://www.zimoja.co.za/articles/poultry-sector-suffering-as-load-shedding-persist

About the Contributors

Sumesh S. Dadwal has 20-years of experience in teaching, academic research, eLearning, and educational quality management. Currently, he is working as Lecturer with Northumbria London campus, UK. He is also a visiting lecturer at ICON College, University of West London and University of Plymouth (London), UK. As a Programme leader of MSc Mass communication, Sumesh, leads a team of experts in teaching and research. He has also been associated with QAA, UK; as a reviewer for educational quality oversight of higher education in the UK. He has successful experience in programme development and the UK HEI quality assurance, using benchmarks from HEI, QAA, HEA, and industrial practices Sumesh is an active researcher and is also involved in PhD supervision. His core areas include International strategic marketing, consumer behaviour & misbehaviour, product launches, prosumers & experience economy, service encounters & sensational experiences, Innovation & technology in marketing, and leadership & organisational change. He has undertaken analysis of brands, markets and consumer behaviours using various qualitative and quantitative techniques. He has written various research papers, book chapters and lead research at various levels. He has successfully undertaken projects that required data mining, editing and detailed statistical analysis using qualitative and quantitative research methods using software: N-Vivo, Excel, SPSS. He is also an external examiner for PG programmes with EduQual UK, and external examiner for PhD (International Expert) with Punjab Technical University, India. He is also a member of advisory and editorial board of academics at Acme Intellects IJRM, India. Sumesh is also a reviewer at Journal of Enterprise Information Management, UK. In addition, Sumesh has hands-on industrial experience in constructions and agricultural supply chain. He is also a freelance consultant (business analysis) for emerging markets.

Pawan Kumar is working as a Professor in the Department of Marketing at Mittal School of Business, Lovely Professional University, Punjab, India. He has 17 years of experience in academics and business research. He is an active researcher and is also involved in PhD supervision. His areas of interest in research include entrepreneurship, marketing, e-commerce, consumer behaviour, marketing research, etc. He is an avid researcher. He is active in Ph.D research supervision and has good number of publications in Q1 and Q2 Journals to his credit in various research papers published Scopus indexed journals namely: The TQM Journal from Emerald, Visions: Journal of Business Perspectives from Sage, International Journal of Business and Globalization, International Journal of Business Information Systems from Inderscience and other national/international journals of repute. He is Editorial Board Member of Scopus Journal namely International Journal of Public Sector Performance Management and International journal of entrepreneurship and small business.

Rajesh Verma is Sr. Dean & Professor of Strategy at Mittal School of Business, LPU, Punjab. His research & teaching interests entails areas like Business Models, Market Orientation & Political Marketing. He is the recipient of Junior Research Fellowship from University Grant Commission of India and other research grants from bodies like UK-India Education and Research Initiative (UKIERI); European Commission; and Department of Science & Technology (DST), Government of India. He is a Wiley Certified Design Thinking Practitioner and has conducted several training programmes on design thinking, selling skills, changing business models, brand building and customer orientation etc. for corporates like India Oil, Radington etc

Gursimranjit Singh is working as an Assistant Professor in the Department of Humanities and Management, Dr. B.R. Ambedkar National Institute of Technology Jalandhar, Punjab, India. He received his Doctoral in Management from the I.K. Gujral Punjab Technical University, Kapurthala, Jalandhar, India. He has published several research articles in international journals of repute. He has also published several book chapters with IGI Global and Taylor and Francis. Further, he has presented research papers in various international conferences.

Bindu Aggarwal is currently an Associate Professor of Marketing in the University School of Business at Chandigarh University, Gharaun, Mohali, Punjab, India. She has teaching experience of 18 years. She completed her Ph.D in marketing from the Lovely Professional University, Punjab, India in the year 2021. Her areas of interest include marketing, human resource management, current issues in management and psychology. She has presented more than 35 research papers related to marketing, human resource management and psychology at the conferences/seminars held at national and international levels. She has also published papers in various reputed national and international journals.

Alfred Akakpo is currently a Senior Lecturer in Business Analytics at University of Northampton. He's research interest are in data mining, business intelligence and forecasting of emerging technologies.

Said Mohammed Ali is a BA Business Management and leadership student at Coventry University. He has interest in governance, SMEs, and developing long-term business models. Said is also interested in social entrepreneurship and discovering new methods to combat global poverty

Manpreet Arora, a Senior Assistant Professor of Management at the Central University of Himachal Pradesh, Dharamshala, India, brings over twenty-two years of rich teaching experience. She holds academic accolades including a Ph.D. in International Trade, an M.Phil, a gold medalist and several other academic distinctions from Himachal Pradesh University, Shimla. Dr. Arora's diverse research interests encompass Accounting, Finance, Strategic Management, Entrepreneurship, Qualitative Research and Microfinance. She works on Mixed methods research. Noteworthy for guiding doctoral research and delving into Microfinance, Entrepreneurship, Behavioral Finance and corporate reporting, she has presented at numerous seminars, delivering talks on various academic subjects across multiple universities and colleges. An accomplished academic, she has an impressive publication record, having authored over 30 papers in esteemed national and international journals listed in Scopus, WOS and Category journals, alongside contributing to fifty-five book chapters in publications by reputed publishers like Emerald, Routledge, CABI, Springer Nature, AAP and more. Her commitment to management research is evident through the editing of four books. Dr. Arora is not only a dedicated researcher but also an ardent advocate for women's rights, combining academia with active social work in that domain. A motivational speaker and workshop facilitator, she inspires through communication and motivation workshops. Her impactful contributions showcase a multifaceted professional excelling in academia, research, and social advocacy.

Gifty Edwin-Akakpo is a Chartered Accountant and lecturer at Coventry University in London. My interest are in Environmental Accounting and Sustainability.

Julius Eziashi is dedicated, motivated, and detailed-oriented professional with extensive experience leading research projects; utilising expert knowledge of qualitative and quantitative research, conducting interviews and developing surveys for data collection. Recognized as a leader in identifying opportunities for efficiency, improvement, and driving development with cutting-edge technologies to achieve solutions. Skilled communicator known as a resourceful consultant who works with integrity and professionalism to consistently meet and exceed all organisational expectations. Dr Eziashi is currently a lecturer in Business and Management at the Northumbria University United Kingdom. He received his Master in Business Administration from Cardiff Metropolitan University in 2012 and his Doctorate in Business Administration in the year 2017 from the Northumbria University Newcastle. Dr Eziashi is a Fellow at the Chartered Management Institute United Kingdom. In addition to his academic career, he has worked as a senior research consultant/ analyst in the United Kingdom. His research interests are Manufacturing, SMEs, Emerging Economy, Strategy, International Business and Operations Management.

David Herzog's first degree is in Medicine (MD) and Structural and Molecular Biology (MSc). He did his PhD at the junction of Computer Science and Psychiatry, which helped to take part in the leading area of research -- IoT, Ambient Assisted Living and Data Analysis. His research interests are information technology applications in healthcare, science and society as a whole.

Nitsa J Herzog has a diverse academic background and extensive experience in the information technology industry. Her main research interest is AI, focusing on Big Data and data science technology, IoT and Machine Learning. Her primary research area is AI in healthcare and medicine, where she developed computer vision and machine learning algorithms for the diagnosis of medical pathology.

Phathutshedzo Madumi is a Lecturer in the Department of Military Economics at Stellenbosch University, South Africa. He is an emerging researcher who is aspired to obtain Phd in Economics. His professional work focuses on Economic, Development, Political economy, Economic Growth, Economic Theory, International economy, Public Economy, Income and Wage Inequality, Human Capital and Training, Labour Economics.

Gargi Malhotra is currently a Research Scholar at Mittal School of Business, Lovely Professional University, Phagwara, Punjab (India). She has completed her Graduation and Masters from Maharshi Dayanand University, Haryana (India). She is a dedicated researcher in the field of Human Resources. In her academic journey she developed a keen interest in the intricacies of managing human capital in organizations. This interest led her to pursue further academic research in the field, aiming to contribute to the knowledge base of HR practices and strategies.

Mridula Mishra - Contributing Author| **Mridula Mishra** is currently Professor in Psychology, School of Liberal and Creative Arts (Social Sciences & Languages), Lovely Professional University, Phagwara, Punjab (India). Dr. Mridula Mishra has done her Ph. D. from Banaras Hindu University (BHU), Varanasi in Psychology. Her Ph.D. was on Rorschach Inkblot Test and SIS. She is the first scholar in the world who did Ph. D on SIS. She has received three times SIS Best Paper Award in 1992, 1996, and 2000, and two-times SIS Best Research Award in 2006 and 2008 from SIS Centre, 2020 Muldoon Rd, # 317, Anchorage, Alaska. 99504. USA. USA. Received best paper award in 2020 on the paper title "Reimagining Indian IT sector to achieve $ 5 Trillion aspiration for India by 2025" from UPES India. Dr. Mridula Mishra has more than 25 years of experience in academics, research and hospitals. In journey of her academic and professional life more than 10 M. Phil. and 15 Ph. D students guided by her. Her interest area of teaching and research is Organizational Behaviour and Psychology. She has 70 research publications with citation 569, H-Index 12 and i10 Index 15 in various Emeralds and Scopus indexed National and International Journals. She has approximately more than 35 FDP/ Workshop/ Seminar attended, conducted and organized on her expertise areas in India and Abroad. She has 6 professional memberships from various national and international organizations. Till the date she has published 25 Copy rights with government of India. Linked in id- or HEAAAAJ&hl=en Scopus Author ID: 57189634625 mishra @mridula03123264 E-4682-202

Siva Kumar Pujari received his Doctoral Degree in Supply Chain Resilience from Department of Management Studies, Indian Institute of Technology Roorkee, India. He obtained his Bachelor of Technology in mechanical engineering from Acharya Nagarjuna University, Guntur, Andhra Pradesh, and Master of Technology in Industrial Engineering from National Institute of Technology Tiruchirappalli, Trichy, Tamil Nadu, India. He Presented his work in reputed International Conferences and has published several research papers in journals of international repute. His areas of interest include Supply Chain Resilience, Supply Chain Disruption Management, Risk Management, Resilience of Small and Medium Enterprises (SMEs), Omni-Channel Supply Chain, etc.

Saibal Kumar Saha (UGC NET Qualified) holds a Ph.D in Management, a first-class master's degree in MBA and a first-class bachelor's degree in Electronics and Communication Engineering. He has over 13 years of experience and has worked in organizations like NIT Silchar, Sikkim Manipal Institute of Technology, Cognizant Technology Solutions and is currently working as Associate Professor in Christ University. He has published more than 60 articles in various journals, conference proceedings and book chapters, indexed in Web of Science, Scopus and ABDC. He has also obtained a couple of copyrights and patents and has authored three books.

Eustathios Sainidis is Senior Lecturer in Strategic Management at Northumbria University and Deputy Director of the Northumbria University London Campus. He is an experienced academic and has taught extensively at undergraduate and postgraduate levels, and has supervised and been examiner to a number of doctoral candidates. Eustathios is an active researcher in the subject of manufacturing strategy in SMEs and has a particular interest in the application of mixed methods in business and management research.

Orhan Şanli works at Aydın Adnan Menderes University Nazilli Faculty of Economics and Administrative Sciences as a doctoral faculty member in the department of economics. His fields of study are general economics. Specifically, he is an expert on international trade, environment, tourism, energy economy, poverty, income distribution, exchange rates, inflation, international integration, European Union, EU-Turkey relations, customs union, trade and currency wars.

Swati Singh is presently working as Assistant Professor in the Department of Management, Maharaja Agrasen University, Baddi, Himachal Pradesh. She has completed her Ph.D. in the area of Microfinance from Central University of Himachal Pradesh. She has presented research papers in many national and international conferences. She also has research publications in Scopus indexed journals and other journals of national and international repute. 4 students are pursuing PhD under her supervision..

Ranjeet Verma is a Doctor of Philosophy from National Institute of Technology, Kurukshetra with specialisation in the field of Marketing and General Management at the Postgraduate level and graduated from Kurukshetra University Kurukshetra and currently working as a Professor in University school of Business, Chandigarh University, Mohali, Panjab Dr. Ranjeet has more than 20 years of teaching and administrative experience published more than 20 research papers in National and International journals of repute (Scopus Indexed), 7 Books Authored titled Brand Management, Fundamentals of Management, Basics of Economics and Management, Micro Business Environment, Macro Business Environment, Business Environment and Production and Operations Management and presented papers in more than 20 national and international conferences.

Luther-King Junior Zogli is a senior lecturer at the Durban University of Technology, Riverside Campus with nine years of experience in higher education. He holds a Ph.D. in Economics and boasts a rich background in academic leadership. Over the years, he has successfully supervised and graduated Ph.D. and several Masters students. With a strong focus on research, Dr. Zogli has contributed significantly to the field of Development Economics and SMME development with a portfolio of over 20 published articles and book chapters.

Mohamad Zreik, a Postdoctoral Fellow at Sun Yat-sen University, is a recognized scholar in International Relations, specializing in China's Arab-region foreign policy. His recent work in soft power diplomacy compares China's methods in the Middle East and East Asia. His extensive knowledge spans Middle Eastern Studies, China-Arab relations, East Asian and Asian Affairs, Eurasian geopolitics, and Political Economy, providing him a unique viewpoint in his field. Dr. Zreik is a proud recipient of a PhD from Central China Normal University (Wuhan). He's written numerous acclaimed papers, many focusing on China's Belt and Road Initiative and its Arab-region impact. His groundbreaking research has established him as a leading expert in his field. Presently, he furthers his research on China's soft power diplomacy tactics at Sun Yat-sen University. His significant contributions make him a crucial figure in understanding contemporary international relations.

Index

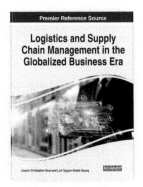

  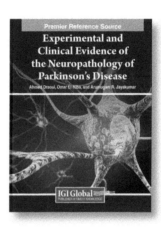 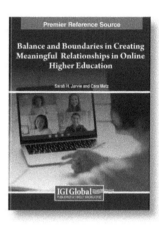

Submit an Open Access Book Proposal

Have Your Work Fully & Freely Available Worldwide After Publication

Seeking the Following Book Classification Types:

Authored & Edited Monographs • Casebooks • Encyclopedias • Handbooks of Research

Gold, Platinum, & Retrospective OA Opportunities to Choose From

Easily Track Your Work in Our Advanced Manuscript Submission System With **Rapid Turnaround Times**

Double-Blind Peer Review by Notable Editorial Boards (*Committee on Publication Ethics* (COPE) Certified)

Publications Adhere to All **Current OA Mandates & Compliances**

Affordable APCs *(Often 50% Lower Than the Industry Average)* Including Robust Editorial Service Provisions

Direct Connections with **Prominent Research Funders** & OA Regulatory Groups

Institution Level OA Agreements Available (Recommend or Contact Your Librarian for Details)

Join a **Diverse Community of 150,000+ Researchers Worldwide** Publishing With IGI Global

Content Spread Widely to Leading Repositories (AGOSR, ResearchGate, CORE, & More)

Premier Reference Source

Food Sustainability, Environmental Awareness, and Adaptation and Mitigation Strategies for Developing Countries

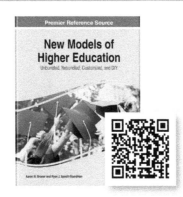

Premier Reference Source

New Models of Higher Education

Unbundled, Rebundled, Customized, and DIY

Handbook of Research on

The Global View of Open Access and Scholarly Communications

DID YOU KNOW?

Retrospective Open Access Publishing

You Can Unlock Your Recently Published Work, Including Full Book & Individual Chapter Content to Enjoy All the Benefits of Open Access Publishing

Learn More

Individual Article
& Chapter Downloads
US$ 37.50/each

Easily Identify, Acquire, and Utilize Published Peer-Reviewed Findings in Support of Your Current Research

- Browse Over **170,000+ Articles & Chapters**
- **Accurate & Advanced** Search
- Affordably Acquire **International Research**
- **Instantly Access** Your Content
- Benefit from the **InfoSci® Platform Features**

THE UNIVERSITY
of NORTH CAROLINA
at CHAPEL HILL

It really provides an excellent entry into the research literature of the field. It presents a manageable number of highly relevant sources on topics of interest to a wide range of researchers. The sources are scholarly, but also accessible to 'practitioners'.

- Ms. Lisa Stimatz, MLS, University of North Carolina at Chapel Hill, USA

9 798369 301111